THE GREAT
WOMEN

Joan Marlow

THE GREAT
WOMEN

A HART BOOK

A & W PUBLISHERS, INC. NEW YORK

~~32084~~

To my father, George Marlow,
and to Donna Kelsh,
whose encouragement
and editorial advice
I deeply appreciate.

PUBLISHED BY
A & W PUBLISHERS, INC.
95 MADISON AVENUE
NEW YORK, NEW YORK 10016

LIBRARY OF CONGRESS CATALOG CARD NO. 79-65342

ISBN: 0-89479-056-0

PRINTED IN THE UNITED STATES OF AMERICA

Contents

FOREWORD

A friend once told me that the most destructive form of racial prejudice he experienced was that during his childhood he had never once seen a black on TV commercials. "It was as if the rest of the world didn't know we existed—or didn't care," he said.

Women have fared better than blacks in the world of advertising; no one doubts that women brush their teeth, drive cars, and perform other routine acts of daily life rather well. But when it comes to obtaining distinction in the world outside the home, women have, until very recently, remained largely invisible. Prior to 1960, the women accorded places in biographical anthologies were more often infamous than great. There were books about sentimental heroines—Pocahontas, Betsy Ross, and Grace Darling—and about women whose celebrity rested on their association with great men—illustrious wives, like Abigail Adams, notorious mistresses like Madame de Pompadour. However, the well-deserved celebrity of a Marie Curie or a Georgia O'Keeffe seemed to be attributed to their supposed uniqueness rather than their accomplishments.

With the rise of feminism, the traditional view that women are unsuited to the "masculine" fields of science, business, art, mathematics, and athletics has been challenged. The past two decades have witnessed a spate of books about outstanding women in these fields. Why then, this book on great women? Because in this age of specialization there is not, to my knowledge, a book that presents to the general reader the lives and accomplishments of a broad spectrum of outstanding women. The present volume is intended to supply that deficiency. For in this transitional age, when women find themselves, in Matthew Arnold's phrase, "Wandering between two worlds, one dead/The other powerless to be born," it seemed to me that a book was needed to show women their common heritage by illustrating how women have transcended the boundaries of time and geography, conflicts and external barriers, to excel in every area of human endeavor. Men, too, need to be acquainted with the female experience and with their own role in shaping that experience, and a collection such as this makes vivid the individual and collective struggle of women as no general history book or list of statistics can.

The purpose of this volume in recounting the achievements and biographies of 60 great women is to provide an overview of what feminist historians today are calling "herstory." For if, as Carlyle wrote, "history is the essence of innumerable biographies," herstory is the essence of innumerable neglected but memorable biographies. This collection encompasses women who lived from the 15th century to the present, who were born into diverse cultural traditions, and who have distinguished themselves in many different types of activity. The only common denominator shared by all is their sex, which has confronted them with the same challenges and obstacles that women have faced, and still face, wherever and whenever they aspire to realize themselves.

Aiming for diversity within the confines of one small volume, I was forced to omit candidates who were outstanding for their individual merit. It was not without a pang that I omitted Mother Theresa, Jane Austen, Edith Cavell, Lillian Wald, and a host of other deserving candidates. Having chosen to represent only one person in any particular field—one nurse, one social worker, one humanitarian, one scientist, etc.—I could not afford to engage in moral debate, for example about whether an athlete deserves equal recognition with a scholar or artist. Interestingly, although it was not my deliberate intention to include women of various religious and socio-economic backgrounds, it happened automatically. The women you will read about here rose from the lowest as well as the highest levels of the societies in which they were born.

Having a surprisingly wide possibility of choices of impressive women, I exercised further limitations. For one thing, I required that all candidates be real women, with documented achievements, rather than legendary or quasi-mythical heroines. Second, I excluded from consideration courtesans, loyal wives, and women whose achievements have been more colorful than important. Such women have already been disproportionately represented in history, and perpetuate the myth that women chiefly influence or inspire great men, rather than gaining distinction in their own right. The women in this book made some significant contribution to human knowledge or human welfare, and to advancing the frontiers for women in general.

You will find in this book well-known figures whose stories cannot be repeated too often, such as Helen Keller or Marie Curie; as well as women who have not, in their own time or subsequently, been accorded the recognition and publicity warranted by their achievements. It is with great pleasure that I attempt to rescue such names as Belva Lockwood, Ramabai Medhavi, or Anna Van Schurman from oblivion.

Although I have researched my material thoroughly and vouch for its factual authenticity, occasionally I have taken the liberty of recreating a dialogue in order to convey a fragment of the dramatic quality of the real life story. Only the wording, not the substance of these conversations, owes anything to my imagination. The portion of each essay that provides brief biographical data emphasizes the factors which contributed to the self-image of these women in their formative years, and the obstacles or aids experienced in achieving their goals.

For the reader who is interested in learning more about any of the women in this book, or who wants to know, in general, where to find information on women not included in standard encyclopedias, I would like to share some of the sources that I employed. First, there is the excellent *Index to Women of the World From Ancient to Modern Times* by Norma O. Ireland, which lists anthologies containing articles about a variety of women. *Biographical Index* contains excellent references to books, media articles, and other sources of information on individuals who lived from 1946 to the present. *Current Biography* is especially commendable for including notable women who are often unaccountably excluded from other biographical encyclopedias. The subject index to *Books in Print* contains listings of available volumes under the listing *Women,* with appropriate subheadings. *Books in Print* also lists biographies of individuals under their book titles.

Of the many collections of biographical essays that I consulted I found Caroline Bird's *Enterprising Women,* Hope Stoddard's *Famous American Women,* and H.J. Mozans's *Women in Science* particularly informative and interesting. As a reference book, *Notable American Women,* a three-volume encyclopedia compiled by scholars at Radcliffe College, is invaluable. *The Book of Women's Achievements* by Joan and Kenneth Macksey was also very helpful.

JOAN MARLOW

Joan of Arc (1412-1431)

SAVIOR OF FRANCE

Revered as the French national heroine, and canonized as a Roman Catholic saint, Joan of Arc is undoubtedly the most prominent female military leader in history. Her courage and faith have inspired many literary works by an array of diverse and outstanding authors. Her remarkable campaign to free France from foreign rule has been celebrated by such varied biographers as historian Jules Michelet and feminist Vita Sackville-West. As an exemplar of faith in the inner light, Joan has been written about by Voltaire, Schiller, Mark Twain, Anatole France, George Bernard Shaw, Maxwell Anderson, and Jules Feiffer.

Joan of Arc was born in Domrémy, a small village in northeastern France, in 1412, at the height of the Hundred Years War. For nearly 75 years, France had been waging a losing battle against England for control of the French throne. Domrémy was one of a few towns loyal to the as-yet-uncrowned Charles VII. As a pivotal post on the Lorraine border, the birthplace of Joan of Arc was frequently besieged by the Burgundians, staunch allies of the English.

As a child, Joan was forced to flee with her family to Neufchatel, eight miles from her home, during one of the Burgundian raids.

Joan was the youngest of five children in a not too poor peasant family. Two of Joan's brothers later served under her standard in the French army. Joan sometimes went with her brothers to the hills to tend her father's flock of sheep and herd of cattle. Joan never received any formal schooling, and remained illiterate all her life. Her mother taught her to spin and sew and say her prayers.

Jeanne D'Arc, as she was called in France, was an unusually devout child. She loved to hear the biblical story of the Annunciation, and her imagination was fired by a local legend that a virgin would presently arise to save war-torn France. Joan regularly attended mass at the village church, and was renowned in the neighborhood for her charitable works.

Statues of three saints, Saint Michael, Saint Catherine of Alexandria, and Saint Margaret of Antioch, stood in the village church. At the age of 13, Joan began to hear "voices" emanating from these statues. Joan told no one of these visitations, which continued throughout her life, for she feared that her stern father would think she was lying. It was not until years later, at her trial at Rouen, that Joan openly confessed her childhood visions.

When Joan was about 17, her voices commanded her to raise the siege of Orléans, and lead the dauphin, Charles, to Reims to be crowned. Joan protested that she was a poor girl, who could neither ride nor fight, but the voices insisted: "It is God who commands it." So in 1428, under the protection of a male relative, Joan presented herself to Robert Baudrecourt, the French garrison commander at Vaucouleurs. The intrepid girl requested a horse, a suit of armor, and an escort to the royal presence, explaining that her mission was to save France. At this point, Baudrecourt judged Joan a lunatic, and dismissed her request as ludicrous.

Joan returned home to Domrémy. But her voices urged her to persevere, and persevere she did. Joan went again to the presidio at Vaucouleurs. Eventually, she overcame Baudrecourt's skepticism when she predicted a French defeat that was later confirmed by official reports. Baudrecourt was impressed by Joan's charisma and common sense. He was the first of numerous French military commanders who were amazed to find themselves paying credence to this incredible girl. He sent Joan, dressed as a male page and flanked by a military escort, to the dauphin's headquarters at Chinon.

Indolent, indecisive, and indigent, Charles had practically abandoned all expectation of ever assuming his rightful place on the French throne. The heir of the Valois dynasty was leading a frivolous existence at the castle of Chinon when Joan arrived with the demand to be admitted into his presence. For two days, she was interrogated by Charles's advisors before they deemed her worthy to see the dauphin. Legend has it that Charles tested Joan, when she was allowed to appear before him, by changing clothes with one of his courtiers and that Joan immediately recognized the imposture. In any event, Joan did ultimately manage to persuade the dauphin of her divine backing, after Charles had subjected her to three weeks of examination by learned theologians. Joan was given a sword, a banner, and a suit of armor and after receiving official ecclesiastical benediction, was placed by Charles at the head of his troops.

Clad in white armor, Joan set out to lead the French army toward the besieged city of Orléans. At first, the soldiers resisted her authority, but Joan exerted her persuasive powers on certain key military commanders, who in turn mustered support for her among their men. Upon reaching Orléans, Joan was taken to the house of one of Charles's supporters to rest. On the evening of May 4, 1429, she suddenly leaped up, and declared that she must go out and attack the English. Guided by her voices, Joan rushed to the fort of St. Loup, where, sure enough, an encounter of which she had not been informed was taking place. Under Joan's leadership, the French captured the fort. This was the first battle the French had won during the many years the war had been raging.

The next day, Joan dictated a letter of defiance to the English, and again rallied her troops to battle. On May 6, at the fort of St. Jean-le-Blanc, the English were routed for the second time; and on May 7, Joan led her forces to victory at Les Tourelles. Although wounded, Joan had continued to fight. Thanks to her tenacity, the French army liberated the city of Orléans from English rule.

The Battle of Orléans was the turning point of the Hundred Years War. The English were thoroughly demoralized by their defeat, which they attributed to diabolical intervention. But if Joan was a witch to the English, she was an angel to her own people.

Henceforth, Joan was known as the Maid of Orléans.

The Maid continued to initiate and win decisive battles to free her country from English domination. In June, she advised Charles that it was time for his coronation. The dauphin, wishy-washy by nature, and easily swayed by his counselors who were all hostile to the Maid, procrastinated. The road to Reims would be fraught with difficulty and danger, he argued. Joan was adamant: "I take no account of all that," she declared. "We *must* go to Reims *now.*" The reluctant Charles succumbed to the Maid's implacable will.

On July 16, the French army arrived at the gates of Reims. The city turned out to welcome the royal troops, and Charles was ushered triumphantly to the cathedral. Joan stood inconspicuously by the altar during the coronation. After the ceremony, she knelt humbly before the king, addressing Charles VII as "my liege."

The Maid had now accomplished the mission outlined for her by her voices, and desired to return to her family at Domrémy, but the king requested her to remain with him. Joan sought counsel from her voices, but her saintly advisors had fallen silent. Bewildered, she yielded to the royal request.

A month of official parades throughout Champagne and the Ile-de-France ensued. Charles VII was hailed by his subjects. Joan was idolized by the French, and felt a surge of reciprocal love for her fellow citizens. The king was content to bask indefinitely in the adulation of the populace, but Joan soon became impatient for action. She urged Charles to launch an attack on Paris. He consented, and in early September joined Joan to begin the campaign.

Joan fought valorously during the siege of Paris, despite a severe wound in the thigh. In the midst of the fighting, the feckless king retreated from battle, and required the Maid to follow him.

When Joan was permitted to resume her military activities, she again led the French to victory. In the spring of 1430, she achieved new triumphs for the king, despite inadequate reinforcements and supplies. In May, she rode to Compiègne. There, a French sortie against the Burgundians was unsuccessful, and Joan was dragged from her horse by the enemy.

Until late autumn, Joan was held prisoner by the duke of Burgundy. With inexplicable ingratitude, neither Charles nor any other Frenchman made the slightest effort to obtain Joan's release.

Meanwhile, the English were clamoring for Burgundy to hand the French sorceress over to them. In January 1431, Joan was sold to the English authorities for the sum of 16,000 francs.

The English imprisoned the Maid in the Castle of Rouen. There she was subjected to continual physical and mental persecution. A preliminary investigation of her case was held from January to March. In April, Joan was charged with witchcraft and fraud.

During the ensuing trial, Joan was scathingly interrogated by political and ecclesiastical authorities who tried to confuse and overwhelm the unlearned girl. But she repeatedly baffled her interlocutors with her simple eloquence, good sense, and sharp wit. Attacking her religious conviction, her accusers suggested that she was defying the Church militant and attempted to convict her of violating the Apostles' Creed. Joan avowed she accepted the Church's authority, but asserted that she was answerable only to God. She supplicated, in vain, that her case be brought before the Pope.

In May, Joan's jurors issued their verdict: guilty. Joan was condemned on a technicality—she was convicted of disregarding an official order to put aside male dress during her imprisonment. It was pretty clear that she had been judged guilty well in advance of the actual trial and any excuse would have served to convict her.

The court advised Joan that she would be turned over to "the secular army," unless she abjured her former testimony. Joan publicly recanted, stipulating that she repented her former statement if it pleased God that she do so. The court then issued a sentence of lifelong imprisonment. When Joan returned to her cell, the voices of Saint Catherine and Saint Margaret castigated her for her treason. Boldly, she summoned her ecclesiastical judges and retracted her recantation. She was summarily condemned as a relapsed heretic, and released to the secular authorities.

On May 30, 1431, at the age of 19, Joan of Arc was burned at the stake by the English authorities. The witnesses of her martyrdom were uniformly impressed by her humble Christian demeanor throughout her immolation. Joan's ashes were tossed unceremoniously into the Seine. An Englishman expressed the consensus of the crowd, when he exclaimed, "We are undone; we have burned a saint!"

Twenty-three years after Joan's death, her mother and brother appealed to Church officials to reopen her case. On July 7, 1456, Joan's conviction was officially overturned by papal edict, and Joan's innocence was confirmed by the Church.

In 1920, nearly 500 years after her immolation, Joan was officially canonized by the Roman Catholic Church. But admiration for the dauntless spirit of the Maid transcends sectarian boundaries. Joan's courage in pursuing her own personal experience of divine dictates serves as inspiration to all who value independent conviction.

As a patriot, Joan's historical importance is undisputed. At the time of her emergence as a national leader, France was hopelessly mired in feudal divisions. Singlehandedly, the Maid achieved national reunification, reestablishing France as a major European power. She was directly responsible for the coronation of Charles VII, safeguarding the continuity of the Valois dynasty. Had Joan not dragged Charles to Reims, Henry V might well have become king of France as well as England, and the course of world history would accordingly have been utterly changed.

In Joan's common sense lay the secret of her success as a military commander. She won the Battle of Orleáns by discerning she must attack the English troops in the north where their fortifications were weakest. Again and again, Joan of Arc took the initiative on the battlefield, and her audacity and stamina inspired her troops to superhuman efforts, even when they were outnumbered. If Joan was no brilliant strategist, the fact is that she led an army with a previous record of unmitigated defeat to a stunning round of victories and turned the tide of the war in favor of the French.

Considering Joan of Arc's age and background, her temerity in undertaking her nation's salvation and her unwavering confidence in her own salvation are astounding. How did an unlettered rustic girl overcome the obstacles to the goal she had chosen as military and inspirational leader of her country? How was she able to disarm sophisticated opponents and persuade them to entrust to her the destiny of her countrymen? The answer is that Joan of Arc was bolstered by the belief that she acted not for herself, but as the instrument of Heaven.

Elizabeth I (1533-1603)

QUEEN OF ENGLAND

When Elizabeth Tudor ascended the throne in 1558, England was at its nadir of power and prestige. The royal treasury was bankrupt; the country was at war with France; and internal religious divisions had paralyzed the national will. Elizabeth I personally effected the great compromise that reconciled warring Protestant factions under the aegis of the Anglican Church. She ended the conflict with the French on better terms than anyone had expected, and restored England to economic solvency. To her countrymen, Queen Elizabeth gave a new sense of national identity and pride, which found expression in a Golden Age of literature, in which, for example, William Shakespeare flourished. Her peaceful and prosperous reign of 45 years was one of the most outstanding periods in English history. During and after her reign, England was established as a major power.

Elizabeth was the daughter of Henry VIII and his second wife, Anne Boleyn. In furthering the Protestant cause by promoting the widespread distribution of William Tyndale's English translation of the Bible, the short-lived Anne set a precedent for her daughter. But

Elizabeth never knew her mother. The infant princess spent the first three years of her life traveling from one royal household to another.

When Queen Anne was executed in 1536, Elizabeth was declared illegitimate by Parliament. A year later, Henry's third wife, Jane Seymour, gave birth to a son, Edward. Elizabeth carried her half-brother's baptismal robe to the christening, and from then on was allowed to remain at court.

As a child, Elizabeth was remarkably precocious. Great pains were taken to give her the best education ever given to a female English child. A series of humanist scholars from Cambridge University served as the princess's tutors, and she studied for many years under Roger Ascham, author of *The Schoolmaster*, who was considered the most brilliant and innovative teacher of his day.

Elizabeth's early mastery of classical and modern languages later enabled her, as queen, to converse directly with foreign envoys, insuring her personal control over England's diplomatic affairs. The knowledge she acquired of history and theology equipped her to later effect far-reaching political and religious reforms.

Elizabeth's exceptional education was largely due to the influence of her father's eighth wife. Catherine Parr, herself an intelligent and cultivated woman, insisted that her ten-year-old stepdaughter receive the same educational opportunities afforded to Prince Edward. On a personal level, Catherine showed great love for the young princess, who remembered her surrogate mother always with affection and respect.

Henry died in 1547, and the next 11 years, during which Elizabeth's half-brother, Edward VI, and later her half-sister, Mary I, ruled were traumatic periods for both Elizabeth and England.

Elizabeth's life was endangered during the reign of Mary I. The aptly-named Bloody Mary was a devout Roman Catholic and during her rule Protestants were persecuted, and many of them executed. In 1554, Sir Thomas Wyatt led an unsuccessful insurrection against Mary, in the hope of putting Elizabeth on the throne as a Protestant monarch. Mary suspected Elizabeth of complicity, and Elizabeth was briefly sequestered in the Tower of London.

Queen Mary became increasingly unpopular with her subjects. When she died in 1558, Elizabeth ascended the throne, to the great joy of the English people. During the coronation ceremonies, the new queen addressed her subjects with heartfelt eloquence. An exceptionally articulate and impassioned speaker, Elizabeth periodically made moving appeals to her subjects, which earned her the nickname "Good Queen Bess."

Elizabeth was equally adept at ingratiating herself to her councilors. She personally selected each of her ministers, and with such shrewd judgment that she was rarely obliged to dismiss anyone. She chose her advisors on the basis of their intelligence and integrity, and listened attentively to their counsel. She also garnered information from direct sources, and made all the final decisions herself. She was not afraid to overrule her male appointees when necessary, not even her most trusted henchman, Secretary of State William Cecil.

In an age of religious strife, characterized by plots and counterplots, Elizabeth was shrewd enough to protect herself. She was acutely aware of the danger posed to her authority by collusion among her male councilors. She kept her cabinet small, and consulted each member individually, using different advisors for different issues. She actually encouraged, and perhaps even instigated, intrigues and rivalries among her ministers and favorites so they would not, as a body, act against her.

Elizabeth's handling of the religious question typified the cautious, deliberative approach that she employed for all knotty affairs of state. She resisted Parliamentary Puritan pressure for radical change and advocated a middle way. The 39 articles comprised in the Elizabethan Compromise established Anglicanism as the national religion and determined the character of the Episcopalian Church as it remains today. The majority of splinter-group Protestants went along with the compromise of 1559 and only the Roman Catholics and Puritans remained unappeased.

In 1568, Elizabeth's Catholic half-sister, Mary Queen of Scots, appealed to the English sovereign for asylum and financial support. Mary had let passion prevail over policy in her management of Scottish affairs, and had accordingly been dethroned. The English Parliamentary consensus was strongly against admitting Mary to English territory, but Elizabeth, though fully cognizant that Mary would provide a focus for Catholic discontent, allowed the potential usurper to enter England and live comfortably at royal expense.

Catholic conspirators promptly began to agitate on Mary's behalf. In 1569, there was an abortive Catholic uprising in northern England. The succeeding decade was punctuated by a string of treasonous plots, in which Mary's personal participation became increasingly obvious. Remembering her own precarious existence under Mary I, Elizabeth repeatedly vetoed Parliamentary bills calling for Mary's execution or for her exclusion from the succession to the throne. But in 1587, weary of her stepsister's intrigues, Elizabeth signed Mary's death warrant.

Parliament was not placated by the execution of the Scottish queen. Throughout Elizabeth's reign, the House of Commons pushed for stronger anti-Catholic bills than the sovereign was willing to sign. She would not persecute the Catholics as Bloody Mary had the Protestants. It was not her business, she declared, "to make windows into men's souls." During the Elizabethan age, the average English Catholic who was not involved in political intrigue was free to practice his faith privately. But Elizabeth did approve laws aimed at containing the power of the Catholic clergy, and after 1570, when a papal bull excommunicated "Elizabeth, the Pretended Queen of England," she returned measure for measure. She vigorously enforced laws prohibiting as potential traitors Catholics educated abroad from returning to England.

Elizabeth's foreign policy was aimed at preventing Catholic hegemony. She supported Protestant uprisings in the Netherlands and France, two countries that might have served as entry ports for a Spanish invasion of England. Catholic Spain posed the greatest threat to English autonomy, but when Philip II's attack was successfully repelled at the Battle of the Armada in 1588, English supremacy on the high seas was established. Explorers like Sir Francis Drake and Sir John Hawkins were allowed to plunder Spanish treasure ships and raid Spanish colonies, and the booty from these expeditions was used to swell the crown coffers. Elizabeth also aided Protestant insurgents in Scotland, opening access to the Scottish throne to Protestant James VI, whom she was to make King of England on her deathbed.

James's peaceful assumption of the English throne vindicated Elizabeth's steadfast refusal throughout her reign either to name a successor or to marry and produce an heir. During the early years of her tenure in particular, Parliament pressured the queen to accept the hand of one of her powerful foreign suitors. These included the king of Spain, the French Duc D'Anjou, and the archduke of Austria. English noblemen, too, urged their suits on the monarch. But Elizabeth knew that a husband would seriously interfere with her omnipotence. An arch-diplomat, she forestalled Parliament with a series of delaying tactics, waiting until her final hour to name a successor. She also promoted her image as the Virgin Queen, gaining popular support for her resistance to the Parliamentary pressure.

Elizabeth's personal mystique has few historical parallels. A cult figure to the populace, she became the first English ruler to have her accession day celebrated as a national holiday, a tradition that endured into the 18th century. Elizabeth showed an unprecedented regard for her subjects' economic welfare. Rather than impose burdensome taxes on the people, she augmented the treasury from her own revenues. Where these were inadequate, she bullied Parliament into voting additional funds. Her reluctance to go to war further minimized stress, securing ease and prosperity for the average Elizabethan Englishman.

In the Golden Age of the Elizabethan reign, the new, exuberant English spirit found its best expression in literature. Among the poets who sought and received the queen's patronage were Sir Philip Sidney, Edmund Spenser, and Sir Walter Raleigh. Elizabeth engaged William Shakespeare's acting company to perform the bard's dramas as private court entertainments. In 1594, she appointed essayist and philosopher Francis Bacon to her learned council.

Elizabeth's declining years were marked by personal and financial misfortune. Circumstances beyond the queen's control, such as poor harvests and corruption among minor officials, caused financial reverses, and the House of Commons became increasingly critical of the queen. Elizabeth silenced her critics with her "golden speech" of 1601. Declaimed two years before her death, the speech is valedictory in tone:

. . . . *It is not my desire to live or reign longer than my life and reign shall be for your [the people's] good. And though you have had, and may have, many mightier and wiser princes sitting in this seat, yet you never had, nor shall have, any that will love you better.*

Elizabeth was too modest. It is doubtful that England—or any other nation—has had many wiser or mightier rulers than Queen Elizabeth I. Her actions were predicated on a belief that it is better to rule through love than through fear, and her achievements amply justify that premise. In ecclesiastical affairs, she eschewed the bloody methods of her predecessors, enforcing harsh measures only where there arose a universally-recognized danger to her throne. As soon as the danger lessened, she mitigated the sanctions. Elizabeth not only created the Anglican Church, she also preserved it from subversive attacks by the Puritans, who presented a powerful and organized Parliamentary opposition. Repeatedly, Elizabeth dared to incur Parliamentary enmity by her vetoes of their proposed anti-Catholic ordinances.

Elizabeth's tolerant, forbearing nature resulted in a refreshingly non-belligerent foreign policy. There was a minimum of bloodshed during Elizabeth's reign. She took the offensive only when her nation's independence was endangered. She was respected and feared by her more bellicose foreign opponents, who tried to woo her with marriage proposals when they could not weaken her by military attacks.

Elizabeth's reign was as prosperous as it was peaceful. Her credit was better than that of any other European monarch. She set a national example by her personal frugality and intolerance of official corruption. As a sovereign, Elizabeth was a shining example of the so-called womanly virtues. Never was a monarch more loyal or more loving toward servants and subjects. Her innate abilities, coupled with her erudition, enabled Elizabeth to express her feelings in speeches that are outstanding for their literary eloquence. Her oration to her troops at Tilbury, made in 1588 in anticipation of an invasion by Parma, illustrates Elizabeth's unique rapport with her land and people:

My loving people. . . . Let tyrants fear. I have always so behaved myself that, under God, I have placed my chiefest strength and safeguard in the loyal hearts and good will of my subjects. . . . I know I have the body of a weak and feeble woman, but I have the heart and stomach of a king, and a king of England, too, and think foul scorn that Parma or Spain, or any prince of Europe should dare to invade the borders of my realm; to which, rather than any dishonour shall grow by me, I myself will take up arms, I myself will be your general, judge, and rewarder of every one of your virtues in the field.

Anna Van Schurman
(1607-1678)

ARTIST, SCHOLAR

Her portrait hangs in the major museums of Europe, but her name is all but forgotten. In the 17th century, Anna van Schurman was variously hailed as the Wonder of the Age, the Tenth Muse, the Dutch Sappho and Corneille, the Learned Maid, the Star of Utrecht. Poet and polyglot, Anna van Schurman's linguistic fluency extended to Hebrew, Samarian, Arabic, Chaldaic, Syriac, Ethiopian, Turkish, and Persian, in addition to French, English, Spanish, Italian, Latin, Greek, and her native German and Dutch. In the fine arts, Anna van Schurman was an accomplished craftsman in ivory and wood-carving, glass-engraving, and paper-cutting, as well as a renowned oil painter, whose canvases commanded good prices. Like Sir Francis Bacon, Anna van Schurman took all knowledge for her province, studying law and theology, teaching history and philosophy, and even dabbling in medicine. Her friends included Descartes and Richelieu, Princess Elizabeth of Bohemia, and Queen Christina of Sweden. In her time, it was said that to go to the Low Countries without seeing Anna van Schurman was like going to France without seeing the king.

But at the age of 48, when she was at the zenith of her fame, Anna van Schurman renounced learning, gave up the *beau monde*, and

23

devoted the remainder of her life to works of charity.

Anna Maria van Schurman was born in 1607, in Cologne, Germany. Her paternal grandparents, members of the Dutch Reformed Church, had migrated to Germany to avoid religious persecution when the Spanish occupied the Netherlands during the Thirty Years War. Anna grew up in the tranquil German countryside, at Castle Dreitorn, the ancestral home of her mother's family, the van Harfs. Her only playmates were her two older brothers.

Anna's intellectual and religious precocity manifested themselves early. By the age of three, she could read the Bible in German; and by the age of four, she knew the lengthy Heidelberg catechism by heart. Anna also liked to read hagiographies of the Christian martyrs. One day, when Anna was out in the meadow gathering herbs with her nurse, she had an important spiritual experience. As she recited the Lutheran litany which begins, "I am not my own, but I belong to my true Saviour Jesus Christ," she reports, "I was penetrated with so great and sweet a joy, and was filled with so strong an inner impulse of love to Christ, that all my after years have not dimmed the lively recollection of that moment."

Educated by her parents at home, Anna proved an apt scholar, quickly learning to read and write in a number of languages and to do mathematics. She also learned to sing and to play instruments, and to weave tapestries. By the age of 11, Anna was tutoring her older brothers in French and Latin. Recognizing Anna's extraordinary gifts, her father also taught her science and philosophy. Of the classical poets, he allowed her to read only Homer and Virgil, but there were no strictures on classical prose writers, and Anna eagerly devoured Plutarch, Tacitus, Livy, Seneca, and Augustine.

Anna's mother took a dim view of her daughter's intellectual pursuits and taught the girl the domestic arts and needlework. Anna became adept at embroidery, and could produce flawless imitations of Flanders-point lace in paper.

In 1615, the van Schurmans moved to Holland, which was now more congenial to Protestants than Germany. At Franeker Anna's brothers could study at the university. Anna continued to study with her father until he died. On his deathbed, Mr. van Schurman enjoined his daughter not to "entangle herself in matrimony," but to consecrate her genius to science and religion.

Leaving her sons at the University of Franeker, the widowed Mrs. van Schurman took Anna and moved into the house of her two unmarried sisters in Utrecht. The three older women were actively engaged in charity work, and left Anna to her own artistic devices. Day after day, Anna read, carved, did tapestry, and drew landscapes, portraits, and still lifes.

One day, Anna's older brother, Gottschalk, showed some portraits she had carved of her family in boxwood to the renowned artist Gerard Honthurst. He declared them remarkable, and showed them to other artists and connoisseurs. Soon Anna was commissioned to carve portraits of the king and queen of France, Queen Christina of Sweden, and other royalty. At Honthurst's art school for women in Utrecht Anna met Elizabeth, the princess of Bohemia, and other celebrated women.

At the age of 16, Anna van Schurman was taken up by Society. A number of men proposed to her, but Anna refused them all. She spent a good part of the next seven years painting fanciful portraits of herself. Anna also established a reputation as a musician. Upon hearing her sing, Marie de' Medici exclaimed, "how pleasant a surprise it was to find Italy in Holland." Anna also won praise for her performances on the lute, the violin, and the cymbals. She frequented the salons, and maintained a regular correspondence with foreign scholars. Among her closest friends was the philosopher Descartes, who publicly extolled Anna's art, command of French and Latin, and piety.

At the age of 28, Anna van Schurman abandoned the fine arts to devote herself exclusively to scholarship and culture. She helped to establish a university in Utrecht, which opened in 1636. She became acquainted with the university's rector, Gisbert Voet, a professor of oriental languages. Voet was also a stern Calvinist and the most powerful influence in the Dutch Reformed Church. Under his influence, Anna abandoned her usual sartorial splendor, exchanged her brocades and pearls for plainer garb, and ceased to curl her hair. Women were not allowed to attend lectures at the University of Utrecht, so Professor Voet had a special box constructed for Anna where she could sit, concealed by curtains, during his lectures. Soon,

Anna was spending most of her time in this box, and learned Syriac, Chaldaic, and other oriental languages.

In the course of her theological reading, Anna became critical of the misogyny of the early Church Fathers. Taking up the cudgels for women's rights, Anna became embroiled in an epistolary controversy with her godfather, Dr. Rivet, a professor of theology at Leyden, who claimed that higher education was not for the common run of women. Anna argued:

My deep regard for learning, my conviction that equal justice is the right of all, impel me to protest against the theory which would allow only a minority of my sex to attain to what is, in the opinion of all men, most worth having. . . . I cannot see why a young girl in whom we admit a desire of self-improvement should not be encouraged to acquire the best that life affords.

Inspired by feminist treatises by her contemporaries Lucessia Marinelli and Maria de Jars, Anna van Schurman published her own defense of women's education, urging that "reason not custom" should prevail. Feeling that her efforts ought to be for the glory of God, and not for self-glorification, Anna did not generally claim authorship for her works, but her feminist manifesto, *Apology for the Female Sex*, was one of the few works that Anna van Schurman allowed to be printed under her name during her lifetime.

In 1653, Anna's mother died. Upon Anna now devolved the housekeeping and the care of her maiden aunts, aged 80 and 82 respectively, who were now blind and suffered from other infirmities of old age. As Anna ministered to their physical needs, and read and talked to them to ease their loneliness, she became sympathetic to the silent suffering of the old. She realized that there must be other aged citizens in Utrecht who were helpless, and ailing, and—not being cared for—joyless.

Now 48 years old, Anna decided to make the care of the elderly and the needy her special mission. She renounced her arcane studies as a luxury, shut her books, closed her doors to society, and terminated her voluminous correspondences. She began to frequent the poorer sections of Utrecht, giving away her money to the poor and visiting the elderly in workhouses. Dismayed to discover how many people could neither read nor write, she began to teach the illiterate.

Around 1654, Anna, her brother Gottschalk, and the two aunts went back to Cologne to live on the van Harf estate. Determined that the only true greatness was moral greatness, Anna continued to devote herself to almsgiving and to contemplation. Gottschalk, who shared her religious fervor, set off for Switzerland to meet Jean de Labadie, a former Jesuit turned Protestant pietist. Upon the death of the aunts, within weeks of each other at the ages of 89 and 91, Gottschalk and Anna went back to Utrecht, where they became ardent mystics and ascetics and followers of Labadie.

When her brother Gottschalk died, to the horror of her former friends, Anna joined Labadie's religious community. After Labadie's death in 1674, Anna continued caring for the poor, and preaching Labadie's gospel of the inner light. In 1677, she wrote her autobiography, which was full of religious and mystical observations. The following year, she died, at the age of 71.

Like Anna van Schurman, in the 18th century, Maria Gaetani Agnesi, one of the most brilliant mathematicians of her day, declined a chair in mathematics at the University of Bologna in order to devote herself to the care of the poor and the afflicted. Agnesi's name is today as unknown to the average person as is van Schurman's. It is perhaps fitting that the annals of *herstory* restore to fame the names of these exceptional women neglected by history. The conflict between home life and career has for centuries been uniquely reserved to women, but the conflict between the goals of personal enhancement and social service is shared by all. Anna van Schurman was lucky enough to be born into circumstances that afforded her every opportunity for self-development. She gave it all up for the greater goal of service to humanity.

Caroline Herschel
(1750-1848)
ASTRONOMER

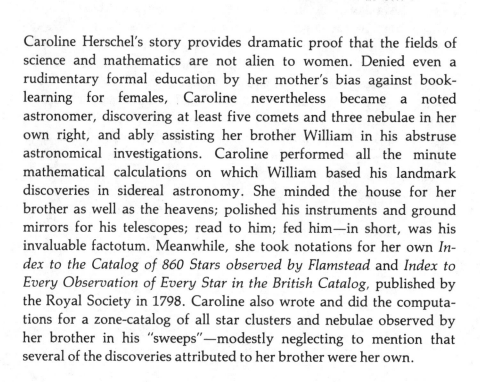

Caroline Herschel's story provides dramatic proof that the fields of science and mathematics are not alien to women. Denied even a rudimentary formal education by her mother's bias against book-learning for females, Caroline nevertheless became a noted astronomer, discovering at least five comets and three nebulae in her own right, and ably assisting her brother William in his abstruse astronomical investigations. Caroline performed all the minute mathematical calculations on which William based his landmark discoveries in sidereal astronomy. She minded the house for her brother as well as the heavens; polished his instruments and ground mirrors for his telescopes; read to him; fed him—in short, was his invaluable factotum. Meanwhile, she took notations for her own *Index to the Catalog of 860 Stars observed by Flamstead* and *Index to Every Observation of Every Star in the British Catalog*, published by the Royal Society in 1798. Caroline also wrote and did the computations for a zone-catalog of all star clusters and nebulae observed by her brother in his "sweeps"—modestly neglecting to mention that several of the discoveries attributed to her brother were her own.

Born in Hanover, Germany, on March 16, 1750, Caroline Herschel was the youngest child of Isaac Herschel, a musician. While her father supervised the musical education of his four sons, Caroline and her sisters learned the domestic arts from their mother. Caroline's father quickly discerned the genius of his youngest child, and tried to let Caroline share in her brothers' music lessons, but Mrs. Herschel would not allow it.

When Caroline was seven years old, her brothers Jacob and William went to England to pursue their musical studies. Caroline's father again attempted to give the girl violin lessons, and was again obstructed by his wife's opposition. Caroline vowed that she would not be "turned into an Abigail or housemaid," and fumed when her mother apprenticed her to a seamstress for three months.

William returned home briefly in 1764, and Caroline was a rapt spectator at local concerts where her brother performed. In 1772, William finally rescued his sister from her dreary round of housework, taking her with him to Bath, where he was a distinguished professor of music and a celebrated organist.

Actually, William's consuming interest was not in music—he was a passionate amateur astronomer. In his spare time, he pursued his own studies in astronomy, and even gave lessons in that science. So consumed was William by his astronomical endeavors, that he all but ignored his sister. Caroline, who had hoped that William would impart to her some of his vast knowledge of music, was sadly disappointed. She attempted to practice by herself, but William hindered her efforts at self-improvement, requiring her to spend her time constructing pasteboard containers for the lenses of a 20-foot telescope which was to arrive shortly from London.

Eventually, William became more considerate of his uncomplaining sister's desires. In appreciation for Caroline's indispensable services, he arranged for her to study with a singing mistress. Caroline showed great promise as a vocalist, singing in local concerts under her brother's direction. Caroline's musical career was abruptly terminated in 1782, when William, who had distinguished himself as the discoverer of the planet Uranus, was appointed Britain's royal astronomer. Being informed by William that she was to be his full-time astronomical assistant, Caroline reports, "my . . . thoughts . . .

were anything but cheerful." Her training in that field would commence, he told her, when William returned from court. In the meantime, Caroline was given some hasty instructions and a Newtonian reflector, with which she was to "sweep" the skies for comets in William's absence.

In August 1782, Caroline began her own journal of her astronomical findings, but, upon his return, William continually hampered Caroline's independent investigations. As they each sat at their telescopes, he would shout across the lawn to her to drop whatever she was doing and come record his latest observation. In the midst of making an observation of her own, Caroline would obediently abandon her reflector to serve as William's amanuensis.   William never followed through on his promise to give Caroline a proper scientific education; his own investigations absorbed all his time. Caroline's training in astronomy was a very slipshod business, and occurred primarily at her own instigation. At the dinner table, she would query her brother about his activities and enter his remarks into a notebook. Later, she would organize these random observations into a coherent system, so that she could understand what her astronomical labors were all about. Caroline's mathematical instruction was equally parsimonious and consisted of piecemeal dictation of mathematical formulae by William, which Caroline diligently applied to the data gathered from their joint observation of the heavens. Only a mind as perspicacious as Caroline's could have made sense of the minimal information she was receiving in this most exacting, abstruse field.

By 1786, the Herschels' astronomical apparatus required more space than their modest yard at Dachet afforded, so Caroline and her brother moved to Slough. Soon after the move, William was sent to Göttingen by King George, to present a ten-foot telescope to the Göttingen Observatory. Caroline was enjoined to continue sweeping the skies and refurbishing the house at Slough. During this separation, brother and sister carried on a heavy correspondence concerning their independent sidereal observations. In a letter dated August 1, William exults that he has seen an object that he believes to be a comet, apparently unaware that this comet had been one of Caroline's previous discoveries. William never publicly acknowledged his sister's original discoveries.

In 1786 and 1787, William Herschel made the important discovery of the Georgian satellites, for which he was granted an annual pension by the king, and an additional lump sum with which to complete the construction of a 40-foot telescope. For her share in the work Caroline, also, was awarded a small annual stipend, an unprecedented royal recognition of a woman. In October 1787, she confided to her diary her delight at receiving the first installment of this grant, "the first money I ever in all my lifetime thought myself to be at liberty to spend to my own liking."

In 1788, William Herschel married. The stunned Caroline found herself relegated to lodgings nearby, as William still required his sister's nightly assistance in his backyard observatory. Left with large blocks of time to herself for the first time in her life, Caroline began to pursue independent investigations. In the next several years, she announced the discovery of eight comets. Five of these were indisputably observed for the first time by Caroline. Her accomplishment brought her widespread recognition as a gifted astronomer in her own right. Batches of congratulatory letters from European scientists arrived in the mails.

In 1805, Caroline Herschel discovered her eighth and last comet. From then until 1822, various members of her family made incessant inroads on her time. Brought up not to believe in her right to her own life, Caroline's talents were largely wasted while she catered to the demands and priorities of her male relatives. A ne'er-do-well brother came to live with Caroline, at her expense, for four years, raising constant shenanigans all the while. Caroline was an affectionate aunt to her several nephews, who also absorbed much of her time. Her major priority, however, was William and on clear evenings, Caroline was always at his beck and call, and would join him outdoors to continue their mutual astronomical endeavors.

In 1882, William Herschel died of overwork. The inconsolable Caroline returned to Hanover after an absence of 50 years. Now 72, Caroline devoted the next six years to charting the zones of her brother's 25,000 nebulae, and published the findings. Her presentation of this catalog to the Royal Society, in 1828, earned her a gold medal and an honorary membership in the society.

At the age of 78, Caroline left off scientific pursuits, and, returning to her childhood passion, resumed attendance at musical and theatrical entertainments. To her amazement and delight, artistic celebrities, including the great violin virtuoso Paganini, requested to meet the renowned lady astronomer, and the last 25 years of her life were full of social activity. She also remained devoted to her siblings and their children. Caroline Herschel died on January 9, 1848.

The story of Caroline Herschel poignantly exemplifies the dilemma of exceptionally bright women who are conditioned, from infancy, to serve in auxiliary roles. From childhood, the self-styled "Cinderella of the family" regarded herself as the mere handmaiden of her brilliant older brother. Although she was content to bask in the reflected glory of her famous brother, her own contribution did not go unnoticed by knowledgeable scientists. At the eighth general meeting of the Astronomical Society of London, Caroline's services and sacrifices for William were publicly extolled:

. . . she it was whose pen conveyed to paper his observations as they issued from his lips; she it was who noted the right ascensions and polar distances of the objects observed; she it was who, having passed the night near the instrument, took the rough manuscript to her cottage at dawn, and produced a fair copy of the night's work on the following morning; she it was who planned the labours of each successive night, who reduced every observation, made every calculation; she it was who arranged everything in systematic order; and she it was who helped him to obtain his imperishable name. Many of the nebulae contained in Sir W. Herschel's catalogues were detected by her.

We can only surmise what this intelligent and industrious woman might have accomplished had the circumstances of her life not prevented her from developing personal ambitions or acquiring a systematic education. Her actual achievement, in spite of being a victim of her time and circumstance, is imposing. As co-founder of modern astronomy, and pioneer in opening up the sciences to women, Caroline Herschel merits a place in the pantheon of great women.

Elizabeth Gurney Fry
(1780-1845)

PRISON REFORMER

In 1819, Virginia congressman John Randolph visited London and sent the following rousing report to an American friend:

I saw the greatest curiosity in London—aye, and in England, too, sir—compared with which Westminster Abbey, the Tower, Somerset House, the British Museum, nay, Parliament itself, sink into utter insignificance. I have seen, sir, Elizabeth Fry in Newgate, and I have witnessed there, sir, miraculous effects of true Christianity upon the most depraved of human beings— bad women, sir, who are worse, if possible, than the Devil himself. And yet the wretched outcasts have been tamed and subdued by the Christian eloquence of Mrs. Fry.

As enthusiastic as he was, what John Randolph failed to comprehend was that to Elizabeth Fry, as to Jesus before her, there were no "bad women," but merely erring sisters.

In two noisome cells, with the bare floor for their beds, no change of clothing or nightclothes, no work or recreational activities, 300 women and their children lived, washed, cooked, and slept. Women convicted of felonies and of misdemeanors, wrongly accused prisoners awaiting trial—all were indiscriminately lodged together. There was no matron to look after them, only a dour male turnkey who scornfully referred to his charges as a "den of wild beasts."

Into this "den" walked Elizabeth Fry, forbearance in her eyes, compassion in her voice, and on her face a smile of infinite kindness for women and children alike. She listened carefully when a prisoner complained that it was harsh that she should be condemned to death for stealing a bit of food for her child, or when a woman soon to be released said she'd like to lead an honest life, but had no trade, no skills. Elizabeth Fry promised to procure a schoolroom, and did. She read the gospel to the women in a gentle voice. She brought them soap and warm clothing, and expressed approval when they took thought for their appearance. She raised the prisoners' self-esteem by appointing monitors from among them.

Then she brought Newgate officials to see the transformation that self-respect and hope had wrought in the prisoners, and persuaded them that rehabilitation, not retribution, was the proper purpose of penal institutions. She carried her message all over Europe, and single-handedly injected the spirit of Christianity into the treatment of prisoners. Wherever she went, Elizabeth Fry was greeted as the Angel of the Prisons.

Born in Norfolk, England, on May 21, 1780, the third of 12 children, Elizabeth Gurney had some personal experience with the effects of being treated as an inferior. She was delicate in health and plagued by migraine headaches. Her two older sisters far excelled her in schoolwork. Years later, Elizabeth commented:

I was considered and called very stupid and obstinate. . . . I think having the name of being stupid really tended to make me so, and discouraged my efforts to learn. I remember having a poor, not to say, low, opinion of myself, and used to think that I was so very inferior to my sisters.

Elizabeth's father was a wealthy banker. Her mother closely supervised her daughters' education, emphasizing not only intellectual attainments, but "gentleness of manner," and this, young Betsy acquired easily. When she was 12, her mother died. At 15, Betsy was engaged to James Lloyd, son of a wealthy landowner, but her fiancé broke off the engagement to pursue a life of dissipation in London.

Her experience with her fiancé left Betsy Gurney permanently altered. No longer one of the "gay Gurney sisters," she became somber and pensive. The Gurney family was nominally Quaker, but they were not "plain Quakers," and Betsy Gurney had hitherto delighted in the dancing and music that filled Gurney Hall in the evenings. Like her sisters, she had derided chapel-going. But now she became introspective and considered that she was frittering away her life aimlessly preening before the mirror and flirting with officers. She confided to her diary, "I feel I am a contemptible fine lady. All outside, no inside. May I be preserved from continuing so is the ardent prayer of my *good* man, but my *evil* man tells me I shall pray in vain."

The following winter her prayer was answered. The visit of an American Quaker named William Savery effected a conversion in her soul, and gave a focus to her life.

As Betsy Gurney set out for chapel on February 4, 1798, she had no sense that the day was to prove cataclysmic. A few hours later, after hearing William Savery deliver his plea for a return to the first principles of Christianity, "peace on earth and good will to men," she felt agitated and upset. She wept most of the way home.

Betsy embarked on a course of self-improvement, reading moral literature and studying grammar. "I am to be a Quaker," she told her diary. For Betsy, being a Quaker meant a renunciation of social frippery. To her father's dismay, she declined invitations to parties and adopted the drab clothing and prim bonnet of a plain Quaker. She began to show what Mr. Gurney regarded as an excessive interest in her poverty-stricken neighbors, and even demanded that her father escort her to the Norfolk House of Correction, that she might obtain some sense of what it was like to be truly wretched.

In 1799 Elizabeth Gurney wrote in her diary: "I overflow with the blessings of this world. I have friends, as many as I wish for, good health, a happy home with all that riches can give, and yet these are nothing without a satisfied contience. [sic]" To begin to ease her conscience, Betsy turned the laundry at Gurney Hall into a schoolroom, and soon she had 70 pupils. Many of her scholars were child laborers in the local factories. Invited to visit her students' homes, Betsy went. She found sickness, and nursed it; she found empty stomachs, and filled them. She did not think of herself as a Lady Bountiful, but as a simple Christian doing her duty. A new sense of joy and purpose came to her.

Betsy's lighthearted sisters found in her school a source of hilarity; "Betsy's imps," they called her students. Mr. Gurney was at first distressed by his daughter's crude scholars, but within a year he was proudly bringing friends to observe her classroom. Still, Mr. Gurney thought he'd better find Betsy a husband, before the mischief went too far. For this purpose, he chose Joseph Fry, a plain Quaker who was also a wealthy banker. Mr. Gurney invited young Fry to spend a weekend at Gurney Hall, and as he hoped, the youth was immediately attracted to the graceful, simply-garbed Elizabeth.

Elizabeth Gurney discouraged Joseph Fry's suit. But Joseph Fry had a strong will of his own, and went straight to Betsy, demanding to know the reason for her disinclination. The young woman told her suitor about Savery, her conversion, and her philanthropic activities. She explained that she felt a vocation to do good in the world, and feared that marriage would prove incompatible with her mission. Joseph Fry professed that his wife would be free to follow her vocation. Thus, on August 19, 1800, Elizabeth Gurney and Josephy Fry exchanged marital vows before the congregation at Goats meeting hall.

The young bride went with her husband to his London manor at Mildred's Court. Elizabeth yearned to be an active Christian. True to his promise, Joseph Fry accepted his wife's striving for a vocation, and in May 1801, though Elizabeth was six months pregnant, she went with his blessing to Southwark, where she had heard that an exciting educational experiment with poor children was taking place.

Elizabeth returned full of enthusiasm. In schoolmaster Joseph Lancaster's classroom in Southwark, she had witnessed an entirely novel approach to education. Lancaster appointed some of the older children as monitors and assistant teachers, and Elizabeth had been impressed with the change that came over former delinquent pupils when they were given positions of responsibility. Elizabeth longed to start a school of her own, but had to content herself with sending Lancaster financial support for his remarkable school.

Giving birth to six children in eight years forced Elizabeth to postpone her project time and again. Meanwhile, she made forays into the London slums to vaccinate children and read the Bible to their parents. Often, her husband accompanied her on these missions, and gave money to the poor to alleviate their distresses. Elizabeth Fry also became a part-time teacher in the London workhouses.

In 1809, Joseph Fry's father died, and the couple moved to the Fry estate at Plashet. Here, Elizabeth, aided by the wife of the local Episcopalian rector, was at last able to establish her school. Then, in 1811, when her father died, Elizabeth felt impelled to stand up in meeting to be recorded as a Quaker minister. She soon became known as an eloquent preacher, with a fine voice, admirable delivery, and sublime message.

In 1817, Joseph Fry found it necessary to sell his country estate and seek modest lodgings in London. Now Elizabeth Fry could really devote herself to the work she dreamed of. She began the prison reform work for which she is famous.

Her first endeavor was to start a school in the Newgate Prison, using the Lancaster monitor system. Next, she established a Ladies Newgate Committee to care for the prisoners' physical wants, conduct Bible classes, and teach sewing and other trades. When the prison authorities witnessed the changes humane treatment had wrought in the inmates of Newgate, they supported Elizabeth's plea for other badly-needed reforms, such as providing a matron and setting up a classification system for prisoners.

Reports of the Newgate miracle spread to all parts of Great Britain and the Continent, and soon foreign monarchs were journeying to London to observe Elizabeth Fry in action. She became an established authority on penal reform, and a visiting consultant to penal institutions throughout the United Kingdom, as well as in many countries in Europe.She also instigated a program to provide homes and jobs in the colonies for felons who were freed and sent to Australia and New Zealand.

Although prison reform was Elizabeth Fry's primary concern, she became involved in other benevolent pursuits. She founded the first shelters for the homeless in England, obtained employment for beggars, established the first organized visiting societies for the destitute, organized libraries in 500 British coast guard stations, and was a pioneer in the field of nursing, founding the first institution for the training of nurses in Devonshire Square. She happily pursued her work for wide-ranging reforms until her death, on October 12, 1845.

For 32 years Elizabeth had served as the vanguard of European penal reform, despite periods of enforced inactivity due to pregnancy and household responsibilities. At the age of 40, the mother of 11 children confided to her journal: "My household cares at times are a weighty burden which particularly cast me down, and appear as if they must swallow up much of my powers. It is what I have no natural taste or aptitude for, and . . . so difficult for me. . . ."

But domestic chores, her husband's eventual bankruptcy and her own deteriorating health could not stay Elizabeth Fry from her prodigious activities. Single-handedly, she changed the emphasis in penal institutions from chastisement to rehabilitation. By fostering self-respect and creating professional opportunities for female prisoners, she reduced the incidence of recidivism to an incalculable degree. She pursued reform of the penal code by publicizing such injustice as having the stealing of a loaf of bread be punishable by death. She was always available to the women incarcerated at Newgate and would come to them at all hours to read the Bible or listen to the final thoughts of women bound for the executioner's block. Elizabeth Fry was the first woman to appear before a Parliamentary committee, the Committee on Prisons, and her testimony was responsible for a massive overhaul of the penal laws. Although she never achieved her goal of abolishing capital punishment, Elizabeth Fry did succeed in diminishing the number of executions of criminals. Over and above all, she established a precedent of humane treatment in penal institutions all over the world.

Emma Hart Willard
(1787-1870)

PIONEER IN EDUCATION

The intention of your being taught needlework, knitting, and such like is not on account of the intrinsic value of all you can do with your hands, which is trifling, but . . . to enable you to fill up, in a tolerably agreeable way, some of the many solitary hours you must necessarily pass at home.

Thus wrote Dr. John Gregory in *A Father's Legacy to his Daughters,* the foremost primer of women's education during the girlhood of Emma Hart Willard. Willard, founder of the first permanent institution for higher education for women in America, had very different views about how women should pass their hours, both in and out of the home, from those ingenuously expressed by Dr. Gregory. Needlework and other ornamental arts were eliminated from the curriculum of Willard's seminary in Troy, New York, and were replaced by zoology, anatomy, geometry, trigonometry, and other subjects considered at that time to be beyond the grasp of female minds. Today, Dr. Gregory and his *Legacy* have passed into oblivion, but the Emma Willard School in Troy is still one of the best college-preparatory institutions in the nation, and Emma Willard's promulgation of higher education for women remains a legacy for the daughters of all generations.

Emma Hart was born on her father's sheep farm in Berlin, Connecticut on February 23, 1787. She was the 16th of her father's 17 children, and the 9th of the 10 children borne by the second Mrs. Hart to her husband. The Hart household provided a good deal of intellectual nourishment—Mr. Hart discoursed to the children on American history and on the philosophies of John Locke and George Berkeley, while Mrs. Hart enthralled them with readings from Chaucer, Shakespeare, and Milton. A Jeffersonian liberal, Mr. Hart encouraged his daughters, especially the inquisitive Emma, to develop their minds. But in the division of the wool sheared from the Hart sheep, the ethic of female inferiority still prevailed—the best wool was used for Mr. Hart's clothing; the second best for his sons'; and the poorest for the women's garments.

As she entered adolescence, Emma found her education becoming increasingly separate from, and unequal to, that of her brothers. She was given no instruction in mathematics or the sciences, neither at school nor at home. She managed to teach herself geometry from one of her brother's textbooks at the age of 13, and aspired to learn astronomy by rising at four to go out and study the constellations.

In 1804, two years after matriculating at the Berlin Academy in Connecticut, Emma Hart became an instructor at a local primary school. Here Emma made her first educational innovation, arranging her students according to educational level instead of age or size as was the custom. Emma's pupils found her a stimulating teacher, and in 1805, Emma opened her own school for older students in the upper rooms of her father's house. The following winter, she taught at the Berlin Academy. Emma also continued her own schooling, paid for by one of her brothers, at a finishing school in Hartford.

As a young teacher, Emma Hart broke no new ground in educational philosophy, but continued to experiment with new teaching techniques, and her reputation as a dynamic pedagogue spread throughout the New England states. In 1807, Emma became the preceptress of the Female Academy in Middlebury, Vermont. Her enthusiasm for learning was infectious, and she quickly attracted a group of 60 adolescent students from all over Vermont.

Middlebury was a hive of social and cultural activity, and Emma enjoyed the companionship of interesting adults. Among the most congenial of her new acquaintances was Dr. John Willard, a prominent Middlebury physician and advocate of women's education. On August 10, 1809, 22-year-old Emma Hart married 50-year-old Dr. Willard, and became stepmother to four children from her husband's two previous marriages. She resigned her teaching post upon marrying, and in 1810 gave birth to a son, John.

After several years of marital bliss, Emma began to feel hemmed in. Her restlessness was fanned into a fire of intellectual discontent when she saw the riches that her husband's nephew, a student who was living with her family, was being exposed to at Middlebury College. Emma rushed to fill the gaps in her education by inducing her husband's nephew to repeat the lectures of his Middlebury professors to her, lend her his books, and allow her to study his examination questions.

In 1814, Emma was rescued from domestic stagnation by financial adversity. The bank in which Dr. Willard served as director was robbed, and the angry depositors demanded that he make up their losses. Emma saw her opportunity, and opened a private seminary for women in her home. Unlike any other seminary of its day, the Middlebury Female Seminary taught higher mathematics, classical literature, and college sciences. Emma continued to imbibe her nephew's college courses secondhand, and passed on her new knowledge to her students. Soon her pupils numbered 70, and a housekeeper was engaged to assume Emma's domestic duties.

Ingrained by her mother with the motto of Chaucer's scholar, "and gladly would he learn and gladly teach," Emma urged her students to do likewise. Several of her pupils became assistant teachers at the school. They learned from Emma to discourage rote-learning. In Emma Willard's classroom, for example, geography was not the mere memorization of maps, but a study of comparative demography and topography. Herself a poet, whose "Rocked in the Cradle of the Deep" is still a popular elocution piece, Emma required her students to write original compositions. She also introduced college-level courses in history and literature into her curriculum.

Seeking support for her campaign for the improved education of women, Emma Willard approached De Witt Clinton, the progressive governor of New York, who agreed to let Emma present her proposals for a state-supported female academy to the legislature, with his recommendation. In 1819, Emma Willard stood before the New York legislators and read them her *Address . . . proposing a plan for improving female education,* thus becoming the first woman lobbyist in America.

Although her views on the role of women were to undergo increasing radicalization, at this stage of her career, Emma Willard was far from a feminist, and the tone of the *Address* was propitiatory. She conceded that women were destined for a humbler sphere than men, and argued that at present women were not even being educated to become good wives. More training in the useful domestic arts, rather than fancy needlework, was required; and women ought to be trained to teach advanced subjects. Society would benefit from the resulting brigade of well-educated women teachers, who, Willard suggested, offered an economic advantage in that they would accept lower salaries than men. In later years, Emma was to become a vehement opponent of unequal pay for equal work.

Moderate as these proposals were, the New York legislature equivocated. However, when the *Address* was endorsed by President James Monroe and former presidents Adams and Jefferson, the legislators approved the first state charter for women's education, with promises of eventual funding. Fifteen years were to pass before the money was forthcoming.

With her *Address,* Willard achieved national prominence. The citizens of Troy, New York, invited her to locate her female seminary in their town. Accordingly, in 1821, the Troy Female Academy was opened in a capacious three-story building renovated at municipal expense. Because New York State law barred married women from owning property, the school was leased to Dr. Willard, business manager and school physician of the seminary. A Committee of Ladies, a precursor of the P.T.A., was formed.

The school drew its student body from all over the United States. The original class included 90 pupils from seven states. There was a staff of Willard-trained teachers, and language and arts professors. The curriculum gradually expanded, and in the 1830s one of the students described the studies thus:

We had reading, writing, spelling, arithmetic, grammar, geography, history, maps, the globe, algebra, geometry, trigonometry, astronomy, natural philosophy, chemistry, botany, physiology, mineralogy, geology, and zoology in the morning, and dancing, drawing, painting, French, Italian, Spanish, and German in the afternoon. Greek and the higher branches of mathematics were only studied by the tall *girls.*

The advanced sciences were taught by Professor Amos Eaton, who instructed Emma Willard and the other teachers as well as the students. Among his star pupils was Emma's younger sister, Almira Hart Lincoln, who later wrote books on botany and chemistry that became standard college texts. Emma herself also wrote textbooks, including *Temple of Time*, which won a gold medal at the 1850 World's Fair in London for its creative use of charts to present historical events in chronological "pillars."

In 1825, Dr. Willard died, and his wife assumed official proprietorship of the school. Her educational philosophy became increasingly progressive. Competition between students was discouraged; no grades or awards were given at the Troy Female Seminary, where learning was considered its own reward. The school maintained an unwavering reputation for excellence. Founded 16 years before Mount Holyoke, the first woman's college in the United States, the Troy Seminary was rated on a par with Harvard and Yale by visiting male educators. Among the school's illustrious alumnae was suffragette Elizabeth Cady Stanton.

Increasingly interested in advancing the curriculum of her school and developing new teaching techniques, Emma Willard turned the day-to-day management of the seminary over to her son and daughter-in-law, a Troy alumna. Despite opposition, Emma added courses in physiology and anatomy to the curriculum. In 1846, she herself wrote a treatise on the circulation of the blood, and became one of the first women admitted to the Association for the Advancement of Science. It was not until a year later that the first woman, Elizabeth Blackwell, was to matriculate at medical school.

At the age of 50, Emma Willard made a second—and unhappy— marriage to Christopher Yates, a seemingly respectable Albany physician, who turned out to be a fortune hunter and a compulsive gambler. Separated after a brief nine months, Emma later obtained a divorce. For the next 20-odd years, Emma Willard served as a national and international lecturer and consultant, promoting higher standards and opportunities for female education. She founded the Willard Association for the Mutual Improvement of Female Teachers, which served as a national network for the exchange of educational ideas and techniques.

Emma Willard died on April 15, 1870. Her name was perpetuated 25 years later, when the Troy Female Seminary was renamed the Emma Willard School.

Emma Willard of Troy helped launch close to 1,000 women's schools, including the still outstanding Wheaton and Mount Holyoke seminaries in Massachusetts, and Catharine Beecher's seminary in Hartford. She was an implacable advocate of continuing education for women, especially for young mothers, like her own daughter-in-law "who with five children performs well the duties of principal of this [Troy Female Seminary] school."

The most definitive tribute to this pioneer is inscribed on Emma Willard's statue on the grounds of her school, "her most enduring monument, the gratitude of educated women."

In 1891, 53 women received B.A. degrees from London University and five women received M.A. degrees.

Dr. James Barry
(1795?-1865)

SURGEON-GENERAL OF THE BRITISH ARMY

On July 25, 1865, "Dr. James Barry," senior inspector-general of Her Majesty's Medical Services, died in London, at the age of 71. About a month after "Dr. Barry's" demise, the following obituary appeared in the *Manchester Guardian*:

. . . . *Our officers quartered at the Cape between 15 and 20 years ago may remember a certain Dr Barry attached to the medical staff there, and enjoying a reputation for considerable skill in his profession, especially for firmness, decision and rapidity in difficult operations. This gentleman had entered the army in 1813, had passed, of course, through the grades of assistant surgeon and surgeon in various regiments, and had served as such in various quarters of the globe. His professional acquirements had procured for him promotion to the staff at the Cape. . . . He died about a month ago, and upon his death was discovered to be a woman. The motives that occasioned, and the time when commenced this singular deception are both shrouded in mystery. But thus it stands as an indubitable fact, that a woman was for 40 years an officer in the British service, and fought one duel and had sought many more, had pursued a legitimate medical education, and received a regular diploma, and had acquired almost a celebrity for skill as a surgical operator.*

By order of the British War Office, not one London daily carried news of "Dr. Barry's" death, for the army was anxious to suppress what could be a major scandal: that one of its most distinguished surgeons with a rank equivalent to major general had been a woman—and no one had ever discovered the hoax.

To this day, not much is actually known about the early life of this remarkable woman, or about the circumstances that led her to assume a male identity. The scanty records at Edinburgh Medical College concerning "Dr. James Barry" indicate the year of her birth as 1795, and her birthplace as London. After her death, colorful stories concerning her parentage and youth were circulated. It was speculated that "James Barry" was the granddaughter, or the daughter, of a wealthy Scots nobleman, or perhaps the illegitimate daughter of the prince regent, or of his brother, the duke of York.

But these romantic stories were disproved in the 1950s, when author Isobel Rae prevailed upon the British War Office and the University of Edinburgh to let her examine their "Barry Papers." This resulted in the publication of *The Strange Story of Dr. James Barry*, the first factual account of the mysterious "Dr. Barry." Even this account leaves much of "Dr. Barry's" story unexplained.

According to Ms. Rae, "Dr. Barry" took her name from the man she called "Uncle," James Barry, R.A., a gifted Irish painter living and working in London. Who her parents actually were is not known. The painter's sister, Mrs. Bulkeley, raised the child until she reached adolescence. Most likely, "Dr. Barry" received her early education from her uncle, a cultivated man and a brilliant conversationalist. As a professional painter, James Barry was well-versed in anatomy, and probably included this subject in his "nephew's" education. When or why Barry's young charge became identified as his nephew is not known, but there is no doubt that he would not have scrupled to educate the youngster regardless of sex. An admirer of Mary Wollstonecraft Godwin, James Barry believed that women should be the "well-instructed companions and associates of men." In 1806, when the girl was eleven, her uncle died.

A good friend of the artist, the Latin American patriot General Francisco de Miranda, who was at that time residing in London, was renowned as the possessor of the best private library in London, containing over 6,000 volumes on every conceivable subject. Some

time between 1808 and 1809, the general invited the deceased painter's "nephew" to avail himself of this library, in preparation for his
medical studies.

Like her uncle, the younger "James Barry" was a gifted talker.
Even at the age of 14, young "James" exuded a good deal of charisma, and soon ingratiated herself with General Miranda. Miranda, in
turn, introduced the young "man" to her uncle's former patron,
David Stuart Erskine, the 11th earl of Buchan. The founder of the
Scots Antiquarian Society, Lord Buchan had a library nearly as "extensive and elegant" as the general's, and placed it at "James Barry's"
disposal when she arrived with her aunt in Edinburgh in 1809.

Armed with letters of introduction from Lord Buchan and from
the physician who had attended her uncle during his final illness,
"James Barry" had no trouble getting admitted to the Edinburgh
Medical School. The 15-year-old "James" pursued studies in the
practice and theory of medicine, botany, anatomy, military surgery,
midwifery, dissection, clinical surgery, and medical jurisprudence.
Her professors were the foremost physicians in Edinburgh. "James
Barry" also received practical training at the local hospitals. Fellow
students later recalled her as an aloof lad, who wore a long overcoat
instead of the shorter jacket sported by her peers. She made only
one close friend at the University, John Jobson. Jobson tried to
teach his young friend to box, but she insisted on keeping her arms
over her chest, "to protect it from blows," and finally persuaded
Jobson to teach her instead the art of the rapier, as "more my style."

Apparently, no one at the University of Edinburgh ever suspected
"James Barry" of being a girl, although she was twitted about her
beardless chin and diminutive stature of five feet. On her brilliant
medical thesis, completed in 1812, "Barry" wrote, "do not consider
my youth, but consider whether I show a man's wisdom." The subject of the thesis, strangely enough, was hernia of the groin. At the
age of 20 she was awarded the M.D.— perhaps the youngest recipient of this degree in Edinburgh's history.

As a new doctor, "Dr. Barry" went to London, where she was a
junior surgeon's apprentice. "Dr. Barry" was given a private
bedroom at St. Thomas Hospital, and was allowed to study surgery
with Sir Astley Cooper, the most eminent surgeon of the day, at St.

Guy's, a hospital across the street from St. Thomas. Within six months, she completed her studies and passed an examination by the College of Surgeons of London. In June 1813, "Dr. Barry" passed the Army Medical Board exam, and was commissioned as a hospital assistant. How she evaded the pre-induction physical exam, we will never know.

In July 1813, "Dr. Barry" accepted a post in Plymouth, England, and after two years she was promoted to assistant surgeon to the forces. In 1816, she was posted to the garrison at Capetown, South Africa. Here she distinguished herself by quashing a cholera epidemic, and successfully performing a Caesarian section—only the second operation of this kind in modern history where both mother and child survived. She worked alone, with primitive equipment and no anesthetic. This was in 1818; the first successful Caesarian in the British Isles was not performed until 1833.

Universally respected for her surgical skill, "Dr. Barry" was often consulted in non-military cases. Within six months of her arrival in Capetown, she saved the life of one of the daughters of His Lord Excellency the governor, Lord Charles Somerset, and became Lord Somerset's private physician and protégée.

"Dr. Barry" was often seen in the company of Lord Somerset's two daughters, and, indeed, her chivalry made her a general favorite with the ladies. But the men considered the little doctor, who wore high-heeled boots and satin waistcoats with elaborately padded shoulders, something of a fop. It also became known that "Dr. Barry" took violent umbrage at comments on her high, squeaky voice or curvacious calves. Few of her subordinates cared to cross the mercurial "Dr. Barry," who was an excellent swordsman and seized on the slightest provocation to suggest a duel.

But the doctor's most famous imbroglios were professional rather than personal. Known as "the most skillful of doctors and the most wayward of men," she was uncompromising in maintaining the highest standards of medical professionalism. Upon her appointment as colonial medical inspector, in 1821, "Dr. Barry" prohibited the administration of patent drugs by persons other than qualified physicians or licensed apothecaries. "To my knowledge," she wrote, "many persons have been poisoned by patent medicines given improperly, and pedlars and hawkers of drugs in the Interior and in Capetown do more real injury to the inhabitants than the most virulent diseases themselves."

"Dr. Barry" incurred the enmity of the governor of the Leper's Institute on Hobbes Island, Dr. Leitner, whom she called "a man opposed to all change, ignorant, intractable." During her inspection of the Leper's Institute, "Dr. Barry" was appalled by the inhuman treatment of the inmates, and immediately drew up a set of *Rules for the General Treatment of Lepers*. The foreword stated:

Good order must be preserved, but no cruelty nor deprivation of food must ever be resorted to. The parties must be considered not as convicts but as unfortunates. . . . The strictest attention must be paid to the personal cleanliness of the lepers, the bedding and clothing must be frequently changed, and they must bathe twice a week at least. . . . The sores must be washed twice daily with tar water and dressed with tar plaister, the old plaister must be thrown away. The School and Church should be encouraged, so should Industry as much as possible.

"Dr. Barry's" next fusillade was aimed at the central prison in Capetown, known as "the Tronk." Outraged by the filth and arbitrary floggings she witnessed there, "Dr. Barry" submitted a graphic report to the governor. This brought quick action, and eventually the Capetown prison became a model penal institution.

"Dr. Barry's" refusal to subordinate medical reform to political amenities won her as many enemies as friends. But she steadfastly did what she felt she must to improve medical practice wherever she worked. She was alternately promoted and demoted, and transferred to various installations as she met support or opposition in her reform campaigns.

In 1845, she succumbed to an epidemic of yellow fever and was forced to take a year's sick leave. After recuperating in London, "Dr. Barry" was sent to Malta as principal military officer, and served there for more than ten years. After relieving a cholera epidemic in 1851, she was promoted to deputy inspector general of hospitals and posted to Corfu. At "Dr. Barry's" request, soldiers wounded in the Crimea were brought to her hospital for treatment. Of the 500 who came, 400 were cured and returned to active duty.

In 1857, at the age of 62, "Dr. Barry" became inspector general of hospitals in Canada. Here she succeeded in altering the soldiers' diet, improving the water and drainage systems, and establishing the first separate quarters for married soldiers and their wives. In May, 1859, "Dr. Barry" contracted influenza and was sent home to England, where a medical board declared her physically unfit for further duty. Against her will, "Dr. Barry" was retired at half pay. She took up residence in London, making weekend visits to the country estates of friends. But she was lonely. On July 25, 1865, "Dr. Barry" was found dead in her bed in Marylebone by John, the Negro valet who had tended her faithfully for 40 years, without ever suspecting that his master was a woman.

"Dr. Barry" might have carried her secret to the grave had her instructions that her corpse be sewn in a sack and immediately interred been honored. Her sex was revealed when a charlady was called in to lay out the body. "What do you mean by calling me to lay out a general, and the corpse a woman's and one who has borne a child?" the scrub woman demanded of the army staff surgeon in charge of the post-mortem. The staff surgeon confirmed the charlady's assertion about the sex of the dead "Dr. Barry," but decided, nevertheless, not to disclose his startling findings in his official report. His superiors, to whom he confided the secret, deemed it best to bury "Dr. Barry" as a man.

Only once during "Dr. Barry's" active career, was the secret of her sex discovered. During her illness with yellow fever in the West Indies, her order that she be quarantined had been defied. "Dr. Barry" awoke from the throes of delirium to find the assistant surgeon general, who had looked in on his ailing superior, gazing, in astonishment, at her female figure beneath the bedclothes. "Dr. Barry" swore the man to secrecy, and he kept his promise until after her death. Wherever she served, the effeminate "Dr. Barry" was presumed to be a hermaphrodite, and was even accused of carrying on homosexual relations with Lord Somerset. The allegation was vociferously denied by both parties, and given "Dr. Barry's" known willingness to defend her honor, the charges were never publicly renewed.

The secret of "Dr. James Barry's" origins and the circumstances of her childbirth went with her to the grave. But it is very tempting to postulate possible explanations. It seems plausible that she was the daughter, rather than the niece, of Mrs. Bulkeley. Her father might well have been General Miranda. With her angular features, and "long, Ciceronian nose," the love-child was clearly not destined to be a beauty. How then, could she overcome the stigma of illegitimate birth? The girl was bright and spirited; it is likely that Mrs. Bulkeley, abetted by her brother, decided the girl might have a better future as a man. With a university degree, she would have no trouble entering a profession. The girl no doubt agreed to the masquerade, knowing that her alternative was to become a governess or a teacher. Of course, it is equally possible that the painter, rather than the general, was the girl's father, and that Mrs. Bulkeley was not her mother. But there is as little evidence for the one hypothesis as for the other. What is a matter of fact and not speculation is the remarkable career achieved by "Dr. James Barry," and this under what must many times have been harrowing circumstances. Colonel N.J.C. Rutherford stated, in the May 1951 issue of the *Journal of the Royal Army Medical Corps:*

Whoever was "James Barry," she has the distinction of being first—THE FIRST WOMAN DOCTOR of the British Isles. Secondly—one who has carried out a long career in the British army, displayed professional attributes of the highest order, served her country in all climates with distinction, and, if she preferred to do so by the only way available in her lifetime, by assuming the outward trappings of the male sex, all the more credit to her courage and pertinacity. A wonderful performance. . .

Despite her heroism, there is something profoundly pathetic in the figure of "the little doctor," whose braggadocio was the talk of the army. Her constant attempts to out-macho her messmates; the winding sheet, found on her bedpost at her death, with which she disguised her womanly breasts; the childbirth marks discovered on her body by the charwoman at the post-mortem—attest to the terrible price of denial "Dr. James Barry" had to pay for her success. Would she have been comforted to know that competing as a man in a man's world brought her posthumous fame as a woman?

Dorothea Dix (1802-1887)
MENTAL HEALTH CRUSADER

One blustery March morning in 1841, a 39-year-old spinster, frail in body but strong in will, crossed the threshold of the Middlesex House of Correction in East Cambridge, Massachusetts. Her name was Dorothea Dix, and she had come to the prison to teach Sunday School to 20 female inmates. A young Harvard divinity student had told Dorothea that the religious education of the young women in the East Cambridge penal institution was being neglected for want of a teacher, and despite ill-health, Dorothea volunteered for the job.

After the lesson, she asked the warden of the jail if she might inspect the premises. He showed her the cells where women convicted of drunkenness, vagrancy, or prostitution were incarcerated. Then he led her to the basement, to a dark, bare, and airless chamber occupied by four women.

"What crime did these women commit?" Dorothea Dix asked the jailer, nearly overcome by the foul stench in the unventilated cell.

"These are the lunatics," her guide informed her.

Dorothea was startled. She had expected to hear that this

malodorous dungeon housed the most hardened criminals. There was no stove in the room, and the walls were caked with frost.

"Why is there no heat in this room?" she inquired.

The jailer leaned toward her conspiratorily. "Now, you and I know it's cold here, Ma'am, but the madwomen don't know it. Crazy people can't feel the cold. They can't feel anything."

Dorothea Dix was indignant. "Of course they feel the cold—just look! These women are shivering. This jail is a disgrace!"

The warden's lip curled, "Why don't you fix the place to suit yourself?" he asked, his voice surly.

"I mean to," Dix replied with quiet determination. And she did.

It did not take long for Dorothea Dix to obtain a court order to install a stove in the insanity ward of the East Cambridge jail. She also demanded a reorganization of all the county jails, so that psychotic patients were not lodged indiscriminately with criminals. Middlesex county was only the starting point of Dorothea Dix's one-woman campaign for humane treatment of the mentally ill. By the time she died, at the age of 85, Dorothea Dix had personally founded 32 hospitals for the insane in the United States, and had been the inspiring force for 123 additional facilities. In addition, this indomitable crusader instigated prison and hospital reforms throughout Europe and Asia, started the first secular nursing order in the United States, and raised more money for charitable purposes than any individual before her. Perhaps her major achievement lay in engendering new public understanding of mental illness, and revolutionizing the treatment of the insane.

Dorothea Dix was born in the wilderness village of Hampden, Maine, on April 4, 1802. Her father was a drunkard and a derelict, who in sober spells earned a livelihood as an itinerant Methodist preacher. Dorothea's mother, 18 years older than her husband, was a chronic invalid. Dorothea was the eldest of three children, and the only daughter.

"I never knew any childhood," was Dorothea's only public comment on her early years. To her best friend, Anne Heath, she confided that she had been an unhappy child: "I was early taught to sorrow, to shed tears. . . ." Dorothea seems to have spent most of her youth caring for her brothers, while her mother lay sick in bed and her father was out on a drunken spree or spreading the gospel among strangers. Her only happy childhood experiences were the occasional trips she made to Boston to visit her paternal grandmother, who was an educated woman. Dorothea enjoyed poring over the books in her grandmother's library. Later, she was to establish many libraries in prisons.

In 1814, Dorothea and her brothers were sent to live with their grandmother in Boston. Dorothea chafed under the iron discipline of the cantankerous old lady, and was shuttled off to a great-aunt's in Worcester. Determined that she would not spend her life rusticating, Dorothea prepared herself for a teaching career as the means of attaining economic independence. At the age of 14, she opened an elementary school. Although she demanded strict conformance, Dorothea won the allegiance of her pupils by transmitting to them her own love of learning.

In 1819, Dorothea returned to Boston, to nurse her ailing grandmother, and in 1821, opened a school for young women. At the same time, she set up a free school for poor children in rooms above her grandmother's stables. In order to run both teaching programs, as well as continue her own education through reading, Dorothea rose at five every morning and went to bed at midnight. Somehow, she found time to compile an anthology, *Hymns for Children*, which included several original compositions, and to publish a book of her lectures, *Conversations on Common Things*. But by 1824 her lungs had begun to hemorrhage and threatened to collapse. The physician ordered a complete rest.

Dorothea panicked. How was she to support herself and her brothers if she had to stop teaching? Her friend Dr. Ellery Channing came to her aid with a plan that eased her troubled physical and financial conditions. The eminent Unitarian minister engaged Dorothea as governess to his children. Dorothea spent the next several years with the benevolent Channings, going with them to Narragansett Bay and to the Virgin Islands, where her health improved. The Channings also seem to have had an impact on Dorothea's troubled soul; she became a Unitarian and wrote several devotional books.

In 1831, Dorothea opened a new school in Boston. She had

learned much during her sojourn with the intellectual Channings, and her school achieved a reputation for excellence. But, in 1836, Dorothea suffered a recurrence of tuberculosis, and the doctor ordered her to go to live in Italy, and she left for Europe.

In 1837, she decided she could return to America. Her grandmother had died, leaving Dorothea a modest inheritance, so she would no longer need to exhaust herself by teaching. For several years, cautious of her health, Dorothea lived aimlessly, visiting friends, wintering in the South, and studying. Then, in 1841, she paid her historic visit to the Middlesex House of Correction, and discovered her life's work.

Wondering whether Middlesex typified conditions for the mentally ill generally, Dorothy embarked on research. She found that there were only six decent institutions for the care of the insane in the whole of the United States, all of these costly private institutions. Dorothea consulted her friends Dr. Channing and Dr. Samuel Howe, head of the Perkins Institute for the Blind, about how to proceed to ameliorate conditions for the insane in Massachusetts. They advised her to find someone to inspect all the jails and almshouses in the state and then report the findings to the state legislature, requesting financial appropriations to effect reforms. Dorothea found someone to undertake the arduous inspection tour—herself.

Eighteen months later, Dorothea Dix stood before the Massachusetts legislators and told them, "I come as an advocate of the helpless, forgotten insane and idiotic men and women, of beings sunk to a condition from which the most unconcerned would start with real horror." She went on to give graphic descriptions of deranged persons "confined . . . in cages, closets, cellars, stalls, pens: chained naked, beaten with rods, and lashed into obedience!" With Swiftian irony, Dorothea reviewed the practice of publicly auctioning mental patients:

I hope there is nothing offensive in the idea of these annual sales of old men and women, the sick, the infirm, and the helpless, the middle-aged and the children. Why should we not sell people, as otherwise blot out human rights? It is only consistent, surely not worse than chaining them and caging naked lunatics upon public roads, or burying them in closets and cellars.

The overseers of the Massachusetts mental asylums attacked Dorothea Dix as deranged herself, or else a liar. Channing, Howe, and Horace Mann rushed to her defense. A blue-ribbon commission corroborated Dorothea's findings, and the legislature voted funds for the enlargement of the Worcester Asylum.

Elated by her first victory, Dorothea went on to conduct similar investigations in other states. For the next three years, despite attacks of malaria and tuberculosis, she covered 3,000 miles and appeared before state legislatures with her "memorials." She also visited wealthy individuals, requesting donations for the establishment of asylums.

At the same time that she conducted her reform activities, Dorothea Dix continued to study the latest scientific theories about mental illness, and to familiarize herself with procedures followed at humane asylums at home and abroad. Gradually, she became recognized as the national authority on mental illness. She was consulted about asylum sites and design, recommended types of occupational therapy for patients, and appointed personnel. She also published a book on American prisons, which eventually led to penal reforms. In 1848, she helped to found a school for the blind in Illinois.

In Europe, Dorothea Dix continued her program of inspecting mental institutions, achieving reforms in Scotland, the Channel Islands, France, Russia, and Italy. Pope Pius IX hailed her as a "modern Saint Theresa."

During the Crimean War, Dorothea Dix went to Turkey to observe the army hospital reforms being carried out by Florence Nightingale. Dix returned to the United States, and when the Civil War erupted, approached the surgeon general with a proposal that she recruit and train a nursing corps of 100 volunteers. To allay his fears that women nurses might create sex scandals in the army, Dix pledged that her volunteers would all be plain women over 30, handpicked by herself, and would observe her own austere style of dress and deportment. The surgeon general could not confute Dix's argument that provision must be made for the wounded, and so the 60-year-old Dorothea Dix was appointed superintendent of nurses, becoming the first woman to hold an executive position in the federal government.

Dix ordered the construction of large, sanitary barracks. She drove her nurses as hard as she drove herself, and performed all the most thankless tasks of nursing herself. She scarcely ate or slept, and her weight plummeted to 95 pounds.

After the war, Dix worked to secure veterans' pensions and stipends for unemployed nurses. When no volunteers could be found to supervise the erection of a monument for the war dead, Dix undertook the job alone, personally selecting the stone for the monument at a granite quarry in Maine, and raising the funds to install the memorial at the National Cemetery in Virginia. Then she resumed her prison and hospital work.

Dix worked actively up to the age of 80, soliciting clothes for orphans, funds for public water fountains, and aid for the victims of the Chicago and Boston fires. In 1881, exhausted, deaf, and half-blind, she retired to the state hospital in Trenton, New Jersey. She suffered for six years from arteriosclerosis, but told visitors, "I think even lying on my bed, I can do something." Dorothea Dix had already done more than her share. On July 18, 1887, she died, in the hospital that she had helped to found some 35 years earlier.

Dorothea Dix's one-woman crusade against mental illness was a landmark of humanitarian reform. She uncovered the gruesome plight of the insane, and exposed their inhumane treatment to the public through her own writings and her legislative testimony. She obtained funding for asylums and hospitals from public and private sources, and precipitated the establishment of humane institutions at the rate of about three a year during her 46 active years. Calling for "regeneration not degeneration," Dix demonstrated that mental patients were capable of rehabilitation through occupational therapy, thereby lighting the way for modern psychological diagnosis and treatment of the insane. Dorothea Dix was the author of countless good works, but it is as a mental health pioneer that she has earned her perdurable place in history.

Angela Burdett-Coutts
(1814-1906)

PHILANTHROPIST

"Money is like muck, not good except it be spread," wrote Sir Francis Bacon. Few millionaires have spent their fortunes as wisely and as well as Baroness Angela Burdett-Coutts. The richest heiress in Victorian England, Angela Burdett-Coutts was eclectic in her charities. Penitent Magdalenes, destitute orphans, and unemployed women were rehabilitated through her aid. The baroness's generosity supplied goats for farmers, boats for fishermen, homes for art students, scholarships for geologists, protection for aborigines, drinking fountains for dogs, and plants for Kew Gardens. The baroness showered myriad gifts on private charities and individuals. Wheresoever there came a legitimate cry for help—from Turkey, Ireland, Scotland, Africa, or her own native England—Lady Burdett-Coutts opened her purse. The first woman to receive the Turkish Order of Medjidie, as well as the keys to the cities of London and Edinburgh, Angela Burdett-Coutts was acclaimed throughout the British Isles as "Queen of the Poor."

Angela Burdett was born on April 24, 1814, in the plush domicile of her maternal grandfather at No. 1 Stratton Place, London. Thomas

Coutts was the proprietor of Britain's largest and most prestigious banking firm, Coutts and Company, whose depositors included the king of England and the royal princes. But it was not her grandfather directly who gave Angela the wherewithal for her munificence. The year before Angela was born, her grandfather married for the second time, and the circumstances of this marriage oddly led to Angela's becoming the heiress to the Coutts fortune.

Thomas Coutts's first marriage had been unorthodox enough, for he had espoused a nursemaid in his brother's family. But the first Mrs. Coutts was respectable if uneducated, and the couple's three daughters all married well-to-do noblemen. Then, less than a week after the death of his first wife, Sir Thomas eloped with an actress named Harriot Mellon. Sir Thomas was 80, his bride 37. Moreover, Harriot was the daughter of obscure gypsy players. The Coutts daughters, Lady Guilford, Lady Bute, and Lady Burdett, were scandalized at the way "the funeral baked meats did coldly furnish forth the marriage tables." The youthful second Mrs. Coutts bore their rebuff with grace and humility, and assured her husband's daughters that she had no wish to deprive them of their rightful inheritances.

Thomas Coutts held tightly to the reins of his fortune until the day he died. Having endowed each daughter with £25,000 on her marriage day, he left them each an additional £20,000 in his will; the rest of the Coutts millions went to Harriot. Remarkably free from rancor, the widow gave each stepdaughter an additional £10,000, and continued to send generous yearly supplements.

Five years after her first husband's death, Harriot married the duke of St. Albans, a man half her age. Keeping in mind Harriot's announced intention of making one of them her heir, the Coutts ladies squelched their rage and their pride just enough to allow Harriot to visit their children. One of Harriot's favorites seemed to be the gentle and compassionate Angela Burdett, one of the five daughters and one son of Sir Francis and Lady Burdett. Angela listened compassionately as her grandmother told of her bitter and impoverished childhood when the two went for drives in Harriot's phaeton at the Burdett estates.

Angela's tranquil temperament may have come from her mother, but her empathy and concern for the plight of the poor probably derived from her volatile father. Sir Francis Burdett, a Radical member of Parliament, championed a number of left-wing causes, ranging from Catholic emancipation, to prison reform, to the abolition of corporal punishment in the army.

From birth, Angela was cosseted by doting nurses and governesses. A studious child, Angela's favorite subject was geology. Later, she was to endow several chairs at Oxford in this subject. As she grew older, Angela was introduced to the *bon ton*, attending royal balls and her father's lavish dinner parties, where she met the poets Thomas Moore, Wordsworth, and Coleridge, and English and foreign politicians of every stripe, including Prime Minister Disraeli.

Harriot died in 1837, and remained true to her promise. She bequeathed to Angela everything except for a £10,000 annuity which was to go to Harriot's husband, the duke of St. Albans. The 23-year-old heiress was now to receive £50,000 a year, and had acquired a bank share worth millions and still growing. Harriot's xenophobia and predilection for marriage made her stipulate that should Angela marry a foreigner or die unmarried, the fortune would revert to one of Angela's older sisters.

Upon coming into her inheritance, Angela Burdett immediately changed her surname to Burdett-Coutts, and moved to London, taking up residence at her birthplace on Stratton Street. There were now many men who aspired to Angela's hand—or to the purse-strings the hand controlled. But the young heiress wanted no husband to spend her fortune for her, and reportedly rejected scores of suitors, from the duke of Wellington to the future Napoleon III, who apparently didn't know about the exclusion clause in Harriot's will.

Angela embarked on a program of generously sharing her wealth with the needy and deserving. By patrician standards, Lady Burdett-Coutts lived modestly, preferring to lay up spiritual treasures that moth and rust would not corrupt. A devout Episcopalian, Angela Burdett-Coutts made the Anglican Church the initial beneficiary of her generosity, endowing a number of churches and parish schools. "No other woman under the rank of a queen ever did so much for the established Church as Lady Burdett-Coutts," an Anglican vicar declared. Her religious endowments included St. Stephen's Church in Westminster, bishoprics in Capetown, Adelaide, and British Columbia. "In no house did you meet so many clergy and churchworkers," observed Lady Helier.

But Angela also entertained in her house princes, peers, prelates, scientists, writers, painters, and actors. No. 1 Stratton Street became a noted salon, where Liszt played the piano, and Alboni sang. Among her most frequent guests and closest friends was novelist Charles Dickens, who was Angela's first private secretary, and who implemented many of her philanthropic endeavors. With Dickens's help, Angela established Urania Cottage, where former prostitutes received training in various trades, and if they desired, could go, at Burdett-Coutts's expense, to one of the British colonies to start life anew. Unlike other reform schools, Urania Cottage allowed its protégées recreational reading and group singing of a non-devotional nature, and gave them colorful dresses instead of prison-type uniforms. Over half the women who entered Urania Cottage renounced the streets forever in favor of respectable jobs, and many of them married.

Angela financed other educational ventures in England. She donated large sums of money to Dickens's Ragged Schools for slum boys, and the first club for working boys, and was founding president of the Destitute Children's Dinners. She paid for the higher education of many youths, including the eldest Dickens son. Another Dickens son became a cadet in the navy through Angela's offices.

"Life, whether in man or beast is sacred," Angela Burdett-Coutts declared, and launched programs to make life more bearable for those who had not been dealt with too kindly. She was a founder of the Society for the Prevention of Cruelty to Children, and the Society for the Prevention of Cruelty to Animals. A goat farm provided a livelihood for farmers and milk for the poor. Evening courses for policemen enabled them to exercise their powers more judiciously.

Working women were of particular interest to Angela Burdett-Coutts. She organized the first union among London's flower girls, and taught the Cockney flower-sellers to make artificial flowers to sell in winter. She established sewing schools to train the destitute women of Spitalfields to be seamstresses, and arranged other employment or relief for those who had no aptitude for needlework.

Lady Burdett-Coutts was a Maecenas to many struggling artists. She patronized two of the great actors of her day, Macready and Irving, and subsidized a number of painters, writers, and scientists. Explorers were also the beneficiaries of the Burdett-Coutts largesse. Angela financed the Livingstone-Stanley African expeditions, as well as General Gordon's incursion into the Sudan.

In Ireland, Lady Burdett-Coutts was known as "the Queen of Baltimore." During the potato famine of 1848-49, she loaned £250,000 to hardscrabble tenant farmers, and during a later agricultural blight instituted sundry relief measures. During the 1860s, Angela Burdett-Coutts single-handedly revived the fishing industry in southwest Ireland, outfitting entire fleets of Irish fishing-boats.

When England was at war, the Coutts millions financed medical aid for the wounded and living accommodations for soldiers' wives. During the Crimean War, Lady Burdett-Coutts sent supplies to Florence Nightingale, and during the South African War, she presided over a ladies' committee that furnished medical care to the British soldiers as well as to their Zulu adversaries.

A pioneer in housing reform, the banking heiress took it upon herself to renovate London's infamous East End. She replaced the shabby tenements with model low-cost dwellings, and provided food, clothing, nurses, and other services for the former slum dwellers.

In recognition of Angela Burdett-Coutts's beneficence, Queen Victoria made her a baroness in 1871. Lady Burdett-Coutts was one of the first English women to be made a peer for performing social service, rather than for serving as favorite to a British king. But the baroness irrevocably alienated her royal patron in 1880, when she announced that she was marrying William Ashmead-Bartlett. Ashmead-Bartlett was 29 and Lady Burdett-Coutts 66 when they were wed, and Victoria was decidedly not amused. "It is positively distressing and ridiculous," the queen wrote in her diary "and will do her much harm by lowering her in people's eyes and taking away their respect."

Angela Burdett-Coutts had met Ashmead-Bartlett when he was a student at Oxford, and he became the last of Dickens's several successors as her secretary. It was Ashmead-Bartlett who went to Turkey in 1877 to present that country with a £43,000 "Compassion Fund" from the baroness. Angela was to enjoy great longevity and the 25 years of her marriage were the happiest years of her life, as she and her husband, who took the name Mr. Burdett-Coutts, went on disbursing her fortune on behalf of worthy causes.

However, her resources suffered limitation. Though raised in England, Mr. Burdett-Coutts had been born in America, and because of the stipulation against a foreign husband in Harriot's will, Angela had to turn a fifth of her capital over to her sister, Clara Money. Clara adopted the name Money-Coutts, provoking a witty jingle in the humor magazine *Punch:*

> *Money takes the name of Coutts,*
> *Superfluous and funny;*
> *For everyone considers Coutts*
> *Synonomous with money.*

Everyone also considered the Baroness Burdett-Coutts synonomous with bounty. By her death on December 30, 1906, Angela Burdett-Coutts had given away over half her fortune. She was buried in Westminster Abbey with the approbation of King Edward VII, who pronounced her "the most remarkable woman in England, next to my mother." The universal consensus was that Baroness Burdett-Coutts had treated her fortune like a public trust, and that no government or foundation could have been more lacking in self-interest over a period of 70 years. This in an era before charitable donations became practically mandatory as tax deductions.

The inscription beneath the Angela Burdett-Coutts window in Lady Chapel, at the Cathedral of Liverpool, aptly reads "God's Almoner."

The Girls' Ragged School, London.

George Eliot (Mary Ann Evans) (1819-1880)

NOVELIST

P. Eliot, G.

Mary Ann Evans was admired by her contemporaries for her protean intellect and the awesome scope of her knowledge. Philosopher Herbert Spencer remarked: "I have known but few men with whom I could discuss a question in philosophy with more satisfaction." But it was under the pseudonym George Eliot that Mary Ann Evans gained her immortality as one of the greatest English novelists.

Born in Warwickshire, England, on November 22, 1819, Mary Ann Evans was the youngest of five children. Her father, Robert Evans, a farm agent, had had two children by a first marriage; Mary Ann and her older brother and sister were born to the second Mrs. Evans, a semi-invalid. Mary Ann was strongly influenced by her father, and she later endowed her fictional characters of Adam Bede and Caleb Garth with many of her father's personal traits. Indeed, she was to use many of her friends and relatives as models in her writing, portraying her puritanical brother, Isaac, for example, as Tom Tulliver in *The Mill on the Floss*.

At the age of five, Mary Ann was sent to boarding school, where her extraordinary intelligence was recognized and developed. When Mary Ann was 15, her ailing mother died, and the girl was forced to leave school. She kept house for her father and her brother Isaac, but continued to study French and Italian privately with tutors, and to read widely and voraciously. Between the ages of 15 to 22, Mary Ann Evans's main interest was religion. Raised in the Church of England, she was caught up in the pietistic fervor of the evangelical movement. She was profoundly influenced by her aunt, Mrs. Samuel Evans, a former Methodist preacher, who was to serve as the model for the portrait of Dinah Morris in *Adam Bede.* Mary Ann became an ascetic and charity worker, like the Dorothea Brooke she created in *Middlemarch.* She taught Sunday School, visited tenant farmers at their cottages, organized rummage sales, and developed the extraordinary sympathy for humble people that pervades her novels.

In 1841, the Evans family moved to Coventry. Here, Mary Ann formed intellectual friendships that caused her to reject evangelicalism and embrace a latitudinarian humanism. In 1846, she published her first book, a translation of D.F. Strauss's controversial *Life of Jesus,* which depicted Jesus as an exceptionally good man, rather than as the son of God. Her translations of works by liberal German theologians brought her to the attention of John Chapman, publisher of the left-wing *Westminster Review.* Chapman decided to recruit the brilliant Mary Ann Evans for his editorial staff.

The year 1851 marked two formative events in the life of Mary Ann Evans; in that year she became an editor of the *Westminster Review,* and she met George Henry Lewes, founder and literary editor of *The Leader.* Lewes and Evans quickly fell in love, but a technicality of English divorce law prevented Lewes from obtaining a divorce from his estranged wife, so he could not marry Mary Ann. However, in 1854 the couple eloped to Germany, where they spent an intellectually productive, as well as romantic, sojourn. Upon their return to England later that year, Lewes and Evans found themselves ostracized by many of their former friends, and Mary Ann was disowned by her family.

Nevertheless, they set up house in Richmond. Mary Ann wrote a series of of short stories called *Scenes of Clerical Life,* which Lewes posted, in 1857, to his friend, the publisher John Blackwood, under the pseudonym of George Eliot lest her anomalous union with Lewes prejudice people against Mary Ann's writing. *Scenes of Clerical Life* was published in Blackwood's Magazine, and was well received by reviewers.

In 1859, George Eliot's first full-length novel, *Adam Bede*, elicited encomiums from such leading literary lights as William Makepeace Thackeray and Charles Dickens. Dickens was sure that the author of *Adam Bede* was a woman, but the pretense that the author was a male was kept up until the appearance of several self-proclaimed male George Eliots so outraged the real author that she revealed her identity.

During the next two decades, George Eliot produced six more novels: *The Mill on the Floss* (1860), *Silas Marner* (1861), *Romola* (1862), *Felix Holt* (1866), *Middlemarch* (1871-72), and *Daniel Deronda* (1874-76). Mary Ann took great pains with both the content and style of her writing. To insure authenticity, on specialized subjects such as law or science she consulted authorities in the field. Her advisor on details of academic life at Cambridge, depicted in *Daniel Deronda*, was Sir Leslie Stephen, the father of Virginia Woolf. Like Virginia Woolf, George Eliot suffered from terrible nervous depressions while writing her novels. Like Leonard Woolf, George Lewes was a supportive editor and critic. Lewes conspired with Mary Ann's publisher, John Blackwood, to have him send her encouraging letters after receiving each installment of a novel in progress.

In 1863, the Lewes moved to Regents Park. By now, attitudes toward the couple's unsanctified union had mellowed, and George and Mary Ann's literary salons were well-attended. George Eliot was admired as a sibyl by the young literary men of the time, and worshipped as a saint by a circle of young women disciples.

George Lewes died in 1878. The bereaved Mary Ann turned for comfort to a close friend of the couple, clergyman John Walter Cross. In 1880, Mary Ann scandalized her friends for the second time by marrying Cross, who was 21 years her junior. However, on December 22, 1880, eight months after her nuptials, the renowned novelist died, at the age of 61.

George Eliot is important primarily as the first great woman writer to enter the arena of the intellectual novel. Other women had previously excelled as fiction writers. In fact, the first great French novel, the psychological romance *La Princesse de Cleves* (1678), had been the work of the Countess de Lafayette. George Sand and Mme. de Stael earned acclaim as the authors of popular romances, and Jane Austen chiselled the novel of manners to perfection. But prior to George Eliot, women novelists had restricted their canvas to the feminine worlds of the drawing room and the ballroom, or had transported their readers to exotic, imaginary settings, eschewing the supposedly masculine realms of history, politics, religion, and high culture. George Eliot was the first woman to incorporate major intellectual ideas into her fiction.

Entering the mainstream tradition of the novel of psychological realism, George Eliot not only pioneered new frontiers for women's fiction, she exerted considerable influence on male writers as well. Eliot created a new genre, the novel of provincial life, which was emulated later by eminent novelists like Thomas Hardy, Leo Tolstoi, and D.H. Lawrence. Prior to George Eliot, the "short and simple annals of the poor" had occasionally been celebrated in poems, but the novel was given over to heroic, degraded, or bourgeois personages. Addressing the reader of *Adam Bede*, George Eliot poignantly explains her sympathy for ordinary and rustic characters:

In this world there are so many of these common coarse people, who have no picturesque sentimental wretchedness! It is so needful we should remember their existence, else we may happen to leave them quite out of our religion and philosophy, and frame lofty theories which only fit a world of extremes. Therefore let Art always remind us of them. . . . There are few prophets in the world; few sublimely beautiful women; few heroes. I can't afford to give all my love and reverence to such rarities; I want a great deal of those feelings for my everyday fellow-men, especially for the few . . . whose faces I know, whose hands I touch, for whom I have to make way with kindly courtesy. . . . It is more needful . . . that my heart should swell with loving admiration at some trait of gentle goodness in the faulty people who sit at the same hearth with me . . . than at the deeds of heroes whom I shall never know except by hearsay. . . .

But George Eliot could also paint a vivid picture of English high society, as she proved with *Daniel Deronda*, a novel that had a enormous impact on Henry James. George Eliot's novels, beloved of a large public in her own day, have become classics. Nearly a century after her death, they are valued by the literate public, and are required reading in many high schools and colleges.

Middlemarch, which depicts the stultifying influence of provincial life on ambitious, idealistic minds, is generally considered Eliot's masterpiece. Here Eliot demonstrates her brilliant satiric wit and displays the impressive range of her political and theological learning, as well as her extraordinary insight into the human heart.

But *Daniel Deronda* contains Eliot's best writing. In this book, Eliot made a daring humanitarian effort to combat English anti-Semitism. George Eliot wrote to Harriet Beecher Stowe, the author of *Uncle Tom's Cabin*, that she realized the Jewish subplot of *Daniel Deronda* would alienate many of her former readers, "but precisely because I felt that the usual attitude of Christians towards Jews is—I hardly know whether to say more impious or more stupid when viewed in the light of their professed principles, I therefore felt urged to treat Jews with such sympathy and understanding as my nature and knowledge could attain to." As the eight serialized installments of the novel appeared, Blackwood noted, "Anti-Jews grumbled, but went on." Though not as neatly structured nor as consistently interesting as *Middlemarch*, *Daniel Deronda* is more innovative in technique and more lively in tone. The heroine, Gwendolyn Harleth, is one of the most vivid characters in English fiction. With Gwendolyn, as with her previous heroines, Maggie Tulliver (*The Mill on the Floss*) and Dorothea Brooke (*Middlemarch*), George Eliot dramatized the plight of the 19th-century Englishwoman who has limited choice of occupation.

The character of Daniel Deronda, a Jewish youth raised as an English aristocrat in ignorance of his origins, is almost as fascinating as is that of the mercurial Gwendolyn. Daniel is one of the few interesting virtuous characters in fiction. But a large section of the book comprising a scholarly treatise on Jewish history and tradition is more well-intentioned than interestingly executed.

Contemporary readers may find Eliot's style a bit ponderous, but her convincing and moving dramatizations of the power of love and suffering to transform rigid, vain egoists into mature, compassionate human beings will inspire the modern reader to echo her publisher's tribute: "What a wonderful woman!"

Harriet Ross Tubman
(1820?-1913)

BLACK EMANCIPATOR

"She was . . . the conscience of a nation," declared Postmaster General Benjamin Bailar, announcing the issuance of a U.S. postage stamp in honor of Harriet Tubman on February 1, 1977. The stamp commemorated Black History Week, and Harriet Tubman was indeed a key figure in black history, and in American history. As "conductor" of the Underground Railroad that guided fugitive slaves to safety in pre-Civil War America, Harriet Tubman was personally responsible for the manumission of 300 black slaves. Proudly she proclaimed, "I never ran my train off the track, and I never lost a passenger." And her work did not stop there. During the War Between the States, Harriet served the Union as scout, spy, and nurse. After the war, she helped to establish schools for blacks, joined the women's suffrage movement, and created a rest home for aged Negroes.

Harriet Ross was born a slave, in a family of 11 children, on the Brodas plantation in Bucktown, Maryland. The exact date is unsubstantiated, the year, around 1820. Originally named Araminta, Harriet was renamed after her mother. The child's very black skin, pronounced

Negroid features, and woolly black hair seemed to inspire her masters with particular antipathy. At the age of six, Harriet was sent ten miles away to learn the trade of weaving. Harriet missed her mother, and suffered under the harsh treatment she received, but eventually the weaver remanded the recalcitrant child to her owner.

One day, when she was 13, Harriet was ordered by an overseer to help tie up another slave, who was to be whipped for going into town without permission. Harriet refused. The overseer decided to administer the punishment by himself and, picking up a two-pound iron weight, he hurled it at the truant slave. It missed, and instead hit Harriet in the head, breaking her skull. The injury caused a pressure on the brain that was to exert itself during the remainder of Harriet's life, subjecting her to sudden seizures of sleepiness. These somnolent spells incited taunts from the other slave-children, and, misunderstood as laziness, beatings from her masters.

Harriet's skull wound also marred her appearance. Her expression became perpetually dazed; her head would hang listlessly on her breast. Her master assumed that this dull-looking girl was stupid and slow-witted and sold her to a woman who was looking for a housemaid and nurse. Harriet was unceremoniously lifted into her new mistress's wagon, without a word as to where she was going or why, and without the opportunity to bid her parents good-bye.

The new mistress whipped Harriet mercilessly if her new chores were not done properly. Harriet occasionally fell into one of her narcoleptic spells while rocking the cradle of her infant charge and was soundly whipped. In an emaciated and scarred condition, Harriet was returned to her original master as "not worth a sixpence."

Harriet's mother nursed her back to health. The pious Rosses reminded their daughter that the Lord loved all his children, and urged her to be diligent in her prayers. Without much to hope for for herself, Harriet knelt obediently, and murmured, "Oh Lord, convert Ole Master. Oh, dear Lord, change that man's heart, and make him a Christian." She also prayed that her face would be washed clean, and her heart purified of sin.

In her teens, Harriet worked in the fields. Alongside the men, she plowed and loaded wood. From this heavy physical labor, she developed tremendous muscle power and stamina. In 1844, at her owner's behest, Harriet married another slave, John Tubman. In 1849, Harriet's master died. Two of her brothers had already been sold to a chain gang, and now two more brothers and Harriet herself were destined to the same fate. Harriet rebelled. For some years the young woman had been haunted by a vision. In her fantasy, she saw a line, dividing the slave territories from the land of freedom. On the northern side of the line stood white women, stretching their hands across the boundary to welcome Harriet. Harriet talked her brothers into trying to escape with her across the Mason-Dixon line.

Harriet's brothers quailed on the first night of the journey, and leaving their sister, returned home. Alone, and with no guide but the North Star, Harriet trod on toward liberty. With unerring psychological instinct, she sought sympathetic faces, and applied to them for food and shelter. Often, she saw no sympathetic faces, and was obliged to sleep on the ground.

Eventually, Harriet reached Philadelphia, and found work there. But she kept thinking of her family and friends, still in bondage. A few months later, Harriet returned surreptitiously to the Brodas plantation. She persuaded a number of the slaves there to escape with her to the North. John Tubman declined to go with his wife, and Harriet never saw him again. She led the company of slaves across the Mason-Dixon line, and then headed South again, alone. Within a year, she had led three successful expeditions, and had rescued two of her own brothers and a sister, along with many other slaves.

The Fugitive Slave Act of 1850 compelled Harriet to lead her runaways to Canada. She remained there with her charges for the winter, then returned to Maryland to liberate more blacks. By this time, Harriet had made contacts with some of the Northern abolitionists, such as Quaker Thomas Garrett. Garrett's house in Delaware served as one of the many "stations" on the Underground Railroad, where fugitive slaves could rest on their way to the North.

The Underground Railroad was a risky venture, and Harriet became adept at subterfuges and disguises. She would have been a great actress, her friends said, for she could hollow out her cheeks and cause her body to shrink, and totter about impersonating a very old woman.

Not all of Harriet's charges shared her courage, and she began to carry a revolver, with which she menaced any slave who expressed a desire to return to bondage. Generally, however, Harriet was able to inspirit her followers by her own redoubtable example. She stoked up their courage by leading them in the hymn, "Go down Moses/Go down to the promised land." Harriet became known as "the Moses of her people," or simply "Moses."

In 1857, Harriet rescued her aged parents, and brought them to her home in Auburn, New York. Harriet led a total of 19 emancipation expeditions, working as a cook between trips to finance her sorties. She raised additional funds through appeals to Northern abolitionists. Harriet's exploits had made her a legend in the North, and in the South a $40,000 reward was offered for her capture. Unable to read or write, Harriet Tubman was an honored guest at the homes of Ralph Waldo Emerson and other Boston intellectuals. John Brown called her "the most of a man naturally that I ever met with." Harriet, in turn, lauded Brown as the greatest benefactor of her people. Brown addressed Harriet as "General Tubman," and conferred with her on his plan to raid Harper's Ferry.

At the outbreak of the Civil War, Governor Andrew of Massachusetts asked Harriet to serve in the Union army. Negro scouts and spies were needed because many slaves feared the Yankees even more than they feared their masters. Harriet, who had had another vision in which she had foreseen the proclamation of emancipation readily agreed to join the Union cause. She earned acclaim as a notable spy behind Confederate lines and led many hazardous scouting expeditions in South Carolina. During one campaign alone, she freed over 750 slaves. She also toiled as a nurse and laundress for the Union troops. During an epidemic of dysentery, Harriet concocted a practical remedy from some roots growing near the infected waters. She also invented medicines for other illnesses.

The war ended, but Harriet Tubman's labors continued. She helped to found schools for free blacks in North Carolina, and for black children in Auburn. The federal government reneged on its promise to remunerate Harriet for her war service, but one of Harriet's friends who had written a book, *Scenes in the Life of Harriet Tubman*, contributed the royalties to Harriet.

The little house at Auburn soon became a refuge for needy and elderly blacks. Harriet, now married to Nelson Davis, personally cared for her wards, nursing their rheumatism and listening to their woes. In 1908, an official Harriet Tubman Home for Aged or Indigent Negroes was established in Auburn.

To her dying day, Harriet Tubman championed the rights of the oppressed. She became a leader in the incipient women's suffrage movement, sharing the platform with Susan B. Anthony. On March 10, 1913, Harriet expired peacefully, at the age of 93.

This untutored woman, who rose from slave status to become a leader of her people accomplished as much or more for the cause of black liberation as any other single individual. She personally guided hundreds of slaves to safety, and was an effective publicist and fund raiser for the Abolitionist cause. Uneducated herself, she established educational opportunities for black children and adults. Harriet's courage and probity, as well as her unstinting hard work, have made her an inspiration not only to blacks, but to all humanitarians. Abolitionist Frederick Douglass movingly observed in a letter to Harriet:

The difference between us is very marked. Most that I have done and suffered in the service of our cause has been in public, and I have received encouragement at every step of the way. You, on the other hand, have labored in a private way. I have wrought in the day—you in the night. I have had the applause of the crowd and the satisfaction that comes of being approved by the multitude, while the most that you have done has been witnessed by a few trembling, scared and footsore bondsmen and women, whom you have led out of the house of bondage, and whose heartfelt God bless you has been your only reward. The midnight sky and the silent stars have been the witnesses of your devotion to freedom and of your heroism.

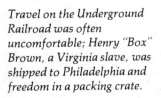

Travel on the Underground Railroad was often uncomfortable; Henry "Box" Brown, a Virginia slave, was shipped to Philadelphia and freedom in a packing crate.

Susan B. Anthony (1820-1906) *and Elizabeth Cady Stanton* (1815-1902)

PIONEER FEMINISTS

The American suffragette movement was spearheaded by an imposing female brain trust: the eloquent Elizabeth Cady Stanton, the egalitarian Lucretia Mott, the militant Lucy Stone, and the flamboyant Victoria Woodhull. But the name that is most closely identified with 19th-century American feminism is Susan B. Anthony. And rightly so; for Susan B. Anthony was unique in serving as the movement's most single-minded general and most dedicated soldier. Her exhaustive canvass of New York State's 60 voting districts has been a model for grass-roots organizers for every feminist cause since early suffragism.

But Susan Brownell Anthony's contribution to female emancipation goes far beyond her leadership of the suffragette campaign. It was Susan B. Anthony who induced the University of Rochester to become coeducational by raising $100,000 to pay the expenses of the first women students. It was Susan B. Anthony who published and edited the feminist weekly *The Revolution*, where such subjects as divorce, prostitution, and the exploitation of women wage-earners were given their first national airing. It was Susan B. Anthony who, propagating the principle "equal pay for equal work," founded the first union of working women.

And it was Susan B. Anthony who declined proposals of marriage, so that she might be free from commitments to husband or child. While Susan minded the children and cooked puddings, Mrs. Stanton penned the fiery speeches that won the public to the cause of women's rights. The right to own property, the right to have custody of their children, the right to vote—these rights, and many others, women owe to the feminist whom Gertrude Stein aptly dubbed "the Mother of us all."

Born on February 5, 1820, Susan Brownell Anthony was the second of eight children of a Quaker cotton-mill owner and a former belle. Susan early imbibed the spirit of reform in the family farmhouse in Adams, Massachusetts. Her parents were among the signers of the first Declaration of Women's Rights drafted at the 1848 convention at Seneca Falls, New York.

When Susan was six, her father became manager of a large cotton mill in Battenville, New York, and the family moved to the Hudson Valley. Her mother, a gay and spirited woman, was gradually worn down by the strain of childbearing and tending to the needs of the Quaker "guests"—as many as 11 at one time—who boarded with the family. Susan's own domestic chores included baking 21 loaves of bread in one day.

Susan worked side-by-side with the local farm girls at her father's mill, hearing their tales of the drunken husbands who beat them and appropriated their earnings—31 cents for a 14-hour day—to buy liquor. Under New York law women had no right to own money or property, and were themselves considered the chattel of their spouses. In 1837, Susan's own family furnished her with evidence of woman's impotence. Her father went bankrupt, and her mother's inheritance was impounded to pay the debtors.

Susan became a schoolteacher at a weekly wage of $2.00—one-fifth of what her male colleagues were paid. Her logical protest that since female students paid the same tuition as male, women teachers should earn the same salary as men teachers put her in disfavor with the school board, and when she persisted in visiting Negroes in their homes, she was fired. But the capable young teacher had no trouble securing another position, and by 1846, Susan was the principal of the Girls' Department at Canajoharie Academy in Rochester. "This woman," one of the Academy's trustees said of Susan, "is the smartest man that ever came to Canajoharie."

Among the Anthonys' friends were many prominent abolitionists and temperance leaders, men like Frederick Douglass, William Lloyd Garrison, and Wendell Philips. Susan was imbued with the reforming spirit, and, undoubtedly influenced by the conversations of the mill wives, she joined the temperance movement. In 1851, as president of the local Daughters of Temperance, she was sent to a convention at Seneca Falls. There she roomed with Amelia Bloomer, editor of the temperance paper *The Lily,* and was introduced by Mrs. Bloomer to suffragette leader Elizabeth Cady Stanton.

Susan had longed to meet this woman for she had cherished an anecdote her father had told about the remarkable Mrs. Stanton after the first Seneca Falls convention. A married minister had upbraided Mrs. Stanton for speaking in public, reminding her that "The Apostle Paul recommends silence to women. Why don't you mind him?" Mrs. Stanton had replied, "The Apostle Paul also recommends celibacy to clergymen. Why don't *you* mind him?"

The momentous meeting between the two women marked the beginning of a fruitful political collaboration and a warm personal friendship. Stanton, five years older than Susan, shared with her the story of her life. She had attempted to compensate her father for the loss of his brilliant only son by excelling in her schoolwork, only have him remark, "Oh my daughter, you should have been a boy." In her father's law office she had listened to the pathetic stories of wives who were plundered of their children and their property under New York's inequitable married women's property laws. She had been refused admission to Union College because she was a woman, and had instead attended Mrs. Willard's female seminary in Troy, New York. In 1840 she had married abolitionist Henry Stanton, and at an anti-slavery convention in London that the couple attended on their honeymoon had been barred, as a woman, from speaking. These experiences had led her to call the first women's rights convention in 1848, which evoked her father's repudiation of her as a madwoman.

Up to that point, Susan had devoted her reforming zeal to the causes of temperance and the abolition of Negro slavery. She had given little thought to woman's right to vote, for the Quakers did not believe in the efficacy of the ballot, but in the power of the inner light. In 1852, Anthony shared Stanton's devastating experience; she was forbidden to address a temperance convention because of her sex. She, too, now embraced political enfranchisement as the keystone of women's equality.

From this time on, Susan B. Anthony became the driving force of the women's movement. She brought an extraordinary political acumen and deft organizational skills to the amorphous assemblage of liberals, radicals, libertarians, and reformers who marched together beneath the suffragette banner. Anthony convened and coordinated a series of state and national conventions on women's rights, and mounted a door-to-door campaign to collect signatures for a petition calling on the New York State legislature to give women the vote and the right to own property. In 1860, after repeated presentation of petitions to the legislators, the women's movement won its first victory when a bill was passed permitting women to control their own earnings and property, enter into contracts, and serve as the guardians of their children. But women were still denied the right to vote.

The momentum of the women's movement was broken by the Civil War, when the suffragettes threw their energies into the struggle for the emancipation of the Negro. The two suffragettes embarked on national and state-wide lecture tours to denounce the inhumanity of slaveholding.

After the war, Anthony and Stanton approached their male abolitionist colleagues to plan a joint strategy to tie in emancipation for blacks with emancipation for women. They received a rude shock; "This is the Negro's hour," Horace Greeley told them. Other members, both male and female, of the Equal Rights Association agreed. In 1869, Anthony and Stanton severed their association with the E.R.A., and formed their own National Woman's Suffrage Association. The women's movement remained divided until 1889, when Susan B. Anthony met with Lucy Stone to merge the two factions into the National American Woman's Suffrage Association.

For over 50 years Susan B. Anthony and Elizabeth Cady Stanton functioned as an ideal team in the cause of women's rights. The energetic Anthony selflessly ceded to the charismatic Stanton the more glamorous role, and took upon herself all the necessary tasks, menial and intellectual. Openly acknowledging Stanton's greater oratorical and literary gifts, Susan became her friend's research assistant and press agent. When the two women arrived in a city where they had a speaking engagement, Susan saw her friend to their hotel. Then, the indefatigable Susan went to the local newspaper offices to assure that their lecture would receive adequate publicity, and to the lecture hall to check security provisions and acoustics. When Susan herself mounted the public platform, she steadfastly ignored the catcalls and rotten eggs that were largely directed at her rather than at Stanton, the respectable and vivacious mother of seven.

In 1872, Susan B. Anthony became a *cause célèbre*, when she led a group of women in Rochester, New York, to vote illegally in the national election in an effort to test the right of women to vote under the Fourteenth Amendment. She was arrested, and tried and fined for this act of civil disobedience, but refused to pay the fine, telling the judge who sentenced her, "Resistance to tyranny is obedience to God; I shall never pay a penny of this unjust claim." Her trial was a travesty of justice. She was barred from testifying in her own behalf; and the judge wrote an opinion instructing the all-male jury to find the defendant guilty before either Anthony's counsel or the prosecuting attorney had delivered their final summations.

Susan B. Anthony never did cast a legal ballot, for at her death on March 13, 1906, only four states had granted suffrage to their female citizens. Fourteen years later, in 1920, Anthony's goal of national universal suffrage was finally realized.

Although Susan B. Anthony did not live to see the accomplishment of this dream, she did certainly receive the gratification of being regarded as a national heroine in her unflagging crusade for women's rights. She published the first three volumes of a six-volume *History of Woman Suffrage*, written largely by herself and Stanton and financed entirely by herself. She was president from 1892 to 1900 of the National American Woman's Suffrage Association, which was responsible in 1890 for the admission of Wyoming to the Union as the first woman suffrage state. Her passionate devotion to the cause of women's rights secured the enlistment of a score of talented young women to the suffragette campaign. Among these young feminists, who called themselves "Aunt Susan's girls," was Carrie Chapman Catt, who was later to be the founder of The League of Women Voters.

Susan B. Anthony's feminism was only part of her larger humanism. As a suffragette, she never missed an opportunity to link the white woman's struggle with the black man's. A staunch pacifist, Anthony told her fellow feminists, "It is evident that if the women of our nation had been counted among the constituents of every state legislature, and of the Congress of the United States, the butchery of the Spanish American War would never have been perpetrated." In her essay "On the Status of Women," Anthony lamented that the energies of the suffragettes could not be "devoted to the needs of government, society, home, instead of being consumed in the struggle to obtain their birthright of individual freedom," and reaffirmed her belief in "the capacity and power of woman for the uplifting of humanity."

Today, as the final legal barriers to women's enfranchisement are crumbling, women activists have followed Susan Anthony's lead in the battle for *human* rights.

Demonstrating for women's rights in Hyde Park, London.

Florence Nightingale
(1820-1910)

NURSE AND PUBLIC HEALTH PIONEER

Comely, clever, cultured, and rich, Florence Nightingale renounced the affluent existence open to her as the daughter of a landed Sheffield banker, and refused two highly eligible suitors in marriage to become a nurse. Indeed, Florence Nightingale established the nobility of the nursing profession, previously the domain of prostitutes and alcoholics. The founder of modern secular nursing, she instituted revolutionary reforms in hospital management and public health.

Born on May 12, 1820, the second of the Nightingales' two daughters was named after her birthplace, Florence, Italy. But when Florence Nightingale was a year old, her family returned to their native England. During their early childhood, Florence and her older sister were taught by governesses. Later, when Florence was 12, Edward Nightingale assumed the tutorship of his daughters, teaching them classical and modern literature, mathematics, and philosophy.

As a young woman, to her mother's dismay, Florence displayed a novel lack of enthusiasm for beaux and balls and showed great interest and concern for the conditions of the poor and the suffering.

Although engaging in charitable activities was customary among Victorian girls of good breeding, Florence's zeal for visiting and tending the sick cottagers on her father's estate was somewhat unusual.

In February, 1837, at the age of 17, Florence wrote in her diary that she had received a direct call from God to enter into His service. At the time, she had no clear idea what form this service should take. She received her first inkling of her vocation later that year, during the Nightingales' two-year tour of the Continent. Florence was moved by the suffering she observed in various European hospitals, and vowed to return to these institutions for further study.

Many dull years passed before Florence was able to realize this goal, as she dutifully attempted to please her parents by leading the life considered appropriate for a young woman of her social station. In 1846, she recorded her dissatisfaction with her prescribed round of activities in her diary:

What in the world have I done this last fortnight? I have read the Daughter at Home *to father, and two chapters of Mackintosh; a volume of* Sybil *to Mama. Learnt seven tunes by heart, written various letters. Ridden with Papa. Paid eight visits. Some company. And that is all.*

In 1850, while traveling abroad, Florence visited the Sisters of St. Vincent de Paul, a Roman Catholic nursing order in Alexandria, Egypt, and was impressed by what they were doing to alleviate human misery. In 1851, she spent three months with a Protestant community of nursing deaconesses at Kaiserswerth, Germany, and later stayed for two weeks with a nursing order in Paris. This was the extent of Florence Nightingale's formal training as a nurse.

By 1853, Florence had determined to make a career of nursing. Her parents, furious at her for refusing a brilliant marriage to Richard Monckton Milnes (Lord Houghton), forbade her to seek a nursing job. But Florence had made up her mind about how she wanted to spend her life. She took a position as superintendent of a nursing home for elderly and indigent governesses, located on Harley Street, London. Her brilliant reorganization of that institution came to the attention of the British secretary of war, Sidney Herbert. Herbert asked Florence to lead an expedition of 38 nurses to

Scutari, Turkey, where British soldiers wounded in the Crimean War were dying in alarming numbers.

Florence eagerly accepted the mission, and departed for Scutari with her force of Catholic, Anglican, and lay nurses. She was appalled by the grim conditions and inadequate supplies at the Scutari hospital. The barracks were dirty and dilapidated; there were no bandages and a dearth of bedding and food; and anarchy reigned among the hospital staff. The situation cried out for a capable coordinator.

Florence Nightingale quickly demonstrated her talents as a take-charge administrator. She ordered the hardier patients to clean up the barracks, and devised schedules for nursing, laundering, and kitchen work, putting the staff on rotation. Day after day, she herself worked 20 hours at a stretch, supervising her subordinates, caring for patients and their families, and drafting urgent appeals to British military authorities to send supplies. Every night, Florence personally patrolled the four miles of hospital corridors, inspecting the wards by the light of a lantern. This image of her was later immortalized by Longfellow in his poem "Lady with a Lamp."

The doctors and military officials at Scutari bitterly resented the iron discipline imposed by their zealous "Lady-in-Chief." They lost no opportunity to harass Florence, and made her onerous task even more burdensome. Nevertheless, within a few months, Florence Nightingale reduced the mortality rate at the Scutari hospital from 42.2% to a mere 2.2%. Her unceasing concern for the suffering of the common soldier earned her the title "Angel of the Crimea."

In 1855, Florence journeyed to Balaclava, where she instituted sanitary reforms that markedly decreased the incidence of typhus, cholera, and dysentery. Unfortunately, she also contracted a severe case of Crimean fever, which was to plague her for the rest of her life. She continued, however, her work to eliminate unsanitary conditions and introduce quality care into Crimean hospitals, and did not leave the area until the war ended, in 1856. Before departing for England, Florence revisited Scutari. Having succored the soldiers' bodies, she now provided for their souls by establishing reading and recreation rooms for the recuperating soldiers.

Florence's return to London was heralded by huge celebrations, which her distaste for frivolity caused her to shun. Instead of attending the gala events in her honor, Florence secluded herself in London, and continued to work. She had carefully compiled statistics on the conditions in Crimean hospitals. In 1856, she sent a proposal for revamping the army medical services to the Ministry of War. But Sidney Herbert was no longer in the War Office, and Florence's recommendations were ignored. After military officials refused to consider her suggestions, the feisty Florence marched to Balmoral to present her proposals to the queen. Victoria was receptive to the national heroine's ideas. In 1857, the queen convened a commission to investigate and implement health reforms in the army.

Based on the royal commission's findings, Florence composed an 800-page treatise, *Notes on Matters Affecting the Health, Efficiency, and Hospital Administration of the British Army*, published in 1858. Soon Florence was besieged by letters from colonial viceroys, seeking her advice on improving sanitary conditions in the British army in India.

In 1860, Florence Nightingale turned her attention to sanitation and care in civil nursing. Her adoring public had presented her with a testimonial of about £45,000 in appreciation of her work in the Crimea. Florence used this fund to found a training school for nurses at St. Thomas Hospital in London. Thousands of nurses were trained at the Nightingale School. Many of them went on to establish nursing schools at other hospitals. Others, under Florence's direct supervision, instituted a network of visiting nursing services in various English districts.

During the decade from 1860 to 1870, Florence Nightingale served as an international consultant on military and civil nursing, hospital planning and management, and public health. The American government consulted her on hospital construction during the Civil War, and other foreign governments enlisted her aid and advice. The British War Office routinely sent Florence all sanitary reports. Meanwhile, she continued to be instrumental in establishing nursing homes, societies, and institutions throughout England.

In 1872, weakened by overwork and by the residual effects of her Crimean illness, Florence Nightingale retired from public life. Nevertheless, a steady stream of potentates, politicians, reformers, writers, and well-wishers invaded her London apartments, seeking her counsel on public health and welfare.

As a young woman, Florence had briefly considered becoming a writer, but had rejected a career in letters as too passive for her passionate nature. Now that her failing health imposed a sedentary existence upon her, she turned her talents to writing. She compiled an anthology of Christian mystic writings, and aided Benjamin Jowett in translating the *Dialogues* of Plato.

This modest humanitarian was not to be overlooked by an appreciative society. In 1883, she had been the given the Royal Award of the Red Cross. In 1907, Florence Nightingale became the first woman to receive the British Order of Merit. When the elderly, aching Florence was discreetly approached with the offer of a State funeral and burial in Westminster Abbey, the unassuming altruist demurred. When she died, on August 13, 1910, according to her express instructions, Florence's remains were deposited in her family's plot in a small Hampshire graveyard. Fittingly, Florence Nightingale's pallbearers consisted of six sergeants in the British army.

As the protagonist of nursing as a reputable secular profession, pioneer of hospital reform, and instigator of improved scientific methods in hospital management and public health, Florence Nightingale was one of humanity's greatest and most selfless benefactors. By shifting the emphasis in medical treatment from corrective care to preventive measures, she saved untold numbers of lives. Her personal achievements as a practical nurse were prodigious, and her influence in her own day was immense. Her inspirational role as a model for women and for would-be nurses in her own time and to the present is immeasurable. Her six official reports and 12 books on various aspects of medical care were responsible for promoting many concrete reforms, such as the institution of proper ventilation and drainage systems in hospitals.

In his allegory *The Faerie Queen*, British Renaissance poet Edmund Spenser narrates the quest of an Everyman-hero, the Red Cross knight, to redeem Man in the service of God. Florence Nightingale, who was divinely inspired to endeavors for the greater good of humanity, might aptly be dubbed the Red Cross Nightingale.

Rachel (1821-1858)
TRAGEDIENNE

A homely, sickly child, with a low, harsh voice and no formal education, Elisa Felix scarcely showed any promise of achieving greatness in any field, let alone in the exacting art of French classic acting. Yet, under the stage name Rachel, Elisa Felix became the peerless interpreter of Corneille and Racine, by her performances rescuing France's two greatest tragic dramatists from oblivion, and the Comédie Française from bankruptcy. Her natural, impassioned style of acting created a revolution in the thespian world. Her delineations turned cardboard characters into real human beings, noble but fallible, with whom literate and illiterate audiences alike could identify.

Elisa Felix was born in Munf, Switzerland, on March 24, 1821. She was the daughter of itinerant Jewish peddlers, who acquired children more easily than money. Only five of the numerous Felix progeny survived infancy.

At the age of four, Elisa was passing the hat for her sister Sarah, who sang with a troupe of Italian children at cafes in Reims. Soon,

Elisa, too, was a streetsinger, performing duets with Sarah in Lyons. When the Felixes moved to Paris in 1830, Sarah and Elisa concertized on the boulevards, giving animated renditions of *La Parisienne* and *La Marseillaise.*

One day, the Felix sisters were discovered by a musical amateur named Morin. Impressed by Sarah's silvery soprano, and by Elisa's flair for the dramatic, Morin gave the girls a letter of introduction to Étienne Choron, a famous singing teacher. Choron was so enthusiastic about the Felix sisters that he took them on as pupils free of charge. He got Sarah accepted at the government School of Sacred Music and arranged for Elisa to study elocution with Pagnon Saint Aulaire, a retired actor from the Théâtre Français. Saint Aulaire had great hopes for the 13-year-old Elisa, and invited members of the French theater companies, such as Samson of the Comédie Française and Monval of the Gymnase, to observe his star pupil's recitals. These men proved valuable to Elisa in her career.

Monval recommended Elisa to the manager of the Gymnase, Monsieur Poirson. Poirson offered the girl a three-year contract at 3,000 francs per year. This salary seemed a fortune to Elisa, who lived with her family in a garret and cooked dinner for them every night. At Poirson's bidding, Elisa adopted the stage name of Rachel.

In April 1837, the 16-year-old Rachel made her debut at the Gymnase, in a melodrama called *La Vendéenne,* based on Scott's *Heart of the Midlothian,* in the part of the peasant heroine. Rachel received an encouraging review by the most influential critic of the day, Jules Janin, of the *Journal de Débats:*

Mlle. Rachel is an unskilled child, but she possesses heart, soul, and intellect. There was something bold, abrupt, uncouth about her aspect, gait, and manner . . . her voice was harsh and untuned, but powerful; she acted without effort or exaggeration; she did not scream or gesticulate unduly; she seemed to perceive intuitively the feeling she was required to express. . . . She was not pretty, but she pleased: in a word, there is a great future in store for this young genius, and she receives a tribute of tears, emotion and interest from the as-yet small audience that comes to do her honor.

Poirson released her from her contract so she could go to the Théâtre Français. Before she moved from the Gymnase to the Français, Rachel was coached intensively by the actor Samson. Samson also engaged his children's tutor to instruct Rachel in history and grammar, that she might be knowledgeable in portraying the ancient queens of classic drama. Then, when Rachel's transformation from German-speaking guttersnipe to French classic actress was complete, Samson secured for her the role of Camille in Corneille's *Les Horaces.* Rachel made her debut at the Théâtre Français on June 12, 1838.

Rachel's Camille evoked a mixed reaction in the galleries. French theatergoers were used to seeing the classics performed in a showy, hyperbolic manner, with the actors chanting their speeches in a sing-song manner, to highlight the rhythms of language instead of the emotions of characters. Rachel's recitation was devoid of bombast or histrionics. She did not declaim; she spoke. Many spectators assumed that the diminutive actress lacked the strength to deliver Camille's imprecation in the usual extravagant rant. There was no applause when Rachel delivered the words in a hoarse whisper with concentrated emotion. Throughout the summer, Rachel played to half empty theaters. It was not until September, when the critic Janin witnessed Rachel's Camille, that she received the acclaim she deserved. A rave review by the powerful French critic finally explained Rachel's genius to the befuddled Parisians, and from then on she played to packed houses.

In her first two years at the Français, Rachel took 34 different roles. She played in some modern dramas by Victor Hugo, Dumas *père*, and de Musset, but excelled particularly in the classics. In 1845, Voltaire's *Oreste*, long off the boards, was revived for her. But the role that was above all identified with Rachel was Racine's Phèdre. Rachel first played Phedre in 1843, after an unhappy love affair had given her a new maturity and understanding of life. One critic observed that Rachel "had not only studied her sobs; she felt them." George Henry Lewes, the consort of novelist George Eliot, wrote after seeing Rachel's Phèdre in Paris:

Nothing I have ever seen surpassed this picture of a soul torn by the conflicts of incestuous passion and struggling conscience; the unutterable mournfulness of her look and tone as she recognized the guilt of her desires, yet felt herself so possessed by them that escape was impossible, are things never to be forgotten. What a picture she was as she entered! You felt that she was wasting away

*within. . . . The whole of the opening scene . . . was inexpressibly affecting
and intensely true. As an ideal representation of real emotion, it belonged to
the highest art. . .*

*In the second act, where Phèdre declares her passion to Hippolyte, Rachel
was transcendent . . . such was the amazing variety and compass of her expression, that when she quitted the stage she left us quivering with an excitement comparable only to that produced by Kean in the third act of
Othello. . . . Like Kean she had a power of concentrating into a single phrase a
world of intense feeling. . . . Whoever saw Rachel play Phèdre may be par-
doned if he doubt whether he will ever see such acting again.*

Rachel's conquests were by no means confined to Parisian audiences. In 1841-42, she was the sensation of the London season; her
success was repeated in Berlin, St. Petersburg, and other European
capitals. Rachel also made frequent tours of the French provinces,
where she earned even more money than at the Théâtre Français. In
1855, Rachel sailed for America, where she hoped to repeat her stu-
pendous successes. Her debut in New York, as Camille, drew a huge
ovation, but on succeeding nights, audience attendance fell off.
Rachel's American tour came near the end of her career; her last appearance was in Philadelphia in *Adriana Lecouvreur*, a melodrama
written especially for her by Scribe and Legouve. Rachel contracted
tuberculosis and was unable to complete her tour.

For 17 years, Rachel had virtually dictated the repertory of the
Théâtre Français, and had received the highest sums ever paid to an actor. She used her earnings to support her family in sumptuous style,
and was noted for her generosity to friends. Leading a volatile emotional life, her love affairs became as legendary as her performances,
and she bore two illegitimate children, whose upbringing she entrusted
to her devoted sister Sarah.

Her health sinking steadily, Rachel retired to Le Cannet, near Nice.
There, in 1858, the actress who had enthralled Europe with her breath-
taking performances breathed her last. Rachel was buried in the Jewish
section at the famous Père Lachaise cemetery.

"Dear God, let me live until I have heard Rachel!" wrote Hans
Christian Andersen, echoing the sentiment of the day. Like Mrs. Siddons before her, and Bernhardt and Duse after her, Rachel created in
her admirers an enthusiasm that bordered on frenzy. Her voice was

regarded as thrilling, and her clear enunciation and precise phrasing as superb. But what probably distinguished Rachel most was the way in which she used her body in her acting. One critic called her silences eloquent: "she relates a whole history by the changes of her facial expression." Another critic lauded Rachel's graceful arms and expressive hands. Supple of movement and electrifying in her intensity, Rachel was known as "the pythoness cast in bronze."

The enthusiastic furor over Rachel's Phèdre finds its only historic parallel in the Lady Macbeth of Sarah Siddons. Perhaps alone of the widely beloved actresses, Rachel owed none of her success to her appearance. She was described by her teacher Samson thus:

Rachel was below the middle height; she had an overhanging brow, a hollow eye which though not large was expressive. . . . She was extremely thin, but wore plain clothes with such art that thinness became a quality. Her gait and gesture were supple, and all her person breathed distinction. . . . Her contralto voice was small in range, yet so skilful was her use of it that there was no shade of meaning which it could not convey. In her earlier years . . . she was declared plain. In her later years, however, people said she was beautiful. Neither statement was true; or let me say that both were true according to the day, the hour, and the expression she willed *her features to assume.*

Will—that was the secret of Rachel's phenomenal success on the stage. In spite of the handicaps imposed on her by nature and by nurture, Rachel willed herself to be a great actress. "I *will* act Phèdre!" she insisted in 1839. "They tell me I am too young, that I am too thin, and a thousand other absurdities. I answer that it is Racine's finest role: I am determined to act it."

Phèdre was Rachel's finest role as well as Racine's, and the great playwright largely owes his posthumous renown to his greatest interpreter. Over and above the powerful impact Rachel had on all who witnessed her reinvigoration of the classics, Rachel performed a tremendous service to posterity by insuring the works of Racine and Corneille a lasting place in the canon of French literature.

Mary Baker Eddy
(1821-1910)

FOUNDER OF THE CHRISTIAN SCIENCE RELIGION

"I hail with joy your voice, speaking an assured word for God and immortality, and my joy is heightened that those words are of woman's divinings."

The speaker was Bronson Alcott, the father of the author of *Little Women;* the subject of his panegyric was a great woman: Mary Baker Eddy. In her lifetime, Mary Baker Eddy restored health, hope, faith, and serenity to millions of unhappy individuals. Today, many years after her death, the Christian Science Church continues to flourish in over 3,000 branches. Theologian, author, teacher, entrepreneur, and founder of one of the best American newspapers, Mary Baker Eddy was among the most remarkable figures in history. A woman who reversed her own fate, prevailing over the most debilitating hardships, she serves as an example and inspiration to all who suffer "the slings and arrows of outrageous fortune."

Mary Baker was born in Concord, New Hampshire, on July 16, 1821. The austerity of farm life proved taxing to Mary's health, and her infancy was constricted due to a congenital spine ailment.

A winsome, mystical child, Mary exercised a strange power over her family, especially her mother. Indeed, Mrs. Baker's predilection for the youngest of her six children verged on veneration: she confessed, "I worship Mary instead of the great Jehovah."

Mary's father, a stern, pious Congregationalist, was extremely solicitous of his daughter's health, but was less doting than his wife, and Mary sometimes resorted to violent temper tantrums to capture her father's attention. Mary did not attend public school, but was tutored at home by her favorite brother, Albert, whenever he was home from Darthmouth College. From the age of nine to thirteen, Mary studied philosophy, Latin, Greek, and Hebrew under Albert's direction. During Albert's absences, she would indulge her partiality for English literature, delving into the 400-page *Lindley Murray's English Reader*.

Mary's father instructed her in the Scriptures, and during the recurrent bouts of back pain and fever that afflicted her, Mary turned to the Bible for solace. Her brother Albert was also of a religious bent, and he and Mary discussed with great zest the mysteries of life, death, and immortality.

In 1836, the Bakers moved to a moderately-sized New Hampshire township, Sanborton Bridge. In this quasi-urban ambiance Mary's health improved, and she was able sporadically to attend the local schools. In 1842, she studied a full year at Sanborton Academy. She continued to write poems and prose, and some of her writings were published in local periodicals.

At the age of 17, Mary was accepted as a member of the Sanborton Congregational Church, despite her open disagreement with certain Congregationalist doctrines. The pastor of Mary's congregation was impressed by the fervor of Mary's faith, and found theological discussions with the girl intellectually stimulating.

In 1841, Albert Baker died. Mary felt her brother's loss deeply, and turned to his friend, George Glover, for consolation. Mutual commiseration ripened into love, and in 1843, Mary Baker became Mrs. George Glover. George's construction business took the couple to North Carolina, where Mary achieved notoriety through her rhymed diatribes against Whig politician Henry Clay. Later, she also published a tirade against the Southern slave trade.

Connubial happiness was short-lived for Mary Baker Glover. In

1844, her husband contracted yellow fever and died, leaving his pregnant, distraught widow to the charity of the Masonic Order. The Masons made funeral arrangements, and nursed Mary until she was well enough to return to her family in Sanborton.

George Glover's death plunged Mary into a state of utter despondency. She suffered hysterical seizures after the birth of her son and was unable to nurse him. George Junior was committed to the care of foster parents and moved with them to the West Coast. Mary did not see her son again until he was a grown man, although she wrote to him occasionally, and eventually sent large sums of money for the support of his family.

The next nine years of Mary's life were a physical hell and a spiritual purgatory. A recurrence of her childhood spinal ailment kept her writhing in perpetual pain, until finally, heavy doses of morphine were administered. Mary lapsed into apathy and exhaustion for weeks at a time. She would sit up in bed and emit piercing screams, filling the entire house with the sound of her anguish. She whimpered for her cradle, and was only mollified when her father rocked her in his arms. Mary's sister had a large cradle constructed, and employed neighborhood children to rock the tormented Mary to and fro, until her cries subsided.

In 1849, Mary's mother died, and the following year, when her father remarried, Mary's other relatives rotated the burden of caring for her. Gradually, Mary's spirit awakened to the humiliation of dependency. She roused herself from her physical and mental torpor, and attempted to support herself through a resumption of her literary endeavors. Mary was able to publish many of her articles, poems, and stories, but she received neither the recognition that might have restored her self-confidence nor the remuneration that would have made her economically self-sufficient. She relapsed into inertia. Except for an occasional temporary teaching position, she remained unemployed, her listlessness intensified by the heavy sedation she was under for her back pain.

Mary's family decided that marriage might be a remedy for her prolonged malaise, and in 1853 she was wed to Daniel Patterson, a charming but irresponsible itinerant dentist. The only common interest of the couple was homeopathy, to which Mary had resorted, with some success, as a panacea for her spinal ailment. Her husband frequently abandoned Mary for protracted intervals during their 13-year marriage. Her back pains became exacerbated by her consort's absences. Mary visited a sanatorium, and here she heard of the miraculous cures effected by a faith-healer named Quimby in Portland, Maine. Mary immediately made a pilgrimage to Portland, and was temporarily cured by Quimby's ministrations. She became interested in his theories of spiritual healing, and although these may have provided the germ of Christian Science, Mary's later theories diverged radically from Quimby's, and she categorically rejected healing by "the laying-on of hands" as quackery.

Separated for many years, Mary and Daniel Patterson were legally divorced in 1873. Mary received no support money—Patterson could barely support himself—and she again subsisted on the meager charity of her relations. Her life became increasingly nomadic and penurious.

In Mary's forty-fifth year, she hit a spiritual bedrock. Her father was now dead; her sister had disowned her; as neither wife nor widow, she felt deeply the stigma of her divorced status. Mary slipped on an icy sidewalk and severely injured her fragile spine. There seemed to be no hope for the homeless, husbandless, friendless, penniless, and jobless Mary. Informed that she would never walk again (and might not even continue to breathe much longer) Mary went from the lethargy of suffering into the panic of despair.

Then occurred the miracle which was to spawn a movement. Mary reached for her Bible, and turning to Matthew 9: 1-8, she read the account of a man cured of his suffering from palsy by the ministrations of Jesus. Suddenly, the pains in Mary's back disappeared. She rose from her bed, and walked.

Too realistic to attribute her regeneration to an unfathomable miracle, she felt a scientific study of the Scriptures would reveal to her the mechanics of her cure, which she then could transmit to other sufferers. "I then withdrew from society about three years—to ponder my mission, to search the Scriptures, to find the science of Mind." Mary's study convinced her that her own mind—in its unwillingness to accept the prognosis of imminent death—had joined with the mind of God to insure her recovery.

Mary journeyed across Massachusetts, boarding with families and lecturing and writing about her evolving theories of spiritual healing. Through her study of the Scriptures, she formulated and taught the basic postulates of the Christian Science religion. A decade later, in 1875, her writings were published as *Science and Health*. The main thesis of that work is that God, Mind, and Good conjoin in a spiritual reality that is capable of controlling matter, and of obliterating the "unrealities" of sin, evil, sorrow, sickness, and injustice. No evil comes from God, who is infinite Good. Only the good is true, eternal, real; evil, disease and death are unreal and mutable. Through unceasing prayer, love, understanding and faith in the goodness of God, sin and sickness can be healed.

Although *Science and Health* would eventually earn Mary $400,000 in royalties, the book was initially a dud. Mary's writing lacked lucidity. She herself recognized the problem, and revised and refined the text in each of its 381 successive printings. Happily, she found a brilliant editor, James Henry Wiggin of Harvard University Press, who could inject the needed clarity and cogency.

It was through teaching rather than writing that Mary initally achieved success in promulgating her theories of Christian Science. At the podium, Mary lacked the self-consciousness that marred her writing. She was an articulate speaker, and her extraordinary presence, enhanced by her mellifluous voice and luminous eyes, won her many recruits. Clergyman Edward Everett Hale wrote that Mary spoke "more truth in 20 minutes than I have heard in 20 years."

In 1877, Mary married Asa Eddy, one of the first and most successful practitioners of Christian Science spiritual healing. Five years later, Mr. Eddy died of an organic heart disease, and Mary carried on the propagation of Christian Science alone. In 1879, she established the Church of Christ, Scientist; in 1881, she founded the Massachusetts Metaphysical College, where she taught for eight years; in 1894, she presided at the laying of the cornerstone of the Mother Church of Christian Science in Boston; in 1895, she became Pastor Emeritus in perpetuum of the Christian Science Church.

At the age of 87, Mary Baker Eddy founded the *Christian Science Monitor*, "to injure no man, but to bless all mankind." She had previously founded two magazines and a publishing company, and was the author of ten books. Her newspaper was to attract particular attention through the excellence of its secular reportage, and is still one of the most respected newspapers in the United States.

Toward the end of her life, Mary was living in semi-seclusion in Concord, New Hampshire, although she refused to relinquish authority over her Christian Science empire. Several of her subalterns and former students turned against her and brought lawsuits, which Mary personally defended and generally won.

On December 3, 1910, the once sickly Mary Baker Eddy died at the age of 89 "of natural causes—probably pneumonia." She willed the bulk of her $2,500,000 estate to the Church of Christ, Scientist, leaving modest legacies to family and friends. After Mary's death, the new religion continued to gain adherents; today, there are Christian Science churches all over North America and in western Europe.

Of the many idealistic philosophies prevalent in Mary Baker Eddy's day, only Transcendentalism and Swedenborgianism have survived at all, and these primarily in literary reference. But Mary Baker Eddy's precepts continue to be actively practiced by stalwart adherents. Even though the romantic, somewhat blowsy rhetoric that rang true to her contemporary followers is no longer fashionable, Christian Science has endured. Spiritual healing continues to work for many people, for whom other systems, including modern medicine, have failed.

It should be noted that Mary Baker Eddy was not, as is commonly believed, an implacable enemy of medical science. She called a physician to treat her (third) husband's heart condition, defended the use of painkillers to allay extreme suffering, and paid for the immunization of her own grandchildren against childhood diseases. In claiming that all disease originates in the mind, Mary Baker Eddy recognized principles that modern medical studies have since substantiated—that much illness is psychosomatic in origin, or is augmented by stress; that psychic well-being is intimately related to physical well-being; and that self-confidence and positive thinking are crucial determinants of worldly success as well as inner peace. In advocating a combination of self-reliance and reliance on God as the means of reestablishing belief in the human capacity to control events, Mary Baker Eddy not only effected her own phenomenal regeneration, but gave new life to millions of tortured individuals, and, perhaps, prevented millions more from experiencing a dark night of the soul.

Antoinette Brown Blackwell (1825-1921)

FIRST ORDAINED WOMAN MINISTER

Antoinette Brown was not the first woman to grace a pulpit. Women had served in the clergy of the Methodist Church in England until forbidden to preach by a ruling at a Wesleyan convention in the early 19th century. The Quakers, an offshoot of the Methodists, continued to allow women to speak in meeting and to be recorded as ministers. And many Protestant women in America, without the sanction of an official denomination, had arrogated to themselves the office of the ministry. The most famous of these was Anne Hutchinson, who was banished from Massachusetts by a Puritan synod convened expressly for the purpose of driving the radical, antinomian woman preacher from the environs of Boston.

However, the Reverend Antoinette Brown was the first woman officially ordained as a minister in America—and probably in the world. She began her ministry as a Congregationalist, but later joined the Unitarian Church. During a long, productive life, in addition to performing clerical duties and lecturing, this gifted woman wrote 10 books, including a novel, a book of poems, and several philosophical treatises. She also worked for women's suffrage, and raised five children. In opening a new profession to women, and in demonstrating that marriage and a significant career or social involvement are not mutually exclusive, Blackwell served as a model.

Antoinette Louisa Brown was born in a log cabin in Henrietta, New York, on May 20, 1825. She was the fourth daughter and the seventh of ten children of devout Congregationalist farmers.

When Antoinette, or Nettie as she was called, was nine years old, she became the youngest person ever admitted to the local Congregationalist church. The Congregationalist elders, impressed by the girl's articulate public confession of faith, voted to admit her to the congregation and henceforth allowed Antoinette to lead prayers and speak in meetings.

Nettie Brown was intellectually as well as religiously precocious. At the age of three, she accompanied her older siblings to the county school. In 1845, she taught school for a year to help finance her tuition, and the following year she entered Oberlin as a member of the junior class. She graduated from the Ladies Literary Course in 1847, without a degree.

At Oberlin, Antoinette became friends with Lucy Stone, an ardent feminist and abolitionist. But even Lucy, who was to become a national suffragette leader and one of the first women to keep her maiden name after marriage, was amazed when Antoinette Brown announced her intention to enter the ministry. Antoinette's father was more than amazed; he was livid with anger, and warned his daughter that he would not finance her theological studies. Oberlin College was similarly opposed to Antoinette's religious ambitions. She was dismissed from her post as an art teacher in the college's preparatory program as soon as she applied for admission to the Department of Theology.

Despite its progressive policy regarding coeducation, Oberlin College drew the line at admitting Antoinette Brown, or her co-applicant, Lettice Smith, to the theology department. Lettice Smith, at least, indicated she had no wish to practice as a minister, but Antoinette Brown made no secret of the fact that she felt a call from God to preach the gospel. She even wrote a stirring essay arguing that the Bible had been wrongly interpreted to bar women from the clergy:

. . . in what portion of the inspired volume do we find any commandment forbidding a woman to act as a public teacher, provided she had a message worth communicating and will deliver it in a manner worthy of her high vocation? . . . . Where have any of the inspired writers said, I suffer not a woman to teach in public, and to stand up in the name of her Redeemer, administering the cup of salvation to the lips of dying mortals, even though her spirit is yearning to break unto them the bread of eternal life. . . .

The Oberlin divines were impressed; they admitted the two women applicants to the theology department. In 1848, Antoinette's essay was published in the *Oberlin Quarterly Review.* But, in 1850, when the two female divinity students completed their studies, they were excluded from graduation ceremonies and denied diplomas. Antoinette Brown was refused a license to preach. For many years, their names failed to appear in the Oberlin alumni catalogue listing of graduates of the theology school. It was not until 1878 that Antoinette Brown was granted an honorary A.M. by her alma mater, and on her 73rd birthday, Antoinette Brown Blackwell was belatedly awarded the Doctor of Divinity Degree by Oberlin.

Since Antoinette believed the only license necessary to preach was a call from God, she was undaunted when official sanction was denied to her ministry. In the course of her three-year theological studies, she had preached widely in Ohio and Michigan. Now she embarked on a two-year lecture tour of the New England and Middle Atlantic states, sermonizing against slavery and drink, and in favor of women's rights. Antoinette joined fellow feminists Susan B. Anthony and Amelia Bloomer on a temperance tour, but did not wear the loose-fitting "bloomer" pantaloons advocated by Ms. Bloomer to replace the onerous bustle.

Her own Congregationalist church denied Antoinette permission to preach in its churches, but liberal Unitarian ministers invited Antoinette Brown to give guest sermons in their pulpits, and she acquired a reputation as an eloquent speaker.

In 1853, Antoinette Brown at last obtained recognition from the Congregationalist hierarchy, and was sent as its delegate to the World Temperance Convention in New York City. When she rose at the first meeting of the convention to thank the delegates for accepting her credentials, she was greeted with a chorus of hoots and catcalls. When the bewildered young woman inquired as to the cause of the rude response, she was told that as a woman she was out of order in addressing a public meeting. Antoinette Brown was incensed, and so were her Unitarian supporters. Editor Horace Greeley rallied to her defense with a mordant editorial in the *New York Tribune*:

This convention has completed three of its four business sessions, and the results may be summed up as follows: First Day—Crowding a woman off the platform. Second Day—Gagging her. Third Day—Voting that she shall stay gagged. Having thus disposed of the main questions, we presume the incidentals will be finished this morning.

Greeley's caustic pen evoked an outpouring of sympathy for Antoinette Brown. When the temperance convention disbanded, a large audience came to hear her speak in the same lecture hall where she had been summarily yanked off the stage. Horace Greeley and Charles Dana of the *New York Sun* were so impressed by Antoinette Brown's command of theology that they offered to pay her one thousand dollars a year, plus board, if she would make New York City her pastorate. But Antoinette Brown declined the honor of preaching in the great metropolis in favor of a position at a small Congregationalist church in South Butler, New York.

A terrible storm broke out on the morning that Antoinette was to be ordained at the South Butler church, and there were snide whispers in some pews that the thunder and lightning expressed divine disapproval of the young woman's effrontery in adopting a man's profession. From her seat on the platform, Antoinette must have guessed what was being whispered; just a few days before, in New York City, her sermon at Metropolitan Hall had been repeatedly interrupted by hissing from male hecklers. But Antoinette had preserved her sangfroid on that occasion, and she preserved it now, at the moment of her ordination. She listened quietly as the Reverend Luther Lee quoted from Galatians 3:28: "there is neither male nor female: for ye are all one in Christ Jesus," and as the Reverend Gerret Smith propounded "Woman's Right to preach the Gospel." When the Reverend Antoinette Brown was congratulated by her brethren, the congregation bowed their heads sensing that they had just witnessed history in the making.

In November, 1853, two months after her ordination, Antoinette wrote in her diary:

This is a very poor and small church, and my salary is three hundred dollars a year, ample I believe for my needs in this small community. My parish will be a miniature world in good and evil. To get humanity condensed into so small a compass that I can study each individual opens a new chapter of experience. . . . Perhaps I shall know some of the feelings with which an Infinite Mind watches the universe.

But Antoinette's experiment in South Butler did not last long. She soon found herself at odds with the elders of the church for disagreeing with the doctrine of infant damnation and other Calvinist dogmas. Antoinette began to realize that she was far too speculative and philosophical for the parochial parish of South Butler, and on July 20, 1854, she resigned her pastorate.

She returned to New York City, where she engaged in philanthropic activities with her friend Abby Hopple Gibbons. Antoinette later described this year of benevolent work thus:

It became our custom to spend one day in the week together, seeking our brethren who were pitiable and forsaken . . . in the slums and institutions of New York. This was before the days of many organized charities. We went wherever the way served, prepared for rescue work. Now, it was down into the heart of darkest New York in search of some suffering family or a stray girl . . . again over to Randall's Island with some mission to strangers in a strange land . . . or perhaps to the Hospital, the workhouse, the Insane Asylum, or the Penitentiary on Blackwell's Island, with some message of good will or moral tonic.

Antoinette Brown and her college friend, Lucy Stone, had remained fast friends. In 1855, Lucy Stone married the abolitionist and reformer, Henry Blackwell, whose sisters, Elizabeth and Emily Blackwell, were physicians and the founders of America's first hospital for women. The wedding ceremony caused a huge sensation, for not only did Lucy Stone insist on retaining her maiden name after marriage, but she and her husband wrote a scorching denunciation of the marriage laws, which the officiating minister, Thomas Wentworth Higginson, incorporated into the marriage service.

In 1856, Antoinette Brown married Samuel Blackwell, brother of Henry, Elizabeth and Emily, and also a feminist. Samuel Blackwell was a hardware merchant and bookkeeper, and his various jobs kept the Blackwells on the move during the early years of their marriage. Antoinette gave birth to seven children, but only five daughters survived infancy. In between accouchements, she appeared on various public platforms. When she was at home she sedulously pursued her philosophical studies for a minimum of three hours daily. She also wrote articles and books, encouraged by her husband, who shared in the household chores. Antoinette shared financial responsibilities with her husband, and undertook a cross-country lecture tour to help pay the expenses of the Blackwell's large menage. In 1901, Samuel Blackwell died. His widow lived on for 20 more years of active work and travel.

In 1908, Antoinette Brown Blackwell helped to found the All Souls' Unitarian Church in Elizabeth, New Jersey. For the next 13 years, she served as pastor emeritus of this church, preaching her last sermon there on Easter Sunday, 1915, at the age of 90. She died seven years later, on November 5, 1921, having cast her vote in the first election open to women in the year of her death.

Mary Harris Jones
(1830?-1930)

LABOR LEADER

"... The working men of America will not halt or will they ever go back. The working man is going forward!" declared Mary Harris (Mother) Jones, during a coal miners' strike in Pennsylvania in 1900. The working man did go forward, in rapid strides, thanks to the dedication of grass-roots union organizers like Mother Jones.

Mary Harris Jones, called by I.W.W. leader, Elizabeth Gurley Flynn, "the greatest woman agitator of our time," was a pervasive figure in the American labor movement. She was one of the first women to support the Knights of Labor in the 1870s, and was pivotal in opening that organization to women members in 1879. In 1905, Mother Jones helped to found the International Workers of the World and was the only woman to appear on the platform at the I.W.W. opening convention. For more than 50 years, Mother Jones worked to publicize and promote the cause of male workers in the coal and steel industries, child laborers in textile mills, women workers in the Milwaukee beer breweries, and Mexican revolutionaries imprisoned in the United States. She organized workers and their wives into brigades, and headed strikes and demonstrations all over the country. She responded unhesitatingly to appeals from workers as expressed, for example, in the following telegram from Shamokin, Pennsylvania:

MOTHER THERE IS A STRIKE AT THE SILK MILLS HERE WILL YOU COME AT ONCE I KNOW YOU CAN DO LOTS OF GOOD COME IF POSSIBLE FROM A MINER

Mother Jones went to Shamokin, as she went to so many other places where American workers required her aid. As Clarence Darrow said, "Wherever the fight was the fiercest, Mother Jones was present to aid and cheer. In both the day and the night, in the poor villages and at the lonely cabin on the mountain side, Mother Jones always appeared in time of need."

Mary Harris was born in Cork, Ireland, but there seems to be some question as to whether the year was 1830, as she reports in her autobiography, or 1838, or 1843. The date, however, is known, and is, appropriately enough, May 1, celebrated today as May Day by labor all over the world. The Harrises and their several children emigrated to the United States when Mary was a young child. They settled first in Burlington, Vermont, where Mr. Harris worked as a railroad construction laborer. The entire family became naturalized American citizens. During Mary's childhood her father's job took the family to Toronto, Canada. Mary attended Canadian public schools, and graduated from the Toronto Normal School, a teacher's college, in 1859.

Mary Harris taught at a convent school in Monroe, Michigan, but "bossing little children" was distasteful to her, so she went to Chicago where she became a dressmaker. In 1861, she married George Jones, an organizer for the Iron Molders Union. Mary Jones joined her husband in what they called "missionary work"—trying to persuade working men to join unions. This was not easy since union members were faced with the constant threats of harassment, blacklisting, firing, and even imprisonment. But Mary and George Jones tried to convince workers that the only way they could improve their condition was by confronting management in a united block and bargaining with employers through their own chosen representatives.

Mary and her husband lived in a run-down section in Memphis, not far from the iron foundry where George Jones worked. During the 1860s, the Joneses had four children—three boys and a girl. In 1867, an epidemic of yellow fever struck Memphis. One by one, the Jones children caught the contagion and died. Then George Jones succumbed to the fever as well.

After the pestilence had subsided, the stricken Mary returned to Chicago, where she resumed the dressmaking trade. She displayed a flair for color and style and her dressmaking establishment prospered. But as she stitched lace fronts and velvet furbelows on the gowns of wealthy ladies, her social conscience made her contemptuous of conspicuous consumption:

. . . the word society, as applied to women of today, stands for idleness, fads, extravagance and display of wealth. . . . It nauseates me to see your average city woman. She is always overdressed, although she is careful to leave her right hand bared so that she can display her fingers crowded to their utmost with jewels.

Nevertheless, she was later to use her skill to give miners' wives a sense of personal dignity by teaching them how to make bonnets to replace their peasant kerchiefs.

In 1871, Mary Jones's dressmaking establishment went up in smoke in the Great Chicago Fire. Her home and all her belongings were also destroyed by the conflagration, making Mary Jones one of the 90,000 Chicagoans left homeless by the calamity.

Mary Jones was billeted with other dispossessed refugees at St. Mary's Church. Close by the church was the hall of the Knights of Labor, chartered as "an organization of working people of every craft . . . skilled and unskilled . . . with members of every creed and color." But not of every sex—women could not, at that time, join the Knights of Labor. Although she was not invited to participate as a member, Mary Jones's labor experience and gift of oratory were appreciated. She was sent out to recruit members among immigrant workers; and she brought them into the union fold in droves. In speaking to immigrants, Mary Jones adopted an Irish brogue, which seemed to please the aliens and put them at ease. Her warmhearted and expansive manner soon inspired the men to identify her as "Mother Jones."

During the last three decades of the 19th century, Mary Jones engaged in varied activities in America and in Europe, studying and promoting the cause of labor. She became particularly sympathetic to the plight of the miners, which she described graphically:

Mining at its best is wretched work, and the life and surroundings of the miner are hard and ugly. His work is down in the black depths of the earth. He works alone in a drift. There can be little friendly companionship as there is in the factory, as there is among men who build bridges and houses, working together in groups. The work is dirty. Coal dust grinds itself into the skin, never to be removed. The miner must stoop as he works in the drift. He becomes bent like a gnome. His work is utterly fatiguing. Muscles and bones ache. His lungs breathe coal dust and the strange damp air of places that are never filled with sunlight. . . . Around his house is mud and slush. Great mounds of culm, black and sullen, surround him. His children are perpetually grimy from play on the culm mounds. The wife struggles with dirt, with inadequate water supply, with small wages, with overcrowded shacks.

In 1890, she became one of the organizers for the United Mine Workers, participating in their valiant struggles to improve the life of the miner, described as follows by Clarence Darrow:

"Some of the fiercest combats in America have been fought by the miners. These fights brought thousands of men and their families close to starvation. They brought contests with police, militia, courts and soldiers. They involved prison sentences, massacres, and hardships without end. . . ."

The wives of striking miners were of as much concern to Mother Jones as the men themselves. She helped the women with housework and childcare, and pressed them to join their men in demonstrating. In 1900, during a strike at the Dripmouth Mine in Arnot, Pennsylvania, Mother Jones organized a women's brigade, telling the men, who were demoralized by the strike, then in its fifth month, "Stay home with the children for a change and let the women attend to the scabs." Armed with washtubs, mops, brooms, and buckets of water, the all-woman army charged the mine, chasing the scabs from the entrance to the pits and knocking down the guards who tried to stop them. One of the scabs who was attacked fell at the feet of his own mother who had joined the women's militia. "For God's sake come back to life . . . and join the union," the woman implored her son, afraid he had fractured his skull in the fall. The man's eyes fluttered open. "Sure," he said, "and I'll go to hell before I'll scab again." Whether this anecdote which Mother Jones often told to union audiences was true or not, what is certain is that the women's march changed the course of the Arnot strike. Morally buttressed by the support of their womenfolk, the miners recovered their nerve and remained on strike until their demands were met.

In 1902, the United Mine Workers achieved a general settlement with the mine owners, which, however, did not cover the miners of bituminous coal in West Virginia. Mother Jones was one of the first union organizers in that state, and established chapters of the U.M.W. in the Fairmont district and the New River coal camps. But when U.M.W. president John Mitchell repudiated a walkout in the Colorado mines in 1903, Mother Jones repudiated Mitchell and quit her job with the U.M.W. She continued to serve as a free-lance troubleshooter for miners, but also directed her efforts toward helping other exploited workers. She joined forces with the striking machinists of the Southern Pacific Railroad, she helped organize the I.W.W. She compelled Congress to open an inquiry into the situation of Mexican revolutionaries who were being held prisoner in the United States.

Mother Jones received the greatest publicity for her work on behalf of the juvenile textile workers of Kensington, Pennsylvania. She led them on the famous March of the Mill Children, from Pennsylvania to Theodore Roosevelt's vacation home in Oyster Bay, New York. All along the way, Mother Jones organized public meetings enlisting sympathy for her young charges. "Here's a textbook in economics," she said, bringing forth James Ashworth, whose young shoulders were stooped from carrying 75-pound bundles of yarn every day. "He gets three dollars a week and his sister who is fourteen gets six dollars. They work in a carpet factory ten hours a day. . ." Thus was the populace introduced to these and other children, prematurely aged from overwork.

The Children's March caused a sensation in the press, receiving daily coverage by the *New York Times*. Railroad men let the marchers travel free of charge; the children were given shelter by sympathizers, including Grover Cleveland, who let the youngsters sleep in his barn in Princeton, New Jersey. Although President Roosevelt refused to meet the youthful delegation, the public pressure aroused by the march forced Pennsylvania to amend its child labor laws.

The other cause for which Mother Jones became famous involved her beloved miners. On April 20, 1914, 20 members of mining families were machine-gunned to death in Ludlow, Colorado, in what came to be known as "the Ludlow Massacre." Mother Jones was incensed by the slaughter at Ludlow. She criss-crossed the country, bringing audiences to tears with her description of the tragedy. She personally petitioned the Congressional Mines and Mining Committee. President Wilson, for whom she had campaigned in 1916, was moved to intervene to establish a truce between mine owners and mine workers. Grievance committees were set up at each mine.

Mother Jones was not active in the suffragette campaigns, claiming, "You don't need a vote to raise hell. You only need a voice and convictions."

Mother Jones was a dynamic force in the labor movement well into her eighties or nineties. In 1915-16, she lent her aid to striking streetcar operators and garment workers in New York City; in 1919, she was active in the Great Steel Strike; and in 1921, she made her third visit to Mexico as an American labor delegate, this time to the Pan American Federation of Labor Convention.

On May 1, 1930, a huge centennial birthday party was held for Mother Jones at the home of Mrs. Walter Burgess of Silver Springs, Maryland, with whom Mother Jones passed her final years. Among the messages of congratulation that rained in was a telegram from John D. Rockefeller, with whom Mother Jones had locked horns on so many occasions. "He's a damn good sport," said Mother Jones. "I've licked him many times, but we've made peace."

Seven months later, Mother Jones was at peace with all the world. She died on November 30, 1930, and was buried at the Union Miners Cemetery at Mount Olive, Illinois, near the graves of miners killed in the 1898 riots at Virden, Illinois.

Despite her white hair and matronly black bonnets, Mother Jones was anything but a sedate little old lady. Flamboyance and salty language were her hallmarks. Typical of her colorful cannonades was this one, fired during the 1912 coal strike in Paint Creek, West Virginia. Mother Jones told striking miners, ". . . I warn this little governor that unless he rids Paint Creek and Cabin Creek of these goddamned Baldwin Felts mine-guard thugs, there is going to be one hell of a lot of bloodletting in these hills." Although she was fond of stating, "The militant, not the meek, shall inherit the earth," Mother Jones did not relish violence. "What is won today by violence will be lost tomorrow," she said. "We must ever and always appeal to reason. . . . The taking of human life has never settled any question." One of the most charismatic revivalist-style speakers in modern times, Mother Jones never used her ability to sway the masses for self-serving ends. Many union members, disillusioned by the opportunism of some of their leaders, found in Mother Jones renewed faith in the labor movement. The simple, honest words of this acccolade addressed to Mother Jones must have pleased her enormously, ". . . [I and my brother would] bet our last cent on Mother Jones . . . you cannot be touched with money, and you don't want a political job. So they can't reach you nohow."

Mother Jones and Coolidge.

Harriet Hosmer (1830-1908)

SCULPTOR

Some years ago, in an art store in Boston, a crowd of persons stood gazing intently upon a famous piece of statuary. The red curtains were drawn aside, and the white marble seemed almost to speak. A group of girls stood together, and looked on in rapt admiration. One of them said, "Just to think that a woman did it!"

"It makes me proud and glad," said another.

"Who is Harriet Hosmer?" said a third. "I wish I knew about her."

And then, one of us, who had stolen all the hours she could get from school life to read art books from the Hartford Athenaeum, and kept crude statues, made by herself from chalk and plaster, secreted in her room, told all she had read about the brilliant creator of "Zenobia."

The statue was seven feet high, queenly in pose and face, yet delicate and beautiful, with the thoughts which genius had wrought in it. . . . Since that time, I have looked upon other masterpieces in all the great galleries of Europe, but perhaps none have ever made a stronger impression upon me than "Zenobia," in those early years.

The above narrative, from a 19th-century schoolgirl's memoir, indicates the impact Harriet Hosmer's achievement had on American girls of her day. Hosmer was one of a very few American sculptors to attain an international reputation in that period.

Harriet Goodhue Hosmer was born in Watertown, Massachusetts, on October 9, 1830. Her upbringing was most unorthodox for a girl of that era. Her father, a physician who had lost his wife and three other children through illness, was determined that Harriet should be a strong, healthy child. "There is a whole lifetime for the education of the mind," observed Dr. Hosmer, "but the body develops in a few years; and during that time nothing should be allowed to interfere with its free and healthy growth."

Consequently, Harriet engaged in outdoor activities that were considered strictly masculine at the time—she rowed; she skated; she rode horseback; she hiked; she hunted; and she fished. The Hosmers' neighbors viewed the tree- and mountain-climbing Harriet as a regular hoyden. Her snake and insect collection was the scandal of Watertown. Unmindful of gossip, Harriet preserved and dissected her specimens of natural history with great gusto. She also enjoyed modeling figures of horses, dogs, and other animals.

Although slight in build, Harriet became an unusually vigorous and rugged child. To her father's dismay, she was also unruly and headstrong. He hired a tutor to discipline and educate Harriet, but the meek Mr. Peabody could not cope with the *enfant terrible.* Dr. Hosmer then sent Harriet to Lenox, Massachusetts, to Mrs. Charles Sedgewick's school, an institution that specialized in "difficult" children.

Harriet thrived under the liberal and understanding tutelage of Mrs. Sedgewick. In her three years at the school, Harriet met a number of distinguished persons, including Ralph Waldo Emerson, Nathaniel Hawthorne, and actress Fanny Kemble. Fanny Kemble was impressed by the little figures that Harriet continued to fashion from clay, and urged the girl to turn from amateur clay-modeling to professional sculpture. Harriet also sparked the interest of the father of one of her school chums, Dr. Wayman Crow, who was to prove instrumental in advancing Harriet's career as a sculptor.

From Mrs. Sedgewick's, Harriet went to Boston. She enrolled in drawing and modeling classes under a Mr. Stephenson, and applied to the Boston Medical School for a course in anatomy. Her application was summarily dismissed because she was a female.

Her friend, Dr. Crow, came to her aid. He invited the girl to live in St. Louis with his family and arranged private lessons in anatomy for Harriet at the St. Louis Medical College. As in Boston, women were customarily barred from anatomy courses, but Dr. Crow's friend, Dr. Joseph McDowall, agreed to take on Harriet as a special pupil. Professor McDowall immediately warmed to his eager young student. She reciprocated his high regard, and later sculpted a medallion-portrait of him. Others at the Medical College were not so well-disposed toward Harriet as Dr. McDowall, however, and she was obliged to take the precaution of carrying a pistol to and from class. She was delighted, however, to be able to resume mountain climbing and, unescorted, scaled one of Missouri's highest mountains. The peak was later named Mount Hosmer, in Harriet's honor.

After receiving a diploma, Harriet set out on an adventure. She hopped a steamer which took her to New Orleans. Harriet then returned to Watertown. Her affluent father, proud of his artistic daughter, procured an atelier, where Harriet passed many hours sculpting marble figures. Harriet's unusual muscular strength and physical stamina, fostered by her athletic childhood, enabled the slight but wiry girl to wield a leaden mallet weighing four-and-a-half pounds for eight to ten hours a day. The tiny Harriet did all the carving and modeling of the stone herself after the block had been reduced to within an inch or two of the desired outlines.

In 1852, when Harriet was 22, she executed her first notable sculpture, a Neoclassical bust of *Hesper*, the Evening Star. *Hesper* brought Harriet to the attention of Charlotte Cushman, the leading American actress of the day, who was so impressed she secured Dr. Hosmer's permission to take Harriet to Rome, where many eminent male sculptors were studying and working. Here, the irrepressible Harriet boldly sought admission to the studio of the most prominent sculptor there, the British John Gibson. At first, Gibson refused to even consider taking Harriet as a pupil, because "women wouldn't apply themselves to study." Stung by this rebuff, Harriet refuted the charge by showing Gibson some daguerreotypes of her work. Gibson was impressed and relented, giving Harriet her own workroom in his atelier. Through Gibson, Harriet met many wealthy British art collectors, who later offered the girl a number of important commissions.

Harriet continued to sculpt in the prevailing Neoclassical mode. Initially, Gibson set her to work copying antique statues. Then he encouraged her in original endeavors. Harriet's early productions were statues of mythological heroines—*Medusa* and *Daphne.* She created the statue of Daphne for her early mentor, Dr. Wayman Crow, who also commissioned a full-length statue of Oenone, the nymph from Greek mythology who was abandoned by her husband, the fickle Paris, in favor of Helen of Troy.

Harriet very much enjoyed living in Rome, and pursued an unconventional nightlife, recklessly galloping through the Campagna on her saddle-horse at midnight. She was abetted in her capers by other members of Charlotte Cushman's maverick menagerie, also women sculptors, or painters. The Cushman coterie became known as "the White Marmorean Flock," and their exploits and affectation of male dress became the scandal of Rome.

In 1854, Harriet Hosmer faced a crisis. Her father wrote that he had suffered financial losses and could no longer pay her tuition abroad. Harriet packed up her bags to return home; then rebelled. "I cannot give up my art, and I won't," she averred, unpacking her trunks. She sold her horse and exercised Draconian economies. She also appealed to her old friend Dr. Crow for financial aid, which, as usual, he gave. Then Harriet Hosmer settled down to sculpt feverishly—her avocation must now be her trade.

Harriet became the only woman sculptor of the day to make her living solely through her art. In 1856, she produced a statue that earned her the incredible sum of $50,000. This work was *Puck*, an uncharacteristically humorous piece, showing a child perched on a toadstool, a lizard in his left hand, a beetle in the right. The prince of Wales was among the many notables who bought copies of *Puck*. A companion piece, *Will-o'-the-Wisp*, sold well, too.

In 1859, Hosmer created her masterpiece, *Zenobia in Chains*, which drew the quoted ecstatic remarks from the Boston schoolgirls. To execute her statue of the Palmyran queen, manacled by her Roman captors, Harriet sedulously pursued a good deal of archeological research. Several replicas of *Zenobia* were sold to wealthy

American collectors, and an exhibition of the work netted $5,000 for the artist. The piece is now in the collection of the New York Metropolitan Museum.

When *Zenobia* was exhibited in London, the critics refused to believe that the statue was the work of a woman. Harriet's *chef d'oeuvre* showed the technique of a master, and had a grandeur of spirit they judged to be beyond the limited scope or capacity of a woman. Several British publications attributed the statue to Harriet's teacher, John Gibson. Harriet speedily slapped her detractors with libel suits and they promptly withdrew the offensive statements.

In 1860, Harriet returned to America to visit her ailing father. While home, she was given the important public commission to execute a colossal bronze statue of Senator Thomas Hart Benton of Missouri. Harriet expressed her gratitude for the commission, ". . . I have also reason to be grateful to you because I am a woman; and, knowing what barriers must in the outset oppose all womanly efforts, I am indebted to the chivalry of the West, which has first overleaped them." The Benton statue was unveiled in 1868.

Harriet continued to support herself through her sculpture, and when her nude statue, *A Sleeping Faun*, was displayed in Dublin in 1865, it sold for $5,000. When Harriet returned to Rome after her sojourn in America universal adulation greeted her. Harriet's friends and admirers included Carlyle, Ruskin, George Eliot, the Hawthornes, Thackeray, Whittier, and the Brownings. At the Brownings' request, she cast a model of their clasped hands in bronze. Harriet also became a great favorite of Pope Pius IX, who admired her spunk and her wit.

Harriet Hosmer died in her hometown, Watertown, Massachusetts, on February 21, 1908, at the age of 78.

Harriet Hosmer's *oeuvre* stands out from among the rather pedestrian Neoclassical statuary produced by her contemporaries by the humanity with which she endowed her marble figures. Her teacher, Gibson, declared that she had "the power of imitating roundness and softness of flesh he had never seen surpassed." The crown princess of Germany, upon viewing Hosmer's *Puck*, exclaimed, "Oh Miss Hosmer, you have such a talent for toes!" Harriet also had a talent for souls: her *Zenobia* is indeed "a queen in spirit, undethroned by calamity."

Harriet did not initiate any revolutionary techniques or styles in 19th century sculpture—but neither did any of her male contemporaries. She did, however, serve as the vanguard of American women sculptors, setting a standard of exceptionality which the great contemporary, avant-garde sculptor, Louise Nevelson, so amply continues.

Harriet was aware of the conflict the women of her day experienced in choosing between emotional or professional fulfillment, and early in her career, she embraced celibacy as the only practicable mode of life for a woman artist. She wrote:

Even if so inclined, an artist had no business to marry. For a man it may be well enough, but for a woman, on whom matrimonial duties and cares weigh more heavily, it is a moral wrong, I think, for she must neglect her profession or her family, becoming neither a good wife and mother nor a good artist. My ambition is to become the latter, so I wage eternal feud with the consolidating knot.

The choice of a career over marriage exposed Harriet to the animosity and derision that has met women aspirants in every field. But this plucky lady was up to her chosen task. In a letter to Phoebe A. Hanaford, one of the first clergywomen in America, Harriet extolled the role of pioneer:

I honor every woman who has strength enough to step out of the beaten path when she feels that her walk lies in another; strength enough to stand up and be laughed at if necessary. That is a bitter pill we must swallow at the beginning: but I regard these pills as tonics quite essential to one's mental salvation. . . . But in a few years, it will not be thought strange that women should be preachers and sculptors, and everyone who comes after us will have to bear fewer and fewer blows. Therefore I say, I honor all those who step boldly forward, and, in spite of ridicule and criticism, pave a broader way for the women of the next generation.

Belva Bennett Lockwood
(1830-1917)

ATTORNEY AND CRUSADER
FOR HUMAN RIGHTS

Belva Bennett Lockwood was born with a sense of destiny. At the age of ten, after reading the Bible, she decided her mission in life was to perform miracles. Her juvenile experiments in miracle-working were failures. But as the first woman to be allowed to plead cases before the U.S. Supreme Court, and as the dauntless champion of the underdog and of international pacifism, Belva Lockwood did indeed work wonders. In her own words: "I have not raised the dead, but I have awakened the living; and if I have not been able to walk on water, the progressive spirit of this age may soon accomplish this feat."

Belva Ann Bennett was born on October 24, 1830 in Royalton, New York, the second of five children. Her parents were farmers. Belva attended local schools until age 15. She taught school in the summers, and attended Royalton Academy in the winters.

At the age of 18, she married Uriah H. McNall, a farmer and sawmill operator. Four years after the marriage, her husband was killed in a sawmill accident. The 23-year-old widow returned to teaching to support herself and her infant daughter. Belva obtained a teaching post at Royalton, at a salary half the amount paid to her male colleagues. She continued her studies and graduated from Genesee College with honors in 1857.

Armed with a B.S. degree, Belva McNall landed a position at the Lockport Union School where she taught higher mathematics, logic, rhetoric, and botany. She was soon elected principal of the school. During the four years of her administration, she introduced a number of innovations into the curriculum. Over heavy protest, she expanded the course offerings for women to include public speaking and physical education, teaching both courses herself.

In 1866, seeking a broader field for her talents, Belva McNall moved to Washington, D.C. Here she opened one of the first private coeducational schools in the capital.

In 1868, Belva married Ezekial Lockwood, a former minister and practicing dentist. Not long after her marriage, Belva, who had been studying law on her own, applied to Columbia College (later George Washington University) Law School. Her application was rejected on the ground that the presence of the 39-year-old woman "would distract the attention of the young men." She was also turned down by the law schools of Georgetown and Howard Universities, but in 1871 was admitted to the newly created National University Law School. Her husband managed her school while Belva devoted herself to her studies.

She completed law school in May, 1873, but was not immediately granted her degree. In fact, Belva obtained her diploma only after writing to President Grant, ex-officio president of the law school, demanding that he intervene on her behalf. In September 1873, after an acrimonious debate, Belva Lockwood was admitted to the bar of the District of Columbia.

At the age of 43, Counselor Lockwood began to practice law in the District, which had only two years before amended its rules to allow female attorneys to appear in court. During the following years, Belva Lockwood mainly represented clients in claims against the government.

In 1875, Belva Lockwood was not allowed to plead her case before the federal Court of Claims because she was a woman, and moreover, a married woman. A bitter contest ensured, with Belva bravely pursuing the battle to gain women lawyers entry to the higher courts. Belva Lockwood filed for admittance to the bar of the U.S. Supreme Court in 1876. Her motion was denied.

Blocked by the government's judicial arm, Lockwood turned to the legislature. She drafted a bill to allow women counselors to plead before the federal Supreme Court, and persuaded some senators who were sympathetic to women's enfranchisement to sponsor the measure. For three years, Belva lobbied energetically for the bill in Congress. She campaigned across the country, drumming up public support for her legislation. In 1879, the bill was passed, and on March 3 of that year Belva Lockwood became the first woman to practice law before the nation's highest tribunal. Singlehandedly, Belva Lockwood had opened every federal court in the land to women attorneys.

Throughout her career, Belva Lockwood was a staunch feminist. In 1867, she helped found Washington's first women's suffrage organization, the Universal Franchise Association. Belva worked closely with Susan B. Anthony. In 1872, Belva campaigned for the first woman candidate for the U.S. presidency, Victoria Woodhull. In 1884, Belva Lockwood was herself nominated for the U.S. presidency by the National Equal Rights Party, and garnered over 4,000 votes.

She also served tirelessly in the cause of international peace. One of the founding members of the Universal Peace Union, Lockwood was also a member of the International Bureau of Peace in Berne, Switzerland, and served on the nominating committee for the Nobel Peace Prize. A year before her death, at the age of 86, she campaigned strenuously for the election of Woodrow Wilson as president. Belva Lockwood died on May 19, 1917.

An astonishing number and variety of reforms may be directly attributed to the efforts of Belva Lockwood. A year after she was admitted to the bar of the U.S. Supreme Court, Lockwood sponsored Samuel R. Lowery, who became the first Southern black to practice before that august body. She was largely responsible for the passage, in 1872, of a bill granting female government employees equal pay for equal work with males. In 1896, she helped secure passage of an ordinance liberalizing the property rights of married women in the District of Columbia.

Belva Lockwood was not the first American woman lawyer; that honor belongs to Myra Bradwell. But Lockwood's incessant labors mark her as the most influential figure in opening opportunities to women in the legal profession. Belva Lockwood brought women lawyers into the big-time. But Lockwood's eminence goes beyond her efficacy in promoting women's causes; she was among the most generous and tireless crusaders for the rights of all the oppressed, and for world peace.

Emily Dickinson (1830-1886)
POET

> This is my letter to the world
> That never wrote to me.

Thus did Emily Dickinson describe her nearly 2,000-poem communication to the human race, whose company she assiduously shunned during her lifetime.

Born in the isolated village of Amherst, Massachusetts, nearly 100 miles from even a quasi-urban center, Emily Dickinson eventually went to great lengths to preserve the solitude that she had inherited. Sequestered in the family residence, with only domestic chores, neighborly visits, and letter-writing to interrupt her work, Emily Dickinson busied herself recording

> The simple news that Nature told—
> With tender majesty.

Her quirky, imagistic compositions have established her as one of the greatest and most original of poets.

Emily Dickinson was born on December 10, 1830. She was the youngest child of Amherst's leading lawyer—later a Massachusetts congressman—and an unassertive, self-effacing mother. Emily's brother Austin was the family's pride and hope, and her sister Lavinia, Emily's childhood protector and champion.

A Puritan of the old school, Squire Dickinson forbade his young children to read any book but the Bible. Nevertheless, Austin, who had access to literary classics through school, occasionally snitched a volume of Longfellow or some other poet for his sisters' edification. The children read these books clandestinely, stashing them under the cover of the pianoforte whenever their father was in the vicinity.

At 15, Emily was sent to Amherst Academy, where the principal encouraged her fondness for books. Two years later, Emily entered Mount Holyoke Seminary, in nearby South Hadley, but her father called her home after only a year of college.

At Mount Holyoke, Emily was notorious for her wit and for her refusal to become a "professing" Christian. Although deeply religious all her life in her own idiosyncratic fashion, Emily professed an aversion for the dogma and rituals of organized religion.

Her formal education and her reading were somewhat limited, but Emily's literary models were of the best: she knew the Bible and Shakespeare; had a smattering of the Greek and Roman classics in translation; and read the leading English and American authors of her day—Emerson, Thoreau, Hawthorne, Keats, Ruskin, Tennyson, and the Brownings. Her correspondence reveals that she was particularly drawn to women writers—she adored Charlotte and "gigantic" Emily Bronte, as well as Elizabeth Barrett Browning. Emily's great idol was George Eliot. She once sent a copy of *Middlemarch* to a friend with the inscription, "I am bringing you a little granite book for you to lean upon."

In her early twenties, Emily began composing poems. In 1858, Emily took her poetry seriously enough that she copied her poems in ink, and bundled them together in little packets tied with thread. She wrote 52 poems that year. Ignorant of traditional stanza and meter forms, she used her hymnbook as a model. Her poetry is characterized by an unusually rich and colorful vocabulary. Although proscribing non-Biblical reading for his children, Squire Dickinson had apparently never thought to keep them from the dictionary. Throughout her life, Emily pored avidly over her lexicon.

Emily Dickinson felt the continual need of an editor. Noting an article in the *Atlantic Monthly* by clergyman and author Thomas Wentworth Higginson soliciting submissions by new writers, Emily selected this total stranger.

Higginson has left the following memoir of his introduction to Emily Dickinson's work:

". . . On April 16, 1862, I took from the post-office the following letter:—

'Mr. Higginson, Are you too deeply occupied to say if my verse is alive?

The mind is so near itself it cannot see distinctly, and I have none to ask.

Should you think it breathed, and had you the leisure to tell me, I should feel quick gratitude.

If I make the mistake, that you dared to tell me would give me sincerer honor toward you.

I inclose my name, asking you, if you please, sir, to tell me what is true?

That you will not betray me it is needless to ask, since honor is its own pawn.'

. . . . Inclosed with the letter were four poems. The impression of a wholly new and original poetic genius was as distinct on my mind at the first reading of these four poems as it is now, after half a century of further knowledge. . . . It is hard to say what answer was made by me, under these circumstances, to this letter. It is probable that the advisor sought to gain time a little and find out with what strange creature he was dealing. I remember to have ventured on some criticism which she afterwards called 'surgery.'"

In her second letter to Higginson, Emily confessed that the "surgery," or editing, was "not so painful as I supposed," and ventured to sign herself "your friend, E. Dickinson."

Higginson was indeed to prove the poet's friend. Had he not, after Emily's death, undertaken the laborious final editing of her work, and combed Publisher's Row in search of a bookseller willing to print such an unconventional and esoteric *oeuvre*, Emily's opus might have perished unread, except for the seven poems that were published anonymously during her lifetime. Although she sought a knowledgeable personal critic for her work, Emily was unwilling to see her works printed, fearing that fame might prove corrupting, or lack of fame, disheartening.

From 1862 on, Emily Dickinson began to send Higginson small batches of selections. Their correspondence indicates frequent rows concerning Higginson's editorial function. To Emily, the substance of her work was sacred; she wished Higginson to attend only to formal elements of style, correcting her spelling, standardizing her punctuation, and performing the other duties of a copy editor. But the somewhat pedantic Higginson could not resist altering what he considered "fracture(s) of grammar and dictionary." Ironically, the neologisms emended by Higginson—and later restored by the unregenerate Emily—are today cited by literary critics as examples of Dickinson's poetic genius. Indeed, her inventions of terms such as *gianture* and *diminuet* are among the more creative coinages in the English language. She regularly flouted grammatical conventions with refreshing effect, as in the lines:

> The grass so little has to do
> I wish I were a hay—

Higginson never did learn to appreciate Dickinson's originality, although he eventually despaired of ever curbing her proclivities for irregular word usage and "spastic" meter. Aware that strict adherence to the sing-song formulas of the hymnbook would render her poetry monotonous, Emily occasionally inserted a line of syncopated rhythm. Her penchant for inexact or "slant" rhymes, in rhyming *defer* with *no more,* and *hope* with *up,* was decried by Higginson, but those "deformities" lend Dickinson's verse some of its magical power, as evinced in the following composition:

> The heart asks pleasure first;
> And then, excuse from pain;
> And then, those little anodynes
> That deaden suffering;

And then to go to sleep;
And then, if it should be
The will of its Inquisitor,
The liberty to die.

    Except for two face-to-face meetings, Dickinson's conferences with her editor were conducted entirely through epistolary exchanges. For eight years, Higginson repeatedly requested an interview with his self-styled "scholar." The reclusive poet begged off: "I should be glad to see you, but think it an apparitional pleasure, not to be fulfilled. I am uncertain of Boston." She added, however, "Is it more far to Amherst?" Apparently, Higginson decided that Amherst was no farther from him than the mountain from Mohammad, and in 1870, he confronted his eccentric correspondent at her father's brick manse. His account of the meeting is enlightening:

". . . . *After a little delay, I heard an extremely faint and pattering footstep, like that of a child, in the hall, and in glided, almost noiselessly, a plain, shy little person, the face without a single good feature, but with eyes, as she herself said, 'like the sherry the guest leaves in the glass,' and with smooth bands of reddish chestnut hair. . . . She came toward me with two day-lilies, which she put in a childlike way into my hand, saying softly, under her breath, 'These are my introduction,' and adding, also under her breath, in childlike fashion, 'Forgive me if I am frightened; I never see strangers, and hardly know what I say.' But soon she began to talk. . . .*
    She went on talking constantly, and saying, in the midst of narrative, things quaint and aphoristic. 'Is it oblivion or absorption when things pass from our minds?' 'Truth is such a rare thing, it is delightful to tell it.' 'I find ecstasy in living; the mere sense of living is joy enough.' When I asked her if she never felt any want of employment, not going off the grounds and rarely seeing a visitor, she answered," I never thought of conceiving that I could ever have the slightest approach to such a want in all future time. . . ." *She told me of her household occupations, that she made all their bread, because her father liked only hers; then saying shyly, 'And people must have puddings,' this very timidly and suggestively, as if they were meteors or comets. . . . she pleased herself with putting into words what the most extravagant might possibly think without saying, as thus: 'How do most people live without any thoughts? There are many people in the world,—you must have noticed them in the street,—how do they live? How*

do they get strength to put on their clothes in the morning?' Or this crown-
ing extravaganza: 'If I read a book and it makes my whole body so cold no
fire can ever warm me, I know that is poetry. If I feel physically as if the
top of my head were taken off, I know that is poetry. These are the only
ways I know it. Is there any other way?'"

After this meeting, among his friends Higginson referred to Emily
as "my half-cocked poetess." But if Emily Dickinson was mad, there
was a definite method to her madness, and as she herself proclaimed, "much madness is divinest sense."

Until her death Dickinson continued to send Higginson her
poems, which, after 1865, averaged 20 a year. During the last decade of her life, Emily refused to leave the house, visiting only with
family and a few close friends on the premises. But she conducted a
voluminous correspondence with more distant friends. Among her
chosen intimates were her sister-in-law, Sue, who lived next door;
her sister Lavinia, who like Emily remained a spinster at home; and
family friend Judge Otis P. Lord, a widower in his sixties. Judge
Lord and Emily apparently fell in love, but both were too set in their
ways to undertake marriage. Although her poetry indicates that
Emily was frequently in love with Love, she was content to lead the
cloistered life of "a wayward nun."

When Emily died, on May 15, 1886, her poetry was known only
to Higginson and a few close friends. Even Lavinia had no idea of
the extent of her sister's literary output until she discovered more
than 1,800 poems in the top drawer of the deceased poet's dresser.
Lavinia instantly carried the bundles next door to Sue, commanding
her to prepare the almost indecipherable jottings for publication.
When Sue proved a dilatory editor, Lavinia retrieved the manuscript
and confided it to Mabel Loomis Todd, the well-read wife of an Amherst professor. Mrs. Todd enlisted the aid of Colonel Higginson. In
1890, he succeeded in having a slim volume of *Poems* by Emily
Dickinson published, although the publisher insisted that the poet's
family underwrite the cost of publication.

The publisher's fears were unfounded: *Poems* went through 16
editions in eight years, and was regularly reprinted thereafter. Mrs.
Todd had created the initial market for the book, publicizing the un-

known author through a series of lectures. After that, word of mouth sent Emily Dickinson's popularity skyrocketing. The poet's colloquial tone, economical style, and universal themes—Nature, Love, Death, and Immortality—captivated the public in spite of her studied vocabulary and the elliptical syntax of some of the poems.

Today, nearly a century after her death, Emily Dickinson's more accessible poems serve as standard inclusions in anthologies of great poetry. Such lines as "Parting is all we know of heaven/And all we need of hell" have become universally familiar quotations. Since the publication of the definitive edition of her work by Harvard University Press in 1950, Dickinson has become a favorite of literary scholars, who view her as the forerunner of the imagist and free-verse movements. Literary historians have traced Dickinson's influence in the works of modern poets, such as e.e. cummings and William Carlos Williams, among others.

The greatness of Dickinson's poetry lies in its easy intelligibility and highly inventive use of language. Her personifications of Death depart refreshingly from the hackneyed image of Death-the-reaper: for Emily, Death comes not with a sickle, but in a carriage. Though she lived quietly in an era of gentility, there is nothing genteel about Dickinson's poetry. With undisguised contempt, she writes:

> What soft cherubic creatures
>   These gentlewomen are;
> One would as soon assault a plush,
>   Or violate a star.

Dickinson had no use for the "dimity convictions" of the Victorian lady; her concern was with "freckled human nature" and the mystery she called Deity. Her poetry is versatile in style as well as subject, ranging from the quietly erotic "Wild Nights," to the journalistic paean to the newly invented railroad, "I like to see it lap the miles." Dickinson's visceral, variegated verses reinvigorated American poetry, and renewed the English language. Her independent spirit and extravagant imagination epitomize American individualism at its best.

Margaret Knight (1838-1914)
INVENTOR

Unlike most men, or indeed most people, Senator John Daniel of Virginia had the insight to recognize an unlikely area of female potential. "Woman's intuitions are proverbial; when she turns them to mechanical invention, the possibilities of achievement surpass the scope of prophecy," he wrote during the Industrial Revolution. The U.S. Patent Office records bear out the senator's prediction. Between the years 1815 and 1910, a total of 8,596 patents were granted to American women, for inventions ranging from corsets and baby carriages to locomotive wheels and mining machines.

Actually, although it is not generally expected or acknowledged, women have been inventors from time immemorial. A woman, Se Ling-she, has been credited with founding the silk industry in China; the culture of grains and cereals in Egypt, as well as the invention of the sailboat are attributed to Isis; and the construction of the first canals and bridges in ancient Assyria to Semiramis.

But in 19th (and even 20th) century America, most people shared the opinion of the farmer who told feminist Mrs. Ada Bowles, "You women may talk about your rights, but why don't you invent something?" Mrs. Bowles was quick to point out that the farmer's feedbag and the head-shade for his horse had been invented by women; she might also have told him that the curry comb, sectional horse shoes, and the snap-hook on his horse's halter were all patented inventions of women. But even Mrs. Bowles was unaware of the range of devices invented by women, for at the time women were by and large timorous about claiming credit for their inventions.

The date of the first American patent issued to a woman, Mary Kies, for a weaving machine, was May 5, 1809. The number rose only gradually at first, and almost all patented inventions had to do with clothing, childcare and household functions and appliances. By 1860, the number of patents issued to women had accelerated vastly. Moreover, women were directing their inventive genius into the field of industrial invention. Women had patented such devices as corn plows, low-water indicators, thermometers, apparatuses for punching corrugated metals and desulphurizing ores.

The rapid increase in inventions by women may relate to the fact that public high schools began admitting women in 1852. Yet, the most prolific American woman inventor, Margaret Knight, with 27 patents in her name, received only the scantiest formal education.

Margaret Knight was born in York, Maine, on February 14, 1838. But though Mattie, as she was called, was born on Valentine's Day, she showed a singular lack of interest in romantic love. Mattie's passion was for making things, useful things. As she wrote:

I never cared for the things that girls usually do; dolls never had any charms for me . . . the only things I wanted were a jacknife, a gimlet and pieces of wood. . . . I was always making things for my brothers. Did they want anything in the line of playthings, they always said, "Mattie will make them for us." I was famous for my kites, and my sleds were the envy and admiration of all the boys in town. I'm not surprised at what I've done; I'm only sorry I couldn't have had as good a chance as a boy, and have been put to my trade regularly.

Mattie contrived her first real invention when she was 12. The Knights were then living in Manchester, New Hampshire, and Mattie's brothers were employed at a cotton textile mill. One day, when Mattie was at the mill, there was an accident. A steel-tipped shuttle fell out of one of the looms, injuring a worker. Having observed what happened, Mattie went home and developed a device to prevent such accidents. But no one suggested to the young girl that she patent the device; nor did anyone encourage her in her unusual talent.

Margaret later took a job in a paper-bag producing factory in Springfield, Massachusetts. The factory had been attempting unsuccessfully to modify the paper-feeding machine so that it would produce square-bottomed paper bags. Mattie tackled the problem. In February, 1867, she constructed a primitive "guide finger and a plate knife folder." The men were skeptical, but even in its rough state, the device produced the long-desired satchel-bottom bags. Next, Mattie constructed a full-scale wooden model of a machine that incorporated her folding mechanism. From this model she drew patterns which she took to Boston in 1869, to have an iron machine made under her direction. She had to overcome resistance from the workers who resented taking orders from a woman, but finally the machine was constructed according to her specifications.

Encouraged by the success of her venture, Margaret Knight went on doing what she enjoyed most in life. She invented a dress and shirt shield (1883); a clasp for holding robes (1884); a spit (1885); and a half dozen machines for shoe-cutting. In 1894, Margaret Knight patented a window frame and sash, and a numbering mechanism. Over the next few years, she started tinkering with rotary engines and motors, and in 1902 patented her first invention in this field. She assigned some of her sleeve-valve engines to the Knight-Davidson Motor Company in New York, a family enterprise.

Margaret Knight's inventions did not apparently bring her great financial remuneration, for at her death at the age of 76, on October 12, 1914, her estate was appraised at a mere $275.05.

A lengthy obituary for Margaret Knight in the *Framingham News* hailed her as "the woman Edison." This is certainly an overstatement, but if there has not been a female Edison, neither has there ever been a second male Edison. With all the advantages of education and cultural encouragement enjoyed by men, few have achieved what Margaret Knight accomplished. Encountering resentment, envy, cynicism, and contempt as a female inventor, yet she persisted, and her pertinacity resulted in at least 27 inventions, ranging from domestic devices to heavy industrial machinery. The example of Margaret Knight should forever lay to rest Voltaire's pronouncement, "We have seen very learned women as well as women warriors, but there have never been any women inventors."

Ellen Swallow Richards
(1842-1911)
FOUNDER OF HOME ECONOMICS

In her lifetime the ground-breaking Ellen Swallow Richards achieved a phenomenal number of "firsts." Ellen Richards was a member of the first graduating class at Vassar College, and the first American woman to attend a scientific college, the Massachusetts Institute of Technology. At M.I.T. Ellen was the first student to earn a doctorate in chemistry, although she was denied the degree because the all-male chemistry faculty did not wish to award its first doctorate to a woman. Ellen was the first woman to teach at M.I.T., where she created the first Woman's Science Laboratory in the world. For her research on copper ores, Ellen was elected the first woman member of the Institute of Mining and Metallurgical Engineers. As the first chemist to make a comprehensive study of the scientific basis of nutrition, Ellen Richards created two new professions, dietetics and home economics. Ellen Richards brought the standards and procedures of the scientific laboratory into the American home, and her unremitting efforts to improve the environment, both in and out of the home, make her the first effective ecologist.

Ellen Swallow was born on a farm in Dunstable, Massachusetts, on December 3, 1842. The only child of two former schoolteachers, Ellen was educated at home for the first 16 years of her life. Her mother taught Ellen her ABC's and elementary math, while her father instructed the girl in history and logic. Mr. Swallow also taught his daughter to pitch hay and plow the fields of the family farm, to the dismay of Ellen's mother, who tried to curb her daughter's tomboy propensities and interest her in the domestic arts. By the age of 13, Ellen was an accomplished housekeeper, and won prizes at a local fair for the best piece of embroidery and the best home-baked bread. Ellen's husband was later to describe his mother-in-law as "a small-minded woman with no conception of what her daughter was." The fact is that neither parent recognized their unusual daughter's brilliance.

In 1859, Mr. Swallow opened a store in Westford, Massachusetts, and Ellen became his assistant shopkeeper. In addition to minding the store and serving as the local postmistress, Ellen tried to continue her education. Aware through charitable visits to jails, hospitals, and asylums of the miseries of the larger world, and depressed by the lack of recognition of her natural abilities, Ellen experienced the years 1865-1867 as "a *Purgatory.*"

But when she finally realized her deepest yearning and entered Vassar College in 1868, Ellen completely recovered her spirits. Ellen found two of her Vassar professors particularly exciting—the astronomy professor, Maria Mitchell, and the chemistry professor, Charles A. Farrar. Only one fault did Ellen find with Vassar: "They won't let us study enough. They are so afraid we shall break down."

Ellen Swallow applied to M.I.T. in 1870, five years after the founding of the college. Her application created a dilemma for the M.I.T. staff; Ellen was clearly qualified for admission, yet the neophyte institution was fearful of ridicule by a world that believed the scientific laboratory was no place for women. After much debate, the college decided on a compromise: Ellen would be admitted free of charge to M.I.T. as a special student in chemistry. The elated young woman thought that she had been offered a scholarship, "but I learned later it was because he [the president of M.I.T.] could say I was not a student, should any of the trustees or students make a fuss about my presence." "The Swallow experiment," as it was called in the university's inner sanctum, was so successful that in 1877 M.I.T. began to admit women as regular students.

Ellen found a warm welcome in the chemistry department of M.I.T., not so much because of the caliber of her scientific work, which was excellent, as because of her proficiency as a housekeeper. Actually, her professors also found her an invaluable research assistant, who neither expected nor got public acknowledgment. "They say I am going ahead because Professor Ordway trusts me to do his work for him, which he never did anybody else," she wrote, "I am only too happy to do anything for him." Ellen's only unhappiness at M.I.T. stemmed from her being the only woman there; all her professors, all her fellow students, were men, and for weeks on end she did not see a single female face on campus.

As an undergraduate at M.I.T., Ellen showed great promise as a pure researcher. She analyzed the rare mineral samarkite and found an insoluble residue that she believed must contain two unknown elements. Ellen's co-workers at M.I.T. encouraged her to go on to isolate these elements, and had she done so, Ellen Richards might have been acclaimed the discoverer of samarium and gadolinium, an honor that fell instead to two French chemists who repeated Ellen's analysis soon afterward. But Ellen Richards was interested in using her scientific knowledge and skill in more practical ways. She renounced recondite research in order to open the sciences generally to women, and concentrated on using the knowledge that she had already acquired to improve people's lives.

In 1873, Ellen Swallow earned a B.S. degree from M.I.T. She was also awarded an M.A. from Vassar for isolating the metal vanadium from a sample of iron ore. Ellen had been encouraged in her mineralogical research by Professor Robert Hallowell Richards, a metallurgist only two years older than Ellen. One day, as they were both doing research in the same laboratory, Professor Richards proposed to Ellen. After a two-year engagement, Ellen Swallow became Ellen Richards on June 4, 1875.

While still an undergraduate at M.I.T., Ellen had taken time from her own studies to teach a chemistry course to students and teachers at an all-girls' school in Boston. The experimental course had been financed by the Women's Education Association of Boston. In November 1875, Ellen appealed to this organization to subsidize a woman's laboratory at M.I.T. They agreed to contribute funds for equipment and student scholarships, and M.I.T. provided lab space in a former gymnasium. Professor Ordway and Ellen directed the women's laboratory, and regularly donated money to its support. After seven years, the successes of her students led M.I.T. to open its regular laboratories to women, eliminating the need for a segregated woman's laboratory.

Remembering her own two years of home-bound "Purgatory," Ellen Richards determined to help bring the world of the intellect to women whose lives were constricted. She organized a correspondence course in science for housewives. Ellen personally corrected her students' papers and wrote to them. She became a friend to whom they confided their tribulations and ambitions. This experience inspired Richards later to formulate the science of home economics, designed to convert housework from mindless drudgery into a more creative and challenging task.

From the beginning of her married life, Ellen Richards made her own house a model of simplicity and comfort, banishing the customary wall-to-wall carpeting and heavy, dust-catching draperies in favor of filmy curtains and light scatter rugs. Richards was among the first owners of a vacuum cleaner and a gas stove. These appliances lightened the burden of housekeeping for the students who boarded with the Richardses in exchange for performing household tasks. Later, when the Richardses could afford it, they hired servants, and, Ellen sent her maids to cooking school to learn the principles of nutrition, and taught them the most efficient ways of doing the chores. By choice, the Richardses remained childless, Ellen's attitude being, "the world will be peopled without my help."

Ellen Richards became an industrial consultant. Her services ranged widely, including testing wallpaper and fabrics for arsenic content and foods for adulterous agents; examining oils for impurities and combustibility; analyzing industrial water supplies. She discovered the process of dry cleaning wool with naphtha. She was responsible for testing the purity of the Massachusetts drinking water until 1897, when a state laboratory was established for the purpose. The first Massachusetts Food and Drug Act was passed as a result of Ellen's report on her pioneer research in public health.

Called "Ellencyclopedia" by her sister-in-law, Ellen Richards became a national authority on air, water, and food. In 1884, Ellen helped to create the country's first department of sanitary chemistry at M.I.T., and trained the world's first public health engineers.

Moved by the difficulty encountered by Boston's impoverished working class in obtaining wholesome, inexpensive meals, Ellen Richards established the New England Kitchen. In 1893, Ellen directed a similar kitchen at the Chicago World's Fair, which was then copied by Jane Addams at Hull House. In 1894, the New England Kitchen became the purveyor of lunches to the Boston public schools, and soon other schools and hospitals were employing Ellen as a dietary consultant. She also found time to write, producing a series of brochures on nutrition for the U.S. Department of Agriculture and publishing ten books on the application of science to daily life. Along with Fannie Farmer, her successor in the field of nutrition, Ellen Richards revolutionized the art of cooking by quantifying measurements and standardizing ingredients.

Ellen Richards was instrumental in creating home economics departments in schools throughout the United States, prescribing the curriculums and bibliographies, and training instructors. She worked to the very end and died of heart disease on March 30, 1911, shortly after completing an address on "The Elevation of Applied Science to the Rank of the Learned Professions."

In her long and distinguished career, Ellen Richards had the satisfaction of accomplishing her goals. She witnessed radical improvement in the American diet and sanitation system; she opened doors for the female population in science education; she elevated the status and eased the burden of housekeeping, making women more productive and happier. Her task had not been easy; opposition grew out of psychological, cultural and political roots. Anthropologists maintain that food habits are more resistant to change than any other human behavior; and when Ellen Richards began her sanitation crusade, an ignorant public and an apathetic government gave her little encouragement and less financial aid. But she prevailed.

Every individual who begins the morning by drinking a glass of orange juice has Ellen Richards to thank for introducing this innovation to the American breakfast; and every community proud of the purity of its water supply should remember this altruistic scientist, who found practical ways of bringing "the considerable body of useful knowledge now lying on our shelves" into every household.

Catherine Konstantinova Breshkovsky (1844-1934)

MOTHER OF THE RUSSIAN REVOLUTION

She was barely 26 years old when she renounced husband and child and her status as a wealthy countess to carry the message of freedom to the Russian serfs. For ten years already, Catherine Breshkovsky had been devoting her energies to establishing schools for the Russian peasants, first on her father's estate, then on her husband's. But with the new wave of czarist oppression in the 1870s, the young countess decided that it was not enough merely to teach the peasants to read and write. She must join the revolutionaries, and organize the serfs for revolt.

So in the summer of 1874, Catherine Breshkovsky stained her face brown like a peasant's, donned coarse garments, learned the dyer's trade, and went to live among the peasants, or *muzhiks*, in order to incite them to rebellion. She was to spend 45 years in prison, mainly in Siberia, before her dream of a Russian revolution was realized. Then with the overthrow of the czar in 1917, Catherine Breshkovsky was borne in triumph to the royal apartments at the St. Petersburg railroad station. There, one of her comrades in the Kerensky government told cheering crowds:

Comrades, the Little Mother of the Russian Revolution has returned at last to a free country. She has been in dungeons, in the penal settlements of the Lena, has been tortured endlessly. Yet here we have her with us, brave and happy. Let us shout "Hurrah" for our dear Baboushka.

Sadly, it was not a long hurrah; with the Bolshevik *putsch*, Catherine Breshkovsky was once again exiled, this time to Czechoslovakia. But Baboushka was undaunted by this final setback to her dream of a free Russia. "We may die in exile," she said, "our children may die in exile, and our children's children may die in exile, but something will come of it at last."

Ekaterina Konstantinova Breshko-Breshkovskaya was born on the Verigo estate, 300 miles south of St. Petersburg (now Leningrad) and 300 miles west of Moscow. The year was 1844, and Czar Nicholas I, "the Autocrat of all the Russians," was enthroned. Catherine's father was a Russian aristocrat, her mother a Polish noble. On the Verigo estate lived well over 100 serfs. Unlike other landowners, Catherine's father did not flog his serfs, or overwork them, or force them to subsist on black bread and water. "Your estate, dear Konstantine," said his neighbors disapprovingly, "is a republic."

Catherine's father was indeed a republican. He read Diderot, Rousseau, and Voltaire, and taught little Katya to read these French liberal philosophers, too. In an age when French was the fashionable language of the Russian aristocracy, Catherine's family persisted in speaking Russian among themselves. Katya's mother also read the Bible to her daughter in Russian. The little girl took literally the Scriptural admonition to give everything to the poor, often returning from a visit to her father's serfs without her coat or dress. "Little fool," her mother said tenderly, when Katya explained she had given her fine raiment to some ill-clad peasant child. "One can do nothing better than help the poor," she insisted. She would fantasize about going to California where she would find gold and return to Russia to buy a tract of land "as huge as the sky" where all could come who lacked enough to eat or a snug roof over their heads.

Catherine refused to go to "silly soirées" with her sisters, preferring to stay home reading works such as Rousseau's *Social Contract*.

When she was 16, Catherine secured her father's permission to establish a school for the peasants on the Verigo estate. She found the older serfs apathetic about learning, and uninterested in social reform. They defended the czar, saying "Our Little Father loves us; it is only the nobles who are evil and cause us to suffer." But the younger peasants shared Catherine's dream of a free, democratic Russia, and applied themselves eagerly to their studies.

On March 3, 1861, Czar Alexander II signed an edict freeing the 40 million Russian peasants from serfdom. But the czar's ukase also ordered the serfs off the land, to starve in their new-found freedom. All the *muzhiks* who defied the order to depart were lined up in the villages for flogging. First every tenth man was whipped, then every fifth man, and finally every man, woman, and child who remained on the land. Many died under the czarist lash; others were crippled for life.

Revolted by the spectacle, Catherine Konstantinova went to St. Petersburg to attend meetings of the young revolutionaries who had congregated there. But Catherine was not yet willing to espouse violence in the cause of liberty. "It is a poor patriot who will not thoroughly try his government before he rises against it," she said, and returned to her father's estate. She established two schools, one for the higher education of women, the other for the elementary education of the peasants, and taught at the schools until her marriage to the wealthy Count Breshkovsky.

Like Catherine, Count Breshkovsky was a political idealist. He established an agricultural school for the peasants on his estate, and Catherine directed it. The Breshkovsky estate became a meeting place for all the liberal local gentry. They decided that in order to effect reforms they must gain control of the *zemstov*, or local government. They started by enfranchising the peasants to vote, and in the next election, the liberals won all the offices. But the corrupt landowners who had been ousted from power charged conspiracy, and had the election declared invalid. The Breshkovskys were placed under police surveillance, and many of their friends were exiled.

Now Catherine Breshkovsky lost hope of obtaining reform through the ballot box. If the czar would not allow equality for the serfs to come through peaceful evolutionary reform, it must be achieved by revolution. Catherine Breshkovsky, seven months pregnant, announced to her husband that she could no longer live as the chatelaine of his estate. She must live among the people, "feeling where the shoe pinches," and "agitating for a New Day." Would he come with her? The count refused, and rebuked his wife for forgetting her family responsibilities. Catherine answered: "This consciousness of duty toward the people is so mighty a force that no personal affection . . . can displace it. When once it has sunk into the depths of one's soul, it drives out all other aspirations and leads mightily toward the chosen goal."

So in 1874, Catherine Breshkovsky set forth to launch the Russian Revolution. She stayed with her widowed sister Olga at Kiev until her son was born. Then, leaving the baby with her brother and his wife, she departed for Tcherkass with two Socialist companions. Armed with false passports and disguised as peasants, the troika was part of a brigade of 2,000 educated revolutionaries who were covering 36 Russian provinces, advocating just taxation and universal ownership of land, representation in the government, and education. It was an uncomfortable journey. They had festering blisters on their feet from marching long distances in primitive shoes; but they rejoiced, like Lear in the storm, "to feel what wretches feel." The three revolutionaries traveled from town to town. By day, Catherine worked at her newly-learned trade of dying clothes; by night, she read Socialist parables to the peasants who gathered in her mud hut.

One evening, as she was reading the fable of *Moses and his Four Brothers* to her fellow-laborers, a gendarme burst into the hovel and arrested her. "So it's revolutionary trash you'd be teaching our simple souls, is it?" he sneered, and he dragged Catherine to the local prison, known as "the black hole." In this noxious dungeon, with vermin and lice as her only cell-mates, Catherine passed a sleepless night, the first of a great, great many to come.

During the next two years, Catherine Breshkovsky was shuttled from one Russian prison to another. She developed partial paralysis and rheumatism from the cold, cramped cells, and was frequently given nothing to eat except tea and potatoes. Finally, she was taken to a jail in St. Petersburg, to await sentencing. One night, as she lay on her straw pallet trying to sleep, she heard a tap-tap-tap from the adjoining cell. Catherine sat up and listened intently. Tap-tap-tap, she heard again, and then there were answering taps from another cell. Catherine quickly realized that the prisoners had devised a code to communicate with one another, and after listening for a while was able to match the taps with the letters of the Russian alphabet. Through this code, the isolated comrades were able to exchange political news, gossip, and ideas; they even told fairy tales and played chess.

In 1878, after 100 of the Petersburg political prisoners had died or had gone insane, the remaining 190 prisoners were brought to trial. As she rose for sentencing, Catherine Breshkovsky told the judge, "I have the honor to belong to the Russian Socialist and Revolutionary Party. I do not recognize the authority of the czar's court over me." She was promptly found in contempt of court and sentenced to five years hard labor in the Siberian mines—the punishment usually assigned to murderers.

It was a 5,000 mile trek over the White Siberian Way to the mining camp in Kara where Catherine was being sent. Long was the way and hard, as the prisoners alternately walked or traveled in flimsy *telegas*, or covered wagons. At night, they slept atop one another in the telegas, or lodged at fetid wayside jails.

When the prisoners finally disembarked at Kara, Catherine found that instead of labor in the mines, her punishment was to be compulsory idleness. When she tried to start a school for children, the guards threatened her with torture. Nor was she allowed to nurse a sick woman, or say prayers over a dying man. "To lie in cold obstruction and to rot"—that was the death-in-life endured by the Siberian exiles.

Nor were the conditions any better 1,000 miles away at Bargazin, where Catherine was later forced to march on foot. After two years in this frigid hamlet, she plotted with three young male revolutionaries, to flee 1,000 miles to Vladivostok, where the fugitives planned to hop a boat to America. They actually managed to traverse 600 miles before being captured by the police. Catherine was transferred to Buriat, a bleak outpost near the Chinese border. Here Catherine Breshkovsky spent seven years in isolation, running and dancing to keep warm in the 45-degree-below-zero weather, and singing arias from Russian operas to remind herself of the civilization from which she was excluded.

Only three times during her exile was Catherine Breshkovsky allowed to see visitors. One of her visitors was George F. Kennan, an American reporter making a study of Russian political prisoners. Kennan emerged from the interview declaring," . . . all my standards of courage, fortitude, and heroic self-sacrifice have been raised for all time, and raised by the hand of a woman."

In 1896, at the age of 52, after 18 years of Siberian exile, Catherine Breshkovsky was returned to Russia. The physical and spiritual hardships she had endured had failed to embitter her: "I was never disillusioned," she wrote, "even as a child, I learned from the biographies of great men that aspiration toward high ideals always leads to cruel penalties."

Catherine found that her parents and husband were dead, and her son had grown into a haughty young aristocrat, totally unsympathetic to his mother's revolutionary ideals. Her brief visits to her relatives and friends at their *dachas,* or country estates, no more enchanted her now than in her youth. "They are worried about their coffee," she wrote, "they are worried about their garden; they are worried about everything. I have had no baggage for 30 years, and I am not worried about anything."

Czar Alexander II had been assassinated in 1881, and after the brief reign of Alexander III, the ineffectual autocrat Nicholas II had ascended the throne. This ill-fated scion of the Romanoffs, the last czar of Russia, refused to fund village schools for the peasants, and forbade the circulation of unofficial newspapers. Catherine returned to revolutionary activity and helped to found the People's Social Revolutionary Party. For six years she journeyed with fellow party members through 26 Russian provinces, circulating revolutionary newsletters printed in Switzerland, and lecturing in cellars, attics, and peasant huts. The police were always hot on her trail, but by this time Catherine had become an accomplished revolutionary, and evaded them by assuming disguises ranging from a peasant cook to a French countess.

In 1904, the Little Mother of the Russian Revolution went to

America, where she was welcomed at Hull House by Jane Addams, and at the Henry Street Settlement by Lillian Wald. In Boston, at Faneuil Hall, Julia Ward Howe helped Catherine to organize The Friends of Russian Freedom. The Little Mother, or *Baboushka*, as her revolutionary compatriots called her, told the Bostonians, "All Russia is an immense prison to every Russian of progressive ideas."

Catherine Breshkovsky raised $10,000 for the Socialist cause from sympathetic Americans. Every time she stepped to the rostrum, she was greeted by a sea of waving handkerchiefs and deafening ovations. Reporter Kellog Durland of the *Boston Transcript* wrote:

To look upon the face of this silver-haired Apostle is like receiving a benediction. Her outward and inward calm are superb. Her hands are beautiful in their delicacy and refinement, despite the years in Siberia. Her voice is low and sweet, her smile winning and childlike. Only her eyes betray the suffering of the years. In repose her face is strong like iron. The shadows of her eyes speak of deepest pathos.

But the Little Mother's sufferings were not yet over. Upon her return to Russia, she was again arrested, and incarcerated in the dread Fortress of St. Peter and St. Paul. Because her friends at Wellesley College in America protested to the czar, the Little Mother was allowed to read books of a non-political nature and carry on a censored correspondence. But during her entire two years at the Fortress, she was not allowed to speak to anyone or to read political literature. Catherine wrote many letters to her American friends and to her son. These were later edited and published by Alice Stone Blackwell, daughter of American feminist Lucy Stone.

In 1909, at the age of 65, Catherine Breshkovsky was sentenced to life imprisonment in Siberia. For seven years, she lived at the northernmost tip of the arctic Russian province, where, she said, "I am kept like a salted herring in a hogshead." Then, on March 2, 1917, came a momentous telegram: RUSSIA IS FREE. COME HOME, BABOUSHKA. The Little Mother and her fellow exiles boarded the Trans-Siberian Railroad and journeyed to Moscow, where they were embraced by the leaders of the Kerensky government. Baboushka was paraded through the streets of Moscow in the gilded carriage of the former czar, then sent on to St. Petersburg in a railroad coach festooned with flowers. In St. Petersburg, the crowd bore Baboushka on their shoulders to the czar's Winter Palace, where she established her headquarters. She began to outline a program whereby every educated Russian would be conscripted to teach an illiterate bother or sister, in order that enlightenment might come to all.

In October 1917, Catherine Breshkovsky was designated temporary chairman of the first provincial Parliament. "We must unite to work together, free and happy, without discord, as one man," she told her fellow citizens. "Let us substitute constitutional liberty for tyranny in the houses of every man, worker, peasant, or noble."

Baboushka was engaged in organizing settlements in the Urals for four million orphaned children when the Bolsheviks gained power over the Socialists and Mensheviks. The Little Mother of the Revolution was exiled for life to Czechoslovakia. There, nearly deaf and blind, she opened a boarding school to train other Russian exiles to be teachers. She also established an elementary school for poor children in Prague. Catherine Breshkovsky had spent most of her life in exile, and in exile she died, on September 12, 1934. She was 90 years old. Fittingly, her elegy, written by Katharine Lee Bates, the author of *America the Beautiful*, concludes:

> *Holy Mother of the free,*
> *Millions more thy sons to be.*
> *Baboushka the Beloved,*
> *What death can silence thee?*

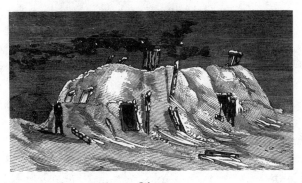

Exterior of convict hut in Siberia

Sonya Kurtovsky Kovalevsky (1850-1891)

MATHEMATICIAN

The year is 1871; the place, Berlin, Germany; the scene, the office of Professor Weierstrass, known to mathematicians as "the father of modern mathematical analysis." A young woman has requested an interview with Doktor Weierstrass; her name is Sonya Kovalevsky. The professor thinks perhaps the youthful emigrée has heard he has young daughters, and is seeking a position as a governess.

"I have come from Heidelberg, where I studied for two years with Professor Helmholtz and Professor Kirshoff," explains Sonya Kovalevsky. "I have brought letters of introduction from these men, and from my other teachers at Heidelberg." The professor is puzzled.

"I wish to study mathematics with you, Herr Doktor," the young woman explains eagerly. "I know that women are not permitted to attend the University of Berlin, but I thought perhaps you would consent to tutor me privately."

Professor Weierstrass suppresses a smile. Are his eminent colleagues in Heidelberg playing a joke on him? "Fraulein Kovalevsky," he begins gently, "I only teach the most advanced students, those

142

who are working toward their doctoral degree in higher mathematics."

"Yes, Herr Doktor, I know that. I would like to take a degree in analytical math. They say you know more about partial differential equations than anyone."

The professor is astounded to hear a woman speak of partial differential equations! "Nevertheless, Fraulein Kovalevsky, women do not take doctorates at German universities."

"But there's no rule against it? Professor Kirshoff assured me there was not," says Sonya anxiously. "Please, Herr Doktor, if you will give me some kind of preliminary examination, I shall show you that I am a worthy student."

The professor shrugs. He has on his desk some problems that he has prepared for his most advanced graduate students. He will let the young woman take them home with her; she will never be able to solve the problems, and that will put an end to the matter.

One week later, Sonya Kovalevsky returned to Professor Weierstrass's office. To the learned doctor's astonishment, she had not only found the correct answers to every one of the difficult problems— some of which had stumped his most promising male students—but her solutions revealed a mind acute and ingenious.

"I shall most certainly accept you as my pupil, Fraulein Kovalevsky," announced the professor. "You have a gift of intuitive genius I have seldom found among men many years older than yourself. I should not be surprised if you won the *Prix Bordin* some day."

Sonya Kovalevsky did win the French Academy of Science's *Prix Bordin*, the most coveted scientific award of the day. Not only was she the first woman to achieve this honor, but so impressed was the Academy with her prize-winning thesis on the rotation of solid bodies which contained the solution to a problem that had long confounded the greatest mathematical geniuses, that they doubled the reward, presenting Sonya Kovalevsky with a purse of 5,000 francs. She was the only woman of her day to hold a chair in mathematics at a European university, the University of Stockholm. Sonya Kovalevsky was also the first woman admitted to the Academy of Science in her native Russia.

Sophia Kurtovsky, known as Sonya, was born on January 15,

1850, in Moscow, the second child of a general in the Russian artillery. Sonya always felt herself an unwanted child. She never quite recovered from her insecurity, and it was only the strong encouragement of her mentors who recognized her mathematical genius that enabled her to persevere in her career.

Sonya wanted to go to college, but Russian universities did not admit women students. When the girls asked their father if they could study abroad, the general flew into a fury. When Sonya was 17, she went to St. Petersburg, where, as their mother had feared, she joined a Nihilist society. A student at the University of Petersburg, Vladimir Kovalevsky, fell in love with Sonya and wanted to marry her. They could live and study together at Heidelberg, he promised. As Kovalevsky was of good family and a brilliant student, Sonya had no qualms about presenting him to her father as a suitor. But the general would not hear of allowing his younger daughter to marry while her older sister was still unwed. So, Sonya decided to force the issue by compromising herself. She went to Kovalevsky's apartments, leaving her father a letter telling him where she was. The general felt compelled to save the family from dishonor and consented to the marriage, which took place in October 1868.

In 1869, the couple set off for Heidelberg. The two bright young Russians were readily accepted at the University of Heidelberg. A friend of Sonya's at the university later recalled, "Sonya immediately attracted her teachers' attention by her unusual capacity for mathematics. Professor Konigsberger, the celebrated natural philosopher, Kirchoff . . . in fact everybody, spoke of her as something extraordinary. She had become so famous in the little town that people would stop in the streets to look after the remarkable Russian lady."

In the summer of 1869, the Kovalevskys went to England, where they met a number of British intellectuals, including Darwin, Spencer, Huxley, and George Eliot. Later, Vladimir Kovalevsky went to Jena to pursue his doctorate in paleontology, and Sonya went to Berlin to study with Professor Weierstrass. There she lived with a girlfriend, who later wrote, "our life in Berlin—with bad lodgings, bad food, ditto air, constant and excessive work, no changes, no amusements—was . . . dreary." The drudgery was relieved when Vladimir visited his wife on weekends, and when they vacationed together during holidays.

In 1874, after three years of studying privately with Professor Weierstrass, Sonya applied to the University of Göttingen for her doctorate, presenting three mathematical theses. Sonya asked to be exempted from the oral examination, as she was timid about appearing before a panel of "unknown men." Professor Weierstrass, to whom Sonya was now like a daughter, vouched for the young woman's oral competence in mathematics, and the university awarded Sonya her Ph.D. on the basis of her brilliant dissertations. She was one of the first women to earn a doctorate at a German university.

In 1878, Sonya gave birth to her only child, a daughter. As there were no positions for women mathematicians in Russia, Sonya decided to become a writer. She published essays in several literary magazines and a novel, *The Private Lecturer*, about life in a small German university town. The novel was well received by both the critics and the general reader.

In 1880, the Kovalevskys moved to Moscow, where Vladimir had been appointed professor of paleontology. But soon Vladimir became involved along with a friend in dubious business speculations, and apparently committed suicide.

Deeply hurt, Sonya had to face reality, and leaving her six-year-old daughter with a friend in Moscow, she went to Stockholm where her friend, the eminent Swedish mathematician Mittgang Leffler, secured for her a position as a lecturer. Sonya's lectures were so well attended, not only by students but by her colleagues in the math department, that in 1884 the university officials offered her a five-year professorship.

The next few years were happy and productive ones for Sonya Kovalevsky. She gave lectures on the theory of partial equations, the theory of potential functions, and other advanced mathematical subjects.

Sonya prepared her thesis for the *Bordin* competition. The most original entry, it was easily chosen for the prize. Since all entries were submitted anonymously, the members of the French Academy of Science were amazed when they discovered that the brilliant thesis they had selected had been submitted by a woman. Sonya Kovalevsky was invited to Paris and on Christmas Eve, 1889, at a solemn session of the Academy, Sonya accepted the highest scientific honor of her time. Upon her return to the University of Stockholm, Sonya Kovalevsky was awarded a chair in mathematics for life.

But not everyone was ready to see such acclaim go to a woman, especially in a field considered a male domain. Sweden's leading playwright, August Strindberg, objected strenuously. ". . . as decidedly as two and two make four, what a monstrosity is a woman who is a professor of mathematics," he wrote, "and how unnecessary, injurious, and out of place she is." Sonya was deeply upset by Strindberg's article, especially by his outlandish allegation that she owed her appointment merely to the gallantry of her male colleagues. But she went on writing articles for scientific journals.

In 1890, Sonya Kovalevsky became the first woman to be elected to the St. Petersburg Academy of Science. She began now to concern herself with encouraging other women to enter the sciences, and undertook another great work of mathematical analysis. But her brilliant career was prematurely cut short when Sonya contracted pneumonia. On February 10, 1891 she died. A monument to her memory was erected in Stockholm, by a group of Russian women.

Sonya Kovalevsky provided another major milestone in the little appreciated tradition of great women mathematicians, joining her exalted predecessor Hypatia, the most celebrated woman in ancient Greece, and Maria Gaetana Agnesi, the most brilliant of a number of astonishing women mathematicians in Italy. Sophie Germaine had won the *Grand Prix* in mathematics as Sonya herself had won the *Prix Bordin,* by submitting her entry anonymously and being identified only after her entry had been proclaimed the winner. Emilie du Chatelet had been pronounced "a genius in geometry." A self-taught Scotswoman named Mary Fairfax Somerville had been one of the first scientists to use mathematical formulas in developing conversion processes in physics. But Sonya probably knew little of these other women, and having experienced the obstacles placed in the path of women with this particular talent, she must have felt herself a lonely pioneer in a field where women were looked upon with suspicion and contempt. But Sonya had no doubt that women could display the same brilliance as men if, as she wrote, "we all had the same education, the same mode of living; if we were all one great society of equals."

Mother Francesca-Xavier Cabrini (1850-1917)

MISSIONARY SAINT

"Rosa, I have founded a convent!"

"A convent? *Macchè*?" Rosa Cabrini stared at her eight-year-old little sister in amused wonderment. "What do you mean, you have founded a convent, Santina?"

"Come see," replied the child, known fondly to her family as Santina, "the little saint." Francesca led her older sister Rosa to her bedroom, where she had set up her collection of dolls clothed in black, like nuns. " There is my convent!" exclaimed the miniature mother superior triumphantly. "We are to be a missionary order," explained Francesca. "We shall sail to China, where there is much misery and spiritual darkness." Francesca had never been outside her native Lombardy, but she had heard from her uncle, a priest, about China.

"Ah, Santina, Santinissima," sighed Rosa. "Do you think you must go to China to find misery and spiritual darkness? Why, right here in Sant'Angelo, there are little girls no older than yourself who haven't enough to eat or anyone to teach them the catechism, let alone a fine collection of dolls."

"Alas!" exclaimed Francesca. "Well, then, my postulants will not go to China after all. I will go to Father Serrati, and have him distribute my dolls to the poor little girls you spoke of." And scooping up her dolls, the little abbess ran off to the parish priest.

Francesca Cabrini's childish play at founding a missionary order ended, prophetically, in a good deed. Years later, as Mother Superior of the Missionary Sisters of the Sacred Heart, Francesca sailed to America, where she was to do many more good deeds, establishing orphanages, schools, and hospitals. Under her leadership of the Sisters of the Sacred Heart, 67 institutions were established, distributed over three continents. A naturalized American, Mother Cabrini became the first U.S. citizen to achieve sainthood. Fittingly, Mother Cabrini was designated the patron saint of immigrants.

Maria Francesca Cabrini was born at Sant'Angelo Lodigiano, about 20 miles from Milan, Italy, on July 15, 1850. Francesca was the youngest of 13 children, of whom only three girls and a boy survived childhood. Francesca's father was a prosperous farmer. Her mother was a devout Roman Catholic and led the family in evening prayers. Her mother was 52 when Francesca was born, and the little girl was largely brought up by her older sister Rosa, a teacher, who took charge of the little saint's secular education.

When she was confirmed, at the age of seven, Francesca Cabrini had her first mystical experience. She seemed to be suddenly "wrapped in light, and was in Heaven. . . . From that moment, I was no longer of the earth . . . I cannot tell why, but I knew the Holy Ghost had come to me." After her confirmation, Francesca insisted on doing the chores that nobody else wanted to do. "Anybody can do the possible," she said. "The real joy is to do the impossible." Later, Mother Cabrini was to counsel her nuns, "It is not enough to do the possible. The thing for us is to attempt the impossible."

At the age of 11, Francesca Cabrini took annual vows of chastity. Two years later, she enrolled at the boarding school of the Daughters of the Sacred Heart in Arluno. Francesca graduated from the school with highest honors, and, at 18, took vows of permanent celibacy. By now, both her parents were dead and Francesca went to earn her living as a teacher.

Her first teaching post was at Vidardo. In 1872, a smallpox epidemic struck the town. Francesca Cabrini nursed the sick, until she contracted the fever herself. On October 15, 1874, Francesca entered the novitiate, and three years later, at the age of 27, took her final vows.

In 1880, Mother Cabrini founded the Missionary Sisters of the Sacred Heart at Codogno. The new order was given no funding from the Church, but this didn't deter Mother Cabrini. As she was later to do many times, Mother Cabrini herself collected furniture for the convent and even helped to lay the bricks for the building. By 1887, she had established seven affiliates of her convent in neighboring towns, including Milan.

But Francesca Cabrini still retained her childhood dream of becoming a Chinese missionary, and so, in 1888, Mother Cabrini went to Rome to petition Pope Leo XIII. The Holy Father gave official sanction to Mother Cabrini's order, but instead of granting the Sisters permission to go to China, instructed them to establish a school for orphans in Rome. Disappointed, Mother Cabrini nevertheless set herself to her assigned task with her usual dedication.

Now Mother Cabrini went to Pope Leo for the second time, and renewed her request to be sent to China. The Pontiff shook his head. "No, my daughter, not to the East but to the West," he said, explaining that a community of Sisters was needed to work among Italian immigrants in the United States.

So, though she spoke no English, Mother Cabrini sailed for America in 1889. The ship's passengers included 1,500 Italian emigrants, and Mother Cabrini and her six nuns immediately began their work by ministering to seasick passengers and allaying their fears about the New World. In accordance with her role as a missionary, Mother Cabrini had by now added Xavier to her name.

On March 31, 1889, Mother Francesca-Xavier Cabrini's ship docked at New York Harbor. To Mother Cabrini's surprise, there was no one to meet the Sisters at the pier. The next day, Mother Cabrini went to see Archbishop Michael Corrigan. To her dismay, he was totally unprepared for her arrival, and suggested that she and her nuns take the next boat back to Italy.

"There is no money for an orphanage," Archbishop Corrigan said flatly, "As for the immigrants, they need someone who can teach them to speak English."

"I will learn English," pledged Mother Cabrini, "And I will find money for the orphanage myself."

And so, Mother Cabrini and her nuns scoured the streets of Little Italy, ducking into shops, apartment buildings, and even saloons, to ask for donations. Within two months, they had collected enough money to house and feed 400 orphans. With the help of Contessa Cesnola, the wealthy wife of the director of the Metropolitan Museum of Art, a convent was established and Archbishop Corrigan pronounced the official benediction at the consecration of the first American motherhouse of the Missionary Sisters of the Sacred Heart.

A Jesuit order had vacated its monastery in West Park, New York, along the Hudson river where acres of land bloomed with trees and flowers. Much healthier surroundings for children than the streets of Little Italy, thought Francesca-Xavier Cabrini, and she determined to move her orphanage to West Park. No one knows how Mother Cabrini got the money to purchase the Jesuit residence, but purchase it she did. Throughout her career, Mother Cabrini claimed to have access to a "heavenly bank," and when one of her novices came to her for funds, the enterprising prioress would open a drawer, and lo and behold, the sum required was there.

In the years that followed, the indefatigable Mother Cabrini spread her most impressive accomplishments far and wide. Hearing of persecution of Italian immigrants in New Orleans, Mother Cabrini and her nuns boarded a train to New Orleans. There they established a convent, a school, and an orphanage, to succor not only the Italian population of the city, but the blacks and Creoles as well.

Denver, Seattle, Los Angeles, Rio de Janeiro, São Paulo, Paris, Madrid, London, Turin—as Mother Cabrini circumnavigated the globe, orphanages and schools sprang up in her wake. Now she embarked on new probjects. Sisters of the Sacred Heart went to Sing-Sing and to the death chambers of the Chicago penitentiaries to work among prisoners. Then it was on to Burbank, California, where Mother Cabrini established the first "preventorium" for children threatened with tuberculosis.

The year 1905 marked the 25th anniversary of the founding of the Sacred Heart missionary order, but the peripatetic Mother Cabrini was too busy to attend the celebrations. There were 50 Houses of the Sacred

Heart in eight countries to oversee, with sites to be chosen for new houses, money to be raised, and construction to be supervised. But the modest Mother was not to be ignored by her church. In 1907, the Missionary Sisters of the Sacred Heart received a final Decree of Approbation from the Pope. In 1910, a year after Mother Cabrini had become a naturalized American citizen, she was made superior general of her order for life. On July 3, 1914, a Jubilee Mass was held for Mother Francesca-Xavier Cabrini at Dobbs Ferry, New York, the site of a Sacred Heart orphanage. Here the Italian government awarded Mother Cabrini a medal and 70,000 lire.

But her health was declining now, as she again suffered an attack of malaria. Mother Cabrini was hospitalized in Chicago, where she died on December 22, 1917. Before departing this world, Mother Cabrini uttered a final prayer. "Dear God," she murmured, "give me a heart that can embrace the universe."

Mother Cabrini's heart had already embraced a considerable portion of the universe. She was known as "the Apostle to Mankind." Her organizational ability and genius for fund-raising had provided shelters for some 5,000 orphaned children, and had ameliorated the lives of many more children and adults. Mother Cabrini had no hesitation about approaching prominent millionaires and telling them, "I am about to confer upon you the privilege of paying for the construction of an orphanage for homeless children." Mother Cabrini's lambent eyes and *cantabile* voice melted their hearts, and the plutocrats would reach for their checkbooks.

In the minds of Mother Cabrini's beneficiaries the philanthropic nun had been more than a mortal woman. The Roman Catholic Church agreed and undertook the canonization of Mother Cabrini. In 1933, she was declared venerable; in 1937, her virtues were acknowledged heroic; in 1938, she was beatified. On July 27, 1946, Santina, the little Santina, grown up to be the famous Mother Francesca-Xavier Cabrini, became the first American saint.

Annie S. Peck (1850-1935)

MOUNTAIN CLIMBER AND EXPLORER

Scholar, sportswoman, linguist, musician, archaeologist, and explorer—the remarkable, versatile Annie S. Peck took up mountain climbing at the age of 35, and conquered heights never before scaled by man. She was a founding member of the American Alpine Club, and the United States delegate to the International Congress of Alpinists in Paris in 1900. In 1904, after having climbed all the famous European peaks, she became the first individual to reach the top of Mount Sorata in Bolivia, climbing its entire 21,300 feet without oxygen. In 1906, Annie Peck explored the Raura Range in Peru, scaling its rocky mountains and reaching the summit of its highest peak (18,000 feet). Then, in 1908, Annie Peck scaled Peru's virgin Huscaran mountain (21,812 feet), reaching the greatest height to be attained on foot in the western hemisphere up until that time. She continued mountaineering until she reached her 82nd birthday.

Nor were Annie's activities limited to her consuming interest in mountaineering. For 25 years she worked to promote closer diplomatic and commercial relations between the Americas. In 1929, Annie Peck made a unique promotional flight of 20,000 miles across Latin America using previously unexplored routes and a dozen kinds of local aircraft.

Annie Smith Peck was born on October 19, 1850, in Providence, Rhode Island, the youngest of five children, and the only surviving daughter. Her father was a lawyer and coal merchant. As a child, Annie was allowed to join her brothers in vigorous outdoor sports. In time, she became an accomplished rower and equestrian.

Annie received an excellent early education at Dr. Stockbridge's School for Young Ladies in Providence. Annie hoped to attend a liberal arts college like her brothers, but her parents refused to support her in this idea. She determined to raise her own money to pay for her higher education and taught for a year in Providence; then became preceptress of the Saginaw, Michigan, High School.

In 1874, Annie Peck entered the University of Michigan, one of the few coeducational colleges in America at that time. She graduated at the top of her class with honors in every subject. Annie Peck went on to earn a master's in Greek in 1881, supporting herself by teaching math at the Bartholomew School for Girls in Cincinnati. From 1881 to 1883, Annie Peck was a professor of Latin and elocution at Purdue University. In 1884, she made her first trip to Europe, studying music and German in Hanover, Germany. In 1885, Annie Peck became the first woman student to be admitted to the American School of Classical Studies in Athens, Greece.

In the summer of 1885, Annie journeyed to Switzerland. As she gazed at the mountain scenery, dominated by the Matterhorn, the Jungfrau, and the Funffingerspitze, Annie's vocation was born. She made her neophyte excursion into mountain-climbing, scaling the "nursery slopes" of the Swiss Alps. But she could not yet afford to pursue a career as a climber, so, returning to the United States, she accepted a chair in Latin at Smith College. She supplemented her teaching salary by lecturing on Greek and Roman archeology, showing stereopticon slides of her own photographs. She was a woman of commanding presence in spite of her slight stature, and being thoroughly versed in her subject, Annie Peck was praised as an archeological lecturer both by academicians and the press.

Meanwhile, Annie Peck was improving her climbing skills. In her first major ascent, she climbed Mount Shasta (14,380 feet) in California. Four years later, she ascended the Matterhorn, and descended from that majestic peak to find herself famous, or, rather, infamous. The story of this diminutive American woman, clad in knickers and sturdy boots, reaching the summit of Europe's most awesome mountain caused a sensation in the American press. But there were no congratulatory messages from public officials awaiting Annie Peck on her return to America. Her unladylike feat and costume had outraged the American public. "Go home where you belong," one man jeered. With only her older brother, George, to encourage her, Annie Peck nevertheless persisted in pursuing a mountain-climbing career.

Annie's exploits became increasingly daring. In 1897, she went to Mexico, where she climbed the live volcano Popocatepetl, and Mount Orizaba, which at 18,314 feet, was the highest peak in the western hemisphere ever to be scaled by a woman. Then it was back to the lecture circuit. A gifted speaker, Annie Peck was able to convey to her audiences her own sense of exhilaration at the "ever-changing vistas" afforded by mountain climbing. Her cross-country lecture jaunts were her main source of income for the rest of her life. With no outside funding, her climbing expeditions were continually hindered by inadequate equipment and inexperienced assistants.

In 1900, Annie Peck did extensive climbing in the Alps, scaling the Funffingerspitze, the Monte Cristallo, and the Jungfrau. Then, seeking to scale "some height where no *man* had previously stood," she turned to the relatively unexplored region of the Andes, in South America. Conquering Mount Sorata in Bolivia in 1904, she next tackled the twin-peaked Mount Huscaran in Peru. After two attempts to climb this mountain failed, Annie planted her feet at the crest of this Peruvian peak in 1908. In 1911, when at the age of 61, Annie Peck became the first climber of another Peruvian slope, Mount Coropena (21,250 feet), she planted a banner advocating "votes for women" on the mountaintop.

The ascent of Mount Huscaran brought Annie Peck international repute. She received a gold medal from the Peruvian government, and the Silver Slipper Award of the Lima Geographical Society, which later named the Huscaran northern peak Cumbre Ana Peck after its first conqueror. Later, on her 80th birthday, Annie Peck was awarded the Chilean Order of Merit.

Meanwhile, her forays into South America had sparked her interest in the South American people, culture, and natural resources, and Annie worked actively to foster closer relations between the United States and its South-of-the-Border neighbors. Fluent in both Spanish and Portuguese, she lectured in these languages on industrial and educational subjects in a number of Latin American countries. She also wrote books to interest and inform United States readers about their Latin neighbors, such as *A Search for the Apex of South America* (1911); *The South American Tour* (1913); and *Industrial and Commercial South America* (1922).

Annie Peck's attraction to the higher atmosphere was not limited to mountain climbing; she was also fascinated by flying, and managed to cover 20,000 miles by air over South America between November 1929 and June 1930. Her account of this voyage, with aerial photos, appears in *Flying Over South America* (1931). She also published articles on aviation and mountaineering in a number of magazines, including *Harper's* and *Scientific American*.

An indefatigable promoter of mountaineering, Annie Peck helped to found the American Alpine Club in 1902. She was also a fellow of the Royal Geographical Society, the National Geographical Society, and the Society of Women Geographers, and vice-president of the All-American Reciprocity Union.

At the age of 82, Annie Peck made her last alpine ascent, climbing 5,380-foot Mount Madison in New Hampshire. Two years later, Annie Peck took to her bed and died on July 18, 1935, at the age of 84. This plucky, determined woman, who had received little sympathy or support in her lifetime, embodied the exultation expressed in Lord Byron's *Childe Harold*:

> . . . *Above me are the Alps,*
> *The Palaces of Nature, whose vast walls*
> *Have pinnacled in clouds their snowy scalps*
> *And throned Eternity in icy halls. . .*
> *All that expands the spirit, yet appals,*
> *Gathered around these summits, as to show*
> *How Earth may pierce to Heaven, yet leave vain man below.*

Ramabai Dongré Medhavi
(1858-1922)
SAVIOR OF INDIAN CHILD-WIDOWS

Before 1888, when Ramabai Dongré Medhavi opened the first shelter and school for child-widows in India, the life of a widow who had not borne a son was unspeakably wretched. According to Hindu belief, widowhood was a divine punishment inflicted on women for sins committed in earlier incarnations. If the widow had not compensated for her previous crimes by bringing male children into the world during her present existence, she was treated as a common criminal. Sonless widows were incarcerated in a dark corner of their husbands' ancestral homes, clothed in sackcloth, given but one meal a day, and barred from all family festivities and from contact with people. Often, the husband's relatives heaped the unfortunate widow with verbal or physical abuse, regarding her as the cause of her spouse's death. If the deceased husband had no relatives, the widow returned to her own family's household, where although she was spared the beatings and was permitted limited contact with her immediate family, her existence was still that of a pariah. The widow who had given her husband's family or her own relations any excuse to disown her—for instance, by marrying out of her caste—was expected to commit suicide. Since most Indian women entered into arranged marriages at the age of nine, many of these hapless widows were still children, consigned to a lifetime of misery before even attaining puberty.

In her lifetime, Ramabai Dongré Medhavi rescued thousands of sonless widows. She sheltered them at her school in Poona and educated them for the few professions open to women, such as teaching or nursing, or trained them in a trade at her farm and industrial school at Kedgaum. Pundita Ramabai's school and farm were the first such institutions in India.

Ramabai was born in 1858 on a sacred mountaintop in the jungles of Gungamal in western India. She was the youngest of three children of Brahmin (the highest Indian caste) parents. Her father, Ananta Dongré, had acquired his child-wife in the customary manner. While bathing in a sacred river, he had met a fellow pilgrim who offered his nine-year-old daughter, Lakshmibai, to Dongré as a bride. Dongré accepted the offer, and the couple was married the following day. But later, Dongré had come to view child-marriage as barbaric. Dongré, an orthodox Hindu and an erudite scholar, held advanced views on the education of women, and to the horror of his friends and relations taught his own child-wife to read and write and instructed her in the Sanskrit language and literature and in the sacred Hindu texts. For this sacrilege the couple was shunned by other members of their caste. They retired to the hinterlands of Gungamal, where they could pursue their study and meditation unmolested.

The Dongrés did not live in complete isolation. The mountain peak on which they built their hut was a sacred Hindu shrine, and was visited by a steady stream of pilgrims. Ramabai's father considered it his religious duty to provide for the visitors, and the Dongré resources were soon depleted. So, Dongré and his wife, their two older children, and six-month-old Ramabai became pilgrims themselves. They joined the crowds of people who wandered from one end of India to the other paying homage to the gods at shrines and temples. Because he was a learned man, Dongré did not, like other pilgrims, have to beg in order to feed his family. Instead, he became a *Puranika*, or popular preacher. The Puranikas read the *Puranas*, the sacred Sanskrit texts, aloud to the illiterate population and translated them into their listeners' dialects. In accordance with Hindu religious custom, in exchange, to be purified of sin, the hearers paid the Puranikas whatever they could afford. Since the people were so poor, the offerings were often meager—a handful of rice, a few small coins, or at best, a night's lodging. The Dongrés frequently went hungry, and spent many nights in public shelters.

Ramabai never attended school in India, but she received an education from her parents. By the time she was 15, she was fluent in half a dozen Indian dialects as well as in Sanskrit, and could recite from memory 23,000 verses of the Hindu *Shastras*.

In 1874, India suffered one of its most severe famines, and both Ramabai's parents and her sister died of hunger. Estranged from their relatives and friendless, Ramabai and her brother pursued the nomadic life of Hindu pilgrims. In three years, they traversed more than 4,000 miles. Although well educated by their father, they had no practical skills and, being Brahmins, were barred from physical labor by the conventions of caste, so they supported themselves by holding public recitations. In 1878, they settled in Calcutta, where they earned their livelihood by reading the sacred Sanskrit writings to large throngs.

Soon Ramabai's fame spread among the pundits of Calcutta. She was summoned before a council of Hindu scholars, who were as intrigued as they were shocked by the reports of Ramabai's sagacity. They subjected her to a searching literary examination, and to an inquisition on her presumption in pursuing male studies. Ramabai showed both self-possession and humility in demonstrating her credentials as a scholar. The hidebound Brahmins were overcome with admiration, and awarded her the titles of *Sarasvati* (Goddess of Wisdom) and *Pundita* (Learned Lady).

When Ramabai was 22, her brother died, and she was left without a male relative in a country where women were completely dependent on male relations. At the Calcutta Christian mission, Ramabai had become friendly with a young Bengali lawyer, Bipin Bihari Medhavi, who now offered to marry her. The obstacles to this marriage were considerable. It would mean cutting themselves off from both their families, for Medhavi was of the Shundra caste, three steps below the Brahmins. No devout Hindu dared speak to a family member who married out of caste—whether higher or lower—because doing so meant risking losing your own caste for millions of reincarnations. But Ramabai and Bipin loved each other and shared liberal social views. In 1880, the couple married and moved to Poona.

Before the Medhavis had celebrated their second wedding anniversary, Bipin contracted cholera and died. Ramabai and her infant daughter, Manorama, were in danger of destitution. The Medhavi family wanted nothing to do with them, and Ramabai's own family despised her for marrying out of caste. Only a young female cousin,

Anandibai Joshee—destined to become the first Hindu woman to earn a medical degree—showed any sympathy for the young widow. Anandibai urged Ramabai to go abroad to study, as she herself was doing.

Ramabai cherished a dream of devoting her life to freeing Indian women from bondage. Particularly, she longed to help the poor, sonless child-widows. She approached the Christian missionaries at Poona for help. They agreed to finance her passage to England and her education there. So in 1883, Ramabai and her baby daughter embarked for the Anglican convent at Wantage. Here Ramabai was welcomed by the Sisters of Saint Mary's. They gave her English lessons, and secured for her a post as professor of Sanskrit at Cheltenham Female College.

The nuns of Saint Mary's took Ramabai to London to visit a shelter for unfortunate women founded by their sisterhood. She acquired many ideas for her own projected shelter for Indian women, and was so moved by her observations of the Christian precept of charity in action, she decided to embrace the Anglican faith.

In 1886, Ramabai attended her cousin Anandibai's graduation from medical school in Philadelphia. Here, Dean Rachel L. Bodley of the Women's Medical College was so impressed with Ramabai's plan of founding a school and shelter for Indian child-widows, she urged Ramabai to remain in America to study.

Ramabai began an intensive survey of American kindergartens and trade schools. During this time, she also managed to complete a book, *The High-Caste Indian Woman,* exposing the problems of female infanticide, child-marriage and child-widows in India. Published in 1887, the book was the first insider's description of the Indian woman's life, and was widely read.

The book brought Ramabai to the attention of a number of American philanthropists, and in 1887, an American Ramabai Association was formed in Boston. Its officers included Ramabai, Edward Everett Hale, Phillips Brooks, Frances E. Willard, and Rachel Bodley. The Association voted to subsidize a nonsectarian school for child-widows in India for a period of ten years. Ramabai was sent on a tour to establish new chapters of the American Ramabai Association, and to solicit funds.

In November, 1888, after being away from her native land for almost six years, Ramabai returned to India to start her school. Within six weeks of her arrival in Bombay, Ramabai established the Sharada Sadan, or Home of Wisdom. Its first pupils were two high-caste child-widows. One of the girls had attempted suicide three times after her husband's death.

By 1893, the Sharada Sadan had 50 pupils. Ramabai had relocated her school and shelter in Poona, and bought a large farm in nearby Kedgaum. Here she established Mukti (Salvation), a Christian home and industrial school. The dairy and vegetable crops produced at Mukti supplied the school at Poona with milk and vegetables and furnished additional income for Ramabai's work.

In 1897, famine struck central India. Ramabai personally rescued over 500 child-widows and deserted child-brides, who otherwise would have been abandoned by relatives to starve. Three hundred of these young waifs were sheltered at Mukti, and Ramabai found homes for the others with charitable Indians or with Christian missionaries.

When the Boston Ramabai Association convened for its decennial review in 1898, it had reports that 350 child-widows had graduated from the Sharada Sadan and had gone on to become teachers, nurses, missionaries, householders in their own right. The Association voted to continue its support indefinitely.

In 1900, Ramabai's American-educated daughter, Manorama, became vice-principal of the Sharada Sadan, and by 1912 had assumed most of her aging mother's responsibilities. In that year the Sharada Sadan numbered 115 pupils, and Mukti 172. Pundita Ramabai Dongré Medhavi died in 1922. The exact date of Ramabai's death is not ascertainable, but the facts of her life stand as a testimony to what one determined individual can do, in spite of tremendous cultural and religious prejudice, to liberate masses of human beings from sexual and social oppression.

Emmeline Goulden Pankhurst (1858-1929)

SUFFRAGIST AND STATESWOMAN

"She should have been a lad!" exclaimed Robert Goulden in the presence of his precocious daughter. Young Emmeline Goulden knew that her father's remark was meant as a compliment, but it rankled nonetheless. Why should a display of ability be considered more appropriate for a male, she asked herself, and vowed that she would devote her talents to enlarging women's opportunities. Emmeline Goulden Pankhurst did become one of the mainsprings of the women's movement in England. With her husband, she formed the Women's Franchise League in 1889; and by herself, in 1903, she founded a political party, the Woman's Social and Political Union.

Emmeline Goulden was born into a prosperous family in Manchester, England, on July 14, 1858. Her father, a calico broker, and her mother were champions of the causes of black emancipation and female enfranchisement. Mr. Goulden was a member of the Manchester Committee to welcome Henry Ward Beecher, and Harriet Beecher Stowe's novel *Uncle Tom's Cabin* was popular bedtime reading for the ten Goulden children. Emmeline's mother gave her a small "lucky bag" to collect pennies for the abolitionist cause. Later, Emmeline accompanied her mother to suffragette lectures.

At home, Emmeline's quick mind was recognized and nourished. Emmeline's brothers nicknamed her "the dictionary." In 1872, Emmeline was sent to the École Normale in Paris, one of the first institutions of higher education for women. When she returned to Manchester a year later, she found it difficult to adjust to the circumscribed life prescribed for her by her ostensibly liberal parents. Her sister, Mary, who had also attended the École Normale, found the restrictions even more intolerable than Emmeline. When Mary, forbidden by her father from becoming an actress, turned to painting and exhibited her canvasses at a local shop, Mr. Goulden complained that if his clients knew that Mary was selling paintings, they would think the family was suffering financial hardship.

Emmeline's ambition was to marry a great man and escape from her dull existence. She found her great man in Dr. Richard Pankhurst, drafter of the first women's suffrage bill. When Emmeline met Pankhurst in 1878, he had already been working for 20 years as a reformer, championing the rights of workers as well as women, and defending popular education. Dr. Pankhurst had also been instrumental in enacting legislation to improve labor, patent, and bankruptcy laws. In 1879, Emmeline Goulden became Emmeline Pankhurst. She bore three daughters and a son within five years.

In 1889, Emmeline's four-year-old son died of diphtheria, misdiagnosed by the local physicians as croup. Emmeline attributed the doctor's negligence to unconcern for the welfare of indigent patients, and vowed that she would make money so that henceforth her children would be treated with respect. She opened a shop in London, selling antiques and decorative furniture. It did well, and with the profits Emmeline opened a salon for radical politicians and philosophers at 8 Russell Street. Socialists, Fabians, free-thinkers, and libertarians from all over the world flocked to Emmeline Pankhurst's gatherings. At last, Emmeline had fulfilled her ambition to become a celebrated hostess. Meanwhile she gave birth to a fifth child, a boy.

Emmeline had been working with her husband in the cause of women's rights. They had been instrumental in securing passage of the Married Women's Property Act of 1882. The Pankhursts were leaders in the Franchise League, the most militant of the various feminist groups. Gradually, Emmeline became more self-confident and began taking an independent role in fighting for justice for the dispossessed. She formed a woman's committee for the relief of the unemployed, and personally distributed soup and bread to the hungry. She also became the most powerful member of the Chorlton Board of Guardians of the Poor Laws. By now, Emmeline Pankhurst had overcome her bashfulness, and spoke regularly in public, and presented papers at conferences.

In 1898, Dr. Pankhurst died. Emmeline mourned the loss of her husband of 19 years, but turned her attention toward supporting herself and her four children. The Chorlton Guardians offered her a position as registrar of births. This job brought Emmeline into direct contact with poor women—mothers of large families, deserted wives, and unwed mothers—and renewed her fervor for the cause of women's rights.

As she became increasingly zealous for the cause of women's rights, Emmeline Pankhurst also became increasingly disenchanted with the Independent Labour Party, which was doing little indeed to secure the enfranchisement of women. Emmeline decided that women must no longer rely on men to fight their battle. In 1903, she formed the Woman's Social and Political Union, the first woman's political party. Only one of the Labor Party leaders, the valiant Keir Hardy, was willing to work with the new woman's group.

Emmeline Pankhurst was greatly aided in her suffrage work by her daughters. Christabel became one of England's first women lawyers, although the all-male courts refused to let her try cases before them. Sylvia became a champion of unwed mothers, and an international pacifist of note.

In 1905, Emmeline's daughter, Christabel, engaged in militant action for women's suffrage and was fined for disorderly conduct. When she refused to pay the fine, Christabel was imprisoned for a week. Emmeline, too, embraced the tactics of civil disobedience. In 1906, Emmeline and 260,000 of her stalwarts assembled in Downing Street, and clung to the railings to prevent the police from dispersing them. She and her followers continually interrupted party caucuses to interrogate the leaders on their stance on women's rights, and were often forcibly evicted.

By 1907, Emmeline Pankhurst was working full time for the W.S.P.U., and had become increasingly militant. Her suffragette demonstrations involved her in frequent scuffles with the police. Emmeline was arrested along with her daughter Christabel in an attempt to enter the House of Commons. The two women were taken to jail in a prison van, put into prison uniforms, and sent to cold, airless cells, where they remained for six weeks. This was not the last time Emmeline's activities were to land her in jail.

In June, 1908, two of the suffragettes smashed the windows of the Prime Minister's official residence. This was the first violent act committed by members of the W.S.P.U. Emmeline Pankhurst endorsed the action. Later, she was to proclaim, "One thing we regard as sacred: human life. With that exception, we are justified in using all methods resorted to in time of War." When Parliament reopened on October 13, Emmeline Pankhurst and her cohorts were at the gates, urging the suffragettes to "RUSH the House of Commons." Emmeline and Christabel were again arrested and imprisoned.

In 1910, when Parliament vetoed the suffragist Conciliation Bill, Emmeline Pankhurst launched a window-breaking campaign and was charged with inciting to violence. She and the participants were given nine-month prison sentences. Emmeline petitioned asking that they be treated as political prisoners rather than as ordinary criminals. After an outpouring of support from universities, political organizations, and notables from all over the world, Emmeline only was accorded political status. In protest, the suffragettes called a hunger strike, and many of them were made to suffer force-feeding.

In 1914, Emmeline Pankhurst published her autobiography, *My Own Story*. With the eruption of World War I, she ordered a suspension of suffragette activities, calling on her troops to join the more pressing cause of World War I relief work. The British government, in turn, gave amnesty to all suffragette prisoners. The W.S.P.U. members worked to establish day-care centers, clinics, low-cost restaurants, and welfare programs for wives and mothers of soldiers at the front.

In the year 1918, the W.S.P.U. at last achieved partial victory. The Representation of the People Act was passed enfranchising women over 30.

Emmeline Pankhurst spent the next six years lecturing in the United States and Canada. When she returned to London, she accepted an invitation by the Conservative Party to run as their candidate in Whitechapel. In spite of poor health, Emmeline campaigned actively, but she died on June 14, 1928, before the election. Neither did she live to see the full fruition of her efforts. One month after her death, Parliament passed a new Representation of the People Act, at last granting women full enfranchisement.

Emmeline Pankhurst was a courageous and self-sacrificing individual. She might easily have used her considerable personal charm and talent to remain a popular socialite, but gave up personal comfort to fight for the emancipation of her sex. She overcame her shyness to become an excellent public speaker for causes she felt deeply about. She employed her managerial talent to organize the suffragettes for concerted and efficacious action.

Emmeline Pankhurst was no mere armchair leader. She entered the fray right in the front lines. When orderly lobbying failed to persuade Parliament to give women the vote, she mobilized her followers to execute militants acts of civil disobedience, in which she herself participated, sharing the indignities of police brutality and maltreatment in prison. Press coverage of these sensationalist episodes served to publicize and gain sympathy for the suffragist cause in a way that peaceful action had not, until finally the battle for women's suffrage was won. A statue to the memory of this stalwart suffragette was later erected in Westminster.

Emmeline Pankhurst and Christabel Pankhurst in prison dress.

Charlotte Perkins Gilman
(1860-1935)
SOCIOLOGIST

"The consuming female . . . the priestess of the temple of consumption, creates a market for sensuous decoration and personal ornament, for all that is luxurious and enervating. . . ."

A quote from Thorstein Veblen? No. One year before the publication of Verblen's *Theory of the Leisure Class*, in a treatise entitled *Women and Economics*, another great American sociologist identified the phenomenon that Veblen labeled *conspicuous consumption*. The sociologist's name was Charlotte Perkins, and her book was perhaps the most important feminist manifesto ever written. *Women and Economics* (1896) contains the first comprehensive analysis of the economic basis of woman's subjection, and presents the first systematic proposal for gaining greater equity for women in industrial society through the reorganization of home and family life.

"Here I come, doll in hand, to obey my mother's command." Charlotte Perkins was three years old when she composed this dutiful little ditty. She could have no idea that she would grow up to challenge every social, political, economic, and moral precept concerning women in the 19th century. But, conquering overwhelming adversities, Charlotte fulfilled her destiny to serve in the public realm. Charlotte was a descendant of the famous Beecher family, and the Beechers were public-spirited people. Charlotte's great-grandfather was abolitionist theologian Lyman Beecher; her great-aunts were educational pioneers. Charlotte's father, Frederic Beecher Perkins, was Boston's head librarian and a respected magazine editor.

Charlotte saw little of her father during her childhood. Seven years after her birth on July 3, 1860, Mr. Perkins left his wife and two children, and although they corresponded, he did not see much of his children.

Though Mr. Perkins was financially well-to-do, he suffered his abandoned family to subsist in genteel poverty. Mrs. Perkins did her best to eke out an independent existence by teaching—and she was a gifted pedagogue—but destitution eventually drove the family to rely on the charity of relations. Bearing the ignominious lot typical of poor relations, they rotated among more prosperous members of the family. In the first 19 years of her life, Charlotte Perkins changed residence 18 times. But the physical hardships of her childhood—frugal meals and hand-me-down clothing—were mitigated by extended visits with her illustrious relatives Harriet Beecher Stowe and Edward Everett Hale. An inquisitive child, Charlotte thrived on the intellectual stimulation in these households.

Charlotte's education was erratic and haphazard. Her mother schooled her in the three R's and sewing, but only four of Charlotte's first 15 years were spent in a classroom, and her formal education was unsystematically acquired among seven different institutions. Nevertheless, the superior intelligence and empirical spirit that were later to make her an outstanding sociologist manifested themselves in Charlotte's early childhood. When she was five, she devised a more efficient mending stitch than the one she had been taught by her grandmother; and at the age of eight, she proved through her own step-by-step solution that the book's answer to a math problem was wrong.

When Charlotte was 14, one of her great-aunts died, leaving a modest estate to the Perkins children. Mrs. Perkins used the inheritance to send her children to private secondary schools. In high school, Charlotte discovered that she had a facility for versifying and for elocution. But her favorite subject was natural philosophy, an amalgam of physics and natural history. She joined a Boston society to pursue the study of ancient history and ethnology, and at the age of 16, wrote to her father of her interest in these disciplines, hoping that Mr. Perkins might finance her higher education, as he was financing her brother's at M.I.T. But instead of a check, Charlotte's father sent her a reading list, accompanied by several issues of the *Popular Science Monthly*. Disappointed, Charlotte nevertheless avidly devoured the magazines and was grateful to have some direction for her further reading.

Charlotte Perkins's teenage years were anything but carefree, as indicated in the title of a chapter in her autobiography: "Girlhood— if any." Her mother forbade her to read novels, attend the theater, or go to parties. Nevertheless, Charlotte found herself an object of interest to young men, although she soon learned that the male concept of an appropriate relationship differed radically from her own. "My theory was that a girl should meet a boy with the same straightforward friendliness she would show another girl; that it was ignominious and wrong to flaunt one's femininity so to speak. It was far too late for popularity before I learned that this was precisely what men wanted, ordinary men that is." Although she occasionally did meet some extraordinary men who shared her intellectual interests, in general she was shunned by the young men of her acquaintance. Determined to understand the cause of her failure with the opposite sex, Charlotte approached the problem directly. She asked a young socialite "just what the game is." The vivacious belle gave her as direct a response: "It is to get a fellow so he cannot keep his hands off you—and then not let him touch you."

In 1882, Charlotte met Charles Walter Stetson, a painter, and thought him "quite the greatest man, near my own age, that I had ever met. After two years of vacillation, Charlotte agreed to marry Stetson. They were wed in 1884, and the following year, Charlotte Stetson gave birth to a daughter, Katharine. But the marriage did not turn out well, and in 1894, Charles and Charlotte Stetson were divorced.

Between 1895 and 1900, Charlotte criss-crossed the United States, lecturing, writing, editing, and educating herself in the current intellectual trends— Socialism, Darwinism, and feminism. She founded and ran her own magazine, and helped to organize a woman's congress in California in 1894, and again in 1895. She met Jane Addams—"her mind had more 'floor space' in it than any other I have known"—and accepted an invitation to visit Hull House.

Though never a member of the Socialist Party, Charlotte was a delegate to the International Socialist Convention in London in 1896. Here she met George Bernard Shaw and Beatrice and Sidney Webb. Her discussions with the British Fabians and with Lester Ward, the first American sociologist, deeply influenced her and were integrated into her own ideas, which she expressed in *Women and Economics,* published in 1896.

Lester Ward considered Social Darwinism a rationalization for the abuses of capitalism. He argued that social status was not the result of natural, and hence unalterable, characteristics, but a product of capitalist exploitation. To illustrate his point, he cited the role of women in the Western world. Ward believed that women were born with the same varied potential as men, but were, from birth, schooled in the functions that would make them most economically useful to men.

In *Women and Economics* Charlotte argued that women need to work outside the home. Such purposeful activity serves both as a source of mental stimulation, and as a practical economic necessity. Charlotte Perkins knew, from her mother's bitter experiences as well as her own, that the current social structure was inimical to unmarried women. Furthermore, she saw the conditioned overdependence of women on men, and the consequent atrophy of women's non-domestic skills, as detrimental to both sexes economically, socially, morally, and psychologically.

To free women from their imprisonment in the home, *Women and Economics* proposed sweeping reforms in family life. Arguing that children, as well as their mothers, are stunted by the isolation imposed by traditional home-rearing, Perkins proposed the establishment of centralized nurseries. She also advocated that professional diaper services, laundries, housecleaning and catering agencies be established to relieve working women from the drudgery of housework. Such services, in the form of nannies and housemaids, had always been available to wealthy women, but Charlotte sought an economically feasible solution to the problems of middle and low-income families. She did not accept modern technology as the best means of easing woman's domestic burdens, pointing out that labor-saving machines still kept women chained to the home for the dreary purpose of loading and unloading. Charlotte also attacked the American success ethic, which equated success with the accumulation of money and luxurious accoutrements. She proposed that a more fulfilling ideal would be humanitarian service and communal cooperation.

Unlike previous feminist documents, *Women and Economics* pinpointed the major problems of modern society in the language of social science rather than moral rhetoric. The book had an immediate impact in America and England, and was soon translated into seven languages, including Russian, Japanese, and Hungarian.

In 1900, Charlotte Perkins married her cousin, George Houghton Gilman, a Beecher who shared common family memories and similar values. Mutual intellectual companionship and encouragement provided the basis for an unusually happy home life. Charlotte wrote, lectured, and attended conventions, and George practiced law in New York.

All her life, Charlotte had been a staunch believer in physical fitness. At the age of 42 she was still playing basketball with her daughter. At 65, she took a turn at the parallel bars at the University of Oklahoma, and was proud that she had remained athletically equal to the endeavor.

In January of 1932, Charlotte Perkins Gilman discovered that she had breast cancer. After her husband's death in 1934, she began stockpiling chloroform, and rather than suffer the slow debilitation of her hopeless disease, in 1935 she committed suicide. She left the following explanation of her death:

Human life consists in mutual service. No grief, pain, misfortune, or "broken heart" is excuse for cutting off one's life while any power of service remains. But when all usefulness is over, when one is assured of un-avoidable and imminent death, it is the simplest of human rights to choose a quick and easy death in place of a slow and horrible one.

One of the first exponents of euthanasia, Charlotte Perkins Gilman was in death as in life ahead of her time.

In her day, Charlotte was praised an an author, lecturer and economist. Today, Charlotte Perkins Gilman stands out as one of the most original sociologists and rational thinkers of her day. Many of her prescriptions for social maladies have happily been enforced. She insisted that economic independence was the key to woman's emancipation—and time has proved her right.

Jane Addams (1860-1935)

HUMANITARIAN

I recall an incident which must have occurred before I was seven years old, for the mill in which my father transacted his business that day was closed in 1867. The mill stood in the neighboring town, adjacent to its poorest quarter. . . . On that day I had my first sight of the poverty which implies squalor. . . . I remember launching at my father the pertinent inquiry why people lived in such horrid little houses so close together, and that after receiving his explanation, I declared with much firmness, when I grew up I should, of course, have a large house, but it would not be built among the other large houses, but right in the midst of horrid little houses like these.

That determined little girl was Jane Addams, and her prophecy was indeed fulfilled. In *Twenty Years at Hull House* she describes the inception of America's first major settlement house. Following her childhood scenario, Jane Adams located Hull House in a spacious mansion in the heart of Chicago's worst slum.

In the beginning, the settlement house served the physical, educational, cultural, and recreational needs of its immigrant neighborhood. Later, Hull House became a center for city and statewide reforms in housing, welfare, and working conditions.

But in Jane Addams's view, the greatest beneficiaries of Hull House were not the underprivileged, but the overprivileged:

. . . . I gradually became convinced that it would be a good thing to rent a house in a part of the city where many primitive and actual needs are found, in which young women who had been given over too exclusively to study might restore a balance of activity along traditional lines and learn of life from life itself; where they might try out some of the things they had been taught and put truth to "the ultimate test of the conduct it dictates or inspires."

The founder of Hull House was born in Cedarville, Illinois, on September 6, 1860. Jane lost her mother at the age of two; and five of her eight siblings died in childhood. When Jane was eight, her father, a prosperous miller and banker, remarried. The second Mrs. Addams, a widow with two sons, gave her young stepdaughter a solid education in music and literature.

As an adolescent, Jane dreamed of attending Smith College, but her father insisted that she matriculate nearer to home, at the Rockford Seminary. Valedictorian and president of her class at Rockford, Jane helped transform the seminary into a degree-awarding college. The headmistress hoped that Jane might be a religious missionary, but although Jane was very much in sympathy with the high ideals and moral tone of Rockford, she had her own ideas about what she wanted to do. Upon graduating from Rockford, Jane entered the Women's Medical College in Philadelphia.

Jane Addams never completed her medical studies. In 1881, her father died suddenly, at the age of 59. Traumatized by grief, and in poor health due to a spinal ailment, Jane left school. During the next several years she underwent a series of spinal operations, and suffered from nervous depression. During this period of tribulation, Jane became deeply religious. Her father was a Quaker but had never been affiliated with any particular congregation. Jane, feeling the need of religious fellowship, joined the Presbyterian Church. But Jane's enormous vitality would not allow her to seek solace in private meditation. Her way of moral comfort was through positive public action.

In 1883, Jane and her stepmother went abroad and stayed two years. Jane was moved by the destitution she observed in the seamier sections of London. On her second trip to Europe Jane discovered her métier in social work. The epiphany occurred while Jane was attending a bullfight in Madrid, in 1889. Jane was revolted by the gratuitous bloodshed involved in the spectacle, and asked herself what she was doing watching such an exhibition instead of doing something constructive with her life. She remembered a phrase from Carlyle, which had often been quoted to her at Rockford: "'Tis not to taste sweet things, but to do noble and true things that the poorest son of Adam dimly longs." At the age of 39, Jane Addams decided to found a settlement house, where noble and true things would be done.

Jane confided her plan to one of her traveling companions, Ellen Starr. Ellen listened enthusiastically, and asked to be allowed to join the endeavor. Before returning to the States, the two girls went to London, where they visited the renowned English settlement house Toynbee Hall, and consulted with the head of that institution about their plan to establish an American counterpart.

When Jane Addams and Ellen Starr returned to America, they began searching in Chicago for a location for their settlement house. They met with considerable opposition among prominent Chicagoans, who protested that communal living led to loose morals. Undeterred by such arguments, the young women enlisted the aid of a former mayor of Chicago, who succeeded in locating a site for their settlement house on the second floor of a tumble-down homestead on Halstead Street. The women used their own savings to restore the building, and in September 1889, Hull House opened its doors to the community.

Hull House provided free educational and cultural activities for the Irish, German, Italian, Greek and Jewish denizens of Chicago's Nineteenth Ward. The first organized activity of the settlement was a kindergarten. For adults, there were weekly informal readings of George Eliot, Hawthorne, and other classic authors. As Addams enticed new volunteer workers to Hull House, the settlement's activities expanded to include classes in handicrafts, cooking, sewing, acting, and music. By 1893, Hull House was a center with some 40 clubs, a day-care program, a gymnasium, a playground, a dispensary, and a cooperative boarding house for working girls. Each week, some 2,000 Chicagoans entered its doors to partake of the course offerings, and to socialize with their neighbors. Jane Addams and her colleagues regularly visited the neighboring tenements in search of elderly, infirm, or lonely individuals, and arranged transportation for them to Hull House.

Hull House flourished and expanded, eventually comprising 13 separate dwellings. Happily, Jane proved an able fund raiser: by the late 1920s Hull House was running on an annual budget of nearly $100,000.

Gradually, Jane Addams diverted her energies from creating a haven for the residents of the Nineteenth Ward to improving the neighborhood itself, and then, to effecting city and statewide reforms to ameliorate the conditions of the tenement dwellers. In 1893, Hull House brought pressure to secure the passage of the first Illinois factory inspection act. Hull House was also directly responsible for the state's first juvenile court law, and first mother's pension law.

In 1895, *Hull House Maps and Papers*, a sociological study of living and working conditions in Chicago, was published. Jane Addams analyzed the report, and earmarked specific areas for reform. She delegated responsibility for each of these areas to her associates on the basis of their experience and fields of expertise. Thus, Florence Kelley led the inquiry into sweatshop conditions; Grace Abbott made a specialty of newly arrived immigrants; Julia Lathrop spearheaded an investigation of public welfare procedures; and Ellen Starr orchestrated the cultural activities of the settlement, which included one of the nation's first "little theaters." As head of Hull House, Jane Addams coordinated all these activities, publicizing their results in lectures and magazine articles.

Hull House became a target for political reactionaries and defenders of the status quo, who viewed the center as a hotbed of social and political agitation. A vituperative hue and cry was raised when Russian anarchist Prince Kropotkin was invited to lecture at Hull House. A firm believer in freedom of speech, Jane Addams continued to allow the settlement to serve as a forum for ideological interchange as well as practical reform. Attacked by the American

Legion and the Daughters of the American Revolution, Addams' activity was, on the other hand, applauded by American philosophers such as John Dewey and William James. James exclaimed, "you utter instinctively the truth we vainly seek."

Although she was a gifted orator, Jane Addams was no mere armchair exponent of reform. Distressed by the ineffectiveness of municipal garbage collection, she obtained a position as a sanitation inspector and rose at dawn to follow the local garbage collector on his rounds, taking notes on procedures to be improved. Once, Jane acted as midwife at the birth of an illegitimate child, because the Irish matrons who normally officiated refused "to touch the likes" of the unwed mother.

Inevitably, Jane Addams' efforts at reform carried her into the national arena. She rallied to the support of Theodore Roosevelt, seconding his nomination at the Progressive Party Convention in 1912, and making a cross-country campaign on behalf of Roosevelt's candidacy. Addams defended her partisanship, saying:

When a great party pledges itself to the protection of children, to the care of the aged, to the relief of overworked girls, to the safeguarding of burdened men, it is inevitable that it should appeal to women, and should seek to draw upon the great reservoir of their moral energy, so long undesired and unutilized in practical politics. . . .

Jane Addams' political activities also included campaigning for women's suffrage, for peace, and for individual rights. In January, 1915, Addams was chosen to chair the newly organized American Women's Peace Party, and in April she was elected president of the International Congress of Women at the Hague.

When the United States entered the war in 1917, Jane Addams joined Hoover's Food Administration. For two years, she toured the country urging increased food production for the benefit of the victims of the war. After the war, Addams continued to work for international disarmament. She helped found, and served as first president of the Women's International League for Peace and Freedom. In 1930, Jane Addams was co-recipient of the Nobel Peace Prize.

In 1920, Jane Addams was instrumental in establishing the

American Civil Liberties Union. She served on the national committee of the A.C.L.U. for nearly ten years. But when the Depression created a financial crisis at Hull House, Jane returned to Chicago and resumed her settlement work. In spite of failing health, she remained active at Hull House until May 21, 1935, when intestinal cancer caused her death. During the two days that her body lay on view in Hull House, untold thousands of Chicagoans came to pay their last respects to the woman who had brightened so many lives.

Jane Addams' humanitarian activities earned her apotheosis in her lifetime, and continued adulation after death. Endowed with great physical beauty and a magnetic personality, she deliberately embraced celibacy in order to devote all her energies to improving the condition of the common man.

The sponsor of many notable achievements, Jane Addams is, nevertheless, most remembered for her first and most beloved project, the founding of Hull House, where the tired, the poor, and the wretched refuse of Chicago's teeming factories were made to feel welcome.

Settlement work at Hull House.

Juliette Gordon Low
(1860-1927)

FOUNDER OF THE GIRL SCOUTS OF AMERICA

Her friends called her Daisy, and Juliette Gordon was in many ways remarkably similar to the heroine of F. Scott Fitzgerald's *The Great Gatsby*. Daisy Gordon was a charming child, a vivacious debutante, and a Southern Belle whose madcap antics were the toast of the Savannah gentry. At the age of 22, Juliette married a wealthy English playboy, and for the next 30 years led the glamorous life of an international socialite. But unlike Daisy Buchanan of *The Great Gatsby*, Daisy Gordon Low was not careless of other people's lives. At the age of 51, she channelled the organizational and social skills that had made her a world-famous hostess into a radically different activity. She established Girl Guide troops in the Scottish highlands and in London slums. The following year, she founded the Girl Scouts of America. Through this organization, millions of American girls acquire basic survival skills and enjoy the opportunity of meeting and making friends with girls of diverse social and cultural backgrounds. The Girl Scouts organization has also given older women who serve as troop leaders an outlet—often their sole outlet—for their energy and talents. For childless women, leading a troop offers the opportunity of vicarious motherhood.

Daisy Gordon was born on October 31, 1860. "Another girl," sighed her mother when her second child was born. But her father, a wealthy Savannah cotton-broker, was delighted with his offspring, and welcomed Juliette into the world with the comment that was to give her her nickname: "My, but she's a daisy!" Although Nellie Gordon had not really wanted any children, she nevertheless proved a loving and responsible mother to her brood of six.

Daisy Gordon was a capricious, even zany child, endearing but hardly demure. When a neighbor complimented Daisy on being "a pretty little girl," Daisy tossed her head defiantly and retorted, "No I'm not! My mama says I am as ugly as ten bears!" Whatever she may have told her daughter, to friends Nellie Gordon described her second daughter as "beautiful and good." Perhaps it was this discrepancy that saved the high-spirited girl from being utterly egocentric.

Indeed, Juliette Gordon seems to have been a remarkably generous and compassionate child. She rarely spent her allowance on herself, but was constantly buying presents for her friends, and giving away her dolls to little girls who had no toys. At the age of 14, Daisy formed a sewing circle called the Helping Hands with the object of making clothing for the poor. The project was less than a complete success, however, because Daisy and the other upper-class girls she had corralled into the club knew little about sewing. This experience may have inspired Juliette to make the learning of practical skills an important facet of Girl Scout activity.

Juliette Gordon received the typical education of girls of her class—she was sent to private girls' schools in Savannah and Virginia, and attended a posh finishing school in New York City. She never mastered spelling or simple mathematics, but won prizes in the arts, particularly in drawing and acting. Always courteous and convivial at the many parties she attended, Juliette seemed to revel in her role as an adorable scatterbrain and accomplished dilettante. But she was prone to moods of dejection, which she carefully concealed from others.

In her early twenties, Juliette made several excursions abroad. In

England she met, and fell in love with, Willy Low, the boon companion of the licentious Prince of Wales. Willy Low was described variously by the women who knew him as: "handsome as a Greek god, and the most charming person I have ever met"; and "He looked like a Greek god, and was the most despicable personality I have ever encountered." Daisy Gordon and Willy Low became secretly engaged, and in 1886, after both families had given their consent, the couple was wed.

Willy's father died and left a vast fortune to his only and idle son. After a grand wedding in Savannah, Juliette slipped into the role of a fairytale princess, spending the summer seasons at Willy's castle in Scotland, and wintering in Edwardian London, where she became the pet of her husband's fashionable friends. The worldly-wise, world-weary members of Willy Low's set found Daisy's innocence refreshing, her gaiety engaging. Daisy Low could display a scintillating wit, but she often preferred to listen, and had a gift for making the most diffident conversationalist feel like an accomplished raconteur.

Daisy's enchantment with life with Willy was brief. She was partially deafened because a grain of wedding rice had become embedded in her ear. The callous Willy seemed to derive amusement from deliberately talking so softly that Daisy missed the gist of his conversation. When the doctor forbade Daisy to participate in the traditional English foxhunts, her husband rode to the hounds without her. As the years passed, Willy's absences became more frequent, and rumors reached Daisy that her husband was having affairs with other women. Juliette did not let these reports interfere with her outward mirth or gracious mien, but she blamed her husband's intransigence on her inability to conceive the children that they had longed for. She filled the emotional vacuum with social engagements and visits to and from her family. But she began to seek more satisfying outlets for her vitality and intelligence.

Willy was emphatically opposed to his wife's engaging in organized charity or settlement work, so Daisy Low found her own way of surreptitiously committing acts of altruism. She would slip away from her estate at Wellesborne, and visit poor and needy people in the neighboring village. At the workhouse in Stratford-on-Avon, she regularly brightened the days of the unfortunate inmates with lively anecdotes and jokes. She invited vagrants to her kitchen for tea.

By 1901, it was an open secret that Willy Low was conducting a liaison with a Mrs. Bateman. Finally, when Willy exiled his wife to an isolated wing of their mansion, replacing her in the master bedroom with his mistress, Juliette fled from her husband's estate at Mealmore, and returned to Savannah.

Before the humiliating divorce proceedings were completed, Willy's life of debauchery and alcoholism caught up with him, and he died. Mrs. Bateman inherited the bulk of her lover's estate. Juliette had to take legal action and eventually she was awarded an adequate settlement from Willy's estate.

Juliette resumed her social activities, but found herself subject to many restrictions as a separated woman. She had, earlier, taken up sculpting and now began to devote more time to it. One afternoon, at a luncheon, Juliette was introduced to another amateur sculptor, General Sir Robert Baden-Powell. This introduction was to change the entire course of Juliette Low's life.

Among his other achievements, Sir Robert was the founder of the English Boy Scouts. As the friendship between them developed, Juliette learned more and more about the scouting movement from Sir Robert. Finally, Juliette decided the Girl Guides would furnish the "useful sphere of work" that she had so long been seeking. With her usual energy and talent, she directed her organizational ability into this channel.

In August 1911, Juliette wrote to her father from Scotland: "I am getting up a corps of Girl Guides here in this glen where the highland girls are so far from the world they remain ignorant in all details of nursing the sick and the way to feed and bring up delicate children." Juliette taught the Girl Guides first aid, and instructed them in other useful arts, such as knot-tying, knitting, cooking, personal hygiene, and carding and spinning wool.

Encouraged by her success in her new enterprise, Juliette established two Girl Guide troops in London. Then she returned to the United States where she founded the American Girl Scouts. She began with two troops with a total membership of 16 girls—the daughters of friends and relations in Savannah. Juliette personally provided the funding for the scouts' activities, and the Low homestead served as the meeting-place for the groups. Their activities included naturalist expeditions, camping trips, and a girls' basketball team.

Juliette was able to allay the mothers' fears about these unladylike activities with her compelling charm and utilitarian logic, and even managed to successfully recruit some of the Savannah matrons as scout leaders. By 1913, requests were coming to Juliette from all over the country for information about the Girl Scouts' activities, and for advice on how to start new Girl Scout patrols. Juliette went to Washington, D.C., and began to lay the groundwork for a national organization of Girl Scouts. She sounded out representatives of the Campfire Girls about merging the two organizations, but they balked at adding to the wilderness skills they emphasized the Girl Scout Laws which were designed to promote sororal relations between girls of different social classes and to encourage useful and altruistic activities.

In 1915, Juliette Gordon Low became president of the Girl Scouts of America. She began a nationwide campaign to establish branches of the Girl Scouts in all parts of the country, and persuaded socially prominent women to assume positions as scout leaders. The organization grew rapidly. During World War I the Girl Scouts responded to President Wilson's call for aid. They knitted sweaters for the troops; raised victory gardens; worked at recreation and Red Cross centers; and conducted Liberty Loan drives.

In 1919, the first International Council of Girl Guides and Girl Scouts convened in London, and Juliette Low represented the American organization. In 1920, when she retired from the office of president of the Girl Scouts, she was given the title of Founder. She continued to develop national and international support for the organization.

On January 18, 1927, Juliette Low died of cancer. Her funeral was attended by all the Girl Scouts of Savannah.

When Juliette Gordon Low died, the Girl Scouts of America comprised 140,000 members. Today, over two million American girls belong to scout troops. The movement undoubtedly owes a major part of its success to the personal charisma and organizational genius of its founder.

Henrietta Szold (1860-1945)

ZIONIST LEADER AND HUMANITARIAN

Give me your tired, your poor,
Your huddled masses yearning to breathe free,
The wretched refuse of your teeming shore,
Send these, the homeless, tempest-tossed, to me;
I lift my lamp beside the golden door.

Emma Lazarus stated this creed, engraved on our Statue of Liberty; and Henrietta Szold lived by it. Beginning in the 1880s, when she founded one of the first schools for the Americanization of immigrants in Baltimore, Henrietta Szold devoted her life to succoring homeless immigrants first in America and then in Palestine. Through her work as editor, organizer, and writer, she imbued thousands of American Jews with a knowledge of their history and a sense of pride in their heritage.

But the achievement for which she is perhaps best known is her work as a Zionist leader of a women's organization that helped to settle persecuted Jews in Palestine, and cared for the health and welfare of Jews and non-Jews already in Palestine. Henrietta Szold was the founding president of Hadassah, an international Zionist women's organization. She sent the first medical unit to Palestine in 1913. Beginning with only two nurses, this unit grew into a Nurses' Settlement House where thousands of Jews, Arabs, and Christians were treated for malaria, typhoid fever, tuberculosis and trachoma.

Henrietta Szold established the Youth Aliyah, an international organization that rescued over 100,000 Jewish children from 72 countries and resettled them in Israel. Countless orphans were helped to become useful, productive citizens. Until she was well into her eighties, Henrietta Szold continued to lift her lamp, and its light embraced young and old; Jew, Moslem, and Christian; American, Israeli, and European. "We must take care of all the underprivileged, economically and socially," she said. And she did.

Henrietta Szold was born during Hannukah, the Jewish festival of lights, on December 21, 1860 in Baltimore, Maryland. Her father, a Hungarian refugee, was a leading Conservative rabbi. Her mother, also from a well-to-do, educated family, had been a private pupil of his in Hungary.

The Szolds had eight daughters, three of whom died in infancy of scarlet fever or diphtheria. Being the oldest, Henrietta was given the education usually accorded to the first-born son in a Jewish family. With her learned father, she read Shakespeare, not only in English but in Schiller's German translation, Homer in the original Greek, Goethe in German, and Voltaire in French. Rabbi Szold also taught Henrietta to speak Hebrew and to read the sacred Jewish writings, the Torah and the Talmud. Henrietta became her father's secretary, handling his correspondence with the members of his congregation, and assisting him in scholarly research. From her mother, Henrietta learned to cook and sew, and to receive with gracious hospitality those who visited the rabbi at his home.

The Szold household provided a stable environment, both economically and emotionally, and Henrietta grew up a happy, healthy child.

In 1877, Henrietta graduated from Baltimore's Western Female High School as valedictorian of her class. For 15 years, she taught French, German, Latin, history, natural science, and mathematics.

At the same time, Henrietta taught Sunday School and adult Bible classes at her father's synagogue.

In 1882, a massive tide of Jews fled eastern Europe, where they had been persecuted under the anti-Semitic "May Laws" that Czar Alexander III imposed on the Russian empire. Most of the refugees came to America, and many settled in Baltimore. Rabbi Szold had great compassion for the refugees; he had himself been driven out of Vienna after participating in an unsuccessful democratic revolution there in 1848. Many immigrants found shelter in the Szold household, where they were fed, clothed, educated and helped with finding jobs in their new homeland. Henrietta was deeply impressed by the newcomers' stories of life in the ghettoes, with their poverty and police pogroms.

So in November 1889, Henrietta Szold established one of the first adult immigrant schools in the United States. She herself found the money and teachers for the night school, and devised the school's curriculum. She went to other prosperous, cultured Jews, and asked them to donate funds or serve as volunteer teachers. When the school opened, there were 30 students. Within days, that number doubled, tripled, and continued to multiply. New classes were formed. Not only Jews, but Christian immigrants—Irish potato-famine refugees, and Italian and Greek political exiles—came to the Szold school, which within a decade numbered 5,000 pupils.

When the United States began to impose stringent quotas on Jewish immigration, Henrietta Szold was troubled. "Where can the victims of anti-Semitic persecution find refuge, if not here in America?" she asked her father. The rabbi reminded his daughter of the ancient Passover prayer, *Hashanah haba b' Yerusholaim*—"the coming year, in Jerusalem." If a Jewish homeland could be established in Palestine, the Jews would no longer have to depend on the sufferance of other nations. But Palestine was ruled by the Turkish sultan, and only a few Jewish farm colonies existed there.

At this time, Henrietta Szold worked as a part time editor at the Jewish Publication Society in Philadelphia. To promote the society's aim to make Jewish writings accessible to English-speaking Jews, Henrietta Szold translated various works, such as a commentary on the Talmud, the four-volume *Ethics of Judaism* by M. Lazarus, and the first two volumes of Louis Ginzberg's *The Legends of the Jews.*

After her father's death, in 1902, Henrietta moved with her mother to New York City. Henrietta took advanced courses in Hebrew at the Jewish Theological Seminary. Here she fell in love with Professor Louis Ginzberg, a man 13 years her junior, and was quite heartbroken when her love was unrequited. To help her recover, her friends at the Jewish Publication Society sent her and her mother on a trip to Palestine.

Under the leadership of Theodore Herzl, the Zionist movement was forging a dream of a Jewish Utopia in Palestine, where Jews could be safe from persecution, with Hebrew as the common language and Jewish culture as the common national heritage.

Henrietta Szold's visit in 1909 was the turning point of her life. She found no "land flowing with milk and honey," but

. . . land that had been abused by generations of bad farming, that had to be carefully nursed back into fertility. . .

Hardships were numerous. Physicians and nurses were too expensive to be thought of. Swamps abounded, and mosquitoes were numerous. Is it to be wondered at that malarial fever was a common occurrence? Water was scarce, and the ideal of biologic protection never had a hearing. As a result, typhoid fever claimed too many victims. The climate differed from that of Eastern Europe whence came most of the colonists; but who was to instruct these people in a necessary change of diet?

There was no provision for caring for maternity cases, except a missionary hospital to which mothers might be admitted only if the child were to be baptised in the Christian church. Naturally, Jewish mothers could not use it . . . the infant death rate was frightful.

Most horrifying of all to Henrietta Szold were the thousands of Palestinian children blinded by trachoma, trembling with fever, phlegmatic, pitiful. Henrietta Szold experienced "a moment of conversion," in which she saw that her life's work was to be the curing of disease in Palestine.

Upon her return to the United States in 1910, Henrietta Szold became secretary of the Federation of American Zionists, working with her fellow visionaries to restore the land of Canaan to its Biblical munificence. She also conceived a plan of forming a women's Zionist organization, to send the much needed medical aid to the Jews in Palestine. During the festival of Purim, in February, 1912, she called a meeting in New York City, and presented her proposal for a national organization of Jewish women, with chapters in every town and city in the United States, with members from all social classes, rich and poor, educated and ignorant, American-born and immigrant, all united in the goal of providing care for the diseased and ill of Palestine.

The women to whom Henrietta presented her proposals had been brought up in the Jewish patriarchal tradition, in which the woman plays the role of "enabler" to her husband. Shouldn't they act as auxiliaries to some male Zionist organization, instead of trying to carry out their own projects, some of the women suggested. Henrietta reminded them of the deeds and words of Queen Esther, the heroine of the festival of Purim:

> *How can I endure to see the evil*
> *that shall come unto my people?*
> *Or how can I endure to see*
> *the destruction of my kindred?*

So the organization of Hadassah—the Hebrew name for Esther—was born, with Henrietta Szold as president. To start, Henrietta appealed to the Jewish philanthropists, Mr. and Mrs. Nathan Straus, for funds to send two Hadassah nurses to Palestine. Henrietta was confident that the nursing venture would succeed, and that other contributions would then be forthcoming. She was right. Within a year, the two Hadassah nurses had treated 5,000 cases of trachoma. With one of the doctors in Jerusalem's Straus Health Center, they trained four native Israeli women as midwives to assist in deliveries. The infant mortality rate was reduced by 50 percent. The nurses started a Big Sisters Club to train Jewish girls as nurses and midwives. The incidence of trachoma, the cause of blindness in over 60 percent of the Palestinian population, was reduced to three percent.

In 1918, Henrietta Szold became director of the education department of the Zionist Organization of America. After the war, Palestine was reopened to foreigners, and Henrietta took the lead in forming the American Zionist Medical Unit, which sent a team of 44 doctors, nurses, nutritionists, dentists, and civil and sanitary engineers, equipped with four-and-a-half tons of medical equipment to the ravaged Holy Land. The team erected a hospital in Jerusalem, and within months, established four additional medical centers in Palestine. In May 1920, Henrietta Szold went to Palestine to take charge of the medical unit herself.

When the Nazi juggernaut began its systematic extermination of the Jews in 1933, a deputation of Jewish refugees went to Palestine to tell Henrietta Szold of their plight. Thousands of Jewish children had been expelled from German schools, and the trades and professions were closed to them. Henrietta Szold was alarmed. She went to Germany to observe conditions, and met with Jewish leaders to work out a plan to save the Jewish youth. The plan was called Aliyah, Hebrew for "going up." Teenagers were to be trained in agricultural work in youth camps; then they would "go up" to start a new life on communal settlements in Palestine.

In 1934, Henrietta Szold met the first Aliyah delegation—63 girls and boys between the ages of 15 and 17—at the pier in Haifa, and settled them in the colony of Ain Harod. Here the teenagers studied Hebrew for two years, and received practical training in agriculture and other trades. Meanwhile, Henrietta Szold worked to secure passage from Germany for the families of the Aliyah youths, and raised funds to bring over additional contingents. Henrietta continued to meet every boat, and to work closely with the transported youths in their new settlements. The total of refugees transported by Henrietta Szold from Europe, where they would have faced almost certain death, came to some 100,000.

Of the many youthful immigrants rehabilitated by Henrietta Szold, perhaps one of the most poignant stories is that of a Polish boy who, because of a club foot, could not pass the rigorous physical standards of the Aliyah camps. The youth determined to come to Palestine anyway, and despite his handicap trudged on foot across Poland, Czechoslovakia, and Italy, to the port of Trieste, where he stowed away on a ship bound for Haifa. His presence was discovered at sea, and at Haifa the ship's captain turned the youngster over to the passport commissioner. The commissioner sent for

Henrietta Szold. She was deeply moved by the boy's tale of desperation, hunger, cold, and fatigue, and interceded to allow him to stay in Palestine. She arranged to have his club foot operated on at the Rothschild-Hadassah Hospital, and placed the boy in an agricultural settlement. Here he was discovered to be gifted musically, and Henrietta Szold arranged a complete musical education for her protégé. To this boy, as to thousands of other children, Henrietta Szold was *Eemah*, the Hebrew word for mother. To the thousands of children whose mothers were murdered in concentration camps, Henrietta Szold was a substitute mother.

On March 13, 1944, Boston University awarded Henrietta Szold an honorary Doctorate of Humanity. Henrietta was too ill to return to the United States to accept the degree in person, but she listened to the ceremony via an international radio hookup in Jerusalem. She died on February 13, 1945.

To Jewish settlers in Palestine, Henrietta Szold was "Mother of the Yishuv." She was a beloved figure to Moslems and Christians as well. Along with Judah Magnes, president of Hebrew University, and the philosopher, Martin Buber, Henrietta Szold worked to foster mutual understanding and tolerance between Jews and Arabs in Palestine. As Rabbi Stephen Wise declared, Henrietta Szold was "a semi-mythical figure, beyond criticism, beyond detraction, beyond blame, and because of her humility, beyond praise. She is world Jewry's Jane Addams, a transcendent spirit which touches the lowly only to lift them up."

Maggie Mitchell Walker (1867-1934)

BANK DIRECTOR, ENTREPRENEUR AND PHILANTHROPIST

Her skin was black, and she was born in a white woman's kitchen where her mother had formerly been a slave. But Maggie Mitchell grew up to become the first woman bank director in America, and one of the nation's most successful entrepreneurs.

The woman who had once "owned" Maggie Mitchell's mother was no cruel taskmaster or maternalistic Southern belle. Elizabeth Van Lew was a feminist and former Union spy who, long before the Civil War, had freed her slaves, and had given them the option of remaining at her mansion as employees with dignified titles and fair salaries. Maggie's mother had chosen to do that and worked as assistant cook. Elizabeth Van Lew took a particular interest in her cook's clever little daughter. The aging feminist made the child believe that she had been born in a kitchen that she might rise to great heights and lead other members of her race and sex out of the kitchen with her. Rise Maggie did.

Maggie's enterprise, the Saint Luke's Mutual Benefit Society, was one of the first black insurance companies in the United States. The organization was most active in helping black men and women to capitalize on the new opportunities created for Negroes in the antebellum South. Nor were black people the only beneficiaries of Maggie Walker's industry and philanthropy. Saint Luke's Bank and

190

Trust Company held the accounts of white Richmond's tax, gas, and water departments. When the Richmond public school system began to founder because white banks refused the city additional loans, it was Saint Luke's that saved the Richmond public schools with a substantial loan.

Richmond was Maggie's birthplace, and she lived in that city all her life. She was born on July 15, 1867, the offspring of a liaison between her mother and abolitionist Eccles Cuthbert. But Cuthbert went back to his family in the North, and the only father Maggie ever knew was William Mitchell, the butler of the Van Lew household, who married Maggie's mother.

Maggie was one of the first black children in the South to attend a public school, the Lancaster School for Negroes. The teachers here were white Southern women who had fought for the right of blacks to learn to read and write; these women were barred from teaching in the white schools for lack of credentials. But education credits do not necessarily create good teachers, and Maggie's teachers were certified by their enthusiasm for learning and their dedication.

One day, William Mitchell was robbed and murdered, and his family was left destitute. Maggie could remain in school only by helping her mother establish a home-laundry business. After class, Maggie would pick up and deliver the clothing, and do the family marketing.

When Maggie was about to graduate from Armstrong High School, she joined the other students in a protest against discrimination. The graduation ceremony for white students was held in a theater, rented at the expense of all the taxpayers. Black students received their diplomas in a separate ceremony which took place in a Negro church, donated without charge. The principal of the white school, to whom the students brought their grievance, offered to allow blacks to share in the commencement ceremony at the theater, provided they observed segregated seating for blacks and whites. The Armstrong students vetoed this compromise.

After her graduation, Maggie became an insurance agent. At this time, white insurance companies either refused to insure blacks or offered them limited policies at exorbitant premiums.

Fraternal orders at that time refused to consider black applicants, so the Negroes had established the Order of Saint Luke as their answer to the Masons and the Elks. Unlike the white social organizations, Saint Luke's was open to women as well as to men. Maggie had joined the order at the age of 14, and soon rose to positions of increasing responsibility within the organization.

The main business of the order, named for the patron saint of the terminally ill, was to assure care for the sick and burial of the dead. The Independent Order of Saint Luke had been founded in 1867 by a former slave, Mary Prout, to provide these services for blacks, to whom they were not available elsewhere. In 1899, Maggie Walker, whose vision, and managerial expertise had made her one of the most popular members of the order, was elected secretary-treasurer. Her male predecessor had drawn a salary of $300 a year; Maggie's salary was $100.

When Maggie Walker became secretary-treasurer, the treasury contained $31.60; dues were sadly in arrears; the books were in disarray; and there were thousands of claims of illness and death to be verified and paid. Maggie Walker recognized that it was necessary to recruit new members to fill the order's coffers; so she took a course in salesmanship to fit herself for a massive membership drive. Within one year, she doubled the order's membership. Under Maggie's continued leadership, the order grew rapidly during the next 25 years, its 57 local chapters burgeoning to 1,500; its 3,400 members increasing to over 50,000; and its treasury swelling. From a room with a single clerk in a dilapidated building, Saint Luke's grew to a staff of 50, housed in a modern four-story building.

Maggie Walker offered generous terms to Saint Luke's insurance subscribers. Depositors earning $50 a month or more were encouraged to buy their own homes with bank support. Maggie liked to tell success stories, such as the following:

There is in the office here a woman who came to us 18 years ago. She did odd jobs of cleaning, and we paid her a dollar a week, which she was glad to get. We encouraged her to fit herself for better things. She studied, took a business course at night school, and has worked her way up until now she is our head bookkeeper, with a salary of one hundred-fifty dollars a month. She owns a comfortable home, well-furnished and fully paid for, and has money in the bank.

As first president of Saint Luke's Penny Savings Bank, Maggie Walker sought out individuals such as this cleaning woman, encouraged them to get more education and better jobs, and provided them the wherewithal to do so. In 1929, Saint Luke's absorbed Richmond's other Negro banks under the name of the Consolidated Bank and Trust Company.

A gifted speaker, Maggie offered her listeners practical advice. She published the *Saint Luke Herald*, a newspaper with evangelical overtones. The commandment that she most stressed was "love thy neighbor as thyself," and she herself set a noble example in charitable endeavors. She raised money for a girls' reform school, established a Community House and visiting nurse service, and helped to found a tuberculosis sanatorium. A paraplegic from 1907 on, Maggie Walker did not let her handicap interfere with her philanthropic or business activities.

In 1925, the University of Richmond awarded Maggie Walker an honorary B.S., and in the city of her birth an integrated high school, a theater and a street are named for her.

Former governor of Virginia, E. Lee Trinkle, paid Maggie this tribute in 1924: "If the state of Virginia had done no more in 50 years with its funds spent on . . . education . . . than educate Mrs. Walker, the state would have been amply repaid for its outlay and efforts."

Marie Sklodovska Curie
(1867-1934)

DISCOVERER OF RADIUM

An abandoned shed on the Rue Llhomond, Paris. A few poor rotting boards thrown together; no floor save a splattering of bitumen; no roof save a precarious skylight. Through cracks in the skylight rain falls on the worn worktables and rusts the pipe of the old cast-iron stove. In this shack behind the School of Physics of the University of Paris, in a former dissecting room condemned by the Department of Medicine as unfit to house cadavers, a man bends over a delicate scientific apparatus. In the courtyard of the flimsy hovel, a woman, wielding an iron rod as large as herself and a good deal heavier, plunges the instrument into a large basin brimming with a volatile liquid. For years they go on thus: the man working in the shack, an inferno in summer, in winter an arctic zone; the woman outside, engrossed in her herculean labors, laying aside the iron rod only to pour the boiling pitchblende from the basin into jars and to drag the jars into the shed. At last, all the jars are full, and the woman joins the man at the worktables, purifying the smelted pitchblende and subjecting it to a process known as fractional crystallization.

One day the man looks up from his apparatus and sighs. "Marie," he addresses the woman.

"Yes, Pierre?" The woman does not remove her gaze from the kilogram of pitchblende she is treating.

"Manyusya," Pierre begins again, using the Polish diminutive of his wife's name.

Marie smiles tenderly, remembering how in the days of their courtship Pierre had stolen precious hours from his research in electricity to learn her native tongue. She opens her mouth to encourage Pierre to go on, but before she can speak, a gust of wind blows a shower of coal dust into the makeshift laboratory, contaminating the pitchblende that Marie Curie had spent weeks in purifying.

"That does it!" explodes Pierre Curie. "Marie, let's quit this—oh, I don't mean forever," he adds hastily, as his wife stares at him in speechless alarm. "But until we are given a proper laboratory, and can pursue our experiments without all this wasted labor. Radioactive research is not the only valuable work to be done in physics. And we've already uncovered radium and plutonium; we have accomplished the main thing." He looks at his wife beseechingly.

Marie's face is inscrutable as she weighs out a fresh kilogram of pitchblende. "We have not accomplished the main thing, Pierre," she says gently. "The main thing is to isolate radium, to study it, and to discover what it is good for—how it can help people. I will not give up this research until that is done."

Pierre stifles a sigh. He is not as sanguine as his wife that the mysterious element they had called radium would prove beneficial to mankind. And he cares less than Marie; Pierre is a pure scientist who lives for discovery and leaves practical applications to others. But Marie Sklodovska Curie is a passionate humanitarian. She can justify her renunciation of her goal of returning to occupied Poland to work to free her homeland from Russian oppression only if she accomplishes some great work for humanity.

After their day's work in the laboratory was done, the Curies returned to their tiny apartment on the Rue de Glacière. Pierre, his rheumatic legs riddled with pain, collapsed on the sofa. Marie took baby Irene from the arms of her father-in-law, who lived with the Curies and babysat for the child while her parents worked at their lab. Marie changed Irene's diapers as the stew she had thrown together simmered on the stove. After dinner, there were dishes to be washed, and there was the modicum of housework that Marie forced herself to do each evening, insisting that Pierre conserve his strength for the next day's work. They both had lesson plans to prepare, Pierre for his advanced students at the School of Physics, Marie for the young women at the Ecole Normale Superieure at Sevres. Just before retiring for the night, Marie Curie reviewed the calculations she had made earlier in the day at the shed on Rue Llhomond. Watching her, Pierre realized that his invincible wife would let nothing interfere with her search for pure radium. And he vowed never again to desist from their joint labors or to attempt to dissuade Marie from the task.

The Curies' perseverance proved fruitful. In 1902, after four years of travail, they succeeded in preparing a decigram of radium and determining its atomic weight. In 1903, Marie and Pierre Curie were awarded the Nobel Prize in physics for this achievement. Marie would go on to discover many medical uses for radium, and, after Pierre's death, would receive a second Nobel Prize, in chemistry, making her the first individual to win two of the coveted awards.

But even with this distinction, and despite the fact that she saved countless lives by her discovery that radium would kill cancerous cells, and laid the groundwork for modern nuclear physics, Marie Curie more often than not found herself a prophet without honor in her adopted country of France.

Manya (Marie) Sklodovska was the daughter of Polish patriots of noble blood. Manya's father was a professor of physics at the University of Warsaw. Her mother, an extremely well-educated woman, ran a private high school for aristocratic young ladies in the early years of her marriage. But by the time Manya was born, on November 7, 1867, Mrs. Sklodovska was already dying of tuberculosis. She managed to conceal her illness from her five children, and it was not until later that Manya was to understand why her mother refused to kiss her and never held her close.

The Sklodovskis cherished no great aspirations for their youngest child. In fact, they showed more consternation than pleasure when four-year-old Manya demonstrated that she could read, and the little girl feared that she would never be forgiven. Whenever the infant prodigy reached for books, her parents would distract her by putting a doll or a block into her outstretched hand. To no avail, however; by the time she was eight, Manyusya was an avid and catholic reader.

Manya's childhood was shadowed by a series of tragedies. In 1873, Professor Sklodovski was demoted to a high school teacher at half salary because Russian officials discovered that he had been teaching his university students their native language, Polish, on the sly. Young Manya herself learned Polish history clandestinely at her boarding school, and was subjected to interrogation by visiting czarist inspectors. Then Manya's eldest sister, Zosia, died of typhus. Barely two years later, when Manya was ten, her mother succumbed to tuberculosis. Shortly before her death, Mme. Sklodovska had learned the trade of cobbling, and repaired the family's old worn-out shoes since they could not afford to buy new ones.

Life went on: Joseph, the elder brother, entered medical school at the University of Warsaw; his sister Bronya, who also longed to become a doctor, abandoned this goal for the time being and took over the housekeeping; and little Manya helped her father by polishing the scientific apparatus in his modest laboratory after coming home from her classes at the Gymnasium. Like her older siblings, Manya was the valedictorian of her high school class. But there was no question of college. The University of Warsaw did not admit women, and besides, Manya had to earn a livelihood. She worked as a private tutor, but managed to continue her studies under the auspices of the "floating University," an underground organization of Polish patriots, who gave classes on sociology, anatomy, and other subjects proscribed by the official curriculum. The floating University combined socialist with scholarly aims, and Manya, in turn, gave academic lessons to dressmakers and other working women. She was amazed at how quickly some of these humble women learned—often much more quickly than her rich and rather spoiled private students. Years later, Marie Curie was to put her awareness that ignorance is not synonymous with stupidity to good use when she was to train French working women to operate X-ray machines and other radiological equipment, thus saving thousands of lives in war-torn France.

In 1885, Manya Sklodovska abandoned private tutoring in favor of the more remunerative profession of governessing. She had a secret ambition—to earn enough money to send her sister Bronya to medical school in Paris. Manya's first post as a governess was a nightmare, but a year later she went to live with the cultivated "Z" family on their estate near Sczuki where she gave lessons to ten-year-old Andzia, and her older sister, Bronka. Manya and Bronka started a school for the local peasant children and taught them for two hours every day.

Casimir, Andzia and Bronka's older brother, fell in love with the brilliant young governess. Manya reciprocated Casimir's affection, and the young man joyously announced their engagement to his parents. "One does not marry a governess," he was told, and that was the end of the engagement. Humiliated, disillusioned, and broken-hearted, Manya swallowed her pride and remained with the Z. family in order to continue to provide Bronya with fifteen rubles a month for her medical studies in Paris. She was sustained by Bronya's letters, promising that once she obtained work as a doctor she would send for Manya and, in turn, finance Manya's education. Manya longed to join her sister in Paris to study mathematics and physics, so that she might return to Poland to teach high school like her father. Meanwhile, she studied independently as best she could, borrowing science textbooks from the library at the Z. factory.

When Bronya married a practicing doctor, a Polish exile, she made good her promise to send for her little sister. In 1891, Manya Sklodovska went to live with her sister and brother-in-law in a suburb of Paris, and enrolled at the Sorbonne. For two years, she devoted herself to improving her French and preparing for her master's in mathematics. Manya enjoyed living with Bronya and Casimir, whose family life was enlivened by visits from other Polish exiles, including a young virtuoso pianist named Ignace Paderewski. But Manya found the long commute to Paris inconvenient and expensive, and in 1892 rented a garret for herself in the Latin Quarter on the Left Bank of Paris. She concentrated on her studies and had neither time nor inclination for cooking and became anemic and malnourished. But in 1893 she placed first in the mathematics exam. Manya wanted to earn a second degree in physics, and through her friend, Mlle. Dydenska, secured the "Alexandrovitch Scholarship" earmarked for young Poles who wished to study abroad.

When Manya began her studies in physics, she discovered that she would need a large laboratory for her apparatus. She consulted a young Polish professor, who suggested that Pierre Curie, of the Faculty of Physics and Chemistry on Rue Llhomond, might have an extra workroom. Pierre Curie was approached, conceded the workroom to Manya with celerity, and shortly afterwards proposed marriage.

After the mortifying episode with Casimir Z., Manya had vowed never to marry. Moreover, Pierre Curie was a Frenchman, and Manya could not imagine making a permanent home in Paris when there was a desperate need for native high school teachers in Poland. Pierre Curie admired his high-minded friend's patriotism, but he tried to dissuade her: political gains were evanescent, scientific gains eternal; she could accomplish more social good working for Science with Pierre at the Rue Llhomond. Or, if Manya insisted upon returning to her homeland, Pierre offered to go with her and teach French until he could afford to resume his scientific research.

Manya Sklodovska refused to accept Pierre Curie's sacrifice, but she could not refuse his love. In 1895, a year after obtaining her master's in physics, Manya Sklodovska became Marie Curie. Her wedding dress, a present from Bronya's mother-in-law, was, at Marie's insistence, a dark suit that could double as a laboratory uniform.

After a brief honeymoon on the Ile-de-France, the Curies set up house on the Rue de Glacière. They refused an offer of furniture from Pierre's father; neither of them would have time to dust it. Marie did learn to cook, and found time to attend to Pierre's wardrobe and keep their financial accounts, in addition to spending eight hours daily in the laboratory.

Pierre Curie was eight years older than his wife, and already a well-known physicist at the time of their marriage. Like Marie, Pierre was from a scientific family—his father was a doctor and medical researcher—but the ease of Pierre's upbringing contrasted sharply with the hardships of Marie's. From birth, Pierre and his brother, Jacques, had been destined for scientific careers. A dreamy, temperamental child, Pierre had not gone to school but had received private instruction from his father. At 16, Pierre obtained his B.S. degree; at 18, his master's in physics. Pierre and Jacques had conducted joint experiments in crystalline physics, and had devised a new electrological technique that had brought them renown. After his marriage to Marie, Pierre continued his research on electricity as well as his teaching at the School of Physics.

Although Marie Curie did not actively begin her research on radium until 1897, she had been interested in the phenomenon she was to denominate "radioactivity" ever since 1895 when she read some articles by Antoine Henri Becquerel. Becquerel had determined that uranium and its compounds emitted mysterious rays, similar to those produced by X-rays; but unlike X-rays, the uranium rays were released without exposure to light. Marie Curie longed to determine the source and nature of the spontaneously produced uranium rays, but could not yet fully devote herself to this task. She earned a master's degree in secondary education in order to qualify as a teacher at the École Normale Supérieure, placing first on the examination. Then she became pregnant. After giving birth to a daughter, Irène Joliot-Curie, who was herself to become a Nobel Prize-winning physicist, Marie took up the study of uranium rays.

When Marie Curie made the important discovery that minerals other than uranium compounds were radioactive, she immediately posited the existence of a new element, which she called radium. But she needed assistance in carrying out the laborious experiments required to isolate the new element. In 1898, Pierre Curie abandoned his own research on electricity, and thus began one of the most productive scientific collaborations in history.

The Curies devoted themselves to verifying the existence of radium and determining its therapeutic properties. The first years of their research were hampered by poverty, illness, lack of cooperation from the French authorities, attacks on Marie by the xenophobic French press, and inadequate equipment and facilities. But in 1903, the year that Marie Curie was awarded her doctorate, the couple shared the Nobel Prize in physics with Antoine Becquerel, and achieved international celebrity. At this point, Pierre posed a delicate question to Marie: they could now patent their discovery, thereby assuring themselves a personal fortune that would guarantee their continued research under ideal conditions, or they could forego the patent and immediately divulge their secrets to American technicians who wanted to use the information to treat disease. Marie Curie did not hesitate for a moment—the scientific spirit required that the Curies forego the patent. Pierre agreed. They had no desire for wealth for its own sake, and the 70,000 francs that they were to receive from the Nobel Institute would free them for their research. It would allow Pierre to leave off teaching at the School of Physics, and pay for servants and a governess for Irène and for the baby Marie was expecting later that year. Indeed, the Curies used a healthy portion of their prize money to subsidize needy friends and struggling students, and allowed themselves only one private luxury: the installation of a modern bathroom in their little house on the Boulevard Kellerman.

Far from seeking personal glory, the Curies resented the intrusions of the press and curiosity-seekers. Public acclaim did little to substantially improve their relations with the French authorities. Pierre was appointed to a chair at the Sorbonne, but his request for a new laboratory was granted only after prolonged dickering, and his request for a laboratory assistant was flatly denied. The Curies hired the assistant at their own expense. In 1904, after a difficult pregnancy, Marie Curie gave birth to another daughter, Eve. Eve Curie was later to write a moving biography of her mother, *Madame Curie.*

In 1906, Pierre Curie was run over by a horse-drawn wagon, and died of a crushed skull. Marie Curie received the news impassively, suffering "the grief that does not speak, but whispers the o'erfraught heart and bids it break." Rousing herself from despondency, she continued her research on radium, working courageously, despite fresh insults hurled at her as a foreigner and a woman by the French press. As no one else was capable of continuing Pierre Curie's lectures at the Sorbonne, his widow became the first woman to teach at the University of Paris.

Shouldering the necessary increased responsibilities, and ignoring the appearance of the first symptoms of radiation sickness, Marie Curie persevered in her radium research. She discovered that the luminous substance that she and Pierre had originally identified as radium was merely a radium salt, and performed the difficult operation that succeeded in isolating the lethal metal itself. She also devised an innovative technique to weigh radioactive substances that proved immensely valuable later to nuclear scientists, and produced the first international standard of radium.

From 1909 to 1914, Marie Curie supervised the construction of the Institute of Radium, co-financed by the Sorbonne and the Pasteur Institute after an ugly political skirmish between the two institutions was resolved. When war came, Marie Curie invented an X-ray apparatus to be attached to ambulances known as "little Curies." Marie Curie herself drove one of the "little Curies" for the duration of the war, as well as training 150 French recruits, drawn from all socio-economic classes, as radiological technicians.

The French government never conferred on Marie Curie the slightest decoration for her heroic war work, which she managed to conduct simultaneously with her research at the Radium Institute. Moreover, in 1911, the year that Marie Curie received her second Nobel Prize, the French Academy of Sciences refused to admit the "foreign woman" to its membership. While her name was before the Academy, Dr. Curie was the victim of a vicious slander campaign, and was harrassed by anonymous letters and phone calls which drove her to the verge of a nervous breakdown. In 1920, Marie Curie's adopted country offered her a final insult when it refused to purchase a second gram of radium (she herself had donated the first gram to her laboratory) for her research—this, after Marie Curie had donated her entire second Nobel Prize award of 200,000 francs to the French government during World War I. But a committee of American women generously came to Dr. Curie's rescue, procuring for her not one, but two, grams of the precious radium.

To radium Marie Curie devoted her life, and from radium she received her death. On July 4, 1934, Dr. Curie expired, a victim of leukemia brought on by excessive exposure to radioactive materials. Her coffin was buried on top of her husband's, at the cemetery in Sceaux, France.

Marie Curie's life was a drama of inspirational bravery in the face of perpetual hardship. To be sure, there had been the sustaining satisfaction of laboring with her husband on important research; and there were occasioned lighter moments when the couple were entertained at their home by dancer Loie Fuller, or went to visit their sculptor friend, Auguste Rodin. But Pierre Curie's premature death permanently darkened the life of his widow. Refusing a widow's pension that would have eased her financial burdens, Marie Curie continued to earn a living by teaching, and persevered in her pioneer research into the nature of radioactivity. Although several other scientists—Rontgen, Becquerel, Poincaré and Pierre Curie—contributed to our knowledge of radioactivity, it is Marie Curie who stands out as the individual who expedited the use of radium to combat disease.

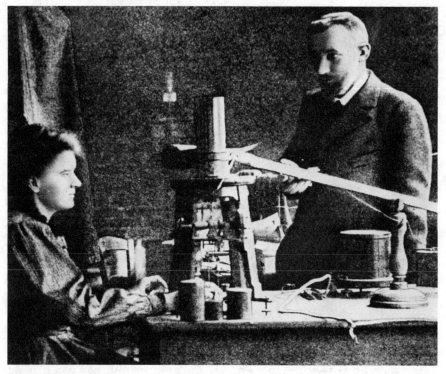

The Curies in their lab.

Constance Gore-Booth Markiewicz

(1868-1927)

IRISH PATRIOT AND POLITICIAN

Whither the Irish nationalists went, Con Markiewicz went with them, from the picket lines, to the soup kitchens, to the battlements. Wherever her fellow patriots lodged, she lodged, in the slums of Dublin and in the prisons of Mountjoy, Aylesbury, Holloway, and Cork. Ireland's people were her people; Ireland's gods were her gods.

Baptised a Protestant, Con Markiewicz converted to the Roman Catholic faith in 1917. She steeped herself in Gaelic mythology, and was an actress and nationalist playwright for the Abbey Theater, as well as founder of the Republican Players Dramatic Society.

The daughter of an Anglo-Irish baronet and an English gentlewoman, and the wife of a Polish count, Constance Gore-Booth Markiewicz renounced family and fortune to join the Sinn Fein revolutionaries and the Daughters of Ireland. She founded the Fianna Boy Scouts, where cadets were trained for the Irish Volunteer Army. She was a leader of the Irish workers' strike of 1913, second in command in the Easter Rebellion of 1916, and the first woman elected to the British Parliament. As Ireland's secretary of labor, Con was also the first woman cabinet minister in Europe.

Never did the banshees howl so mournfully as when Con Markiewicz lay dying in the public ward of a Dublin hospital. The Irish Joan of Arc was given a state funeral, with Irish President

Eamon De Valera presiding. Never did Ireland have a more devoted daughter than Con Markiewicz, the Bride of Ireland.

Constance Gore-Booth was born on February 4, 1868, at the elegant townhouse of her mother's family at No. 7, Buckingham Gate, London. She grew up on her grandfather's estate, Lissadell, in the western coastal county of Sligo, Ireland. When Constance was eight, her father became the fifth baronet of Lissadell, and followed his father's example as a humane landlord. During the potato famine of 1878-80, Sir Henry Gore-Booth, his wife, and their children personally distributed food and clothing to the tenants on their estate.

"Miss Con" was well-liked by her father's tenants, for there was nothing condescending in her visits to their cottages. When she found the pregnant wife of one of the grooms bent with exhaustion over a wash tub, Constance gently lifted the woman into a chair, and finished the washing herself. When a tenant was ill, Constance would sit up all night nursing the patient back to health.

Constance's father was often absent on polar explorations in his private yacht, and the girl was largely raised by women—her mother; her maternal grandmother, Lady Hill; and her father's sister, Aunt Augusta. All three were strong, authoritative women who could ride a horse or shoot a gun as well as any man. From the age of five, Constance, too, learned to ride and shoot. By the time she was 14, Constance Gore-Booth was acknowledged to be the best rider County Sligo had ever seen.

Constance, her two sisters, and her brother were all educated at home. There were lessons in drawing, music, and literature, but never any discussion of politics or Irish history. Later, Constance wrote:

No one was interested in politics in our house. It was rare that anyone mentioned them. Everyone accepted the status quo, almost as if it had been the will of God. . . . It was unlucky that landlords had been so bad, for if only they had done what they ought, everything would have been all right now. . . . Irish history was also taboo, for "what is the good of brooding over past grievances?". . . .

When she was 18, Constance Gore-Booth made her formal entrance into Dublin and London society. In 1887, she was presented to Queen Victoria, at Buckingham Palace. Then it was back to Sligo for a constant whirl of parties, hunts, balls, shopping, visiting, and amateur theatricals. Bored with the life of a dilettante, she begged her parents to let her study painting in Paris, but in vain. She had to content herself with drawing courses .

Frustrated by the powerlessness of women, she joined her sisters, Eva and Mabel, in founding the Sligo Woman's Suffrage Society, and was elected president. In her maiden speech to the society, Constance sounded the themes she was later to develop as a firebrand of the Irish Rebellion:

Now in order to attain to any Political Reform, you know that the first step is to form societies to agitate and force the government to realize that a very large class have a grievance, and will never stop making themselves disagreeable till it is righted. John Stuart Mill said thirty years ago that the only forcible argument against giving women the suffrage was "that they did not demand it with sufficient force and noise." Silence is an evil that might easily be remedied, and the sooner we begin to make a row the better.

In 1898, her parents at last consented to let her study art in Paris, and she enrolled at the Atélier Julien. In Paris, Constance met Count Casimir Dunin-Markiewicz, a Polish widower who had renounced a prosperous law practice to become an artist and playwright. The two aristocratic bohemians were married on September 29, 1900.

Constance and Casimir and his son lived briefly on the bride's family estate at Lissadell, where Constance's only child, Maeve, was born in November, 1901. Then the Count and Countess de Markiewicz went to Dublin, where they held several joint exhibits of their paintings. The count also founded an acting company to put on his plays, and Constance became a leading actress in her husband's troupe.

The Markiewiczes were prominent members of Dublin high society. One night, as Constance and Casimir were on their way to a ball at Dublin Castle, their coach was stopped by a little girl in tattered clothing. She had been instructed by her mother, who was stationed on the sidewalk nearby, to run up to the fine carriage to beg for alms. The child reached out toward the window of the brougham, but, overwhelmed by the diamonds that glittered at Constance's throat and ears, forgot to make her plea and merely stared. The

Markiewicz coach rolled on, and as Constance glanced back, she saw the little beggar wince with pain as her irate mother slapped her hard across the face. It was as if that slap had landed on Constance's face, for she "saw the hollowness of all that Castle business, and I wanted to do something for the people."

Constance Markiewicz began her career as an Irish patriot by joining the Inghinidhe na hEireann, or Daughters of Ireland, a feminist nationalist organization established by the noted activist Maud Gonne in 1900 to promote Irish economic, political, and cultural independence. Later, when Con Markiewicz became president of the Daughters of Ireland, she made rousing appeals for action, such as this:

. . . go out in the world and get elected on to as many public bodies as possible. By degrees through your exertions no public institution—whether hospital, workhouse, asylum or any other—and no private house but will be supporting the industries of your country. . . . Regard yourselves as Irish, believe in yourselves as Irish. Arm yourselves with weapons to fight your nation's cause. Arm your souls with noble and free ideas. Arm your minds with the histories and memories of your country and her martyrs, her language, and a knowledge of her arts, and her industries. And if in your day the call should come for your body to arm, do not shirk that either.

Con Markiewicz made equally rousing speeches when she went to Manchester, England, in 1908 to work with her sister Eva in a campaign to elect William Joynson-Hicks. The primary issue in the election was a bill to prevent women from working as bar maids, one of the few jobs open to unskilled, uneducated women. Joynson-Hicks opposed this bill and won the support of the Markiewicz sisters. As the countess drove her electioneering wagon through the streets of Manchester, she was taunted by hostile men who supported the opposing candidate, Winston Churchill.

"Hey, there, lady, can you cook a dinner?" one of the hecklers called out.

"Yes, I can," retorted Countess Markiewicz. "And you—can you drive a coach-and-four?"

Madame, as Con Markiewicz was commonly called, won the hearts of the Manchester voters—and cost Winston Churchill the election.

Con Markiewicz now devoted herself fully to the cause that had the greatest priority for her: "A free Ireland with no sex disabilities in her Constitution." She felt that the key to Irish independence lay in the formation of a strong youth movement, well-trained in the martial arts. To this end, she founded the Fianna na hEireann in 1909. The Fianna, a militant scout organization comprised mainly of boys, conducted military drills, studied the Gaelic language and Irish history, and promulgated the ideal of a free Irish republic. Having been exposed to the sexism that permeated the Sinn Fein and other Irish nationalist organizations, Constance was determined that the Fianna should be headed by females who would change the Irish male concept of women. She recruited her friend, Helena Molony to her cause. They took care to emphasize the role of great women in Irish history in the Fianna meetings; and they personally instructed the members in shooting and in the care of guns.

The center for Fianna operations was Surrey House, Madame's seditious salon in Dublin, where patriots, labor leaders, and visiting journalists were also welcome. A printing press at Surrey House churned out leaflets and brochures, which were distributed to every house in Dublin by the Fianna boys. The press also turned out posters which Madame and her scouts affixed to buildings, standing on their bicycle seats so the bills would be out of the reach of the Dublin police, who tore down the revolutionary posters at every opportunity.

Con Markiewicz was arrested for the first time in 1911, when she stood up to speak at a public meeting and was grabbed by police, who then charged her with resisting arrest. After she was released, she continued her insurrectionary activities. In 1912, Con Markiewicz participated in the first mass meeting of Irish suffragettes in Dublin. She supported Helena Molony in her efforts to form an Irish Women Workers Union. In 1913, when Dublin laborers went on strike for several months, Madame opened a soup kitchen and clothing shop at Union headquarters in Liberty Hall. One of the kitchen workers remembers especially her compassion:

The children ever the hungriest and the most eager, used to file past with mugs, tin cans, porringers, old jam crocks, which she filled, and with a jolly word for all, for Madame had a personal contact and real sympathy with the poor that removed all taint of the Lady Bountiful and made her a comrade among comrades. One day a youngster came along, a boy of about ten, with his little soup-can, only to be recognized and pushed aside scornfully by the others with a taunt, "Go away, your father is a scab." Madame, seeing the hurt look in the child's face and the quick withdrawal, called him back. "No child is going to be called a scab. He can't help his father. When he grows up he'll be all right himself, won't you sonny? And now have some soup."

The Great Strike of 1913 was a failure, and starving workers gradually drifted back to work at the old rates—14 shillings for 70 hours a week for men, and five shillings for 90 hours a week for women. Police brutality during the strike confirmed Con Markiewicz' conviction about the need for militant action. She joined the Citizen Army organized by union leader, James Connolly. As a member of the Women's Franchise League, Madame urged women to:

Dress suitably in short skirts and strong boots, leave your jewels in the bank and buy a revolver. Don't trust to your "feminine charm" and your capacity for getting on the soft side of men, but take up your responsibilities and be prepared to go on your own way depending for safety on your own courage, your own truth, and your own common sense, and not on the problematic chivalry of the men you may meet on the way. The two brilliant classes of women who follow this higher ideal are suffragettes and the Trades Union or Labour women. In them lies the hope of the future.

As a lieutenant in the Citizen Army, Madame participated in the planning sessions for the armed rebellion that occurred on Easter Monday, April 24, 1916. Madame took charge of an outpost at Stephens Green, commanding 123 men and 15 women. For six days, the Irish rebels withstood the onslaughts of the considerably larger and better-equipped British forces; then they were defeated. The leaders of the uprising, among them Constance Markiewicz, were court-martialed. Fifteen of the rebels were executed; Madame's life was spared because she was a woman, but she was sentenced to life imprisonment.

She spent the next year in various Irish prisons, but was released in 1917 under a general amnesty. Continuing her activism, she became one of four women elected to the 24-member executive board of Sinn Fein, but in April, 1918 was arrested again on charges of seditious activity. Not to be deterred by iron bars, Madame ran as a nationalist candidate in the December parliamentary elections from Holloway prison, and won her district by a large majority. She thus became the first woman ever to be elected to the British Parliament. When she was released from prison on March 10, 1919, Madame joined the other Irish parliamentarians, refusing to take their seats in the House of Commons, and forming instead their own Parliament, the Dail, in Dublin. Madame was chosen by President Eamon de Valera as his minister of labor. She was twice imprisoned by the British during her ministry, in conjunction with the Black-and-Tan terror, and was finally released as a result of the truce between the British government and the Irish Free State, on July 24, 1921.

Con Markiewicz's next imprisonment, in 1924, was startling, for this time her jailers were not the British but her own colleagues in the de Valera government. She had actively opposed the establishment of a compromise Irish Free State, which swore fealty to the king of England, and urged her fellow members of the Dail not to sign the treaty but to hold out for the Free Irish Republic long dreamed-of by the Sinn Feiners. But the treaty was signed.

Nevertheless, Con continued to organize and agitate, to write plays and work with the Abbey Theater. During Dublin's fuel shortage of 1926-27, the 59-year-old Countess personally carried large sacks of coal up the staircases of Dublin tenements to the shivering poor. In 1926, she presided at the formation of a new party, the Fianna Fail, and was one of 44 of the party's candidates elected to the Dail.

But Madame had lost her youthful vigor. In early July, she entered Sir Patrick Dun's hospital in Dublin. On July 15, 1927, as throngs of Irish citizens stood in the corridor outside her ward, praying for Madame's recovery, she gave up the ghost.

Con Markiewicz was given a huge Irish funeral. The procession included the highest dignitaries of both Church and State, as well as representatives of the various youth, feminist, labor, and nationalist organizations she had headed in her lifetime. The streets were lined with "old veterans of the Citizen Army, poorly clad, hungry, worn. Mothers from the slums crowded together, silent, fiercely sad." Among the eulogizers was Nora Connolly, the wife of the labor leader, who celebrated Madame as follows:

Her gaiety, her friendliness, her courage, her generosity, her love of the people which had grown out of her understanding of their problems, and amazed appreciation of their powers of endurance. It was a love which was returned a thousandfold while she lived, and lined the streets through which her funeral passed with sorrowing hearts. She was a great woman of great heart.

Maria Montessori
(1870-1952)

EDUCATOR AND PHYSICIAN

When I was at school we had a teacher whose fixed idea was to make us learn by heart the lives of famous women, in order to incite us to imitate them. The exhortation which accompanied these narrations was always the same: "You too should try to become famous. Would you not like to become famous?" "Oh no," I replied drily, one day, "I shall never be that. I care too much for the children of the future, to add yet another biography to the list."

When Maria Montessori shared the above anecdote with her disciple, E. M. Standing, she may already have known that her name added to the list, far from burdening "the children of the future," served to free them. But even before she developed the principles that were to have worldwide repercussions in education and child psychology, Maria Montessori was renowned as Italy's first woman physician. She had also gained a reputation as a miracle-worker with mentally retarded children.

Maria Montessori was born in the province of Ancona, Italy, on August 31, 1870. Maria's father was a government accountant.

Maria's mother, an aristocrat, was unusually well-educated for a woman of the period, and her constant absorption in books set a studious example for her daughter. Renilde Montesorri, a firm disciplinarian and believer in charity, set little Maria to do a daily quota of knitting for her less fortunate neighbors.

When Maria was five, the family moved to Rome, and Maria attended local schools, where, in first grade she received an award for good behavior, and in second grade an award for excellence in "women's work"—sewing and fancy needlework. Although uncompetitive by nature, Maria found that learning came easily, and concluded "that it would be nonsense" not to obtain academic honors.

Even as a child, Maria had a strong sense of purpose. During a bout of serious illness when she was ten, Maria assured her anxious mother, "Do not worry, Mother, I cannot die; I have too much to do."

At the age of 12, Maria announced to her parents that she wished to attend technical school to become an engineer. She had been exposed early to mathematics, and had always excelled in the subject. Maria's choice of vocation was logical, but unfeminine, and her parents urged her to become a teacher instead. "Never!" Maria replied. "Anything but teaching!" Had she found it necessary to maintain this negative resolve, the world might have lost one of its best educational innovators.

Renilde Montessori listened sympathetically to her brilliant daughter's strivings for the future, and then took up the cudgels for Maria with her disgruntled husband, who couldn't see that a girl needed any career beyond that of wife and mother. In 1883, Maria Montessori entered the Michelangelo Buonarroti Technical School. She was 13, and the only girl in the student body.

In 1889, after completing her technical studies, Maria informed her parents that she no longer aspired to an engineering career. Her father was overjoyed—until Maria explained that she now wished to become a doctor. The opposition to this goal surpassed the objections to engineering, but the determined Maria Montessori did become a doctor, in spite of almost insuperable obstacles. Her fellow students at the University of Rome barely tolerated her presence.

Nevertheless, unimpeded by her status as a social pariah, Maria completed her subjects with high marks, and then applied for the M.D. program. She was told her ambition was unthinkable—the University of Rome Medical School had never accepted a woman student; it never could; it never would; it never should. Maria was not to be dissuaded. When her appeals to medical authorities fell on deaf ears, Maria turned to the most powerful man in Rome—Pope Leo XIII. From the Holy See she obtained the statement that "the best profession a woman could enter was medicine." Thus, in 1893, Maria Montessori became the first woman medical student in Italy.

To the pre-med students, Maria had been a joke; to the medical students, she was a threat. Maria's distinguished marks procured her the most coveted prizes and scholarships—and incurred the jealousy of her male colleagues. She met the bursts of taunts with good-humored determination. "Blow away, my friends," she called to her detractors, "the harder you blow, the higher I shall go."

Laboratory work was usually performed by student teams, but it was considered unseemly that a woman should dissect naked corpses in the company of men, so at night, when the other students had gone home to their families, Maria performed her lone dissections in the deserted, dimly-lit laboratory.

Maria's father had disowned her for making him a laughing-stock among his friends, so she supplemented her scholarship income by tutoring. Her mother helped her daughter cram for her exams, since Maria's fellow students were unwilling to study with her.

In her final year of medical school, following the tradition of the time, Maria delivered a public lecture to the medical faculty. There was a large turn-out for her address, which was electrifying, and the spectators, who had come to jeer, stayed to deliver a resounding ovation. In the audience was Maria's estranged father, who had been dragged, unwillingly to the presentation. Amid the congratulations, a rapprochement between father and daughter occurred.

Maria Montessori obtained her medical diploma in 1896. Her experiences in the male-dominated world had made her sensitive to the injustices leveled at her sex. As the Italian delegate to a feminist congress in Berlin, she made a speech on behalf of women laborers that earned her plaudits in the international press. A later speech, in London, on child-labor practices in Sicily was equally impressive.

For ten years, Maria Montessori practiced medicine in Rome. She took on many poor patients without charge, and managed to support herself by lecturing on biological anthropology at the University of Rome. In 1897, she joined the staff of the psychiatric clinic of the university as an unpaid assistant. Her responsibilities included touring the city's insane asylums, which at that time housed not only the mentally unbalanced, but mentally-retarded children as well. Maria was disturbed that so-called idiot children, were mixed in with psychotic adults. Watching a group of retarded children scrambling under the table for crumbs after lunch one day, Maria realized that the youngsters were not hungry, but bored. Without toys or learning materials, they had themselves made a game out of foraging for crumbs. Gradually, Montessori became convinced that retarded children were capable of learning, given the opportunity.

Maria Montessori became engrossed with the theories of French doctors Jean Itard and Edouard Seguin about the educability of mentally-defective children. She continued her field work with subnormal children at the Italian insane asylums, and published articles and gave lectures on the subject .

In 1898, the founders of the Orthophrenic School for the education of retarded and slow-learning children in Rome asked Maria Montessori to serve as director. The methods she devised for teaching mentally-retarded children to read and write were inordinately successful. Maria's pupils learned so well that they were able to pass the national examinations designed for normal children of their age group. Maria Montessori was acclaimed in the press as a miracle-worker. "While everyone was admiring my idiots, I was searching for the reasons which could keep back the healthy and happy children of the ordinary schools on so low a plane that they could be equalled in tests of intelligence by my unfortunate pupils."

In 1901, Maria Montessori became pregnant and retired to the country to bear her child in secret. Had her status as an unwed mother become known, Montessori's credibility as a doctor and an educator would have been destroyed. Maria left her newborn son in the country to be brought up privately, and only visited him secretly. Later, Mario Montessori joined his mother in her educational programs and continued his mother's work after her death.

When Maria Montessori assumed the directorship of the Casa dei Bambini, or Children's Home, in the disreputable San Lorenzo quarter of the Italian capital, her medical colleagues criticized her for lowering the prestige of the medical profession. Doctors should practice medicine, not childcare, they argued. But Montessori saw the Children's Home as an opportunity for experimentation. She was eager to test her hunch that the educational methods she had used so successfully with subnormal children would be equally effective with ordinary children.

In the one-room school that authorities had designated as the learning-quarters of the "little vandals," Maria faced her charges: "Sixty tearful, frightened children, so shy that it was impossible to get them to speak; their faces were expressionless . . . poor abandoned children who had grown up in dark tumble-down cottages, without anything to stimulate their minds—dejected, uncared for."

The children ranged from three to six years in age. At first, Dr. Montessori and her assistant simply sat back and observed the behavior of their charges when left to their own devices. They found that the children showed a spontaneous interest in learning; that they preferred work to play, order to disorder, and the reward of accomplishment to artificial prizes. The children, Montessori concluded, required teachers, not to show them how to do things, but to create opportunities for them to learn by doing for themselves. Montessori gradually evolved a system whereby the teacher provides learning materials in the form of sequenced games and exercises—for example, three-dimensional geometric shapes, paper letters of the alphabet, zippers and snaps—through which children may progress in developing sensory and motor skills and abstract concepts. Children were to exercise their own initiative in manipulating the materials to master the tasks themselves. Under the Montessori method, children were encouraged to proceed at their own pace, and to follow their creative bents rather than slavishly imitating the teacher.

Soon, visitors were coming from all over the world to observe Maria Montessori's phenomenal results. Her charges, none over six years of age, could read, write, and count; moreover, they showed more sustained concentration than had been thought possible for children so young, and had achieved a happy balance between taking initiative and submitting obediently to directives.

Montessori was besieged by requests from teachers all over the world for training in her teaching methods. Montessori schools sprang up throughout Italy, and eventually in England, Ireland, Holland, Denmark, Germany, France, the United States, India, and Pakistan.

While her disciples were starting Montessori kindergartens all over the world, Maria turned her attention to the learning needs of older children, and developed materials through which children over six could engage in independent study to learn grammar, higher math, music, geography, history, biology, and earth science. Later, she became interested in the learning processes of newborn babies and young preschoolers, and laid the groundwork for innovative work in this field. Dr. Montessori also recorded her theories of child psychology in a number of published books, including *The Montessori Method* (1912), *The Secret of Childhood* (1936), and *The Absorbent Mind* (1949).

In 1922, Montessori was appointed government inspector of the Italian school system. In 1934, when Fascist authorities closed the Montessori schools in Italy, Dr. Montessori removed the center of her operations to Barcelona, Spain. In 1936, the outbreak of the Spanish Civil War again forced her to relocate, this time in the Netherlands, where she died in 1952.

An American Montessori Society was formed by Alexander Graham Bell; in Italy, Queen Mother Margherita served as patroness of the Roman Montessori Society. For over 49 years, Dr. Montessori lectured at training centers in every corner of the earth. Today, special Montessori schools continue to operate in all parts of the world, and Montessori methods have penetrated the curriculums of ordinary nursery schools, kindergartens, and primary schools everywhere.

Lillian Moller Gilbreth
(1878-1972)

ENGINEER AND INDUSTRIAL PSYCHOLOGIST

When Lillian Moller was chosen as valedictorian for her graduating class at the University of California in 1900, her mother was distressed.

"Oh, Lillian," fretted Mrs. Moller. "I suppose this means that your name will appear in the newspaper?"

"I imagine it will, Mother," replied Lillian absently. Her mind was still on her morning interview with Dr. Wheeler, the president of the University, in which he had advised her that as the first woman to appear on the University's Commencement Day program she had a special responsibility to be a credit to her sex. "Don't imitate a man," he had told her. "Look and speak like a woman."

What exactly had Dr. Wheeler meant? Lillian asked herself. She didn't see how being a woman should affect the way she conducted herself. Manners were manners, weren't they? She supposed Dr. Wheeler had been worried about her costume; he kept urging her to wear something frilly—as if her dress would even show beneath the heavy graduation robes. Well, Dr. Wheeler needn't worry—no Moller woman had ever been known to stray enough from established convention to don bloomers.

218

"Oh, Lillie, your name is in the papers," the timid Mrs. Moller went on. "What is the world coming to? Haven't I always told you a woman's name should appear in the newspaper but three times: once at her birth, once at her marriage, and finally, when she dies?"

Poor Mrs. Moller. Not only Lillian Moller's name, but also her picture (with a ruffled bodice peeking out from her graduation gown) appeared in the San Francisco and Oakland newspaper accounts of the graduation ceremonies. "Miss Moller made the most interesting speech of the day," observed one newspaper, "that is, it contained more original ideas and was not so much the stereotyped graduation essay."

Lillian Moller's original ideas were to get her name in the newspapers time and time again during the next 68 years. As Lillian Gilbreth, America's foremost woman industrial engineer, and a pioneer in studies of motion and in the psychology of management (known technically as psychotechnics), Lillian's accomplishments were to be noted in every major American and European newspaper. Articles by her were to appear in a number of technical and popular magazines. With her husband, Frank Gilbreth, and by herself for nearly 50 years after Frank's death, Lillian Gilbreth was to introduce the principles of scientific management into factories, offices, and homes all over the world.

Lillian Evelyn Moller was born on May 24, 1878, in Oakland, California. The eldest of nine children of an affluent businessman, Lillian enjoyed helping her mother bring up her five sisters and three brothers. Lillian was so timid her parents did not send her to public school until she was nine years old.

When Lillian finally entered the Oakland public schools, she easily mastered the educational requirements. But the social hurdles were something else. Having constantly been unfavorably compared to her pretty little sister, she felt she was unattractive. "I . . . decided very young, that since I couldn't be pretty, I *had* to be smart," Lillian later recalled.

Smart she was. Lillian became the teachers' pet, though her classmates were less than thrilled by her familiarity with the works of Emerson, Thoreau, Irving, Cooper, Louisa May Alcott, Longfellow, Whittier, and Lowell.

In high school, Lillian Moller was an honor student and an amateur poet and musician. She showed so much promise in music that her parents engaged composer John Metcalfe to give her lessons. Lillian wrote the lyrics for one of Metcalfe's songs, "Sunrise." But the composer refused to continue the lessons when Lillian decided to go to college. She must choose—music or books. For Lillian it was simple—she chose books.

Lillian felt quite fortunate to be allowed to attend the University of California. Sharing her parents' view that becoming a good wife and mother was her primary role in life, it had taken her a whole year to persuade her father that higher education would not interfere with this goal. Actually, she secretly doubted that any man would ever find her attractive enough to marry, and prepared herself for teaching as an alternate career.

As an undergraduate, Lillian's goal to make Phi Beta Kappa was frustrated, not by her failure to meet the honorary society's high standards, but because it was decided that no woman should be given the honor, since men had more need of the status conferred by a Phi Beta Kappa key in finding good jobs after college. Lillian received her B.A. in English literature in 1900, and went on to take a masters' degree in English, also at the University of California.

Before embarking on a doctorate program in English, Lillian decided to go abroad with some friends from Oakland. She left for Boston to board the ship. Here Lillian met Frank Gilbreth. Ten years Lillian's senior, Gilbreth was a self-made man. A former bricklayer's apprentice, he had become one of the biggest industrial contractors in the United States. Frank Gilbreth was also a self-taught engineer, and had acquired a reputation as an efficiency expert through his work eliminating extra motions in the performance of factory and office tasks. Frank showered attention on Lillian during her stay in Boston, and when she returned from Europe, renewed the acquaintance. The Gilbreths were married on October 19, 1904.

Lillian soon discovered that Frank Gilbreth's ideas about a wife's role were very different from her own and her father's. Frank came from a family of accomplished women; his sister Anne had studied music with Franz Liszt, and his sister Mary had been a brilliant botanist before her early death. To Lillian's surprise the Moller woman Frank most admired was Lillian's aunt of the same name. The

Mollers had always regarded Dr. Lillian Powers as the black sheep of the family, a divorced woman who had gone to medical school when her son was already in college.

Frank Gilbreth wanted his wife to have a career—or rather, to share his career. At Frank's instigation, Lillian changed her field of study from English to psychology, and began to investigate the operation of the human factor in employer-worker relations. Meanwhile, Frank taught Lillian the practical side of the construction business. Soon Lillian felt at ease climbing a scaffold and inspecting brickwork. She even learned to operate a steam engine. But Lillian persuaded Frank that he could put his engineering genius to greater use in industrial engineering rather than in the construction business.

When Lillian questioned workers and made suggestions as she accompanied her husband on his inspection tours, Frank Gilbreth began to realize that his wife had her own ideas about industrial management, and good ones. Frank tended to assume that all men thought as he did about all matters, and did not readily understand or cope with differing viewpoints. Lillian, considerably less self-confident than Frank and tending to be less absolute in her opinions, felt an empathy which enabled her to reconcile the conflicting interests of workers, employers, and middlemen, in order to effect solutions satisfactory to all parties. For instance, recognizing that assembly-line jobs were often monotonous, Frank offered the men job variations that he would have found interesting. Lillian, instead, elicited suggestions from the men themselves about what they would like to do, then offered job modifications based on these suggestions. The workers felt they had a certain degree of control over their jobs and weren't merely following the orders of higher-ups. In this way, the work got done faster and better, and Frank Gilbreth found himself confronting fewer personality conflicts.

Although he appreciated his wife's brilliance, Frank couldn't quite relinquish to her the role of innovator. Frequently, he would propose new sugestions to Lillian that had actually originated with her. Lillian had no need to point this out and would merely smile and approve the ideas, and ultimately, Frank would acknowledge her role with a sheepish grin.

The Gilbreth family was growing steadily. Frank wanted 12

children, six boys and six girls. Lillian managed to produce the requisite number of offspring in the desired proportions, although one little daughter died. Just as Lillian served as an equal partner in the business, Frank served as an equal partner in raising the children. The task was made easy since Frank's mother and aunt were members of the Gilbreth household and helped with the children. Also, there was ample money to secure additional help, which ultimately included a housekeeper, a handyman, a college-student babysitter, a secretary, and, during Lillian's confinements, a professional nurse.

The Gilbreth household became a testing ground for the couple's ideas of industrial management. Their rambling house in Montclair, New Jersey, was divided into work centers, and charts were kept on the Gilbreth "One Best Way" of doing everything. As the children grew up, they participated in the home management—for example, a family council made joint decisions; a family newspaper served as the medium for answering the mail; a family member was charged with securing for each Gilbreth an appropriate remembrance on his or her birthday. This extraordinary household was immortalized in the book *Cheaper by the Dozen*, written by two of the Gilbreth children, and in the motion picture of the same title.

Before the Gilbreths settled in Montclair, they had lived in New York City and Providence, Rhode Island. The sojourn in Providence was necessary because Brown University was the only institution in the East that would give a woman a Ph.D. degree in applied management. Lillian had run into difficulty previously when she had come to New York City to study English with Brander Matthews, only to discover that Matthews and many other male professors would not accept female graduate students. Frank Gilbreth, who had been unaware of the massive discrimination against women in higher education, flew into a towering rage at the affronts to his wife. It was because Gilbreth had many friends on the Brown faculty, that Lillian was admitted to the doctoral program in management there. But Frank found he couldn't sell Lillian's groundbreaking dissertation, *The Psychology of Management*, to book publishers with a woman's name on it. In 1912, the magazine *Industrial Engineering* agreed to serialize the manuscript under the by-line of L.M. Gilbreth, and using the same subterfuge, Lillian was able to have

The Psychology of Management published as a book in 1914. The publisher stipulated that no publicity would be given to the author, lest her sex be discovered. When Frank Gilbreth was asked by colleagues if the illustrious L.M. Gilbreth was a relation, he would reply sardonically, "only by marriage."

Lillian's thesis was that consideration of the human factor was crucial in meeting management's production aims. She advocated making the worker a partner in industrial projects, and instituting efficiency methods only with the cooperation of labor unions.

Lillian and Frank expanded their theories of psychological management in *A Primer of Scientific Management* (1912), but Lillian was given no credit for her co-authorship of this book because the publisher objected. As she established a reputation as an equal partner in Gilbreth, Inc. Industrial Engineering Firm, Lillian was allowed a by-line on the couple's later books, which included *Motion Models* (1915), *Applied Motion Study* (1917), and *Motion Study for the Handicapped* (1920). The Gilbreths' prestigious summer school of scientific management was attended by industrial personnel and teachers in business programs.

By the 1920s, Frank and Lillian Gilbreth were internationally famous as consulting engineers, and their travel commitments had greatly increased. But on the eve of his departure for Europe on June 14, 1924, Frank Gilbreth suffered a fatal heart attack. Lillian Gilbreth went abroad in her husband's stead, attending a London power conference, and reading a paper at the Masaryk Academy in Prague that she and her husband had written together. The Masaryk Academy had planned to make Frank Gilbreth an honorary member, and conferred this honor on his widow. Frank would probably have preferred it that way; he had never been more pleased than when the Society of Industrial Engineers made Lillian Gilbreth the first female honorary member in 1921.

In spite of her independent contribution to industrial engineering, 46-year-old Lillian Gilbreth found that firms that had retained Gilbreth, Inc. during Frank's lifetime were reluctant to confide their affairs to Lillian's sole management. Instead, they asked Lillian to train male personnel in Gilbreth techniques. In 1925, Lillian opened a school for motion-study at her home in Montclair. Within a year, representatives from Macy's department store, Sears Roebuck, Johnson and Johnson pharmaceutical supplies, the Dennison Company, and Cadbury Chocolates were attending the Gilbreth school. These men were so impressed by Lillian's grasp of technical problems and by her psychological acuity, that on their recommendations, their firms hired her as an independent consultant. The problem of how to finance some 44 years of college education for her 11 children began to loom less large for Frank Gilbreth's widow. She found, too, that she was able to enter industry though "the kitchen door" by designing an efficiency kitchen for the Brooklyn Gas Company. She developed an electric food mixer and other electrical devices for this kitchen. She also introduced many of the convenience features she had used for years in her own kitchen, such as cabinets at reachable levels, and counters at heights that would not prove fatiguing for a person engaged in rolling dough or slicing vegetables.

Ultimately, Lillian Gilbreth carved out a whole new career for herself in which she showed how business methods could be applied to ease homemaking and childrearing tasks. Her books *The Homemaker and Her Job* (1927) and *Living With Our Children* (1928) were lauded by reviewers as provocative, stimulating, and revolutionary.

For several decades, Lillian Gilbreth performed many important professional and social services, serving on presidential committees, and on the New Jersey State Board of Regents, holding government and teaching jobs. She was a professor of management at Purdue University, the first woman to serve on the faculty of an engineering college. She became dean of women at Purdue, succeeding Amelia Earhart after her death. She continued to write and publish, collaborating on *Normal Lives for the Disabled* with Edna Yost, and on *The Foreman in Manpower Management* with Alice Rice Cook. She contributed the chapter "Work and Science" in *Toward Civilization*, edited by Charles A. Beard, and the article on scientific management in the *New International Encyclopedia*.

In spite of her undisputed credentials as an industrial engineer, Lillian Gilbreth was twice refused admission to American Society of Mechanical Engineers meetings because they were held at all-male clubs. However, she was finally allowed to chair a meeting of the

A.S.M.E., at the Engineer's Club in New York City, opening that male enclave to women for the first time. As a woman in a field almost exclusively dominated by men, she broke ground for women, achieving many "firsts," including an honorary Master's of Engineering degree from the University of Michigan, an honorary Doctorate of Engineering from Rutgers University, an appointment as the first woman delegate to the World Engineering Congress in Tokyo, and the Washington Award awarded by engineers to a fellow engineer. Lillian Gilbreth shared with her husband the Gantt Medal, the highest award of the American Society of Mechanical Engineers. She was also the recipient of the gold medal from the National Institute of Social Science "for distinguished service to humanity," and earned the highest honor given by the International Association of Management Groups.

Lillian Gilbreth continued to serve as an industrial consultant and lecturer until her death on January 2, 1972, at the age of almost 94. This remarkable woman, who had started out as a shy youngster with very circumscribed goals, managed to make major contributions in a competitive field previously out of bounds to women.

Isadora Duncan (1878-1927)

DANCER

"She moved as no one had ever seen anyone move before," commented stage designer Gordon Craig about Isadora Duncan's revolutionary mode of dancing. Isadora rejected the stylized, artificial movements of traditional ballet, and improvised her own movements to reflect the spontaneous rhythms of nature and the human body. Isadora made of dancing an organic art. By wearing costumes patterned on classical paintings and statues, and dancing to music (not written for dance) of the great composers, she demonstrated the unity among all the arts. A consummate artist, Isadora was both the darling of the coterie, and the popularizer of high art among the masses. Isadora's iconoclasm opened the dance world to later innovators, such as Agnes de Mille and Martha Graham.

On May 27, 1878, Isadora Duncan was born in San Francisco, by the Pacific Ocean that was to serve as the original inspiration for her dance movements. Isadora's mother divorced her husband, a philanderer, poet, and sharper, just after the birth of Isadora, their fourth child and second daughter. A skilled musician, Mrs. Duncan

226

endeavored to support her progeny by giving piano lessons, but neither teaching nor the handiwork she later made and sold produced a sufficient income. The Duncans were often forced to flee from their quarters on rent day, and the family frequently fasted for days on end.

Needless to say, a babysitter was a luxury that Mrs. Duncan could ill afford. When she was out giving piano lessons or peddling her knitted wares, the children played by themselves, untrammeled by adult supervision. Isadora and her sister enjoyed running along the shore, imitating the lapping rhythm of the ocean, or trying to float like the clouds above them.

In the evenings, as Mrs. Duncan declaimed poetry and played music by Schubert, Chopin, Mozart, and Beethoven, Isadora was inspired to dance extemporaneously. Mrs. Duncan recognized her daughter's talent, and enrolled Isadora in ballet school, but Isadora found dancing on her toes unnatural, and therefore distasteful. Preferring to create her own free-style dances to practicing the stereotyped exercises of the ballet, Isadora left the class in a huff after the third lesson.

At the age of six, Isadora reconnoitered the neighborhood, dragooning all the available babies for a dancing lesson. Lining the toddlers up on the floor, Isadora taught them to sway their arms like flowers in the wind. This was the beginning of Isadora's first dance school, which was soon to become a lucrative venture. As a child of ten, Isadora quit public school, which she found hateful and boring, to devote herself full time to her dance pupils. A year later, Isadora and her sister were also teaching "society dancing" to adults.

Isadora haunted the Oakland Public Library, to satisfy her omnivorous appetite for novels. Reading George Eliot's *Adam Bede*, Isadora entered vicariously into the life of Hetty Sorrel, an unwed mother. Isadora vowed that she would never marry and put herself at any man's mercy.

When Isadora was 18, the Duncan clan headed east. Isadora went to New York, where she located a position as a dancer and actress with the Augustin Daly Shakespearean Troupe. Two years later, she arranged a concert at Carnegie Hall. She also danced in private performances at the homes of local social lions.

Deciding that her destiny lay in Europe, Isadora herded her family aboard a cattleboat bound for London. With no money on hand, Isadora's initial performances took place in public parks. A spectactor at one of these open-air representations, Mrs. Patrick Campbell, took Isadora under her wing, and introduced her to other wealthy Londoners. Soon Isadora was making the circuit of the fashionable soirées, and was supporting her family with her emoluments. The Duncans frequented the British Museum to study the classic Greek depictions of the human body and costuming.

From London, the Duncans went to Paris, where Isadora became a salon entertainer. She danced barefoot, in loose tunics and gauzy veils. Her patrons were so impressed by Isadora's dancing that they enlisted their own children to learn from her. Soon Isadora had an entourage of dance pupils. Irma, a pupil, whom Isadora later adopted as her own daughter, described a lesson interpreting the Brahms song "If I were a Bird":

I flew about the room as if I were a bird. When I stopped I saw "that look" on Isadora's face. No, she explained, the song did not say "I am a bird"; it said "If I were a bird." It meant "I wish I could fly to you but I am earth-bound" . . . . She demonstrated with beautiful gestures how the dance should have been done.

In Paris, Isadora met Loie Fuller, an innovative American dancer who invited Isadora to accompany her troupe on a Continental tour. In Vienna, in 1902, while performing with the Fuller company, Isadora was discovered by impresario Alexander Grosz. Grosz lured Isadora away from Loie Fuller, and booked solo performances for her in theaters all over Europe. In Budapest, Isadora won universal acclaim, and lost her virginity to a Hungarian sculptor. Isadora created a sensation at the Bayreuth Festival, where she had been invited to dance by Richard Wagner's widow. Isadora also made her first tour of Russia. With the proceeds, she started a dance school in Grunewald, Germany.

Here, Isadora lived with her lover, the brilliant stage director Gordon Craig. She became pregnant, and entrusting the newly formed dance school to her sister, Elizabeth, Isadora retired to Holland for her accouchement. In the small Dutch town where Isadora resided, she suffered from loneliness and inactivity, declaring herself "miserable and defeated." She was cheered by occasional visits from Craig, and by the birth of a daughter, Deirdre, on September 24, 1905.

Following Deirdre's birth, Isadora again took to the road. For three years, she performed in Scandinavia, Holland, and Germany, and twice revisited Russia. Isadora introduced Russian director Konstantin Stanislavski to her former lover, Gordon Craig, and although her own liaison with the stage designer had been plagued by a perpetual war "between the genius of Gordon Craig and my art," the association between Stanislavski and Craig proved to be one of the most creative theatrical partnerships in history.

In 1908, Isadora returned, for the first time in nine years, to America. Her unsophisticated compatriots did not rise to the challenge of Isadora's innovative work, and she danced to indifferent audiences. But to Walter Damrosch, conductor of the New York Symphony, Isadora Duncan was a revelation: she "opened my eyes to the significant connection between the art of music and dance." Damrosch invited Isadora to perform at the Metropolitan Opera House, accompanied by his own orchestra. Buoyed by the triumph of her Metropolitan debut, Isadora went on to make successful appearances in other major American cities, and even danced before President Theodore Roosevelt in the nation's capital.

Back in Paris, her two performances at the Gaieté-Lyrique marked the apex of Isadora's fame. She became the darling of the culture-vultures, who packed the theaters for her performances, and the muse of painters and poets, who attempted to incarnate her in their works. The Théâtre des Champs Elysees had bas-reliefs and murals modeled after Isadora, and author Max Eastman hailed her as "an apparition of creative genius."

In Paris, Isadora found a new patron and lover in Eugene Singer, heir to the Singer sewing machine fortune. In 1910, she gave birth to a son. She was once again obliged to suspend her dancing for the period of her pregnancy, and found herself "wondering if a woman can ever really be an artist, since Art is a hard taskmaster who demands everything, whereas a woman who loves gives up everything to life."

Although she resented the thralldom of pregnancy, Isadora adored her offspring. When Deirdre and Patrick were drowned in a car accident in 1913, their mother's grief knew no bounds. Only the comfort extended to her by her friend Eleonora Duse, the famed Italian tragedienne, revived Isadora's will to live.

An affair with an Italian sculptor led to Isadora's third pregnancy. When her baby was stillborn, Isadora was disconsolate, and was again plunged in the clutches of despair. She insisted that she would never dance again, and entertained thoughts of suicide. Her suffering aroused the consternation of Eugene Singer. He purchased a mansion near Paris, and urged Isadora to start a dancing school there. The new project proved restorative to her spirits.

When France went to war in 1914, Isadora liquidated her dancing school, and donated the building to the Red Cross for use as a hospital. She took her students to New York, where she unsuccessfully attempted to obtain municipal funding for a new school. One of Isadora's wealthy American admirers rented a theater where she presented Euripides' *Iphigenia in Tauris.* The next few years were spent restlessly touring Europe and the Americas, and in a second abortive attempt to found a dancing school in Athens. Then she accepted an invitation by the Bolshevist government of Russia to start a school in Moscow. After a year, the Bolsheviks rescinded their financial support, and Isadora prepared to return to America. Before departing, she married Russian poet Sergei Yessinin, so that he could accompany her to the United States.

Isadora's American tour of 1922 was a fiasco. She and her husband were accused of being Communist spies, and the enraged dancer added fuel to the flames by shouting from the stage that she *was* a "Red," and waving a red veil. Meanwhile, her pathological husband was on a perpetual drunken rampage, and created an emotional and financial crisis for Isadora. The couple returned to Russia, where in August 1923, Isadora played to worshipful audiences for 18 consecutive performances. After a farewell performance in Moscow, Isadora returned to Paris, alone. Yessinin had eloped with the daughter of Leo Tolstoi.

In 1925, hearing of Yessinin's suicide, Isadora experienced the most severe of her recurrent depressions. In order to earn some money, she began to write her memoirs, which were published in 1927 under the title *My Life*. Isadora was unhappy with the finished manuscript, complaining that "I wanted to write about my art, mostly, but my publishers were not interested . . . It's a crazed century that can only find interest in me as a female Casanova." Nevertheless, *My Life* contained enough of Isadora's artistic theories to prove an enormous inspiration to young artists.

Unfortunately, Isadora did not live to witness the impact of her autobiography. She died in Nice, on September 14, 1927, when her fateful scarf became entangled in the rear wheels of her automobile, strangling Isadora as the unaware chauffeur drove ahead. A month before her death, Isadora had made a triumphant comeback at the Théâtre Magdalen. Her final words, as she stepped into the fatal racing car, had been, *"Je vais à la gloire."*

"I sometimes feel that Isadora Duncan is the greatest woman the world has ever known," declared French sculptor Auguste Rodin. Indeed, Isadora's contribution to the arts is immeasurable. She created a radically new style of modern dance based on the theory that all human motion originates in the solar plexus. Her success gave legitimacy to naturalism in modern dance. Although Isadora's dances were not recorded and have not been preserved, she established a tradition of interpretive dancing that has been an inspiration to dancers and choreographers who came later.

Not only the pioneers of modern dance, but the practitioners of classical ballet, as well, came under Isadora's influence. The legendary impresario Diaghilev remarked, "She gave an irreparable jolt to the classic ballet of Imperial Russia." Choreographer Michel Fokine incorporated Isadora's Greek themes and flowing movements into his ballets. Russian ballet authority Prince Peter Lieven observed that Isadora "was the first to bring out in her dancing the meaning of music, the first to *dance* the music, and not dance *to* the music."

Isadora's choice of music was as significant for setting a new trend in dance as was her impromptu style. She spurned the light, trite compositions that generally served as background music for the dancers of her day, turning instead to the great composers: Beethoven, Tchaikovsky, Wagner, Chopin, and Gluck. Isadora did not restrict her choice to ballet music; she created dances to symphonic compositions and operatic selections.

Isadora was a trend-setter. She wore her diaphanous tunics and light sandals on the street as well as on the stage, and couturiers took to copying the popular idol's simple lines and gossamer fabrics in their designs.

When Isadora left the United States in 1922, she rebuked her countrymen: "You know nothing of Love, Food, or Art . . . so good-bye America. I shall never see you again." But her influence ultimately penetrated and enhanced American culture and America has continued to respond to Isadora's influence.

Isadora's free-flowing costumes and naturalistic movements heralded the new art form known as modern dance.

Helen Keller (1880-1968) and *Anne Sullivan Macy* (1866-1936)

HUMANITARIANS AND HELPERS OF THE HANDICAPPED

Blindfold your eyes, and stuff your ears with cotton. Now attempt the simplest daily acts—dressing, eating, walking up stairs. Do you feel disoriented, isolated, even panicked? Yet you have the comfort of knowing that one flick of your hand will restore to you light and sound. Now consider Helen Keller; nothing could remove her darkness, reverse her deafness. And yet this woman, blind and deaf from her second year of life, learned the survival skills that we who see and hear simply take for granted; and indeed rose to heights of achievement that few of us are privileged or gifted enough to attain. In her life, she epitomized the triumph of an indomitable spirit over incredibly restricting physical handicaps; and in her work, she opened new frontiers for the afflicted. Supporting Helen Keller was another great woman, Anne Sullivan Macy, teacher and faithful friend.

On July 27, 1880, in Tuscumbia, Alabama, a healthy, vibrant baby, with lovely pale blue eyes, was born to Captain Keller, a newspaper editor and lawyer,· and his second wife. The Kellers named the baby girl Helen. Helen was a precocious infant; at the age of six months, she was already enunciating words and on her first birthday, Helen began to walk, to the delight of her proud parents. But at the beginning of 1882, Helen Keller was afflicted with an acute congestion of the brain and stomach. The fever passed, but Helen Keller's sight and hearing were irrevocably lost.

The next six years were hell on earth at the Keller homestead. Deprived of her hearing, Helen could not continue to acquire language and speech, and, enraged at her inability to communicate with the surrounding world, behaved like a little animal. At mealtime, Helen's fingers groped randomly in all the plates. When the Kellers had company, Helen would thrash about wildly and tear and scratch at the guests—having no other means of making contact or claiming their attention. Among themselves, the Kellers' friends whispered, "It would have been more merciful if she had died of the fever." Helen's uncle told her mother, "You really ought to put that child away. It really is not pleasant to see her about." Yet, the energy and drive that made her so intractable were undoubtedly the same forces that saved her from a life of oblivion, and enabled her to rise to such heights of achievement.

One day, Mrs. Keller read in Charles Dickens' *American Notes* the story of Laura Bridgman, a blind and deaf girl who had been educated by Dr. Samuel Howe of the Perkins Institution for the Blind in Boston. But the renowned educator was now dead. A famous oculist in Baltimore referred the Kellers to Alexander Graham Bell, the inventor of the telephone, and a gifted teacher of the deaf. Dr. Bell observed Helen, and advised the Kellers to write to the director of the Perkins Institution, Michael Anagnos, the son- in-law of the renowned Dr. Howe. Upon receipt of the Keller letter, Mr. Anagnos began to ponder who should be sent to Tuscumbia. He chose the recent Perkins graduate, Annie Sullivan. Although Annie was barely 20 years old, the adversities of her own childhood had developed in her the compassion and patience that would be required of Helen Keller's teacher.

The child of Irish-born parents who had emigrated to America during the potato famine, Annie was blinded by trachoma at age five. When she was eight, her mother died, worn out by poverty and by the abuses of her alcoholic, malingering husband. Two years after his wife's death, Mr. Sullivan deserted his three children. Annie and her younger brother were sent to an almshouse in Tewksbury, Massachusetts. In this atmosphere of neglect, Anne Sullivan's brother died. Four years later, the squalid conditions of the almshouse had become so infamous that a citizens' committee was sent to investigate. The 14-year-old Annie Sullivan rushed up to one of the investigators, clutched him about the waist, and blurted out, "Oh, please, sir, please—I want to go to school!" The piteous cry of the blind girl went straight to the man's heart, and he arranged for Annie Sullivan to be transferred to the Perkins Institution.

At Perkins, Annie underwent several eye operations. She was restored to near-normal vision, but was warned never to overstrain her eyes. In 1886, Annie graduated from the Institution at the head of her class. When Mr. Anagnos told Annie about Helen Keller, she immediately accepted the challenge.

Thus, on March 3, 1887, what is perhaps the most moving teacher-pupil relationship in history began. The first few weeks were difficult, for Helen had never been disciplined and the child lived in a state of furious anarchy. Anne attempted to teach Helen language by having her touch an object and then, using the manual alphabet, Anne quickly spelled the name of the object into the child's palm. But Helen showed no sign of recognition. One day, Anne pressed into Helen's hand a sewing card and began to spell the word *card* into Helen's palm. She got as far as c-a- when Helen, who had previously been taught the word c-a-k-e, began to make primitive eating gestures. She pushed her teacher toward the door, gesturing to her to go downstairs for cake. Anne Sullivan realized that the girl's powers of association and memory were phenomenal, and was now hopeful that Helen would soon learn that "everything has a name."

The great breakthrough occurred on April 5, 1887. The scene, at a water-pump in the Kellers' backyard, was later immortalized in

William Gibson's play *The Miracle Worker*. Annie Sullivan describes it:

I made Helen hold her mug under the spout while I pumped. As the cold water gushed forth, filling the mug, I spelled w-a-t-e-r in Helen's free hand. The word coming so close upon the sensation of cold water rushing over her hand seemed to startle her. She dropped the mug and stood as one transfixed. A new light came into her face. She spelled "water" several times. Then she dropped on the ground and asked for its name, and pointed to the pump and trellis, and suddenly turning round, she asked for my name.

The experience at the pump opened up to Helen more than the mystery of language; she also learned that to *con*struct was better than to *de*struct. As Helen returned to the house with Anne Sullivan, she suddenly broke away and began to feel her way toward a doll that she had torn apart in the morning. Picking up the scattered pieces, Helen attempted to put the doll together again. When she realized that the effort was futile, she began to cry. She understood that she had "murdered" the doll, and "for the first time I felt repentance and sorrow." That night, Helen Keller crept into bed and for the first time returned her teacher's bedtime kiss. A few weeks later, as Anne Sullivan was attempting to explain to her pupil the meaning of the word *love*, Helen interrupted her, "Yes, Teacher, I understand what love is. I love *you*."

Over the next several years, Helen made phenomenal progress. She mastered Braille and learned to read and write not only in English, but in Latin, Greek, French, German, and Italian as well. She also learned to use a Braille writer and typewriter. Accompanied by Anne, Helen journeyed to Boston, where another gifted teacher, Sarah Fuller of the Horace Mann School, taught her to speak. At her 11th lesson, Helen announced, "I am not dumb now."

Helen told her family that she wanted to go to college; indeed, not just to any college, but to Radcliffe, the women's division of the most prestigious institution of higher learning in America—Harvard University. The determined Helen wanted "to try my strength by the standards of those who see and hear." Helen Keller entered Radcliffe in the fall of 1900, at the age of 20. Helen's beloved teacher was always at her side. Anne Sullivan had written to Mr. Anagnos, "I know the education of this child will be the distinguishing event of my life, if I have the brains and perseverance to accomplish it."

Helen's professors at Harvard included William James and Josiah Royce in philosophy, and Charles Townsend Copeland in English composition. The lectures were transmitted to Helen through the fingers of Anne Sullivan. Helen's favorite course was Shakespeare, taught by George Lyman Kittredge, one of the most gifted teachers of English literature. Both Shakespeare and Dr. Kittredge, Helen wrote, "gave new sight to the blind." Helen's writing talent was fostered by Dr. Copeland. "You have something of your own to say, Miss Keller, and you have a manner of your own in saying it," he told her, and suggested that she write a book-length autobiography. With the encouragement and editorial assistance of Anne Sullivan and literary critic, John Macy, Helen wrote *The Story of My Life*, an eloquent profile in human courage and superhuman endurance.

In 1905, the year after Helen graduated with honors from Radcliffe College, Anne Sullivan and John Macy were married. One of the conditions of the marriage was that Helen Keller was to live with them always. Unfortunately, the union did not last, and soon the two women were on their own again. Helen and Anne embarked on the lecture circuit. Helen told her story and urged her audiences to help the handicapped. She was also an ardent advocate of women's suffrage and of the right of industrial workers to organize into unions. Helen devoted many speeches to the blue-color workers' "right to a life better than the soul-quenching struggle for bread." Helen became a member of the American Socialist Party, and was among the first individuals to excoriate the evils of the military-industrial complex. Her anti-capitalistic sentiments were disturbing, and Helen was attacked as "mentally deficient" by the press. Bitterly, she wrote:

So long as I confine my activities to social service and to the blind, they compliment me extravagantly, calling me the "archpriestess of the sightless," "wonder woman," and "modern miracle," but when it comes to a discussion of a burning social or political issue, especially if I happen to be

. . . on the unpopular side, the tone changes completely. . . . I do not object to harsh criticism, so long as I am treated like a human being, with a mind of my own.

In 1924, Helen decided to concentrate her life's work on promoting the cause of the blind and the deaf-blind. She did extensive fundraising for the American Foundation for the Blind; lobbied for legislative appropriations to provide books on records and rehabilitative services for the blind, and served on the Massachusetts Commission for the Blind to secure increased opportunities for training and employment of sightless adults. Helen Keller toured every continent, and almost every country in the world, persuading government officials and private citizens to establish training facilities and schools for the handicapped. During World War II, Helen Keller personally visited thousands of soldiers who had lost their sight in the war.

Over the years, Anne Sullivan gradually lost her vision. In 1936, Helen's devoted teacher died. Aided by her personal secretary, Polly Thompson, Helen Keller continued lecturing and writing. In 1955, Helen published an elegiac tribute to Anne Sullivan, *Teacher*. She also wrote many other books, including *Out of the Dark*, *Midstream: My Later Life*, *Peace at Eventide*, and *Let Us Have Faith*, and conducted a massive correspondence right up until the day of her death. On June 1, 1968, Helen Keller died peacefully in her sleep, at the age of 88.

Helen Keller's life had been rich in inner and outer rewards. She had many friends who knew her worth, including her early supporter, Dr. Bell; her publisher, Frank Doubleday; Socialist leader, Eugene Debs ("that neglected St. Francis of the twentieth century"); and authors Oliver Wendell Holmes, William Dean Howells, Van Wyck Brooks, and Mark Twain. The author of *Huckleberry Finn* called Helen "the greatest woman since Joan of Arc," and told her "The world is full of unseeing eyes, and vacant, staring souls." Helen Keller's eyes were sightless, but her soul was visionary; and though her ears were closed to sound, her spirit was ever awake to what Wordsworth called "the still, sad music of humanity."

Margaret Higgins Sanger
(1883-1966)

BIRTH CONTROL
PIONEER

"I am the protagonist of women who have nothing to laugh at," said Margaret Sanger. The despairing women whose cause Margaret Sanger had adopted were the wives of poor working men who had little energy left, and no hope, for anything else in life but year after year of child bearing. She recognized a need; coined a word; started a movement. Architect and standard bearer of the American birth control movement, Margaret Sanger was the first individual to openly disseminate contraceptive information. Through her lectures, her writings, the conferences and clinics she started, Sanger brought help and hope to countless individuals, and paved the road for nations to solve one of the most pressing problems of modern times: overpopulation. Almost single-handedly she persisted against all odds to win over a hostile public and law system, until today birth control in some form is legal and accepted in most states and lands.

Margaret Higgins knew firsthand the liabilities of unplanned families. The sixth of 11 children, Margaret was born on September 14, 1883, in Corning, New York. Each of the Higgins children had weighed at least ten pounds at birth, and Margaret's consumptive mother died at the age of 48, exhausted by the rigors of rearing her large family. Margaret's father later endorsed his daughter's birth control activities, saying, "Your mother would have been alive today if we had known all this then."

Mr. Higgins, a stone-cutter, found it difficult to get work because of his reputation as a radical. When local authorities prohibited agnostic Robert Ingersoll from speaking at the town hall, Mr. Higgins invited the free-thinker to his house to lecture. "The one thing I've been able to give you is a free mind," Mr. Higgins told his children proudly. Margaret was to carry out his exhortation, "Leave the world better because you, my child, have dwelt in it."

Margaret was a clever child, and her older sisters arranged for her to attend boarding school. Here, courses in public speaking turned the timid little girl into an articulate exponent of her father's unpopular ideas. When her mother died, the 17-year-old girl had to serve as housekeeper, and as mother to the younger children.

Margaret finally left home to enter nurses' training a hospital. She was especially drawn to maternity work, often delivering babies herself, in the absence of a doctor. In her autobiography, Sanger wrote, "Birth, to me, has always been more awe-inspiring than death. As often as I have witnessed the miracle, held the perfect creature with its tiny hands and tiny feet, each time I have felt as though I were entering a cathedral with prayer in my heart."

Later, when she was working at a hospital on the lower East Side of New York City, Margaret was exposed to the attitude of the prematurely aged and worn-out wives of impoverished pushcart vendors, sweatshop workers, and small tradesmen, who were faced with unwanted pregnancies. The doctors would give these women no information about contraception. Under the 1873 Comstock Act, birth control information was considered "obscene, lewd, lascivious, and filthy," and could not be distributed through the mails.

In 1902, when Margaret was working at the Manhattan Eye and Ear Hospital, she met Bill Sanger, an artist and architect. The couple eloped, and within a year, Margaret was pregnant. Margaret's residual tuberculosis flared up, and during the last three months of an agonizingly painful pregnancy, she was confined to a sanatorium. She gave birth to a son, but suffered a severe postpartum depression. Over the next six years, Margaret bore two more children.

Margaret Sanger played the role of a dutiful suburban wife and mother in the luxurious home built by her husband in Hastings-on-Hudson. The Sangers' friends included such reformers as Lincoln Steffens, Mabel Dodge, Walter Lippmann, and Max Eastman. But after eight years, Margaret longed to return to Manhattan and to nursing, so the family moved into the city. As a visiting nurse in the slums, Margaret learned of the deaths of young women from self-induced or botched abortions. She wrote a column, "What Every Girl Should Know," on women's health problems for the Socialist journal *The Call*, until that paper was seized by the anti-vice crusader, U.S. postal chief, Anthony Comstock. Margaret's column on gonorrhea was judged "obscene material."

At this same time, Margaret had a particularly poignant experience which was to prove the turning point of her life. Jake Sachs telephoned Margaret with a frantic plea for help for his 28-year-old wife. Sadie was dying of blood poisoning, the result of a home abortion. Two weeks of intensive, around-the-clock care rescued her from death. During her recuperation, Sadie explained to the attendant doctor that she and Jake could not afford any more children, and asked how she could avoid getting pregnant again.

"Tell your husband to sleep on the roof," the doctor replied indifferently. Three months later Sadie Sachs was dead of another self-inflicted abortion.

The impact on Margaret was definitive. "I came to a sudden realization that my work as a nurse and my activities in social service were entirely palliative and consequently futile and useless to relieve the misery I saw about me." Coupled with the harassment by Comstock, Sadie's death galvanized Margaret Sanger to action and pointed her in the direction of her lifelong work. "When women have raised the standard of sex ideals and purged the human mind of its unclean conception of sex, the fountain of the race will have been cleaned," she proclaimed to Socialist gatherings. She began to propound her own brand of feminism, with this her basic tenet: "No woman can call herself free until she can choose consciously whether she will or will not be a mother."

Margaret was determined to make birth control information available to every woman in the United States, but found herself

stymied. Her medical colleagues were either uncooperative or as ignorant as herself; the public library shelves had been purged of sex
literature by her antagonist, Anthony Comstock.

Margaret decided that she must go to Europe to garner birth control information. She knew that the women of France had been lim-
iting their families ever since the Napoleonic Code had decreed the
equal distribution of wealth among all children in a family.

In October, 1913, Margaret and Bill Sanger and their children
sailed for Paris. Margaret talked to French doctors, midwives, drug-
gists, and mothers. She found that French women employed tam-
pons, suppositories, and contraceptive douches to prevent conception, and that birth control recipes were passed down from mother
to daughter with the same respect and pride as culinary secrets.

Back in New York, Margaret founded a monthly magazine, *The
Woman Rebel*, to "stimulate working women to think for themselves
and to build up a conscious fighting character." The first issue dealt
with birth control, a phrase coined by Sanger herself.

In the eight months of its publication, *The Woman Rebel* received 10,000 letters to the editor, and achieved a circulation of
2,000. Then Anthony Comstock moved to halt the presses. On August 25, 1914, she was called to court to face a nine-count indict-
ment for violating federal statutes.

The judge who presided at Sanger's hearing was moved by her
eloquent account of the Sadie Sachs episode, and impressed by the
statistics that Margaret produced: in 1913, one-fifth of all babies
born in the United States. had died within the year, and over 15,000
women had died in childbirth. Sanger's trial was postponed. Meanwhile, Margaret had 100,000 copies printed of her book, *Family
Limitation*, which explained with diagrams how to employ contraception. Sanger's friends hid the books, promising to release them
should Margaret be sentenced to imprisonment.

On October 20, 1914, the case of *The People vs. Margaret Sanger* came to trial. The judge ordered a postponement until the next
morning, warning Margaret that she had better get herself a lawyer
and prepare a plea. After agonizing about what course of action to
take, Margaret packed a valise and wrote to inform the court that
she was sailing to England.

When Margaret Sanger landed on British soil, she received word that 10,000 copies of *Family Limitation* were in the mails. This bible of the birth control movement was eventually to sell ten million copies and was translated into 13 languages. In London, she met invaluable allies, among them the C.V. Drysdales, founders of the British birth control movement, feminists Olive Schreiner and Marie Stopes, and sexologist Havelock Ellis. From her new friends, Margaret learned that in Holland, where birth control was legal, infant mortality and illegitimate birth rates were very low, and the rates of prostitution and venereal disease were at a minimum. Margaret visited the Rutgers Clinic and found the model she was later to adopt. Here 15 different methods of contraception were employed, including the diaphragm, a recent invention.

In September 1915, Margaret Sanger returned to America, to prepare for her trial. Her powerful British allies wrote to President Wilson reminding him that birth control was legal "in every civilized country except the United States." The case of *The People vs. Margaret Sanger* was postponed and eventually dismissed.

She now barnstormed the country, preaching the right of every woman to be "mistress of her own body," and of every child "to be wanted, to be desired, to be prepared for with an intensity of love that gives it its title to being." In most places, she encountered hostility from the Catholic Church and from women's clubs, and was locked out of lecture halls and theaters. In Portland, Oregon, Margaret was jailed. But in Denver, Sanger was welcomed by municipal authorities; and in Indiana, the National Social Workers Convention invited her to speak to their members.

When she returned to New York, Margaret and her sister, Ethel Byrne, opened the nation's first birth control clinic, in the Brownsville section of Brooklyn on October 16, 1916. That day, 140 women stood patiently in line from dawn until the closing hours of the clinic. Each day, the clinic was jammed by women who had read circulars in English, Italian, and Yiddish, inviting them to obtain "information [on birth control] from trained nurses at 46 Amboy St."

Despite the great demand for its services, the clinic was closed as a public nuisance. Ethel Byrne was sentenced to 30 days in jail. Margaret was also sentenced to 30 days, in the Queens Penitentiary. Upon her release from prison, Margaret started a new magazine, the *Birth Control Review*, and published *Women and the New Race*, publicizing the problems of women workers.

In 1922, Margaret Sanger embarked on a lecture tour of Japan, China, and India. She and Bill Sanger had been divorced, and in London she married the oil, magnate, Noah Slee, who offered to contribute his life and capital to the cause of birth control. In 1925, the couple founded the Clinical Research Bureau, to test and produce new contraceptive devices. An inexpensive version of the German birth control jelly was developed. Slee also subsidized an American company in the mass-production of the diaphragm. Slee and Sanger could have profited by marketing birth control devices commercially, but were only interested in thei wide dissemination.

In 1928, the Sanger Clinic was raided by police. However, this resulted in a legal victory for the birth control movement. The judge declared, "The law is plain that if the doctor in good faith believes that the patient is a married woman and that her health requires prevention of conception, it is no crime to so advise and instruct therein." Margaret Sanger won another judicial victory in the case of *the United States vs. One Package*, which resulted in the legalization of the distribution of contraceptive devices through the mails.

Finally, the birth control movement gained legitimacy in the United States. The dean of the American Gynecologists Association joined the advisory board of the Sanger Clinic, and the American Medical Association endorsed contraception as a legitimate medical procedure. On September 14, 1966, Margaret Sanger died. She had lived to fulfill her dream: birth control, no longer the prerogative of the rich, was available to all "women with nothing to laugh at."

Today, the Sanger Clinic still operates in New York City. Its services include the dissemination of birth control information and devices, help with problems of infertility, sexual dysfunction, or other impediments to family happiness.

In 1920, H.G. Wells predicted, "When the history of our civilization is written, it will be a biological history, and Margaret Sanger will be its heroine." In her lifetime, Margaret Sanger was vilified as a "lascivious monster." Today, with 250 Planned Parenthood chapters in 150 American cities, and centers in 88 foreign countries, Margaret Sanger is recognized as a heroine of modern civilization. Her slogan "voluntary motherhood" has been embraced by staid women's organizations, as well as by feminist revolutionaries.

Eleanor Roosevelt
(1884-1962)

HUMANITARIAN AND DIPLOMAT

"Mrs. Roosevelt has done more good deeds on a bigger scale than any woman who ever appeared on our public scene. No woman ever so comforted the distressed, or so distressed the comfortable." The occasion was a testimonial dinner honoring Eleanor Roosevelt on her 70th birthday. The speaker was author Clare Booth Luce, whose own foray into the congressional arena was encouraged by the example of Eleanor Roosevelt.

America's 32nd First Lady was the first president's wife to pursue an independent career in public service and to speak out on controversial issues, thereby revolutionizing the role of women in American politics and government. A paragon of compassion, Eleanor Roosevelt's little nameless acts of kindness were unnumbered but not unremembered. Adlai Stevenson, delivering the official eulogy at her funeral, spoke for millions when he said simply, "We are lonelier." As First Lady, Eleanor Roosevelt restored to the nation a sense of values; in the words of poet Archibald MacLeish, "things got simpler where she was. Good became good again, and nonsense nonsense, and evil evil, and a man could live again and even pity." As her husband's goodwill ambassador, and in her own right, Eleanor Roosevelt was the champion of human rights, the defender of human freedoms, and the universally recognized "First Lady of the World."

Eleanor Roosevelt was born on October 11, 1884, the eldest child of one of New York City's most socially prominent couples and members of a distinguished clan. An ugly ducking child, with buck teeth and thick glasses, Eleanor was clearly not destined to be a belle. Her mother, Anna Roosevelt, one of the great beauties of her day, urged her to compensate with charm for what she lacked in looks. The shy and gawky Eleanor only grew more self-conscious when her mother affectionately told guests, "She is such a funny child, so old fashioned, that we always call her 'Granny.'" Eleanor would stand wistfully in the doorway, feeling excluded as she watched her mother caress her two attractive brothers.

Eleanor adored her fun-loving alcoholic father who did not reject her. He often took the solemn little girl out with him. Once, when Eleanor accompanied her father to a Thanksgiving charity dinner for newsboys, Elliott Roosevelt fostered his daughter's social awareness by calling her attention to the contrast between her own holiday finery and the shabby, threadbare clothing of the newsboys, telling her about the precarious existence of these homeless youths, many of whom slept in the lobbies of apartment buildings.

When Eleanor was eight, her mother and one of her brothers died of diphtheria. Her beloved father died two years later. Eleanor and her surviving brother, Hall, were sent to their maternal grandmother's, to be reared with two alcoholic uncles and a deranged aunt.

At Grandmother Hall's, Eleanor led a cheerless poor-little-rich-girl existence. Mrs. Hall subjected the children to a spartan regime: a cold bath every morning, no sweets, and for Eleanor, a steel back-brace to improve her posture. Eleanor and Hall were advised never to complain of illness or unhappiness. Eleanor accepted this stoic code for herself, but tried to compensate her younger brother for his deprivation by giving him the love and sympathy of a mother. She remained Hall's surrogate parent until 1941, when he died of illness induced by alcoholism.

Eleanor was not a studious child, preferring her own daydreams to the lectures of her governesses. But when she was 15, her interest was sparked and her intellectual horizons considerably widened when she was sent to school in London where she became the protégée of the headmistress, Mlle. Souvestre. The Frenchwoman stimulated in Eleanor an inteest in current events, literature, art, philosophy, and languages. Eleanor learned to converse easily with her French and Italian schoolmates, and for the first time in her life made friends. Much later, her Italian and French were to serve her in good stead in the diplomatic arena.

During school vacations, Eleanor accompanied Mlle. Souvestre on her Continental travels, and was encouraged to make the travel arrangements, converse with Europeans, and even wander through Florence alone. Mlle. Souvestre was the diametric opposite of Eleanor's rigid, overprotective grandmother, and under the Frenchwoman's tutelage, Eleanor blossomed and developed poise, selfconfidence, and a greater appreciation of the world around her.

After graduating, Eleanor entreated her grandmother to let her attend college. The elderly dowager refused peremptorily. "All you need, child, are a few of the social graces to see you through life." The word "social" was anathema to Eleanor, as was the unceasing round of teas, luncheons, cotillions, balls, and visits that constituted her "coming out" ritual.

However, Eleanor was happy to engage in the philanthropic activities newly embraced by the American debutante population. Eleanor was one of the first members of the charitable Junior League, and enjoyed teaching dance and calisthenics at the Rivington Street Settlement House. As a volunteer for the Consumer's League, Eleanor toured factories and department stores, inspecting washrooms and working conditions. She was struck by the injustice of poor women toiling long hours in sweatshops to make the fashionable items of clothing that wealthy women could purchase in minutes at prices many times the weekly wages of the workers.

In 1903, Eleanor's relationship with her childhood playmate and distant cousin, Franklin Delano Roosevelt, was renewed. A Harvard undergraduate, Franklin came to New York on weekends to escort Eleanor to the theater and to restaurants. Eleanor told her cousin about her charitable activities, and invited him to accompany her to the tenement apartment of one of her settlement pupils. As they emerged from the ramshackle dwelling, Franklin exclaimed, "My God! I didn't know people lived like that!" Throughout their marriage, Eleanor was to open Franklin's eyes to the degradation suffered by the poor and the dispossessed.

After a year of courtship, Franklin proposed to Eleanor. Franklin's overpowering mother, Sara Roosevelt, tried to prevent the engagement. Franklin was too young, Sara said publicly; in private, she added that his fiancée was not pretty enough. Franklin insisted that he wanted a wife he could talk to, and in March, 1905, the cousins were married. Eleanor was given away by her Uncle Theodore, the president of the United States.

Eleanor accepted marriage as a duty, and was prepared to devote herself to her husband and family. In the next 12 years she gave birth to six children, one of whom died in infancy.

During the first decade of her marriage, Eleanor was cowed by her omnipresent mother-in-law. She and Franklin lived next door to Sara, who ruled both households and selected Eleanor's servants and nurses. Eleanor lunched with her mother-in-law every day, and listened to her orders. Inwardly, however, she seethed with helpless anger. In 1910, when Franklin became governor of New York State and the couple moved to Albany, Eleanor rejoiced to escape her mother-in-law's dictatorship. Still, her life was not really her own; her time was consumed in transporting family and servants back and forth from Albany to Manhattan to Hyde Park to Campobello, or with the political entertaining that was required of the wife of a public official.

In 1913, President Wilson named Franklin Roosevelt assistant secretary of the navy, and Eleanor accompanied her husband to Washington. For three years, she was a slave to political protocol. Every afternoon, Eleanor paid between ten and 30 social calls, and in the evenings there were receptions to give or attend. Her spare time was devoted to her children; she bore her last two children in this period. Eleanor later recalled her early years in Washington as follows: "I looked at everything from the point of view of what I ought to do, rarely from the standpoint of what I wanted to do."

World War I liberated Eleanor from her servitude to social formalities and gave her a more rewarding outlet for her energies. She took charge of a Red Cross canteen, doing everything from managing its finances and soliciting funds to mopping the floors. She accompanied Franklin on inspection tours of naval installations, and paid weekly calls to wounded servicemen at naval hospitals.

Eleanor found herself appalled, not by the patients, but by their forbidding living quarters and by the hopeless attitude of the hospital staff. She marched straight to the secretary of the navy, and demanded that he rectify the situation. An investigating commission substantiated Eleanor's allegations, and Congress appropriated the necessary funds for rehabilitation.

Eleanor Roosevelt developed enormous stamina and a new opinion of herself and her aptitudes. She was pleased to be recognized as the "dynamo" of the canteen.

In 1918, Eleanor Roosevelt made another discovery which was to further motivate her to develop a life apart from her husband's. She found out that Franklin and her own personal secretary, Lucy Mercer Rutherford, had been having an affair. Eleanor was deeply wounded by the liaison, which endured right up until FDR's death in 1945. Eleanor considered divorce, but ultimately opted to continue in the marriage, but as an independent partner.

In 1921, Franklin Delano Roosevelt was stricken with polio. Eleanor nursed her husband through his convalescence, and took over his role as athletic role-model to their children. She learned to drive a car and to swim, and became an expert horsewoman. She refused to let Franklin view himself as a hopeless cripple, and encouraged him to strengthen his limbs through therapeutic exercises, over the opposition of Sara Roosevelt, who urged her son to retire to Hyde Park for a life of reading, writing, and stamp-collecting. Eleanor was supported in her insistence that Franklin was destined for a life of public service by her husband's campaign manager, Louis Howe, who predicted that Franklin Roosevelt would become president of the United States.

"How can we revive Franklin's interest in politics?" Eleanor asked her husband's political mentor. "Easy," replied Howe, "*You* go into politics." By engaging in political activities, Eleanor could keep FDR informed on the issues, and make valuable personal contacts for him.

Eleanor's first step was to resume her active membership in the National Consumer's League. She lobbied on behalf of child-labor legislation. She also renewed her activities with the League of Women Voters, heading a committee to keep the public abreast of congressional developments. She joined the women's division of the Democratic State Committee, conducting a statewide canvass of women voters, editing a newsletter, and stumping for local candidates. She also joined the Women's Trade Union League, and began an investigation of women's working conditions. At the 1924 Democratic Convention, Eleanor Roosevelt presented feminist plans to the party platform committee. Howe taught Eleanor to speak so that her voice stayed on pitch and lost its tremulous quality. Her political career was in full swing.

Meanwhile, Eleanor was also developing some nonpolitical activities of her own. With a friend, she bought the Todhunter School in New York City. Renamed the Dalton School, this institution is still today one of the best progressive private schools in the country. Eleanor taught literature and history classes at the Todhunter School, and took her middle- and upper-class students on field trips to the slums, business districts, and police courts, in an effort to awaken in them a social conscience.

Later, when Franklin became governor of New York, in 1928, and when he was elected president of the United States in 1932, Eleanor refused to revert to the colorless image of a political wife. She pursued the goal of justice for women, minorities, the unemployed and the poor by continuing actively to support women's organizations, consumer and youth groups.

She did not shirk the official entertaining required of First Ladies, but Eleanor Roosevelt adapted her role as Washington's most publicized social hostess to her own reforming ends. For instance, in addition to giving a garden party for the ladies of the Senate, she held a fête for the National Training School for Girls in order to call attention to the deplorable condition their school was in. The public was outraged; the president's wife was inviting delinquent girls—many of them black—to the White House! But it worked. The training school was renovated. Eleanor publicized the destitution of the unemployed by serving a 19-cent lunch at the White House. Giving a literal interpretation to the maxim "Charity begins at home," the wife of the president provided recreational facilities for the White

House servants, and renovated the antiquated kitchen. She traveled without ostentation, using ordinary transport, and inaugurated an era of simplicity and informality in the White House. She would answer the door herself instead of sending servants to greet her guests.

Eleanor made sure that her husband heard various voices urging reform by inviting people of different political persuasions to dinner, and seating them next to the president. She called attention to the conditions of the poor by leading expeditions of cabinet wives and reporters through Washington's most squalid neighborhoods.

When the Daughters of the American Revolution closed Constitution Hall to black contralto Marian Anderson, Eleanor Roosevelt resigned from the D.A.R., and invited Anderson to sing at the White House. On her cross-country tours, Eleanor Roosevelt always sat in the Negro section of segregated lecture halls. She investigated allegations of racial discrimination in labor, and brought these practices to her husband's attention.

She supported the cause of women as well as of blacks. When the National Recovery Act was passed, she made sure it provided equal pay for women in industry. She secured 4,000 postal jobs for women in all parts of the country. She advocated the appointment of women to the highest cabinet posts, and insisted that her husband retain qualified female appointees from the previous administration. Learning that women reporters were excluded from presidential press conferences, Eleanor inaugurated the first press conferences ever to be held by a First Lady. She staged a shindig for the "gridiron widows" on the night the press gave a stag party for the president.

Eleanor campaigned to improve the lot of the needy by assuming a public service role on the national and international levels. She visited coal mines in West Virginia, shipyards in Portsmouth, Maine, rural schools in Puerto Rico, prisons in Baltimore, and during World War II served as goodwill ambassador to American troops abroad.

She was a tireless author and lecturer who donated her royalties and stipends to charity, and used her newspaper and magazine columns to awaken the national conscience, and gain public support for legislative reforms. Many thousands of readers came to know and love this humane woman through her newspaper column, *My Day*.

When FDR died in 1945, Eleanor Roosevelt did not retire from public life; she expanded her activities; lecturing, teaching at Brandeis, appearing on radio and T.V., and authoring books. Over the opposition of John Foster Dulles and others, President Truman appointed Eleanor Roosevelt to the five-member U.S. delegation to the United Nations. As a member of the General Assembly, Eleanor attacked U.N. discrimination against women, noting that female delegates were excluded from the powerful political committees. She established and chaired the Human Rights Commission, and tangled with Soviet committee members over the question of war refugees who did not wish to be repatriated. Representing the United States in the debate against the Russians before the U.N. General Assembly, Eleanor planned her strategy shrewdly. Aware of the danger of a walkout by Latin American delegates, she kept the South Americans riveted to their seats with an eloquent discourse on Simon Bolivar's fight for freedom. The *New York Times* eulogized her speech as "the most dramatic event of the session," and she carried the day for the refugees.

Eleanor Roosevelt continued to serve in various capacities during the Eisenhower and Kennedy administrations. She spoke to women's and citizens' groups all over the world, and was a liaison to black organizations and youth groups in the United States. She served on the Peace Corps Advisory Council and counseled the United States to stay out of the Vietnam War. She remained politically active up to the day of her death, on November 7, 1962.

Speaking of Eleanor's influence on FDR, Texas governor W. Lee O'Daniel observed: "Any good things he may have done during his political career are due to her, and any mistakes he may have made are due to his not taking up the matter with his wife." This may be an overstatement, but there is no doubt that as a staunch New Dealer and diplomat without portfolio, Eleanor Roosevelt made an immeasurable contribution

Perhaps a *New York Times* editorial offers the best summary of Eleanor Roosevelt's achievements: "No First Lady could touch her for causes espoused, opinions expressed, distance spanned, people spoken to, words printed, precedents shattered, honors conferred, degrees garnered."

Karen Danielssen Horney (1885-1952)

PIONEER IN PSYCHOANALYSIS

Karen Horney was a seminal force in modern psychoanalytic theory. Pioneering successively at the Berlin Psychoanalytic Institute, the New York Psychoanalytic Institute, and the American Institute for Psychoanalysis, Horney's career divides into three periods, each marked by a breakthrough contribution to neo-Freudian theory.

From 1919 to 1932, Horney was one of the guiding spirits of the celebrated Berlin Psychoanalytic Institute. Her formulation of a feminine psychology, and her analysis of conflict between the sexes made her a heroine of the German youth movement.

With the Nazi takeover of Germany in the thirties, Horney emigrated to the United States, where she became a training analyst at the New York Psychoanalytic Institute. Here Horney aroused increasing antagonism among orthodox Freudians, as she challenged their belief in the primacy of instinct and genetics as the basis of human behavior. Horney argued that social and cultural factors were as important as biology in determining man's complex psychic makeup. In later restatements by Erik Erikson and other neo-

Freudian psychologists, this theory was to gain wide acceptance, but in 1941 Horney was ousted from the New York Institute for her apostasy.

She then became the leading founder of the American Institute for Psychoanalysis, where she made further contributions to the study and treatment of neurosis. Her nonauthoritarian approach to analysis is widely emulated by practicing psychiatrists today.

Karen Danielssen was born near Hamburg, Germany, on September 16, 1885. Her father, a Norwegian ship captain, was 17 years older than Karen's Dutch mother. During Karen's childhood, the family sometimes accompanied Captain Danielssen on voyages around Cape Horn and Karen developed an early love of travel and foreign cultures.

Captain Danielssen, a member of the country aristocracy, was a stern father. A firm believer that *kinder, küche* and *kirche* were woman's proper sphere, he would periodically dismiss the maid and order Karen to assume responsibility for the housekeeping. Karen complied, but inwardly rebelled.

After attending private schools, Karen entered high school at the age of 11. Karen obtained high marks at the all-girls high school, where she studied languages, the humanities, math, and science. The private tutoring she received in declamation was later to stand her in good stead when she was to become one of the most effective psychoanalytic lecturers of her day. She also showed considerable dramatic talent.

In 1906, Karen entered pre-clinical medical studies at the University of Freiburg. Here, Karen met a brilliant young lawyer, Oscar Horney. After a three-year courtship, they were married. Karen bore three daughters.

Karen's doctoral thesis was accepted in 1915. There were few women doctors in Germany at the time, and even fewer women neurologists. Horney had decided on a career in psychiatry. In 1919, when the Berlin Psychoanalytic Clinic was opened, Horney was asked to join the staff as an instructor. She was assigned the job of setting up a training program for other analysts.

The Berlin Clinic, which changed its name in 1924 to the Psychoanalytic Institute, had become one of Europe's outstanding training centers. Its faculty included Theodore Reik and Sandor Rado, and Anna Freud and Helene Deutsch were among the frequent guest lecturers. In Berlin, Horney also became friendly with the influential psychological theoreticians Erich Fromm, Melanie Klein, and Wilhelm Reich.

Throughout the 1920s, Horney was a popular and highly regarded lecturer, dealing with such topics as female sexuality, psychoanalytic techniques, and pedagogic theory for early childhood. Her rapt audiences never guessed the extreme stagefright she suffered at the podium.

In 1927, Horney presented a paper to an international psychoanalytic congress on "The Monogamous Ideal," which addressed the conflict between expectations and realities in marriage, perhaps drawing on her own far from ideal marriage. Oscar Horney took a traditional view of the family, and disapproved of his wife's demanding career and feminist attitudes. The marriage crumbled under the strain of the divergent careers. The Horney's were divorced in 1929.

Karen was idolized by young, emancipation-oriented woman, who jammed her lectures at the Humboldt Hochschule on "The Role of Women in Society." But Horney's male colleagues were made uneasy by her repudiation of the phallocentric doctrines of Freudian psychology, and by her assertion that it was the opportunities and social prerogatives enjoyed by men, rather than the male genitals, that aroused envy and feelings of inadequacy in women.

In 1932, while Dr. Horney was secretary of the Berlin Institute, she received an invitation from Dr. Franz Alexander, head of the Chicago Institute of Psychoanalysis, to become his assistant. Alexander considered Horney one of the most original thinkers of the Berlin School, and had been impressed by her clinical observations. Horney accepted the position, but her two years in Chicago were not happy. Close up, Alexander and his staid colleagues found Horney too revolutionary. In 1934, they parted by mutual consent. Dr. Horney went to New York City.

In New York, Horney resumed her friendships with Fromm, Reich, and other German refugees whom she had known in Berlin. They referred patients to her for psychoanalysis, and Dr. Horney soon had a thriving private practice. She was invited to join the staff of the New York Psychoanalytic Institute, and to lecture at the New York School for Social Research.

From 1940 on, Horney was also one of the leading members of an intellectual salon that included poet Carl Sandburg, theologian Paul Tillich, and social psychologist Abraham Maslow.

In 1937, Horney published her first book, *The Neurotic Personality of Our Time*, in which she minimized the role of infant sexuality in personality development. The author was calumniated by her Freudian colleagues, but some analysts recognized the book as a major contribution to the understanding of the human psyche. Horney was one of the first psychoanalysts to distinguish between the need for intimacy and the drive for sex, in such statements as: "A great part of what appears as sexuality has in reality very little to do with it, but is an expression of the desire for reassurance."

In 1939-1940, a schism developed at the New York Institute between the upholders of Freud's libido theory, and adherents of Horney's psychoanalytic doctrines which emphasized cultural and environmental factors. Horney's paper, "The Value and Debatable Aspects of Freud's Genetic Viewpoints," created pandemonium at the Institute, and prompted Horney, four of her colleagues, and 14 of their students to walk out. A few days later, Horney and her cohorts formally resigned from the Institute, stating: "Reverence for dogma has replaced free inquiry; academic freedom has been abrogated; students have been intimidated; scientific sessions have degenerated into political machinations."

In 1941, Horney founded the Association for the Advancement of Psychoanalysis, and was elected dean of its training center, the American Institute for Psychoanalysis. The American Institute strove to be open to new ideas and techniques, and, for example, in 1943 became one of the pioneers in group therapy. In 1950, Horney became interested in Zen Buddhism, and visited Zen monasteries in Japan. Karen Horney remained dean of the American Institute until her death. On December 4, 1952, she died of lung cancer.

In the final decade of her life, she had published a number of books elaborating and refining her modifications of Freudian orthodoxy. Although writing did not come easily to Dr. Horney, and she often had her secretary retype a single page seven or eight times, she communicated the tenets of psychoanalysis to the lay public more effectively than any of her august predecessors. Avoiding the obscurantist, jargon-ridden prose typically employed by her colleagues, Horney wrote clear, readable statements.

On May 6, 1955, the Karen Horney Foundation was opened, to continue Horney's pioneer work in the reformulation of Freudian theory, and its practical application in therapy with patients. In her writings, Horney made many innovative changes in psychoanalytic theory. "The relevant factor in the genesis of a neurosis," she wrote, "is neither the Oedipus complex nor any kind of infantile pleasure strivings, but all those adverse influences which make a child feel helpless and defenseless and which make him conceive the world as potentially menacing."

Horney regarded wars and other acts of aggression not as sublimated destructive instincts, but as manifestations of feelings of frustration due to social inferiority. She ascribed the inferior status of women to cultural factors rather than to biological inferiority, and countered male taunts of "penis envy" with the evidence that men as well as women suffered from feelings of sexual inadequacy. The current sexual research of Masters and Johnson seems to support these ideas.

Believing that human beings are basically creative, and always capable of change, Dr. Horney's theory of psychic growth is a positive one. Departing from the orthodox Freudian emphasis that ego development is definitive before age six, she maintained that social and cultural factors influence personality and behavior as much or more than biological instinct. This theory, which takes into account the whole array of forces that contribute to the makeup of personality, is known as *holistic* psychology. Horney was one of the first to embrace an anthropological perspective toward psychology, and is considered the originator of holistic psychology.

In light of the contemporary reevaluations that constitute the sexual revolution, Horney's most pertinent contribution to psychoanalytic theory may perhaps be found in her emphasis on sex as the expression of general emotional needs. Horney was among the first psychologists to credit the human need for tenderness, and the role of cuddling and foreplay in sexual relations. She also stressed the rewards of pregnancy and motherhood as a supplement to and not a substitute for other areas of fulfillment.

As a practicing analyst, Dr. Horney decried the tendency to treat patients as helpless creatures, kept in a state of dependency by therapists whose own shaky egos were bolstered by the subjection of their patients. Instead, Horney tried to strengthen the positive self-image of her patients, and to equip people with techniques of self-analysis, so they could continue in their independent growth. Horney advanced the concept that man was distinguished from other animals by the capacity for self-understanding. She was one of the most original psychoanalytic theorists—and one of the most humane.

Elizabeth Kenny (1886-1952)

MEDICAL REVOLUTIONARY

One autumn evening in 1910, a 24-year-old Australian nurse knocked at the door of a cattle drover in the bush country of New South Wales. Nurse Kenny knew the family well, just six months earlier she had delivered their fourth baby. Now, she had been summoned because the only daughter, Nurse Kenny's special favorite, was ill. The nurse found the little girl writhing in pain, her limbs contorted.

When Nurse Kenny attempted to move the knee that was drawn up to the child's face, the little girl howled with pain. An attempt to straighten the child's arm bent catatonically across her chest brought the same response. Nurse Kenny was stymied. Just out of nursing school, she had never before seen such symptoms.

The nearest doctor was 40 miles away, in Toowoomba. Nurse Kenny sent a telegram. While she waited for the reply, a distraught father of seven came to her announcing that his ten-year-old son and four-year-old daughter had been unable to rise from their beds that morning. "They went lame yesterday, just like the cows have been doing for the past few weeks," the man said, "and today, they can't move."

Nurse Kenny's heart began to beat faster. If there was an epidemic among the cattle, and there were already three cases of "cow disease" among humans, the ailment must surely be contagious. There were no doctors in Pilton Hills; how would she possibly cope with an epidemic alone? But, reminding herself that "panic plays no part in the training of a nurse," Elizabeth Kenny waited calmly for the reply to her telegram.

The answering cable from Nurse Kenny's old friend, Dr. Aeneas J. McDonnell, was anything but reassuring:

INFANTILE PARALYSIS.   NO KNOWN TREATMENT.   DO THE BEST YOU CAN.

So Nurse Kenny did her best. Noting that the little girl's muscles were contracted, she decided to apply heat to relax the muscles. But a heating pad filled with warmed salt brought no relief to the young patient, and a linseed-meal poultice only increased the pain. Finally, Nurse Kenny tore a wool blanket into strips, immersed the strips in boiling water, and then wrapped the hot compresses around the child's arms and legs. Within moments, the agonized screams ceased. Soon the child was slumbering peacefully. When she awoke, her first words were, "I want them rags that wells my legs!"

Thousands of sufferers from poliomyelitis were to feel better after the ministrations of Elizabeth Kenny's heat-massage and muscle-re-education techniques. Before Nurse Kenny developed her radical new treatment, the victims of this virus-caused inflammation of the brain and spinal chord became permanent cripples. Indeed, the usual treatment of tying the afflicted limbs in splints or encasing them in heavy casts immobilized the muscles, killing the already weakened nerves.

You would have expected that the medical world would have been delighted when Elizabeth Kenny announced that she had found an efficacious treatment for a disease that had been crippling people since the days of the ancient Egyptians. Far from it. When the young nurse informed Dr. McDonnell she had cured the victims of infantile paralysis, the good doctor shook his head sadly. Though he believed her and was proud of her, he knew his colleagues and tried to warn her.

"Elizabeth," he told her, "you have followed a procedure that is exactly the opposite of what orthodox medical men do today—you treated the spasm instead of the paralysis."

"I treated muscle spasms," the spunky young nurse defended herself, "because I saw muscle spasms—there was a telltale groove in the neck, and I could feel the pulsations beneath my fingers."

The elderly medical practitioner took his protégée's hand. "Elizabeth, I'm not saying you're wrong. On the contrary, I believe you have discovered the first successful treatment for poliomyelitis. I congratulate you. But oh, Elizabeth," the sage physician heaved a gloomy sigh, "you know nothing of the world of professional medicine. Do you think the specialists will acknowledge that the first major Australian contribution to medical science has come from a woman, a woman moreover who doesn't even have a medical diploma? Prepare yourself for the most disheartening opposition."

Dr. McDonnell's words proved only too prophetic. For the next 30 years, Elizabeth Kenny found herself the target of organized medicine. It was not until 1950 that Sister Kenny methods were appreciated. Where poliomyelitis was treated with Kenny methods, 87 percent of the patients recovered the use of their limbs.

Elizabeth Kenny was born in the outback of Queensland, Australia, in 1886. A hardy child, Elizabeth from the age of six rode all over the Australian bush on horseback. Elizabeth was also fearless. One day, when she was eight, an adder glided out of the brush and darted its poisonous fangs in her direction. Elizabeth reached for the nearest stick and gave the venomous snake a resounding whack on the head. The adder lay still. Elizabeth picked up the limp carcass, and brought it back to the farm. Triumphantly, she lay her trophy at her mother's feet. To the surprise of both child and mother, the adder lifted its head and slithered off into a nearby thicket.

A daredevil on horseback, in her early adolescence she was thrown from the saddle of a skittish mount, fracturing her wrist. Elizabeth's parents took her to Toowoomba, and left her with Dr. Aeneas J. McDonnell to receive proper medical treatment. Elizabeth, whose only schooling had come from her mother, enjoyed poring over Dr. McDonnell's medical books.

One day, Elizabeth came upon a tome on muscle development in Dr. McDonnell's library. "I wonder if this might contain anything to help my brother Bill," Elizabeth said to Dr. McDonnell, explaining that her brother was so weak-limbed that the other children took turns carrying him around piggyback-style.

"Why don't you take the book home with you?" Dr. McDonnell suggested. Back at her parents' farmhouse, Elizabeth studied human anatomy. She constructed a "mechanical man," a wooden dummy with pulleys and strings, to demonstrate to Bill the workings of the muscular system and to teach him to do voluntary muscle contractions. Soon Bill was as strong as the other children. At the age of 14, Elizabeth Kenny had effected her first cure.

Elizabeth enrolled in a nursing program and three years later, she obtained her nurse's certificate. Professional nurses were in scarce supply on the Australian frontier.

Elizabeth was engaged to be married. One day, a nursing summons arrived for Elizabeth just as she and Dan were preparing to go to a picnic. Miles away in the outlands a woman was struggling in premature labor.

"Let someone else go!" Elizabeth's fiancé said savagely. "Why does it always have to be you, Liz?"

Elizabeth sighed. "There is no one else, Dan. If I don't go, mother and child may die."

Her fiancé glowered at the cowboy who had come to fetch the nurse on horseback. "Well, at least let me drive you out there in the buggy."

Elizabeth laid a conciliatory hand on her fiance's arm, "Dan, the trail's too rough for a horse and buggy, and you know it."

Dan jerked his arm away angrily. "You'll have to decide right now, Elizabeth. Either you are to be married to me or to your vocation. Now which is it?"

Elizabeth blanched, but she knew what her decision must be. "Wait one moment," she told the embarrassed messenger, "while I change my dress." She choked back tears as she heard Dan's carriage tear out of the yard, never to return.

Soon after, Elizabeth confronted the polio epidemic in Pilton Hills. After her discussion with Dr. McDonnell, she set up a modest polio clinic. Dr. McDonnell brought other medical practitioners to the clinic, to observe Elizabeth soothing the distorted limbs with hot compresses, and massaging the ailing muscles back to health.

Although the children she treated recovered within a few weeks, most of the visiting doctors were skeptical. "The books say to use splints, and we're going to keep using splints," the purblind medical men insisted. What the books did not mention was that splints had proved effective in only 13 percent of poliomyelitic cases. Again and again, Elizabeth Kenny demonstrated that splints further immobilized the muscles and killed the nerves, while heat, massage, and therapeutic exercises relaxed the muscle spasms.

In 1914, Australia entered World War I. Elizabeth Kenny closed her clinic temporarily, and became an army transport nurse. "I have spent more time on dark ships in danger zones than any other woman in the world," she reported at the war's end. She had also invented a canopied stretcher on wheels, which greatly facilitated the transportation of emergency patients.

The Elizabeth Kenny who returned to Australia at the end of the war was not the hale and hearty young woman who had set out for London in 1914. A chunk of German shrapnel was permanently embedded in one leg, and she had suffered a near-fatal bout with heart disease. But Nurse Kenny's heroism had been recognized and she had been rewarded with the title "Sister," bestowed on head nurses in the British army.

Sister Kenny resumed her work with the victims of infantile paralysis. For the next quarter of a century, she waged an incessant battle with the Australian medical authorities. "We don't want any witch doctors here," they told her. But to the grateful parents who saw their crippled children restored to health, Sister Kenny was an archangel.

Despite the attempts of Australian doctors to suppress information about her work, news of Sister Kenny's miraculous cures spread. People heard about baby Jean, who had been born with a deformity of both feet. The local physician told Jean's parents that their daughter required expensive surgery and even then would not be completely cured. Jean's parents were humble farmers, who could not afford the stiff fees of orthopedic surgery. So they took Jean to Sister Kenny's low-cost clinic, and within four months Jean was a perfectly normal infant.

Elizabeth Kenny wrote books about her treatment methods and

made films of her patients, but the doctors ignored them. In the wards of the Queensland hospitals, where she was allowed to enter only at the patients' request, Sister Kenny was regarded with hostility by the resident surgeons. One day, as she was removing the splints from a young boy's legs, one of the hospital physicians entered the room. Observing the boy's flaccid feet and inert toes, the doctor sneered, "And tell me, Sister Kenny, how long will it take you to readjust these dropped feet?"

The unflappable Sister Kenny began to apply moist heat to the boy's limbs. "Come back tomorrow and you will see these feet in their proper place," she said.

The next day, the doctor arrived to find the young patient wriggling his toes and flexing his ankles in all directions. Three weeks later, the boy walked out of the hospital room completely cured.

Sister Kenny charged no fee for her own services. After the war, she had patented her stretcher, and was able to live on the modest royalties from this invention. The orthopedists of Queensland were finding their waiting rooms empty. A royal commission was convened to investigate the Kenny treatment for polio, and issued a 300-page philippic denouncing Sister Kenny. She was denied funds for new clinics and for the training of hospital personnel.

Sister Kenny became discouraged. But, remembering her mother's adage, "He who angers you, conquers you," she decided that if Australia was not ready for the Kenny treatment, she would go elsewhere. So, in 1939 Elizabeth Kenny accepted an invitation to go to London to demonstrate her methods there.

"I will come back," Sister Kenny promised, and 11 years later, she did. By then, having worked polio cures in England, Poland, France, and the United States, Sister Kenny was a celebrated medical pioneer. It was in America that Sister Kenny found the first official medical sanction of her treatment. In 1940, Sister Kenny was invited to demonstrate her methods at the Mayo Clinic in Rochester, Minnesota. Although the Minnesota doctors were cynical, American pragmatism triumphed over professional myopia. One year after Kenny treatments had been instituted in Minneapolis hospitals, 74 of 84 polio victims had recovered full use of their limbs.

During the following years, the Kenny method successfully controlled polio epidemics in many large cities. The National Institute of

Infantile Paralysis endorsed the Kenny treatment, and the editorial board of the *American Medical Journal* conceded that Sister Kenny had revolutionized the treatment of poliomyelitis in the United States. When Sister Kenny prepared to return to Australia in 1950, a grateful U.S. government told her that she was welcome in America at any time—no passport or visa necessary.

But working 18 hours a day for 40 years had undermined Sister Kenny's health. Her right side paralyzed by Parkinson's disease, Sister Kenny retired to Queensland, where she discovered that the schoolchildren began the day with a prayer on her behalf. Content in the knowledge that her life's work had finally found universal acceptance, Sister Kenny expired peacefully, on November 30, 1952.

By this time, there were eight Kenny clinics in the dominion of Australia, and at least twice that number in the United States, with a national Kenny Institute in Minneapolis. In her lifetime, Sister Kenny had trained hundreds of doctors, nurses, and physiotherapists in her methods, and her books and articles reached even more medical personnel.

In 1953, a year after Sister Kenny's death, Dr. Jonas Salk announced that he had developed a preventive vaccine for poliomyelitis. Today, we have both the Salk and Sabine vaccines to prevent polio epidemics. Nevertheless, the disabling disease continues to strike hapless victims, and no drug has yet been found that can kill the polio virus, or prevent its spread in the body. The Kenny treatment continues to be the only effective method of curbing the crippling consequences of poliomyelitis.

The first woman, and the only individual without an M.D. degree, to receive a Distinguished Service Gold Key from the American Congress of Physiotherapy, Elizabeth Kenny was a most deserving recipient of that award. "And they shall walk," she said of children lamed by infantile paralysis. Thanks to Sister Kenny's tireless crusade, few polio victims need go through life on crutches.

Nadia Boulanger
(1887-   )
MUSICIAN

Composer, conductor, musicologist, lecturer, performer, and music teacher *par excellence*—Nadia Boulanger is a consummate musician. Composer Virgil Thomson, one of Mlle. Boulanger's former pupils, has called her "the greatest teacher the world has ever known." This opinion is echoed by other alumni of Nadia Boulanger's "one-woman graduate school," who include composers George Gershwin, Walter Piston, Elliott Carter, and Roger Sessions. Musical godmother to a generation of leading American composers, Nadia Boulanger also counts among her protégés the French composers Darius Milhaud, Jean Françaix, and Leo Preger; the Russian composer Igor Markevitch; and the Rumanian pianists Clara Haskil and Dinu Lipatti.

An excellent pianist, Nadia Boulanger is also considered one of France's finest organists. As a conductor, Mlle. Boulanger has led the London Philharmonic, the Boston Symphony, and the New York Philharmonic, among other major orchestras. Walter Damrosch has cited Nadia Boulanger as "the best reader of orchestral scores I have ever known."

But it is as "a one-woman U.N.," in Virgil Thomson's phrase, that Nadia Boulanger has made what is perhaps her greatest contribution to musical history. By introducing modern American music to European conductors like Serge Koussevitzky, and musical rarities from the French and Italian Renaissance to her students, Mlle. Boulanger has facilitated a cultural interchange fruitful for both the Old and the New Worlds. Future generations of musicologists will probably cite Nadia Boulanger as a foremost single influence on 20th-century music.

Nadia Boulanger was born in Paris, France on September 16, 1887. Her mother, Russian Princess Raissa Mytchetsky, had been a music student who married her teacher at the Conservatoire National de Musique de Paris. A composer, Nadia's father, M. Boulanger came from a distinguished musical family; Nadia's grandfather, who also had taught at the Conservatoire, was an eminent French cellist, and Nadia's grandmother had been a well-known singer.

Nadia and her younger sister, Lili, were taught at home, largely by their mother. Today, as a music teacher, Nadia Boulanger deplores the fact that most American musicians do not begin serious musical training until later in life. She has described her work with infants as a paradigm for other music teachers:

For one year, every day, I took the hand of a little boy of three, and played and sang one note, adding one more each day. He has never made a mistake reading music since, and that training will remain with him all of his life. . . . In music, never is the ear training started early enough.

In 1897, Nadia Boulanger entered the Conservatoire National, where she studied under the composer Gabriel Fauré. In competition with fellow students Maurice Ravel, Georges Enesco, and others, Nadia won first prizes in every category—solfege, counterpoint, fugue, organ, and keyboard harmony. She graduated in 1904, at the age of 16.

After leaving the Conservatoire, Nadia composed and taught music. Her compositions include several short orchestral, instrumental, and vocal pieces, as well as an opera, *La Ville Morte,* co-authored with Raoul Pugno. In 1908, Nadia Boulanger won second prize in the Grand Prix de Rome for her cantata *La Sirène.*

Musicologists have called Nadia Boulanger's scores "strong," "rich," and "original." But by the age of 30, Nadia Boulanger felt sure that teaching, not composition, was her vocation. Nadia became a teaching assistant at the Conservatoire National in 1909 and was also giving private lessons.

In 1921, Nadia Boulanger took on three promising American students—composers Aaron Copeland and Virgil Thomson, and Melville Smith. Copeland recalls his three years with Mlle. Boulanger as *anni mirabilli:*

Nadia Boulanger knew everything there was to know about music. She knew the oldest and the latest music, pre-Bach and post-Stravinsky, and knew it cold. All technical know-how was at her fingertips; harmonic transposition, the figured bass, score reading, organ registration, instrumental techniques, structural analyses, the school fugue and the free fugue, the Greek modes and the Gregorian chant . . . . most important to the budding composer . . . was her way of surrounding him with an air of confidence.

Copeland, Thomson, and Smith wrote home to musical friends in the United States about their marvelous teacher in Paris. Soon Nadia Boulanger was inundated with American pupils, jazz artists like Quincy Jones, as well as classical composers like Roger Sessions and Walter Piston. For her advanced pupils, Mlle. Boulanger instituted a series of "Wednesday afternoons," at the apartment.

The Wednesday salons would begin with score readings by Mlle. Boulanger and her students. Sometimes, the score for the day would be a work in progress by Stravinsky or Schoenberg, still in manuscript form, or perhaps a composition by Gustav Mahler, the wellspring of the avant-garde. Sometimes the lesson pieces consisted of older music, a madrigal by Monteverdi or Gesualdo di Venosa. For two hours, Nadia Boulanger would play the selection on the piano, eliciting comments from her eclectic group of students, and raising their musical consciousness. Then, after the lesson, guest composers would arrive. These included such maestros as Stravinsky, Poulenc, Milhaud, Roussel, and even octogenarian Saint-Saens.

Nadia's mother would ply the gathering with tea and cakes, while the established masters and fledgling composers exchanged ideas.

Meanwhile, Nadia Boulanger's reputation as an organist was growing. On February 20, 1925, she was the organ soloist with the Boston Symphony Orchestra in Boston, playing Handel's *Concerto in D Minor;* an organ symphony by Aaron Copeland, which Mlle. Boulanger commissioned for the occasion.

Mlle. Boulanger also played the Handel concerto with the Symphony Society of New York, leading one reviewer to praise her "perfection of style. The artist's taste in the employment of stops and her classic reticence were exquisite. Her transitions from one manual to another were played with the same impeccable taste. . . ."

By 1932, Nadia Boulanger was the second organist at the great Église de la Madeleine in Paris. The 1930s also found Nadia Boulanger conducting the Paris Symphony and a number of smaller French orchestras.

In 1938, Nadia visited the United States for the second time. Having conducted the Royal Philharmonic in London to critical acclaim in 1936 and 1937, she now became the first woman to conduct the Boston Symphony. At the same concert, she also played the organ solo in the Saint-Saens *C-Major Symphony*, under the baton of Serge Koussevitzky. Asked by a Boston journalist how it felt to be the first woman conductor of a major American orchestra, Mlle. Boulanger answered drily, "I've been a woman for a little more than fifty years, and I've gotten over my initial astonishment."

On February 11, 1939, Nadia Boulanger became the first woman to conduct the New York Philharmonic. The reviews were universally favorable, praising Boulanger's "virile intellectuality," and "mastery of style." The critic for the *New York World Telegram* wrote, "Conducting (without a baton and also without a trace of self-consciousness), she disclosed signal ability as a leader, whether the composition were instrumental or vocal, and she brought fluency and authority to her piano playing. . ."

In 1939, Nadia Boulanger accepted teaching positions at Wellesley College and at Radcliffe College. The Radcliffe course was open to Harvard students as well as to Cliffies—the first coeducational class in Harvard's history.

By the early 1960s, Nadia Boulanger had become an international figure, making guest appearances in Poland, Hungary, and Rumania, as well as in western Europe. She also began to record for RCA during this period. In 1967, on her 80th birthday, Nadia Boulanger was feted in Monaco by Prince Rainier.

Today, at the age of 91, Nadia Boulanger is still giving lessons at her apartment on Rue Ballu, near the Boulevard Clichy. Her working day begins at seven A.M. and ends at midnight. Still interested in fostering international interchange in music, Nadia today draws most of her students from Third World countries—Japan, Korea, Turkey, Lebanon, India, and Egypt.

Mlle. Boulanger seats her pupils to the right of the piano, with herself at the piano bench, and together teacher and pupil silently peruse the score the student has composed. Then Mlle. Boulanger plays the composition on the piano, occasionally commenting on the musical syntax or sound, or asking the student a question about his musical sources or harmonic arrangement. Virgil Thomson has said that Nadia Boulanger's greatest strength as a musician is her enormous critical acumen. "She can understand at sight almost any piece of music, its meaning, its nature, its motivation, its unique existence, and she can repeat this back to the student like a mirror." Both for her own achievement, and as a source of inspiration, Nadia Boulanger's name will go down in music history.

Chingling Soong Sun
(1890-   )

CHINESE PATRIOT
AND FEMINIST

The Soong sisters have been called "the world's most remarkable daughters." Together, these three women had an enormous impact on United States policy toward China. Via radio broadcasts, public appearances, newsreels, and contacts with highly placed officials, the Soong sisters have tried to project the image of a modern China. All three sisters married important Chinese political leaders, yet each established her own identity as a prominent patriot. The eldest, Ai-ling, married banker H.H. Kung and became, in her own right, one of the wealthiest women in China. The baby of the family, Meiling, became world-famous as Mme. Chiang Kai-shek, ambassador without portfolio for her husband's Nationalist government, and architect of the New Life Movement for the rehabilitation of the Chinese people.

But it is Chingling, the shy, retiring middle sister, the widow of Dr. Sun Yat-sen, "the George Washington of China," who is, perhaps, the most renowned. Revered for her honesty, integrity, courage, and dignity in perpetuating her husband's egalitarian principles, Chingling Soong Sun has been called, even by her critics, "the conscience of China" and "the most beloved woman in China." Madame Sun is still active in the People's Republic of China, where she is a vice-premier in the Communist government.

After meeting her in 1927, writer Vincent Sheehan described her as follows:

It did not occur to me that this exquisite apparition, so fragile and timorous, could be the lady herself, the most celebrated woman revolutionary in the world. She was in a truer sense than the merely physical one intended by the headline writers, "China's Joan of Arc," but you had to know her for a good while before you realized the power of the spirit beneath that exquisite, tremulous envelope.

The Soong sisters (and their three also famous brothers) were very lucky in their parents. Their mother, whose feet had been bound at birth, had become so ill and feverish from pain, that her parents had decided to unwrap the bandages, in defiance of the custom begun in the year 950 to remind women of their inferiority to men. Ni, whose mind was as unfettered as her feet, became a teacher. Their father, Charles Jones Soong, who later became a wealthy merchant prince, had gone to America as a penniless youth to study, and had returned to Shanghai as a Methodist minister with his own Bible-printing business. Charles Soong was also actively engaged with his close friend, Dr. Sun Yat-sen, in revolutionary activity opposing the oppressive rule of the Manchu dynasty and working for a democratic socialist China, ruled by Chinese, with freedom from want for all.

Charles Soong met Ni at a Methodist social gathering and proposed without first going to her parents to ask their permission to court the young woman. Assured by her suitor that he wanted a wife who would help him work for the Chinese Revolution, Ni accepted and they were married. She bore her husband three sons and three daughters. Chingling, born in 1890, was her mother's favorite child, for she was "the obedient one."

The Soongs wanted the best education for their children, for the girls as well as for their brothers. When she was seven, Chingling was sent to the McTyeire School for Girls, established in 1892 for the daughters of Chinese aristocrats. Both her sisters also attended the McTyeire School, an occidental-style seminary. Chingling was the most studious member of the family. Even as a child, she was intrigued by philosophy and by Chinese history. She listened eagerly to her father and Dr. Sun, as they discussed the future of her country.

"We must drive the Manchus out of power, and restore China to the Chinese," Dr. Sun declared. "There must be a democratic government, in which all can participate, and the land must belong to the peasants who have worked it, not to the warlords who have persecuted them. We must make a revolution."

Young Chingling's eyes glistened with excitement. "I would like to work for the revolution," she said wistfully.

"And you shall," her father promised, "but first you must complete your studies."

When she was 18, Chingling joined her older sister, Ailing, at Wesleyan College in Macon, Georgia. Twelve-year-old Meiling also went with her sister to America.

Chingling's interest in the Chinese Revolution did not abate while she was at school in America, and great was her joy when Dr. Sun's People's Party, the Kuomintang, overthrew the Manchu government in the Great Revolution of October 1911. In January 1912, Dr. Sun became president of the new Republic of China, but resigned a few months later in favor of Yuan Shin-kai, and served instead as director of transport and trade, and leader of the Kuomintang. In April 1912, Chingling Soong, who had followed reports of the Chinese upheavals in the American newspapers, published an article in the Wesleyan College newsletter entitled "The Greatest Event of the Twentieth Century." Hailing the Chinese Revolution as "the greatest event since Waterloo," Chingling wrote:

It is a most glorious achievement. It means the emancipation of four hundred million souls from the thralldom of an absolute monarchy, which has been in existence for over four thousand years, and under whose rule "life, liberty, and the pursuit of happiness" have been denied.

The essay concluded with Chingling's vision of a united China as the harbinger of international entente:

A race amounting to one-quarter of the world population, and inhabiting the largest empire of the globe, whose civilization displays so many manifestations of excellence, can not help but be influential in the uplifting of mankind. China was the first possessor of a criminal code; her philosophers gave to the world some of the noblest contributions to human thinking; while her extensive literature and her exquisite code of social and moral ethics are hardly paralleled elsewhere. . . . China, with its multitudinous population, and its love of peace . . . shall stand as the incarnation of Peace.

But when Chingling returned to China in 1913, after obtaining her B.A. from Wesleyan, she found China anything but peaceful. A few months after her arrival, in July 1913, Dr. Sun led an unsuccessful Second Revolution, with southern provinces attacking the government in the north. When the rebellion failed, Dr. Sun fled to Japan. With him went his principal followers in the Kuomintang, including the Soongs.

Chingling became Dr. Sun's secretary, replacing her sister Ailing in the job when Ailing married. Dr. Sun's wife, a traditonal Chinese woman, was little informed of her husband's activities. The marriage had been arranged when they were both very young. Chingling fell in love with Dr. Sun and announced to her parents that she wished to marry him and devote herself wholeheartedly to his reinstatement as president of China. The Soongs opposed the match. Dr. Sun was twice Chingling's age and already married, but Dr. Sun divorced his first wife, and on October 25, 1914, Chingling Soong became the second Mme. Sun Yat-sen in a quiet ceremony at the home of a prominent Japanese lawyer.

In 1916, Dr. Sun and his young wife returned to China to reestablish the political base of the Kuomintang. In 1920, when Dr. Sun was again elected president of China, Chingling became her husband's liaison with various Chinese youth groups and set a new precedent for the wives of Chinese political leaders by appearing regularly with her husband on the public platform, where she was "stared at, mobbed by enthusiastic crowds, and photographed within an inch of her life." After much strife within China between the feudal lords and the revolutionary forces led by Dr. Sun's Kuomintang, the Chinese republic was established, backed by the U.S.S.R., the only country willing to support Dr. Sun's democratic regime. On March 12, 1925, Dr. Sun, "the Father of the Chinese Revolution," died of cancer in Peking.

The Kuomintang immediately turned to 33-year-old Chingling Soong Sun for leadership. Dr. Sun's widow was elected to the 33-member Central Executive Committee of the Kuomintang, to the party's Political Council, and to other governing bodies. She also continued to work with Soviet advisors in revolutionary schools. Mme. Sun worked to strengthen the role of women in the Kuomintang. She created a Women's Institute of Political Training in Hangchow, working closely with young Chinese feminists, who idolized her. She also instituted several birth control clinics in China.

In the spring of 1927, General Chiang Kai-shek, commander-in-chief of the Kuomintang army, set up his own Nationalist government at Nanking, in opposition to the established government at Hangchow. General Chiang's financial support came from wealthy Shanghai bankers, who made their aid conditional on Chiang's repudiation of Communist allies. A terrible massacre ensued, with Communist and trade unionists tortured and slaughtered en masse. Dr. Sun's widow never forgave Chiang Kai-shek for this carnage, parting company with the rest of her famly who supported the general. Mme. Sun fled to Moscow, issuing a farewell message to her people:

Some members of the party executive are so defining the principles and policies of Dr. Sun Yat-sen that they seem to me to do violence to Dr. Sun's ideas and ideals. Feeling thus, I must disassociate myself from active participation in carrying out the new policies of the party. In the last analysis, all revolutions must be social revolutions, based upon fundamental changes in society; otherwise it is not a revolution, but merely a change in government.

Despite the fact that her sister, Meiling, had married Chiang Kai-shek, she continued to denounce the reactionary Nanking government.

Earlier that spring, Mme. Sun had been elected, *in absentia*, to the Central Executive Committee of the Kuomintang, but, still opposed to Chiang Kai-shek's Nationalist government, she refused to legitimize that body with her presence at its congresses. Chingling took modest lodgings in the French Concession of Shanghai, where she was visited by a deputy of the Nanking government, who told her, "If you were anyone but Mme. Sun, we would cut your head off." Mme. Sun smiled, and replied, "If you were the revolutionists you pretend to be, you'd cut it off anyway."

In 1940, Chingling visited her sisters in Chungking, a Nationalist stronghold, but continued to inveigh against her brother-in-law's military government and to call for a guarantee of civil rights for all Chinese.

In 1947, Mme. Sun was asked by the left wing of the Kuomintang to run against Chiang Kai-shek in the presidential election, but her health was poor and she declined the nomination. Chiang was re-elected, but two years later, he was ousted when the People's Republic of China was established under the leadership of Mao Tse- tung. Supporting the Communist coup, Mme. Sun told Chinese audiences:

For the first time in China's history, there is a widely representative group of the people forming a real united front to carry out a common program and establish a genuine people's democratic government. . . . Our task does not end until every hovel has been rebuilt into a decent house, until the products of the earth are within easy reach of all, until the profits from the factories are returned in equal amounts to the effort exerted, until the family can have complete medical care from the cradle to the grave.

Chingling Sun continues to be revered in Peking, and to serve as an example to women all over the world that even in the mightiest bastions of male chauvinism, women can rise to positions of great leadership.

Dorothy Thompson
(1894-1961)

JOURNALIST AND
POLITICAL
COMMENTATOR

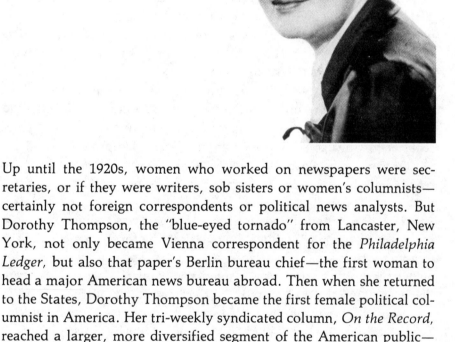

Up until the 1920s, women who worked on newspapers were secretaries, or if they were writers, sob sisters or women's columnists—
certainly not foreign correspondents or political news analysts. But
Dorothy Thompson, the "blue-eyed tornado" from Lancaster, New
York, not only became Vienna correspondent for the *Philadelphia
Ledger*, but also that paper's Berlin bureau chief—the first woman to
head a major American news bureau abroad. Then when she returned
to the States, Dorothy Thompson became the first female political columnist in America. Her tri-weekly syndicated column, *On the Record*,
reached a larger, more diversified segment of the American public—
including males as well as females—than any other political column
of the 1930s.

A vigorous and clear writer, with a thorough and often prescient
knowledge of foreign affairs, Dorothy Thompson was noted as much
for her compassion as for her urbanity. She is remembered for her
brave crusades against Hitler, Stalin, and Franco, and even braver support of Franklin Delano Roosevelt's New Deal, writing in a

Republican-owned newspaper. Her newspaper and radio sponsors often canceled her contracts because of it, but she never wavered in telling her readers the truth as she saw it about international and national affairs. Called by *Time* magazine the most influential woman in America next to Eleanor Roosevelt, Dorothy Thompson was one of the pivotal figures in destroying the myth that women could not be taken seriously in the realm of ideas.

Born July 9, 1894, in Lancaster, New York, Dorothy Thompson was the eldest of three children. Her father was a Methodist minister, and was transferred from one upstate New York pastorate to another throughout Dorothy's childhood. As a youngster, Dorothy entertained herself with the novels of George Eliot, Dickens, Thackeray, Scott, and Victor Hugo, the plays of Shakespeare, and the essays of Emerson. As punishment when she misbehaved, Dorothy was required to memorize Biblical passages and great poetry. She soon knew most of the Bible and Palgrave's *Golden Treasury* by heart.

When Dorothy was ten, her mother died of a miscarriage. Two years later, her father married the organist of his church. Dorothy did not get along with her stepmother; and when she was 14, her father sent her to Chicago to live with an aunt. Here Dorothy attended the prestigious Lewis Institute, where she was transformed from a rebellious hobbledehoy into a popular social leader, and a brilliant student in English and history.

In 1911, Dorothy entered Syracuse University as a junior. Syracuse had a strong feminist heritage, having been the first American college to admit a female undergraduate, and having opened the doors of its medical school to the first American woman doctor, Elizabeth Blackwell. Dorothy was active in the Syracuse Equal Suffrage Club.

Dorothy Thompson graduated from Syracuse *cum laude* in 1914. Twenty-three years later, when she returned to the Syracuse campus as the first woman commencement speaker in the university's 66-year history, she would hear herself described as an "alumna of Syracuse—orator—fearless journalist—foreign newspaper correspondent—author—clear thinker—and master of the art of exposition."

After graduation, Dorothy went to work as a suffrage organizer in Buffalo, where she was a dynamic and enthusiastic fund raiser. After the ratification of the New York State Equal Suffrage Act in 1917,

Dorothy went to New York to try to break into journalism.

Dorothy found the New York newspaper and magazine world supremely indifferent to backwater female reporters with no professional experience or powerful friends. By dint of her persistence in making the rounds, however, Dorothy was able to persuade several Sunday supplement editors to run her feature stories, *without paying her.* She soon was selling articles to a number of national newspapers and magazines. Already, her vivid, incandescent writing was earning Dorothy the respect of fellow journalists. But her efforts to obtain a staff job were unsuccessful. Having failed to achieve the possible, Dorothy Thompson decided to attempt the impossible. She set sail for Europe in June, 1920 to try to land a job as a foreign correspndent.

Dorothy made her first journalist coup in Ireland, where her brilliant coverage of the Sinn Fein's skirmishes with the British Black-and-Tans persuaded of the International News Service to make her a string correspondent.

Although she was barely 27 years old, and in Europe for the first time, Dorothy Thompson had an uncanny knack for sensing where a story was about to break. Again and again, she scooped more experienced reporters—writing about the world's first massive sit-down strike at the Fiat factory in Italy, obtaining an exclusive interview with the deposed King Charles in Austria-Hungary, and startling foreign minister Edward Benes of Czechoslovakia with her audacious questions. At first, Dorothy sold her stories on a free-lance basis to American newspapers, but eventually, she persuaded the *Philadelphia Ledger* to hire her as its Vienna correspondent. Initially, Dorothy was paid space rates, but her output was so prodigious, her prose so lively, and her reportorial instinct so keen that she was soon put on salary. "Two things happened to central Europe during the decade of the 20s," wrote John Gunther, ". . . the world economic crisis and Dorothy Thompson." Dorothy became known as "the only woman newspaperman of our time."

In 1922, Dorothy Thompson became acting chief of the *Ledger's* bureau in Berlin, Germany. Dorothy had recently married Josef Bard, a Hungarian writer, but her journalistic career proved to be a stumbling block to the marriage, for Bard, increasingly disgruntled with his wife's constant travels and enormous success, was chronically unfaithful. In 1927, Josef Bard divorced Dorothy, to marry a more conventional woman. Dorothy's vibrant personality made her a favorite with both men and women. Among her chief admirers was Pulitzer Prize-winning novelist, Sinclair Lewis, who followed her to Moscow in 1927, and courted her as she chronicled the Soviet scene. The following year, Dorothy Thompson and Sinclair Lewis were married.

After her second marriage, Dorothy Thompson resigned her job, and she and her husband returned to America to live in their farmhouse in Vermont. Here, she wrote the first of her eight books magazine and newspaper articles. Thomas Costain, editor of the *Saturday Evening Post*, was a friend of her husband's and for the next several years the *Post* was the major outlet for Dorothy's articles. In 1930, she gave birth to her only child, Michael. Dorothy also became very close to Sinclair Lewis's son by a former marriage.

"Show me a woman married to an artist who can succeed in her marriage without making a full-time profession out of it," Dorothy wrote to a friend. As she pursued her career as a writer and lecturer, her marriage to the hard-drinking Lewis began to founder. Though they were not formally divorced until 1942, there were frequent separations, and Dorothy Thompson once again returned to Europe as a foreign correspondent. In 1931, she was sent by *Cosmopolitan* magazine to interview Adolph Hitler in Germany, and in 1932, published an unfavorable book-length portrait of the future Führer. She was expelled from Nazi Germany in 1935, and the Lewis farm in Vermont became a haven for anti-Nazi emigrants and Dorothy Thompson became one of the most ardent advocates of opening America's doors to Jewish refugees on an unlimited basis.

According to Dorothy Thompson's own view in her autobiography, her career really began in 1935, when she was invited to become a columnist for the *New York Herald Tribune.* From its inception, Dorothy's sprightly, informed column appealed to a large constituency, and within a year, *On the Record* was appearing in more than 130 newspapers.

Dorothy Thompson became known as "The First Lady of American Journalism." She was the only woman ever to address such famous male bulwarks as the Harvard Club of New York, the Union Club of New York, and the New York State Chamber of

Commerce. In 1937, Dorothy Thompson was writing a column in the *Ladies' Home Journal,* and was also a popular radio commentator. Her household had mushroomed to include three secretaries, a housekeeper, several maids, a governess for Michael, and assorted German refugees.

One of Dorothy Thompson's special gifts as a journalist was her ability to dramatize an abstract issue through an individual case. For example, she used the case of Herschel Grynzspan, whose parents were concentration-camp victims, to publicize the plight of Jews under the Nazi reign of terror. Herschel Grynzspan was a 17-year-old Jew who was seeking refuge from Germany in France. When his French visa expired, and no other country would permit him to enter, in desperation he shot a secretary in the German Embassy in Paris. In 1938, Dorothy Thompson started a Journalists' Defense Fund for Herschel Grynzspan, telling her radio audience of five million that "we who are not Jews must speak, speak our sorrow, and disgust, and indignation. . . ." Her book *Refugees: Anarchy or Organization* (1938) influenced President Roosevelt to convene a conference on refugees at Evian, France.

Called the American "self-appointed anti-fascist Joan of Arc," Dorothy Thompson gradually became a liberal crusader on other issues as well. She championed *Esquire* magazine in its battle against censorship, and deprecated a smear-campaign launched by anti-Communist zealots against Bertrand Russell. Dorothy's shift of allegiance from Wendell Willkie to FDR on the grounds that "the President knows the world . . . better than any other living democratic head of state. . ." incited the *Herald Tribune* to cancel Dorothy's contract in 1941, although Willkie himself harbored no rancor toward Thompson, citing her as "the first to see clearly the threat of totalitarianism, not only in its military aspect, but in its economic, social, and revolutionary aspects."

Dorothy Thompson was married for the third time in 1942, to artist Maxim Kopf. She continued writing her column *On the Record* as a nationally syndicated column until 1958, when she retired from journalism. In that year, Maxim Kopf died, and Dorothy's own robust health began to decline. Over the next three years, she suffered several heart attacks, and on January 31, 1961, her heart failed permanently.

Beginning with her early days as a dewy-eyed but intrepid European reporter, through her years of renown as the arch-enemy of totalitarianism at home and abroad, Dorothy Thompson was noted for her integrity and for her concern for human suffering. She used her power and prestige judiciously, focusing her attacks on causes rather than taking potshots at her enemies. She lived by her own high standards of social concern, and personally made generous contributions for refugee relief, including the donation to this cause of the proceeds from her Broadway play, *Another Sun* (1940).

Undoubtedly, one of Dorothy Thompson's most admirable traits and her major strength was her uncompromising honesty, her willingness to express views that might alienate her readership. To Christians, she spoke of anti-Semitism, to Jews of the displaced Arabs, to Republicans of the strengths of Franklin Roosevelt, to Democrats of the virtues of Dwight D. Eisenhower. If Dorothy Thompson's writing on political candidates annoyed her critics, her consistent humanism won her many admirers. Among these was Winston Churchill, who said, "Miss Dorothy Thompson has won a famous name. She has shown what one valiant woman can do with the power of the pen. Freedom and humanity are grateful debtors."

Rosa Ponselle (1897-)
OPERA DIVA

"When you hear the voice of Rosa Ponselle, you hear a fountain of melody blessed by the Lord," observed another great diva, Geraldine Farrar. Opera buffs who have heard Ponselle, live or on records, will agree that hers was a voice of exquisite beauty. Rosa Ponselle was the first American-born and American-trained singer to debut in a principal role at the Metropolitan Opera. Her success created opportunities for succeeding American singers.

Rosa Ponzillo was born in Meriden, Connecticut, on January 22, 1897. Her parents, poor, illiterate Neapolitan immigrants, produced three children—Rosa, her brother Antonio, and her sister Carmela— gifted with exceptional, natural operatic voices. Rosa never had a singing lesson in her entire life, and only received coaching sessions as a mature artist. As a child, Rosa and her older sister, Carmela, studied piano, and it was as a piano player in a silent-movie house that Rosa began her career.

Here is Ponselle's own account of her meteoric rise during her childhood:

My sister Carmela, who had all the drive and ambition I lacked, took me to the manager of the Bristol movie house in Meriden, because she was convinced that I was old enough to start earning my keep. Before long, the manager of the rival theater in town made me a better offer, and I took it. This same fellow had a second movie house near Wallingford . . . and he paid me extra to play there on weekends. From there, I got a very good position as a soloist in a fashionable New Haven restaurant. . . .

At the age of 18, Rosa ceased her activities as an accompanist, and began to perform as a singer. Her older sister again provided the impetus. Carmela, a contralto, was already embarked on a highly successful career in vaudeville. Her manager, noting that sister variety acts were the rage, asked Carmela if she had a girl friend who could sing soprano and would pose as her sister. Carmela was delighted to arrange for her actual sister, Rosa, to come to New York to audition.

Rosa has described this audition, which took place in her sister's apartment:

. . . I was my own accompanist. Before Hughes heard me sing, he took one look at my waistline . . . and then gestured to Carmela that I was too plump for the stage. Then he heard me, and all he said was, "I don't give a good damn how fat she is, when can she open with you?"

Booked as "Those Tailored Italian Girls," Rosa and Carmela toured the vaudeville houses of New York, winning popular and critical acclaim. Beginning in 1916 in the Fox Theater in the Bronx, they rapidly moved up the entertainment circuit to become a headline act at the famed Palace Theater in late 1917. The sisters' act was essentially operatic—they sang a duet version of the prison scene from Gounod's *Faust*, and arias by Offenbach, Victor Herbert, and other light classical composers.

One night, the opera conductor and composer Romano Romani heard the girls perform at the Riverside Theater. Captivated by Rosa's expressive soprano voice and her dramatic talent, he introduced the girls to William Thorner, later Rosa's and Carmela's manager. In May, 1918, Thorner arranged for the celebrated tenor, En-rico Caruso, to come to his studio to hear Romani accompany the sisters in selected opera arias and duets. Ponselle recalls Caruso's encouraging response to her singing:

After he heard me, he told me confidently that I had everything I needed in the throat and in the heart, and that what remained was for me to get what I needed musically in my head. Then he told me flatly, "You'll sing with me." That next fall I made my debut opposite him in Forza del Destino, *and it seemed just that—the force of destiny.*

The forces of destiny, it seemed, included a happy combination of Ponselle's unique talent, and helpful circumstances. Caruso conveyed his enthusiasm to Giulio Gatti Cassazza, the general manager of the Metropolitan Opera. He, in turn, arranged for Rosa to audition at the Met, which was experiencing a shortage of leading dramatic sopranos, due to the war. After her somewhat less than brilliant audition, Gatti took Rosa into his office, closed the door, and went to his desk. Expecting to be turned down, Rosa was surprised to be offered a one-year contract for the 1918-1919 seasons.

Ponselle's historic debut on November 15, 1918 was a triumph. The 21-year-old soprano, who had only twice attended the Met as a spectator, and who was suffering from an acute case of opening-night nerves, took the audience by storm. She was singing one of the most demanding Verdi roles, the dramatic Leonora in *La Forza del Destino*. It was, in fact, a perfect part for Ponselle's pure, warm soprano, but she nearly collapsed from stage-fright before making her entrance. Rosa's debut drew kudos from the reviewers, but after the performance, she spent several days in the hospital recuperating from emotional exhaustion. Rosa suffered from hypersensitivity throughout her career.

Jubilant over Ponselle's smashing success, the Metropolitan management immediately offered her a long-term contract. Ponselle sang at the Met for nearly two decades. Among her most memorable roles were the heroines of *La Gioconda and Norma*. The Met revived exclusively for her such classical operas as Spontini's *La Vestale, Luisa Miller, Don Giovanni,* and she premiered in works such as Breil's *The Legend,* and Montemezzi's *The Night of Zoraima.* An affecting singing-actress, Ponselle particularly excelled as the type of heroine described by the Italians as *dolce*, literally meaning sweet, but perhaps more aptly interpreted as innocent.

Ponselle rapidly became a legend among American operagoers. She would surely have enjoyed international success, had not timidity dissuaded her from performing abroad, where audiences have few qualms about booing or hissing a singer who is having an off-night, or is becoming a threat to the local favorite. Rosa was terrified of the Continental claques, particularly of Italian audiences. However, she did consent to sing at the Florence Festival of 1933, and she spent three seasons at Covent Garden. She opened at the British Opera house in May 1929, in the difficult dramatic role of Norma. Her melting pianissimos won the hearts of her listeners, and Ponselle was proclaimed *prima donna assoluta*.

On December 27, 1935, Ponselle sang the title role in *Carmen* at the Met, and drew the first strongly negative reviews of her career. In 1937, the Met refused her request to revive *Adriana Lecouvreur*. Ponselle gave her last operatic performance in Cleveland in April 1937 in *Carmen*. In 1938, she asked that her name be removed from the Met rosters and formally ended her operatic career.

Following her retirement, at age 40, Ponselle married Baltimore insurance executive Carle A. Jackson. After making an emotional readjustment, Ponselle resumed her activity in the music world, helping to further the careers of promising young singers. In 1950, she and Jackson were divorced. Since 1950, she has served as artistic director of the Baltimore Civic Opera where she continues to champion new musical talent. In 1976, she commissioned and produced an opera, *Inez de Castro*, by the young but extraordinarily gifted opera composer Thomas Pasatieri.

Velvet, seamless, sinuous, molten, ductile, liquid, expressive—these are the adjectives that have been used to describe Ponselle's voice. Hers was a soprano of incredible range, plummeting from the mellow middle register to creamy contralto tones, and then soaring above the staff into dazzling displays of coloratura pyrotechnics. Register breaks were never apparent in Ponselle's singing: she executed perilous chromatic passages with enviable ease, and her *legato*, or long line, was all of a piece. Her pitch was unerringly accurate; her breath control, awesome; her trills, lush; her *pianissimos*, sublime.

Doubtless, Ponselle possessed from birth extraordinary vocal equipment, the elastic vocal chords and muscles and an expansive diaphragm that are necessary for opera singing. But that alone does not account for her special genius. Ponselle put a dramatic and expressive emphasis into *bel canto* music unmatched until the arrival of Maria Callas on the operatic stage. Ponselle was rare among sopranos in possessing a richly-colored instrument, and like Callas, she acted with her voice. Her characterizations are harrowing in their emotional authenticity. Never has there been a more eloquent plea for peace than Ponselle's *pace, pace, il mio Dio*, from *Forza*. In all her roles, Ponselle combined superb psychological penetration with sure technique and ineffable tonal beauty. Her diction was precise; her phrasing exquisite. She set a standard of artistry in opera that has rarely been equalled, and never surpassed.

Ponselle has also made a valuable contribution to the history of opera in bringing to the stage lesser known works of composers. Ponselle had a penchant for the operatic rarities of Bellini and Spontini, and took advantage of her superstar status to induce opera houses to revive them.

Ponselle performed an immense service by opening the Met's doors to native-born singers, including her sister Carmela, whose Metropolitan debut occurred five years after Rosa's.

Puccini, on his deathbed, summoned Rosa Ponselle to sing for him, lamenting that he would not live to create a role for the diva. For this honorific occasion, Ponselle aptly chose one of Puccini's arias from *Tosca, Vissi d'arte*—"I lived for art." At the age of 81, Rosa Ponselle continues to live for art—and thanks to her superb RCA and Columbia recordings, her art will live forever.

Amelia Earhart (1897-1937)
AVIATOR

Eleven-year-old Amelia Earhart shut her book with a dissatisfied bang. "I wish," she told her younger sister, "that just once someone would write a book—a pleasant one—about a girl shipping on an oil-tanker, say, finding the crew about to mutiny, and saving the captain's life. I'm so tired of stories where the men have all the adventures and the women just sit at home waiting for the men to return."

Muriel shrugged her shoulders. "But that's how it is in real life, Amelia. The men do have the adventures, and the women do stay at home."

"Well, it's not right," insisted Amelia. "And it doesn't have to be that way. When I grow up, I'm going to have adventures and show the world that women can be heroic as well as men."

Amelia fulfilled her childhood pledge. The first woman to fly solo across the Atlantic, and the first individual to fly 2,400 miles across the Pacific from Hawaii to the U.S. mainland, unaccompanied, Earhart was a modern Ulysses. Her aerial odysseys finally demolished the sex-stereotypes of wandering males returning to their waiting Penelopes—it was her husband, George Putnam, who stayed by the fire and awaited Amelia's return from her speed and altitude record-setting flights.

Amelia Earhart was born on July 24, 1897, in Atchison, Kansas. Amelia's father was an itinerant railroad lawyer, and her mother a member of one of Atchison's leading families. The marital alliance was filled with strife because of Mr. Earhart's drinking problem.

Amelia and her sister Muriel, three years Amelia's junior, enjoyed more freedom from restraint than was generally afforded girls. They often accompanied their father on fishing trips, and shared a rough-and-tumble outdoor existence unusual for girls of their time. The girls scorned to ride sitting properly on "girls' sleds" with wooden runners; they had their father build them low-slung steel-runner sleds so they could "belly whop" down the slopes the way boys did. But it was always Amelia, rather than the more demure Muriel, who challenged the standards of the day as to what was appropriate for young females. It was Amelia who constructed a roller coaster from the ridgepole of her grandparents' shed roof to the yard some distance below, and descended the daredevil course in a little car mounted on roller skates. Amelia's parents eyed the jerry-built roller coaster with alarm, and dismantled the contraption one night when the girls were aseep.

But Amelia's adventurous spirit continued to seek new outlets. Her wanderlust was whetted by the vagabond lifestyle imposed on the family by Mr. Earhart's job. Long periods of her childhood were spent in the private coach of a railroad train, traveling between midwestern American towns. This perambulatory lifestyle prevented Amelia from attending school regularly. She was a student at six different high schools in four years, before graduating from Hyde Park high school in Chicago in 1915. By that time, Mr. Earhart's dipsomania had cost him his job, and the family till was empty. But an inheritance from her maternal grandmother enabled Amelia to enroll at the Ogontz Preparatory School in Philadelphia.

During World War I, in December 1917, Amelia spent Christmas vacation with her sister in Toronto, Canada. Seeing some soldiers on crutches in the street, Amelia impetuously decided to remain in Canada as a Red Cross aide instead of returning to her school in Philadelphia. Amelia was assigned as a nurse's aide and worked long hours in the kitchen and dispensary.

In Canada, Amelia became enthralled with the romantic exploits of the Royal Flying Corps, and decided she would like to fly; and in 1919, she enrolled in a pre-medical program at Columbia University, simultaneously taking liberal arts courses at Barnard College.

But during her first semester of school, Amelia discovered that her parents were on the brink of a divorce, and in the hope of keeping the marriage together, went to live with them in Los Angeles. In California, Amelia's interest in flying was renewed when she and her father attended an exhibition of stunt-flying at a local airfield. Amelia was spellbound by the aerial acrobatics, and arranged to go up in a small plane. By the time the plane was 300 feet off the ground, Amelia knew she had to learn to fly a plane herself.

But flying lessons were expensive, and the money the family had inherited had been dissipated in unprofitable speculations. So Amelia took a mundane job with the telephone company, "putting marks on paper all day," to finance her aeronautical education. Amelia's first flying teacher was a woman aviator, Neta Snook.

In June, 1921, Amelia Earhart made her first solo flight. On her 25th birthday, with financial help from her mother, Amelia bought her own plane, a secondhand Kinner Canary. Soon, she was swooping about the skies practicing stalls, spins, wingovers, and vertical drops. Toward the end of 1922, Amelia Earhart set a new altitude record for women, of 14,000 feet.

Amelia's efforts to reconcile her parents were unsuccessful, and in 1924, Amelia and her divorced mother headed east. Amelia briefly resumed her pre-medical studies, but decided a medical career was not for her. What then, could she do? It did not occur to Amelia at this time to make a career of flying. She had sold her plane before leaving Los Angeles. Still committed to the ideal of social service, Amelia decided to emulate her sister and become a teacher. Amelia and Mrs. Earhart went to Medford, Massachusetts to live with Muriel, and Amelia enrolled in education courses at Harvard University Summer School. After a brief stint teaching English to immigrants, she became a social worker at the Denison Settlement House in Boston.

Amelia joined the Boston chapter of the National Aeronautics Association "for the fun of it," but her salary of $60 a month did not leave much to be saved for purchasing another plane.

One day in 1928, Amelia Earhart was called out of the girls' class she was teaching at Denison House to answer a phone call from the National Aeronautics Board in New York City. It seemed that Mrs. Frederick Guest, a wealthy American transplanted to England, wished to sponsor a goodwill flight between her native and adopted countries. A pilot, Wilmer Stultz, and a mechanic, Lou Gordon, had already been selected for the flight, but Mrs. Guest insisted that a woman passenger accompany the two men. In fact, Mrs. Guest had originally planned to play the passenger role herself, but her family had objected. Finding Amelia's name on the N.A.A. rolls, the N.A.B. called to ask if Amelia would be interested in substituting for Mrs. Guest. Would she! Amelia took the next train to New York for an interview with the sponsoring committee.

The chairman of the interviewing committee was George Palmer Putnam, a book publisher whose authors included Charles A. Lindbergh. Putnam was struck by Amelia's physical resemblance to the male aviator-hero. Perhaps this goodwill flight might produce another best-selling author for the G.P. Putnam Publishing Company. So Amelia Earhart was chosen to make the trip, and commissioned to write up the voyage for G.P. Putnam's.

On June 17, 1928, the *Friendship* airplane took off from Trepassy Bay, Newfoundland. Wedged between the gas tanks, Amelia Earhart logged the plane's flight, which took 20 hours and 40 minutes. She also took a brief turn in the cockpit. Due to heavy fog, the triumvirate had to land in Burry Port, Wales, and from there they flew to Southampton, England the following day. When the *Friendship* landed at Southampton, Amelia Earhart was given a hero's welcome. On her return to New York, Amelia was also feted with a tickertape parade and a message of congratulation from President Coolidge. The short-haired woman aviator had captured the public imagination, and "Lady Lindy" found herself a national heroine.

But Amelia Earhart was anything but thrilled by her celebrity. She felt she had been a mere mascot on the transatlantic flight, and the international fanfare seemed disproportionate. Moreover, Amelia was disturbed by the implication that a back seat was the proper place for women in aviation. She determined to cross the Atlantic again—but in the cockpit.

Her unsought notoriety did have one fortunate consequence.

Amelia Earhart would now be able to finance her career in aviation. She was offered high-salaried positions as aviation editor of *Cosmopolitan* magazine, and as vice-president of Luddington Airlines. Token positions, perhaps, but Amelia decided to accept these jobs and to capitalize on her public image as the exuberant, teetotalling, all-American aviatrix to obtain parity for women in aviation. Remembering her childhood longing to read stories about women adventurers, she determined to give little girls a real woman explorer to read about.

In 1929, Amelia Earhart placed third in the first Women's Air Derby from Santa Monica, California to Cleveland. The following year, she set a new woman's speed record of 181 miles per hour. In 1931, Amelia made several transcontinental flights in an autogyro, a precursor of the helicopter, as a publicity stunt for the Beech-Nut Company. Her manager was George Putnam, who had promoted Amelia's first transatlantic flight and published her account of it.

In 1931, Amelia Earhart and George Putnam were married. Earhart made the continuation of her career as an aviator a condition of the marriage. (The couple never had any children, though Putnam had two sons by a previous marriage.) George Putnam not only encouraged his wife's flying exploits, he turned them to commercial advantage, bringing out a line of flight luggage and sports clothing in her name, and publishing Amelia's successive books about her flights.

But Earhart was still troubled by the sense that she was an aviation mascot, and planned to destroy this impression by making a solo transatlantic flight. On May 21, 1932, Amelia Earhart made her flight and became the first individual to cross the Atlantic by airplane twice. In her secondhand, one-engine, high-wing, red Vega monoplane, Amelia flew from Newfoundland to Ireland in just under 15 hours. Her altimeter failed before the last 2,000 miles of the voyage were completed, and she landed with part of the plane's mechanism on fire. But mishaps like these were common in those early days of aviation, and Amelia bitterly resented the occasional insinuations that her share of accidents was somehow related to her sex. She frequently iterated that "in anything that requires intelligence, coordination, spirit, coolness, will power, and not too heavy muscular strength, women can meet men on their own ground."

In 1932, Amelia Earhart published *The Fun of It.* Her famed transatlantic flight brought her international celebrity. She became the second non-British honorary member of the British Guild of Air Pilots and Navigators; a decorated Chevalier of the French Legion of Honor; a Chevalier in the Belgian Order of Leopold; and the recipient of the Harmon International Trophy, the Distinguished Flying Cross awarded by the U.S. Congress, and the gold medal of the National Geographic Society. Amelia's response to her apotheosis was, "I think that the appreciation of the deed is out of proportion to the deed itself," but added, "I shall be happy if my small exploit has drawn attention to the fact that women, too, are flying."

And fly she did. That same year, she set a new woman's record for a nonstop transcontinental flight from Los Angeles to Newark, New Jersey, at 19 hours and five minutes. Within a year, Earhart broke her own record, flying the same 2,448 miles in 17 hours, seven minutes, and 30 seconds.

But Amelia Earhart was not satisfied to replicate men's achievements in aviation. In 1935, she accomplished three feats never before achieved by man or woman. In January, Amelia Earhart became the first person to fly solo from Hawaii to North America. Three months later, she completed the first solo flight between Los Angeles and Mexico City. Three weeks after this, she flew nonstop from Mexico City to Newark, another aeronautical milestone.

Earhart sought ways to be of direct service to women. In June, 1935, she found her opportunity, when Purdue University offered her a job as career counselor for women, and special advisor in aeronautics. She was very popular as a dean of women at Purdue, where she advised the young women students, "A girl must nowadays believe completely in herself as an individual. She must realize at the outset that a woman must do the same job better than a man to get as much credit for it."

The Purdue trustees purchased a "Flying Laboratory," an $80,000 Lockheed Electra plane. Now Amelia began to dream of making as "just one last flight" an aerial circumnavigation of the globe by a never before traveled Equator route. Her object was not to establish a speed record, but to pioneer in air-safety studies. The voyage would test long-range human reactions and mechanical performances at high altitudes and extreme temperatures. Microscopic samples of the upper atmosphere would be collected; and world airport facilities would be inspected.

The Electra, manned by Amelia Earhart and a crew of three, took off from California on March 17, 1937. At Honolulu, their first stop, a take-off accident required that the Electra be returned to California for repairs. Also, weather conditions dictated a change of route. On June 1, 1937, Earhart and navigator Fred Noonan set out together from Miami, Florida, heading east. In order to lighten the Electra's load, they had removed the plane's 250-foot antenna, thus inhibiting the plane's capacity to transmit radio signals.

As planned, Earhart and Noonan made stops at Puerto Rico, Venezuela, Brazil, and Dutch Guiana. Then they headed for Howland Island and for the last leg of the journey which would include stops in Honolulu and California. But the Electra never landed at Howland Island. Early on July 2, a Coast Guard cutter received feeble radio messages that the Electra was running short of fuel, with no land in sight. At 8:45 a.m. came the message "overcast . . . circling—cannot see island." Then, "gas running low . . . running north and south." The Electra was never heard from again.

United States ships and planes combed the Pacific searching for remnants of the Electra; but neither the plane nor the bodies of Amelia Earhart and Fred Noonan were ever found. Rumors that the two aviators had landed on an atoll in the Pacific and had been captured—and perhaps executed—by the Japanese were rife throughout the 1950s, but these reports were never verified.

We shall probably never discover the true fate of the brave woman whose exploits continue to inspire women to ascend the empyrean heights. Anticipating the possibility that she would not return from her final long flight, Amelia left a letter to be opened in the event she died. "Hooray for the last great adventure," she wrote. "I wish I had won but it was worthwhile anyway. . . ." To this, posterity can only add a heartfelt *amen*.

Dorothy Day (1897-   )

HUMANITARIAN AND FOUNDER OF THE CATHOLIC WORKER MOVEMENT

The Bowery—what fearful images are evoked; drunkards in door-ways, wearing clothes as seedy as out-of-season cucumbers; puffy-eyed women of indeterminate age stationed on curbstones beneath eye-less tenements, begging small change from each passerby. By day, these woeful vagrants forage in the garbage cans of every New York neighborhood, or aimlessly ride the subways, clutching brown paper bags stuffed with their findings. At twilight, the scavengers return to the Bowery to join their companions, darting into traffic to attempt to wipe a rolled-up car window: "Please sir, 25 cents for a cup of coffee. Gold bless you, sir."

Bums, loafers, junkies, sots, vagabonds, outcasts, soiled, un-shaven, reeking of gin or cheap wine—there is nothing romantic about the Bowery poor. Those who have entered here have abandoned every hope, and have been abandoned as hopeless by the rest of humanity. But Dorothy Day and her Catholic Worker movement have not for-saken the Bowery dwellers. On East Third Street stands Maryhouse; on East First Street St. Joseph's; at these houses of hospitality, the flotsam and jetsam of New York's forgotten men and women can find sustenance, shelter, and sympathy.

There are also Catholic Worker hospices in other major American cities, and Catholic Worker farms in many rural areas. *The Catholic Worker*, Dorothy Day's eight-page newspaper, publicizes the plight of the homeless and heartsore, and scores the need for government intervention in the poverty of "the other America." *The Catholic Worker* still sells at the price established in 1933—a penny a copy. And Dorothy Day is still the polestar of a movement dedicated to voluntary poverty, absolute pacifism, communal living, and regeneration of the downtrodden. Few Christians have ever lived their Christianity as literally as Dorothy Day does. No wonder that, when asked to name a great American Catholic, Archbishop Jean Jabot said he could think of only one: Dorothy Day.

Dorothy Day was not born into the Roman Catholic Church. Her father was a Congregationalist, her mother an Episcopalian, and the little religious upbringing that the Days gave their three sons and two daughters was lukewarm Episcopalianism. Born in Brooklyn Heights, New York, on November 8, 1897, Dorothy was the third child. When she was six years old, the family moved to the San Francisco area, where her father worked as a sportswriter on a California newspaper. Dorothy's mother was one of the first women trained as a stenographer.

During the San Francisco earthquake of 1906, Dorothy pitched in to help the victims of the disaster, and so discovered very early "the joy of doing good, of sharing whatever we had with others." Her father decided to quit the disaster area, and moved his family to Chicago. Mr. Day, who often worked at home, refused to let his children bring visitors to the house. An authoritarian with rigorous intellectual standards, he established a ban on light literature, picture books, and detective stories. When Dorothy was ten, she and her siblings began their own newspaper, but Mr. Day did not approve of his daughters engaging in journalism. Dorothy turned her attention toward religion, becoming a member of a local Episcopalian Church.

At Robert Waller High School in Chicago, Dorothy showed a facility for languages, and the Classics teacher, Mr. Matheson, tutored her privately in Greek and Latin. At the same time, Dorothy was devouring the works of Dostoevsky, Tolstoi, Peter Kropotkin, Jack London, and Upton Sinclair. Impressed by Sinclair's exposé in *The Jungle* of the unsanitary conditions in Chicago's meat-packing industry, Dorothy and her young brother explored the *abattoirs* and the slums of Chicago's West Side. Dorothy felt that her lot was irrevocably cast with the poor. "I had received a call, a vocation, a direction to my life."

At the age of 16, Dorothy graduated from high school, and won a $300 Hearst scholarship to the University of Illinois at Urbana. She supplemented her scholarship by doing housework, babysitting, and newspaper writing. Disaffected by "the ugliness of life in a world which professed itself to be Christian," Dorothy Day joined the Socialist Party during her first year of college. Frequently she fasted and during her second year at college, she wrote an article about the experience of going hungry that brought her to the attention of a brilliant and wealthy fellow student, Rayna Prohme. Ten years later, this extraordinary woman was to smuggle Mme. Sun Yat-sen from China to Russia. At college, Rayna Prohme shared Dorothy's left-wing proclivities, and the two women became close friends. Rayna took Dorothy under her wing, paying the rent for their shared apartment and introducing Dorothy to a number of aspiring writers. With Rayna, Dorothy attended lectures by visiting Socialists and other radical activists.

After studying English, history, Latin, and science for two years, Dorothy left Urbana in 1916, and went to New York, where her father was now racing editor of the *Morning Telegraph*. But Mr. Day objected to both Dorothy's Socialism and her journalistic ambitions, so she left home. She describes this period of her life as a slough of despond. "I found no friends; I had no work; I was separated from my fellows . . . My own silence, the feeling that I had no one to talk to, overwhelmed me so that my very throat was constricted . . . I wanted to weep my loneliness away."

Finally, Dorothy landed a job as a reporter and columnist for the Socialist newspaper *The Call*. She covered strikes, picket lines, bread riots, and demonstrations at City Hall, and interviewed various radical leaders, including Leon Trotsky. Living in Greenwich Village, Dorothy attended lectures by anarchists Emma Goldman and Alexander Birkman, and by Wobbly agitators Elizabeth Gurley Flynn and Bill Haywood. Attracted by the organization's direct-action techniques, Dorothy joined the International Workers of the World.

In 1917, Dorothy joined the staff of the spirited radical monthly *The Masses*. Edited by Max Eastman, Floyd Dell, and Merrill Rogers, *The Masses* was a gathering ground for such left-wing intellectuals as Malcolm Cowley, John Dos Passos, and Eugene O'Neill. Dorothy was dismayed that her collaborators at *The Masses* were not as liberal on race relations as on other political issues. She told one of the gazette's editors that if she ever heard him use the term "niggers" again, she would slap his face.

Six months after Dorothy joined *The Masses*, the paper was suppressed because of its pacifist stance during World War I. Some of Dorothy's colleagues were harassed, beaten, and even murdered. She took work as a model for art classes, and began to interest herself in the inchoate suffragette movement. In June, 1917, Dorothy joined a feminist picket-line at the White House and was arrested and taken to jail, where she was beaten and mauled by the prison guards. She was thrown into a cell where one of the suffragette leaders was chained to the prison bars with handcuffs. The women were denied the right of legal consultation. When they went on a hunger strike in protest, they were forcibly fed. Prison was a horrifying eye-opener for Dorothy Day:

I lost consciousness of any cause. I had no sense of being a radical, making a protest against a government. I lost all feeling of my own identity. I reflected on the desolation of poverty, of destitution, of sickness and sin. That I would be free again after thirty days meant nothing to me. I would never be free again.

After her release, Dorothy worked for a short while at a new radical newspaper, *The Liberator*. But in 1918, responding to the wartime need for nurses, she became a probationary nurse at Kings County Hospital in Brooklyn. A year later, she went to Europe, where she wrote a novel, *The Eleventh Virgin*. The movie rights to her novel were sold for $5,000, assuring her economic independence for the while.

Dorothy had had some fleeting love affairs, but her only serious relationship with a man was with Forster Batterham. "The man I loved, with whom I entered into a common-law marriage, was an anarchist, an Englishman by descent, and a biologist." For four years, Dorothy lived with Batterham.

In March 1927, at the age of 29, Dorothy Day gave birth to her only child, Tamar. Childbirth was a revelation for Dorothy. "To think that this thing of beauty . . . had come from my flesh, was my own child. Such a great feeling of happiness filled me that I was hungry for someone to thank, to love. . . ." The someone Dorothy turned to was God. Drawn by the meditations of Saint Thomas à Kempis and the *Confessions* of Saint Augustine to the Roman Catholic Church, Dorothy had her daughter baptized in the Catholic faith in July, 1927. The following December, Dorothy herself joined the Church. Forster Batterham, an atheist, had no sympathy for Roman Catholicism, or any other religion. Dorothy's conversion meant the end of their relationship, and also sundered her from her other Bohemian friends.

She supported herself and her daughter by taking a job as a scriptwriter for Pathé films in Hollywood. But the Babylon of screenland was not a congenial environemnt for a practicing Catholic, and not meeting kindred spirits, Dorothy found herself "lonely, dead lonely." In her autobiography, *The Long Loneliness*, Dorothy wrote:

I was to find out then, as I found out so many times, over and over again, that women especially are social beings, who are not content with just husband and family, but must have a community, a group, an exchange with others. A child is not enough. A husband and children, no matter how busy one may be kept by them, are not enough. Young and old, even in the busiest years of our lives, we women especially are victims of the long loneliness.

During three years as a practising Catholic, Dorothy had not found a single Catholic friend. Her conversion was viewed with hostility and suspicion by many Catholics, who thought that Dorothy might be a Communist infiltrator plotting some nefarious scheme against the Church. Dorothy, in turn, was dismayed by the Church's lack of involvement in social causes. Covering a hunger march in Washington for *Commonweal* in 1932, Dorothy noted that there were no Catholic organizations participating in the demonstration. As she watched the representatives of the 12 million unemployed Americans parade down Pennsylvania Avenue, Dorothy thought:

Far dearer in the sight of God, perhaps, are these hungry ragged ones, than all those smug well-fed Christians who sit in their homes cowering in fear of the Communist menace. . . . How little, how puny, my work had been since becoming a Catholic. How self-centered, how ingrown, how lacking in a sense of community.

Dorothy recalled an essay by William James, in *The Varieties of Religious Experience*, where James wrote:

Poverty is indeed the strenuous life—without brass bands or uniforms or hysteric popular applause or lies or circumlocutions; and when one sees the way in which wealth-getting enters as an ideal into the very bone and marrow of our generation, one wonders whether the revival of the belief that poverty is a worthy religious vocation may not be the transformation of military courage, and the spiritual reform which our time stands most in need of.

She became obsessed by the ideal of voluntary poverty. But how to realize it? Then, on December 10, 1932, Dorothy was visited by Peter Maurin, a French-born Roman Catholic utopian visionary. Maurin had read Day's articles in *Commonweal*, and sensed in her a kindred spirit, a personalist Christian who might help him implement his dream of a "green revolution," which would bring intellectuals and workers together in urban houses of hospitality for the needy and in rural farming communes. Maurin had been roaming the United States as a lecturer, promulgating his ideas in "easy essays," which he recited in public places like New York's Union Square. Now Maurin wanted to start a newspaper. Dorothy Day agreed to participate in the venture, and the Catholic Worker newspaper and movement were born.

On May 1, 1933, within four months of Dorothy's meeting with Maurin, the first issue of *The Catholic Worker* was published. The newspaper was sold in Union Square at the price of a penny a copy.

When Irishmen objected to the use of the British word *penny*, it was changed in the next issue to *cent*. Then a black man complained that the colophon showed two white workers, so it was changed in the third issue to depict a white laborer and a black laborer.

By 1934, the circulation of *The Catholic Worker* had grown to 100,000; by 1936 to 150,000. By 1939, every reform-conscious Catholic in America was reading what *The Catholic Worker* had to say about unemployment, labor, race relations, Catholic literature, and other topics. Maurin was the inspirational force behind the paper, but it was Dorothy Day who did the legwork, as publisher, editor-in-chief, and business manager. Although Dorothy credits Peter Maurin with founding the Catholic Worker movement, he seems to have been a combination Mr. Micawber and Saint Francis of Assisi, optimistically trusting to Providence. Dorothy took a more realistic Heaven-helps-those-who-help-themselves stance, doing all the hard, nitty-gritty work herself.

From its inception, the Catholic Worker movement was besieged by needy men and women looking for a bowl of soup, a night's lodging, or a kind word. For women, the housing problem was particularly acute, for the cheap Bowery flophouses excluded women, as they do to this day. So Dorothy Day established Saint Joseph's House of Hospitality, moving from one location to another in lower Manhattan until it finally settled in its current home on First Street. Begun as a soup kitchen and hospice for both men and women, Saint Joseph's restricted its lodgings to male wayfarers when a sister institution, Maryhouse, now on Third Street, opened its facilities to women. Today, both hospices are open to both sexes.

During the 1930s, Catholic Worker houses sprang up in 30 cities across the United States, and Catholic Worker farms were established as work retreats for country dwellers. The Catholic Worker staff draw no salaries.

At the age of 82, Dorothy Day is still the head of the Catholic Worker movement. She has been variously eyed as a potentially dangerous maverick, or tacitly acknowledged as a modern day saint. She has gone to jail many times in the past 40 years in connection with her war resistance work, and during the Vietnam War was the friend and champion of the Berrigans and other Catholic war resisters.

It was Dorothy Day who, during World War II, was the prime mover in securing conscientious objector status for Catholic pacifists. Since 1955, the Catholic Workers have actively opposed nuclear preparedness and other manifestations of militarism in American society. In her editorial column "On Pilgrimage," Dorothy Day continues to provide, nine times a year, cogent analyses of such problems as poverty and affluence in the modern world, the role of women in the 20th century, the relation between prayer and politics, and the responsibilities of Catholics in secular causes.

The poor we will always have with us; thank God we also have our Dorothy Days.

Catholic Workers protest.

Golda Mabovitch Meir
(1898-1978)

ISRAELI PATRIOT AND PRIME MINISTER

In 1921, a young American couple named Myerson applied for admission to the agricultural collective, or *kibbutz*, of Merhavia, near Tel Aviv, Israel. Their application was rejected; the *kibbutz* members had no objection to Morris Myerson, but they doubted that his wife, an American girl, would be able to withstand the rigors of *kibbutz* life. Morris accepted the decision and was prepared to settle in Tel Aviv, but Golda would not leave Merhavia. She had come to Israel to work on a *kibbutz*, and work at Merhavia she would. A few days later, Golda Myerson was threshing grain for the cooperative settlement. Her fortitude—and the hornless phonograph that she offered the *kibbutz* as her "dowry"—had so impressed the kibbutzniks that they reversed their decision and accepted the Myersons as members of their commune. Little did they realize that the gutsy 23-year-old former Milwaukee school teacher would go on to become ambassador to Moscow; minister of labor; foreign minister; and finally, prime minister of Israel.

The world's second woman prime minister (Indira Ghandi of India was the first), Golda Mabovitch was born in Kiev, Russia on May 3, 1898. She was the second of three surviving daughters of a Jewish carpenter and his energetic wife. Mrs. Mabovitch had the independent spirit that her middle daughter was apparently to inherit; she had by-passed the marriage broker and had chosen her own husband, who was then a soldier in the Russian army.

One of Golda Mabovitch's earliest memories was of boarding up the house in preparation for a *pogrom.* Turn-of-the-century Russia was not a congenial climate for Jews; and in 1903, Golda's father decided to go to America, to see if he could establish a home for his family in a land where they would not be persecuted for their religion. When she was eight, Golda's father sent for his family, and they left Russia to settle in Milwaukee, Wisconsin.

In Milwaukee, Golda's enterprising mother opened a small shop, which was the bane of Golda's existence. She had to mind the store every morning, so Golda was always late for school. "So it will take you an extra day to become a learned lady," the imperturbable Mrs. Mabovitch told Golda, with the same philosophical wit her daughter was later to display.

With three independent-minded girls, there were frequent clashes in the Mabovitch household. Golda's older sister, who had belonged to a clandestine Socialist-Zionist party in Russia, disowned her parents as "petty bourgeois," and left home for Colorado. Against her parents' will, Golda persisted in her goal of becoming a teacher, and enrolled in high school instead of secretarial school. The Mabovitches did not want Golda to become a teacher because Wisconsin law prohibited married women from teaching, and they feared their middle daughter would turn into a bluestocking old maid.

Eventually, Golda made peace with her parents, and entered the Teachers' Training College at Madison, Wisconsin. But her parents were again chagrined when she joined a radical Zionist organization and lectured on streetcorners despite her father's threat that he would pull her off the podium by her braid. When Golda and her sister announced, in 1921 that they were going to Palestine to live, the Mabovitches were disconsolate. But later, in 1926, they joined their daughters in the Jewish homeland.

Golda Meir did not sail for Palestine alone. While in Denver, she had fallen in love with Morris Myerson, a gentle intellectual. She refused to marry Myerson until he consented to go with her to build *Eretz Israel.* Before Golda's 19th birthday, Morris agreed to emigrate.

For three years, the Myersons lived on the Merhavia kibbutz, where Golda helped to produce grain and raise poultry, established nurseries for the children, and introduced dietary innovations—such as oatmeal instead of herring for breakfast. In 1924, Morris Myerson, exhausted by the strenuous agricultural labor that never seemed to tire his wife, suggested that they leave the kibbutz and move to the city and begin a family. Moris disapproved of collective child-rearing, and wanted Golda to become a full-time homemaker. Reluctantly, she agreed to the move, and for four years the couple lived in dire poverty, first in Tel Aviv and then in Jerusalem. During this time, Golda gave birth to two children, a son and a daughter. But home and family could not contain Golda's driving energy, nor her hunger to contribute to the building of a labor-Zionist state. She joined the Histradut, the general federation of Jewish labor, and in 1928, she was appointed executive secretary of the Women's Labor Council. From 1932 to 1934, she went to work in the United States, as a representative of the Pioneer Women's Organization.

Morris Myerson objected to his wife's prolonged absences and the couple separated, although they were never legally divorced and remained friendly. Golda was rent by the conflict between family and career. In a poignant essay, "Women's Lib—1930," she asked:

Am I at fault, if after giving (my children) and the one other person nearest to me a place in my heart, some part of me still demands to be filled by activities outside the family and home?. . . . If a woman does remain exclusively with her children . . . does that really prove that she is more devoted than the less conventional mother?

Having made her choice, the dynamic Golda rose rapidly in the Palestinian labor movement. During World War II, she pleaded before the British Mandatory authorities for the establishment of a Jewish state. When words were ineffective, Golda resorted to more dramatic measures. She fasted for 101 hours, along with eleven of her colleagues, until the British lifted their blockade and allowed a ship with Italian refugees to enter Palestine.

In 1946, the male leaders of the Jewish Agency to Establish a Homeland in Palestine were arrested, and Golda Myerson became head of the agency.

In 1948, the dream of the Jewish people from time immemorial, and the hope of Golda and her fellow pioneers, was realized. The state of Israel was established by edict of the United Nations. But when the British soldiers were withdrawn, Israel found itself surrounded by hostile Arab nations. Golda Myerson, disguised as a man, embarked on a secret midnight meeting with Jordan's King Abdullah, in an effort to persuade him not to enter the war. The daring attempt failed.

Golda went to America to raise funds for her embattled fledgling country, and became an eloquent spokeswoman for Zionism among American Jewry as well as among non-Jewish humanitarians. The war was won, but not the battle for survival. The Jewish Zionist state existed in a hostile enclave of Arab kingdoms. As one of the signers of the Declaration of Independence of the new nation of Israel, and later as head of state, Golda was to be called upon time and again to justify the right of the Jews to a homeland in Israel.

In the new state of Israel, Golda Myerson was appointed the first ambassador to Moscow. Here she succeeded in obtaining a building for the Israeli legation, and established trade relations between her country and the U.S.S.R. In November, 1948, she was appointed deputy foreign minister of Israel, and joined the foreign minister in Paris to participate in the United Nations negotiations on the partitioning of Palestine.

In 1949, Golda Myerson was elected to the Knesset, the Israeli Parliament, and was chosen minister of labor and social security in the Ben Gurion administration. Golda Myerson carried out major housing and road construction programs; set standards for workers; and authorized an ambitious public works program to provide jobs for the unemployed. She also continued to be a vocal proponent of a policy of unrestricted Jewish immigration to Israel.

In 1956, Prime Minister Ben Gurion insisted that his newly appointed foreign minister adopt a Hebrew name, and Golda Myerson became Golda Meir. Asked how it felt to be the first woman foreign minister of Israel, Golda Meir replied blandly, "I don't know, I was never a man minister." Her sense of humor and her gift for the unerring riposte were to serve her well in the difficult years ahead.

As foreign minister, Golda Meir strengthened Israel's diplomatic ties to Africa by procuring financial aid for the newly emerging African nations. She also represented her country in United Nations negotiations following the 1956 war with Egypt.

Few people could express as movingly as Golda the Jewish dream of a state of their own where they could live without fear of persecution or annihilation. In 1961, Golda Meir, as foreign minister went to President Kennedy to plead for arms. Elie Wiesel suggests what she said:

"You see, Mr. President, I belong to an ancient people. Twice in our history our country has been destroyed, our capital demolished, our Temple reduced to ashes, our sovereignty robbed and our children dispersed to the four corners of the earth—yet somehow we have managed to remain alive. Do you know how? I will tell you. Because of the shopkeeper in Bialystok and the tailor in Kiev, the industrialist in New York and the diamond merchant in Amsterdam, the student in Paris and the visionary in Safed. Though they came from different backgrounds, different lands, speaking different tongues, they had one thing in common—a dream that one day our sovereignty would be restored, our children ingathered and our Temple rebuilt . . . Mr. President, our Temple has not been rebuilt yet, we have just begun. But should this beginning be erased, then the shopkeeper in Bialystok and the watchmaker in Paris, the tailor in Kiev and the rebel in Leningrad, the talmudist in Brooklyn and the visionary in Safed—all these Jews who have one dream in common—would no longer even be capable of dreaming."

In 1966, plagued by illness, Golda Meir resigned as foreign minister, although she continued to represent Israel on foreign missions and at the United Nations, and became a leader of the ruling Mapai Party. In 1967, she was instrumental in bringing about a coalition between the Mapai and two smaller parties, forming the Israeli Labor Party.

When Golda Meir left her post as foreign minister, she envisioned a life of semi-retirement, and perhaps a return to kibbutz life. Her husband had died in 1951; her children were grown, with children of their own. She had accomplished her goal of helping to establish the state of Israel. But in 1969, Prime Minister Levi Eshkol died in office, and Golda Meir was asked to become the head of state. In December, 1969, the 70-year-old grandmother became the fourth prime minister of Israel, inheriting from her predecessor a constituency demoralized by constant war and economic hardship.

Throughout the early seventies, Golda attempted to achieve an end to hostilities in the Mideast through diplomatic negotiations. She met with Rumanian Premier Nicolai Ceausescu, American President Richard Nixon, and Pope Paul VI, and in 1973 welcomed West German Chancellor Willy Brandt to Israel. Meanwhile, she mediated between "hawks" and "doves" within the Israeli cabinet, and served as a rallying point for moderates who were firmly committed to the state of Israel but sought a reconciliation with their Arab neighbors.

She was not, however, to live to see Israel officially at peace with its Arab neighbors. The Yom Kippur attack by Egypt on October 6, 1973, left this brave warrior utterly disconsolate. On April 10, 1974, she resigned as prime minister. At the age of 75, Golda Meir had served her country for nearly half a century, and was ready to make way for younger patriots to assume the reins of power. A highlight of the historic occasion of Egyptian President Anwar Sadat's landing in Israel was the embrace between these two formidable old enemies. After a 12-year bout with leukemia, Golda, the beloved Jewish grandmother, died on December 8, 1978.

Golda Meir was a nonpareil among women rulers, for she rose to power not through hereditary privilege, nor powerful male connections, nor exploitation of sexual charms. Almost 50 years of devoted service to the state of Israel had demonstrated her political acumen and diplomatic facility under extreme adversity. As a wartime leader, she showed military determination, but also compassion for her adversaries. Among her many memorable utterances was: "Someday, when peace comes, we may forgive the Arabs for having killed our sons, but it will be harder for us to forgive them for having forced us to kill their sons."

Dorothy Arzner (1900-   )
MOTION-PICTURE DIRECTOR

When the Directors' Guild of America fêted Dorothy Arzner on January 25, 1975, record numbers of people vied with one another for the 1,000 spectator seats available for the occasion. Congratulatory telegrams poured in from Katharine Hepburn, Joan Crawford, Frank Capra, Joseph L. Mankiewicz, Frederic March, Lee Grant, and Los Angeles mayor Tom Bradley.

Dorothy Arzner, the first woman member of the D.G.A., was a pioneer in many areas of the motion-picture industry. One of Hollywood's Top Ten directors in the 1930s and 1940s, she was from 1930 to 1943 the only woman director in screenland. When sound first came to the screen, Dorothy Arzner was one of the first directors to make "talkie" films. She introduced the use of theme music and the overhead microphone. She was perhaps the prime mover in strengthening the role of the director in film-making.

Prior to her debut as a director, Dorothy Arzner made technical innovations in film-cutting and editing for the silent screen. A former scriptwriter, Arzner also strengthened the role of scenarists in movie-making. Scriptwriter Mary McCall Jr., who collaborated with Arzner on a number of films, said, "[Dorothy] made us part and partner of the enterprise."

On every level, Dorothy Arzner shored up the role of women in films. She employed women as scriptwriters, film-cutters, super-visors, and business managers, and rewrote scenarios to alter the heroines' roles from stereotyped vamps and virgins to complex, dynamic characters. Among the film actresses Arzner propelled to fame were Katharine Hepburn, Ruth Chatterton, Rosalind Russell, and Ginger Rogers. Three decades before Agnes Varda's *One Sings and the Other Doesn't* and Claudia Weill's *Girlfriends*, Dorothy Arzner was exploring relationships between women as no film director had ever done before, and few have done since.

Dorothy Arzner was born in San Francisco on January 3, 1900. In her childhood, Dorothy met the leading stars of stage and screen, but harbored no intention of entering the entertainment world herself. She wanted "to serve humanity by becoming a physician," and she enrolled at the University of Southern California as a pre-med major. Dorothy also studied art and architecture in college, and was an "A" student.

After driving an ambulance for many months in Los Angeles and New York, Dorothy decided a medical career was too grisly for her. Upon her return to Beverly Hills, she began to seek another means of earning a living. One day, Dorothy went on a sightseeing tour of the Famous Players-Lasky Studio. In the course of the tour, she saw William de Mille directing a movie, and decided that directing was the career for her. She went to Mr. de Mille and asked for a job. "I'm willing to start anywhere," Dorothy told him, "I'll start at the bottom."

Where she started was as a studio stenographer, earning $15 a week. Later, Dorothy looked back on the seven years she spent lear-ning the movie business from the ground up as invaluable, and recommended that all would-be movie directors first familiarize themselves with the technical and business ends of the industry.

After three months as a script typist and synopsizer, Dorothy was sent to the Nazimova Company to be a script holder, that is, the person who sits on the set and checks the script for the director.

Six months later, Dorothy was transferred to another Paramount subsidiary, Realart. In one year, Dorothy Arzner edited 32 scripts, as well as supervising a department in film-cutting and splicing.

By 1922, Dorothy Arzner had a reputation as one of the best film cutters in the industry. She introduced a new, crisper method of film-splicing and arrangement, which was soon adopted by other studios. Dorothy's editing of the silent film *Blood and Sand*, starring Rudolph Valentino, brought her to the attention of director James Cruze, who asked her to edit *The Covered Wagon* for him in 1923. The Hollywood pros were flabbergasted at 23-year-old Dorothy's masterful editing.

After two years as a film editor, Dorothy began writing screenplays. She became noted for her "galloping Western" scenarios. Then, in 1925, James Cruze asked Dorothy to serve as both scenarist and film editor for *Old Ironsides*. This movie is considered the best job of film-editing in screen history.

While on location with *Old Ironsides*, Dorothy confided to colleague James Stallings that her real ambition was to become a director. Stallings talked to Cruze, and together the two men approached Paramount mogul Jesse L. Lasky. "There's a woman here who can direct pictures if she is given the opportunity," they told him.

Women directors were not a complete novelty in Hollywood at this time. Starting with Alice Guy Blache, who came to the United States from Paris in 1910, there had been an estimated 26 women directors in this country by the year 1927. But Lasky hesitated. Finally, he had Dorothy promoted to an assistant director. She soon discovered that this was a glorified flunky job; her main duties were to see that the stars arrived on the set punctually, and to fetch coffee for the film casts and crews.

So in 1927, Dorothy Arzner went to Paramount executive Ben Schulberg, and told him she was going over to Columbia Studio, "where there didn't seem to be any prejudice against women directors." Schulberg assured Dorothy that he would make her a director at Paramount, but Dorothy was skeptical. She gave Schulberg a deadline: either she was behind a camera within the month, or she would go to Columbia. Schulberg rummaged through the papers on his desk, picked up a French farce called *The Best Dressed Women*, and said, "Here. Write yourself a script, find an actress to play the lead, and you can direct the film."

Within two weeks, Dorothy had written the script for *Fashions for Women*. Blonde bombshell Esther Ralston playing the heroine, a cigarette-girl who impersonates a well-known beauty, revealed her considerable talents as a comedienne. *Fashions* won first prize in the London International Festival of Women's Films. The movie was also a box-office smash. After another successful Ralston vehicle, *Ten Modern Commandments* (1927), Paramount gave Dorothy Arzner a major film to direct. This movie, *Get Your Man*, with Clara Bow and Buddy Rogers, was a hit, and was followed by *Manhattan Cocktail* (1928).

"Hey, a *broad* is going to direct this film—what do you think of that?" announced one of the crew men for *The Wild Party*, one of the first talking pictures in movie history. His colleagues thought that a woman director meant bad news—until they met Dorothy Arzner. After one meeting with the studio men, they were convinced that "intelligence has no sex." Both cast and crew found Dorothy a delight to work with. Eschewing the blustery manner and theatrical mannerisms adopted by many film directors, she exhibited great self-command and patience. Instead of the traditional roar, "Roll 'em," Dorothy set the cameras in motion with a quiet but firm "Go."

Wild Party proved an important film for its stars, Clara Bow and Frederic March. Clara, nervous about making the transition from silent films to talkies, had a stammering problem, which Dorothy helped her to overcome. Under Dorothy's direction, Clara also proved that she could create a character instead of merely batting her beautiful long eyelashes as she had been encouraged to do on the silent screen.

In 1930, Dorothy Arzner left Paramount to work as an independent director. Although there had been two other women directors in Hollywood when Dorothy made *Fashions for Women*, by now she was the only woman director in the industry. But Dorothy had no trouble getting work. "I made one box-office movie after another. If I had [had] a failure in the middle, I would have been fired." She worked for major studios, such as RKO, United Artists, MGM, and Columbia.

Among Arzner's hit films of the thirties were *Sarah and Son* (1930), with Ruth Chatterton; *Anybody's Woman* (1930), with Chatterton and Clive Brook; *Honor Among Lovers*, with Claudette Colbert, Frederic March, and Ginger Rogers, whom Dorothy had brought from the stage to the screen; *Merrily We Go to Hell* (1932), with Sylvia Sidney and Frederic March; *Christopher Strong* (1933), with Katharine Hepburn, Colin Clive, and Billie Burke; *Nana* (1934), with Anna Sten, United Artists' answer to Dietrich and Garbo; *Craig's Wife* (1936), with Rosalind Russell and Billie Burke; and *The Bride Wore Red* (1937), with Joan Crawford and Franchot Tone.

Sarah and Son, the story of an opera singer's fight for custody of her son, broke all box-office records for Paramount in New York. *Christopher Strong* was another major film, for it was Katharine Hepburn's second appearance on the screen. Hepburn had made her debut as a simpering Daddy's girl in *Bill of Divorcement*, with John Barrymore. The role of aviator Cynthia Darrington in *Christopher Strong* gave her the opportunity to play an entirely different type of character. The part of Lady Darrington was actually based on Amy Lovell, a British altitude record-setting aviator, but the film came out when Amelia Earhart was in her heyday, and most filmgoers were reminded of Earhart by the boyish Hepburn, who sported a tight-fitting leather coat and a beret pulled low over her mop of red curls.

When Dorothy Arzner directed *Craig's Wife*, based on a play by George Kelly, she chose for the role of Harriet Craig (a desperate, ruthless woman who will do anything to obtain possession of her husband's house which for her symbolizes financial security) an obscure young starlet named Rosalind Russell. The rest is film history, as far as Russell's career goes.

But Dorothy Arzner's career began to founder after the minor flop of *The Bride Wore Red*, in which MGM had given her only limited control over the mediocre script. The film fraternity, which rushed to the aid of male directors after unsuccessful films, did nothing for Dorothy Arzner. She was not blacklisted; there was no overt discrimination; but for three years the phone failed to ring with requests for Dorothy Arzner to direct films. The classic situation of the woman who sits by the phone, vainly waiting for the man who said he will call her, immortalized in a humorous short story by Dorothy Parker, was a bitter reality for Dorothy Arzner. For what was at stake was no Saturday night date, but the whole of her working life.

Finally, in 1940, came the long-awaited call. RKO was in trouble with *Dance, Girl, Dance.* The male director could do nothing with Lucille Ball and Maureen O'Hara. The script was a mess; the production snafued. Would Dorothy bail them out?

She would. She did. *Dance, Girl, Dance* is Dorothy Arzner's finest film, a period piece that has survived its period and still packs in capacity crowds in revivals at New York's art cinemas. A contemporary reviewer praised Arzner's "clever brisk treatment" of the story, and wrote, "By the simple expedient of being natural and less concerned with the tinsel than the temper of the accepted screen musical, *Dance, Girl, Dance* avoids monotonous clichés, and for them substitutes some of the most acceptable touches of realism it has been our pleasure to see."

Arzner's final film, *First Comes Courage* (1943), starring Merle Oberon as a Norwegian Resistance spy married to a Nazi officer, also drew favorable reviews. The *New York Times* lauded Arzner for "crisp cutting, swift tempo, sinuous camera work, exquisite lighting, effective gestures, and a brilliantly handled chase sequence at the end."

During World War II, Arzner made a series of short films for the Women's Army Corps, on such subjects as "How to Groom Oneself," and trained four women to cut and edit these films. The army was so pleased with the WAC training clips that they offered Dorothy Arzner the rank of major, which she declined.

While filming *First Comes Courage*, Dorothy Arzner contracted pneumonia, and after 20 years as a successful director, retired from films. In addition to her poor health, she cited disgust with the bureaucracy and razzmatazz atmosphere of Hollywood as the reasons for her retirement. She had directed 17 movies, and had won the esteem of the entire film industry for her assertiveness in dealing with the front office, and her kindheartedness toward colleagues and stars.

Dorothy Arzner had dedicated herself entirely to her career as a director, had never married, and had shunned the Hollywood nightlife. But she had made many close friends among the film stars whose careers she had launched or given new impetus. One of these friends, Joan Crawford, persuaded Dorothy to make 50 Pepsi-Cola commercials for her. Dorothy Arzner also instituted the first course in film-making at the Pasadena Playhouse. In 1960, she became a lecturer at UCLA's graduate program in film. One of her students was Francis Ford Coppola, whose self-esteem was bolstered considerably by Dorothy's encouragement. Now a leading American film director, Coppola remembers Dorothy Arzner as a dynamic and thoughtful teacher, who baked cookies for her often lean and hungry students.

Forced to retire from UCLA at the age of 65, Dorothy Arzner has happily witnessed a strong revival of enthusiasm for her work among film critics and audiences in the 1970s.

"That's one career all females have in common—whether we like it or not—being a woman," Bette Davis says in the movie *All About Eve.* Dorothy Arzner was the first director to probe on the screen every facet of a woman's role—as wife, mistress, girl-of-the-streets, adventurer, artist, patriot, or homebody. She portrays the conventional woman, as well as the active heroine, and the anti-heroine. Her sympathy embraces a rejected wife like Billie Burke in *Christopher Strong,* and also a burlesque hellcat like Lucille Ball in *Dance, Girl, Dance.* Arzner speaks proudly of the role she created for Rosalind Russell in *Craig's Wife:* "[This was] practically the first time a leading lady was a heavy all through the picture—they always had to be sweet and virtuous."

On the set, Arzner herself demonstrated sororal solidarity, employing women scriptwriters like Mary McCall Jr., women film-cutters like Viola Lawrence, and women supervisors, like Elsie Jarvis.

Today, there are many top-notch women directors and women are entering film schools in increasing numbers. But Dorothy Arzner was the first (and as yet unsurpassed) director to produce an opus so relentlessly scrutinizing of the female experience. No other person in the film industry has created as many opportunities for women, on all levels, as did Arzner.

Tillie Ehrlich Lewis
(1901-1977)

INDUSTRIALIST

The legendary "rags to riches" hero, Horatio Alger, had nothing on Tillie Lewis. At the age of 12, Tillie was folding kimonos in a Brooklyn garment factory. At 20, Tillie was a divorcée without a trade, sleeping in a hallway and subsisting on crackers and bananas. But by her 40th birthday, Tillie Lewis, the woman who put the San Joaquin Valley on the agricultural map, was president of a booming tomato canning industry. By her 50th birthday, Tillie owned the fifth largest cannery in the United States, and her net income after taxes easily put her in the millionaire bracket. And by 1973, the septuagenarian "tomato queen" was one of the ten highest-ranking big businesswomen in the United States.

Tillie Lewis was born Myrtle Ehrlich, in Brooklyn, New York, on July 13, 1901. Her mother died before Myrtle's first birthday, and her father, a Jewish immigrant and proprietor of a small phonograph store, soon remarried. Friction was rife between the second Mrs. Ehrlich and her stepdaughter, and Tillie, as Myrtle was called by everyone, resolved to become economically independent of her fami-

316

ly as soon as possible. She quit school after one semester of junior high, and lying about her age, secured work at a sweatshop. A few years later, Tillie found a better job working for a wholesale grocer. At the age of 15, she married her boss, who was twice her age.

A year after her marriage, as Tillie was taking stock of the canned goods in her husband's warehouse, she noted that the most costly tomatoes and tomato products were imported from Italy. She saw from the pictures on the cans that the Italian variety was oblong in shape, like small pears and they were called *pomodoros*, the Italian word for tomatoes.

That evening, Tillie made spaghetti sauce for dinner, using a can of pomodoros that she had taken home from the warehouse, and found that the Italian tomatoes had a more pungent flavor than the American brands. She began to think. It seemed to her that some American could make a fortune by importing pomodoro seeds from Italy and growing the superior tomato in the United States. American pomodoro products could then be sold more cheaply than the Italian imports. Tillie broached the idea to her husband.

The experienced grocer smiled condescendingly. Bright girl, his Tillie, but naive. "Can't be done," Tillie's husband told her. "The climate here is not right for pomodoros, the soil's no good."

The next day, Tillie walked to the Brooklyn Botanical Gardens, to consult the horticulturalists there. The Brooklyn botanists confirmed what Tillie's husband had told her—the American soil and climate were wrong for pomodoros. But they couldn't explain why. Tillie did some research on her own, but could find no explanation of why the American climate was deemed unsuitable for pomodoro cultivation. Tillie had gleaned from her library research that Naples was the heart of the pomodoro industry. Surely the temperature and soil of southern California were comparable.

Tillie's husband began to tire of his wife's consuming obsession with pomodoros. He was older, wiser and more experienced in vegetable growing; he had told her the pomodoro scheme wouldn't work, and that, so far as he was concerned, should have been the end of it. For Tillie, it was the end, not of the pomodoro dream, but of the marriage. Now 20, she saw that her hasty teenage marriage was inhibiting her growth. And so, packing a few clothes, she struck out on her own.

Tillie had never been out of Brooklyn in her life. Aware that she would need capital to realize her pomodoro scheme, she decided to start by going to Manhattan to learn about the business world. So in 1921, Tillie enrolled in business school. She soon secured a job on Wall Street and showed such great acumen that within ten years she was selling securities on commission, with a reported annual income of $12,000. This was in 1932, when the Great Depression was engulfing her fellow Americans. Now she decided to take a vacation in Naples—pomodoro country.

Fortuitously, one of Tillie's fellow passengers on the S.S. *Vulcania* was Florindo del Gaizo, Naples' largest exporter of pomodoros to the United States. Del Gaizo took a liking to his spunky American shipmate, and invited Tillie to inspect his pomodoro farms and cannery in Naples, and entertained her in the bosom of his family.

During the next two years, Tillie Ehrlich rose to an executive position in her securities firm, and began to accumulate a nest egg for her pomodoro project. In 1934, as she was reading the office ticker-tape, she saw that the United States had just raised the duty on imported tomatoes by 50 percent. Tillie decided the time was ripe to implement her scheme for growing pomodoros domestically. She immediately contacted del Gaizo, who she knew would be seriously affected by the augmented import duty, and invited him to share her scheme. Del Gaizo agreed to become Tillie's silent partner, and sent $10,000 and four bags of pomodoro seedlings to the young woman. According to their agreement, Tillie would find a location for a pomodoro farm and cannery, and del Gaizo would send her canning machinery and technicians. Tillie would undertake to raise, can, and market the pomodoros. In gratitude to her Italian godfather—"the first person to believe in me"—Tillie named her company Flotill Industries, blending her sponsor's first name with her own.

In the spring of 1934, Tillie Ehrlich was busy scanning southern California in search of a locale like the farms she had seen in Naples. She settled upon the San Joaquin Valley, and located Flotill Industries in the town of Stockton. The climate was temperate, and Stockton was a harbor town, serviced by two major railroads. Moreover, there were a number of small independent vegetable farmers in the environs, whom Tillie hoped to induce to raise the first American crop of pomodoros.

The San Joaquin farmers were unanimously skeptical when Tillie Ehrlich unfolded her plan to them. They looked at the young woman's high-heeled shoes and flaming red pageboy haircut and declined. But finally, Tillie Ehrlich prevailed upon three farmers to plant her pomodoro seedlings. She prevailed, not with her arguments, but with her pocketbook; Tillie offered a cash bonus to the pomodoro-growing farmers. Finding a canner for the tomatoes was equally difficult, but again the almighty dollar vanquished resistance. For payment in advance, a canner offered his services.

Now Tillie returned to the East Coast to sell her new product to the vegetable wholesalers. Here, Tillie's prosperous appearance overcame doubt. Before a single pomodoro seedling had borne fruit, Tillie Lewis had disposed of her entire crop.

Came harvest time and the vines in the San Joaquin Valley gleamed with rich, red pomodoros. But not enough. Instead of the 100,000 cases of pomodoros promised and sold in advance, Flotill Industries produced only 700 cases; and instead of the 100,000 cases of tomato paste ordered, there were a mere 2,800. What had happened? Simply this: the wary farmers, reluctant to risk their land on the visionary pomodoro scheme, had planted only a fraction of the seedlings that Tillie had paid them to plant. Tillie was devastated, and the wholesalers were enraged, but the demonstrated quality of her pomodoros placated her customers and they renewed their orders for the following year. This time, Tillie visited her pomodoro fields herself, and made sure that the entire crop had been planted. She secured the needed funding from her ever-obliging sponsor del Gaizo, who was undeterred by the net loss of $11,000 by Flotill Industries in its first year.

In its second year of operation, Flotill Industries faced a major crisis. At the height of the tomato season, the cannery's main steam boiler broke down and the year's profits again hung in the balance. Tillie Ehrlich did not panic. With typical determination and ingenuity, she telephoned the Santa Fe Railroad, who agreed to rush two locomotives to Flotill Industries to pipe in the needed steam.

By 1937, its third year, Flotill Industries was showing a profit. But that year, Florindo del Gaizo died. Tillie Ehrlich needed $100,000 to buy out del Gaizo's shares in the company, and carried her ledgers to the local banks. She was unable to obtain a penny from American bankers, but the vice-president of the Bank of Naples in New York approved the loan. The appreciative Tillie told the banker that she never forgot a favor, and she was to have an oppotunity to demonstrate this in 1945. When the United States declared war on Italy, the American branches of the Bank of Naples closed, and her benefactor, the vice-president, found himself unemployed. Tillie Ehrlich paid transportation costs for the banker and his family to come to California, and for the next 27 years the man worked as vice-president and treasurer of Tillie's canning empire.

After del Gaizo's death, Tillie Ehrlich became sole owner and manager of Flotill Industries. She began to branch out, canning asparagus, spinach, and other vegetables as well as tomatoes. She established additional warehouses, and an experimental laboratory staffed by chemists and agricultural experts. She continued to expand, building two more canning plants in Modesto, 30 miles from Stockton. During the Korean War, Tillie's company was the largest producer of combat rations for American G.I.s. After the war, Tillie continued to can an annual 300,000 to 400,000 cases of Hormel meat products, as a sideline.

In 1940, the American Federation of Labor called cannery workers out on strike at all California plants. Flotill Industries was already paying higher salaries than the workers demanded, and Tillie Ehrlich was also offering her employees unheard of benefits, such as day-care centers, transportation for workers who lived on the outskirts, and rest periods for elderly workers. One of Flotill's employees brought these facts to the attention of the western director of the American Federation of Labor, Meyer Lewis. Lewis visited Tillie's plant, was impressed with it, and called off the strike there. Tillie was equally impressed with Lewis, and the following year he became her plant manager. Seven years later, Tillie Ehrlich and Meyer Lewis were married, and the name of Flotill Industries was changed to Tillie Lewis Foods.

By 1952, Tillie Lewis Foods was one of the top five canning industries in the United States, and its proprietor was voted Woman of the Year by the women's page editors of the Associated Press. Always the innovator, with an uncanny sense for profitable new products, in 1952 Tillie started the enormously successful Tasti-Diet line, making her pioneer in the production of artificially sweetened foods. In 1966, Tillie Lewis sold her empire to the Ogden Corporation for $9 million, and became the company's first woman director. Tillie Lewis died at the age 76 on April 30, 1977, a millionaire.

Tillie Lewis was not only an enormously successful industrial magnate, she was also a humane and progressive employer, providing equitable working conditions unusual for her day. From its inception, Flotill Industries paid its employees generous salaries. Tillie also offered her workers an incentive plan, steady raises, nursery facilities, and low-cost housing.

In 1935, the year that Tillie Ehrlich dug the first spadeful of dirt at the site of her first cannery, the San Joaquin Valley did not even appear on the list of the top 50 tomato-producing regions in the United States. By 1951, Tillie Lewis had made San Joaquin the country's leading tomato producer, and had created thousands of jobs for agricultural laborers. That March, the citizens of Stockton celebrated a "Tillie Lewis Day," and the California state senate passed a resolution of acclaim in her honor. Tillie Lewis well merited these accolades. Defying the scientists, businessmen, farmers, and bankers who had scoffed at her, Tillie Lewis singlehandedly built up one of the nation's largest—and most progressive—industrial enterprises. Not bad for a penniless runaway from Brooklyn.

A Flotill Industries highmark.

Margaret Mead (1901-1978)
ANTHROPOLOGIST

Margaret Mead was the foremost anthropologist of our day. When she began her research, anthropology—the study of man, particularly in primitive cultures—was a relatively esoteric discipline whose findings were familiar only to the few scientists and students who specialized in this area. Through such best-selling books as *Growing Up in Samoa* and *Sex and Temperament*, Margaret Mead made anthropology a fascinating subject to the public at large. Mead acquainted westerners with the customs of exotic cultures, and demonstrated that many of the traits we call innate are actually culturally conditioned. A popular columnist and lecturer, Margaret Mead was an astute critic of contemporary American life, expressing challenging views on the major issues facing the modern world.

Margaret Mead was born on December 16, 1901, in Philadelphia, the City of Brotherly Love. Margaret was the first of four children, all wanted and loved by their mother, a sociologist working on a Ph.D., and their father, a professor of economics at the Wharton School of Business. Margaret's paternal grandmother, a former high school principal, also lived with the family.

322

Margaret's mother was a feminist, who urged her daughters to keep their maiden names and individual identity after marriage. Margaret was dressed in bloomers, instead of the frilly dresses others girls wore, and she was brought up on feminist writings. Margaret often went with her mother on field trips and was encouraged to record her observations in a notebook supplied her for this purpose.

Margaret also enjoyed an especially warm relationship with her grandmother. Influenced by her father's maxim that the most valuable contribution a person could make to the world was to add to the sum of human knowledge, Margaret determined to be a minister's wife with six children.

Margaret's education took place largely in the home, where she was exposed to the classics, and given lessons in drawing, pottery, woodcarving, music, and basketry by local craftsmen. She also attended two excellent schools, a private progressive kindergarten, and the prestigious Holmquist High School in New Hope.

In 1919, Margaret enrolled at DePauw University, in Greencastle, Indiana, full of intellectual ambitions, which were soon dashed. She did not dress or act or talk like the other coeds. She was not pledged by a sorority, and was excluded from the campus social life. Her experience at DePauw gave her a lesson in discrimination which opened her eyes to social injustice, and taught her to empathize with its victims. But as an 18-year-old freshman, she was bitter and unhappy; and in 1920, she transferred to Barnard, where intellectual women were the norm, and where there was a great tolerance of ethnic and individual diversity.

At Barnard, Margaret became a campus activist, staging demonstrations for Sacco and Vanzetti and the Amalgamated Clothing Workers. Torn between doing graduate work in psychology or in sociology, she consulted her professor and friend, anthropologist Ruth Benedict. Benedict, noted for her pioneer studies of American Indians, suggested that she, too, consider a career in anthropology, although she added the only incentive would be "the opportunity to do work that matters." That was all Margaret had to hear; she decided to become an anthropologist.

Margaret married Luther Cressman, a divinity student, and obtained a fellowship for graduate work at Columbia University.

When she completed her course work, she elected to do field work for her doctorate in Samoa.

Margaret Mead's male mentors were violently opposed to a woman undertaking field work in Polynesia. Edward Sapir, the dean of American anthropologists, told Margaret bluntly that she ought to forget field work, and stay home and have children. Bronislaw Malinowski, the noted English ethnologist, had never even met Margaret, but scoffed publicly, predicting that she would probably fail even to learn the complicated Polynesian languages. Margaret's own faculty advisor, Franz Boas, tried to dissuade her from the dangerous experiment, and urged her to study the American Indian.

Then Ruth Benedict interceded and a compromise was reached—Margaret wanted to study cultural change among the Polynesians; Boas wanted her to do research on adolescent American Indian girls; Margaret offered to study adolescent girls in Polynesia. Boas sponsored Margaret Mead's application for a National Research Council grant. In 1925, Mead sailed for Pago Pago.

She studied the Samoan language and social etiquette, and then went to the island of Tau to begin her field work. Here, she quickly won the trust of the natives by living as they did, in open quarters under a thatched roof, eating raw fish, and showering publicly in the marketplace. Accepted as a friend, she was able to conduct interviews with the adolescent girls, observe their behavior, and record her findings.

When she returned to New York in 1926, Mead wrote up her study in the remarkable book *Growing Up in Samoa*. The impact of her research was the realization that much of what we regard as human nature is in fact the result of social conditioning. She found that human nature is remarkably pliant, and adapts itself to cultural expectations. Mead reported that Samoans often thought and acted in ways that western minds would consider contrary to human nature, because Samoan culture reinforced a different set of values and behavior patterns. Specifically, Mead suggested that the trauma of adolescence was a western cultural phenomenon, which did not occur in Samoan society, with its freer sexual mores. Repression and guilt rather than sex cause sexual neurosis in western societies, argued Mead. Her plea for more relaxed sexual attitudes in our society unleashed moralistic attacks from puritanical critics, despite Mead's protestations that she was not advocating promiscuity.

Growing Up in Samoa was a startling book, not only in terms of its content and conclusions, but it also represented a departure from the usual anthropological method of research. Mead demonstrated that fresher, more profound results resulted when the observer was freed from the distinctions that came from viewing everything in terms of western concepts. For example, traditional concepts of rank and status could not explain Samoan social hierarchies, where chiefs did not exactly correspond to kings or presidents. Mead was one of the first anthropologists to give accurate eyewitness accounts of what she observed without trying to interpret primitive peoples in western terms, or to conduct controlled experiments among them. She tried to make alien societies and customs intelligible to the Judeo-Christian world, and helped the western world to understand how arbitrary its own conventions are.

When she returned from Samoa, Margaret Mead became a curator at the American Museum of Natural History in New York. For the rest of her life, this was to be her permanent home in between field trips. In 1970, she was made curator emeritus of ethnology at the museum.

Margaret was divorced from her husband who had decided to leave the ministry and was teaching sociology. In 1928, she married Dr. Reo Fortune, also an anthropologist. They went together to New Guinea, where for the next 11 years they studied personality differences and child-rearing practices among four New Guinea tribes.

The New Guinea research resulted in several milestone contributions to comparative anthropology. They found, for example, that the gentle, peace-loving Arapesh tribe most prized affability and tenderness in both men and women. The competitive, cannibalistic Mundugumors, by contrast, encouraged hostile, aggressive behavior in both sexes. In the Tchambuli tribe, traditional sex roles were reversed—the women were the executives and heads of the household, while the men gossiped and did handiwork. Moreover, the Tchambuli women were brisk, hearty, alert and cheerful, while the men were catty, moody, and prone to vanity and petty rivalries.

Based on the New Guinea research, Mead wrote several books,

the most controversial of which was *Sex and Temperament*. Here Mead argued that "masculine" and "feminine" behavior were largely culturally induced rather than inherent. She also suggested that temperament was a more important factor than sex in determining an individual's personality.

Between field trips, Mead and Fortune lived in New York. There was a good deal of tension between the couple. In her autobiography, Mead describes the conflicts that eventually led to the breakup of the marriage:

I was willing to pretend that I never did housework, and I tried to be good-tempered when, after buying food and carrying the packages for four blocks and, finally, up three flights of stairs, I was greeted with the suggestion, "let's go out to dinner"—which we could not afford. But when it came to intellectual matters, I was not prepared to make use of feminine wiles. . . .

I thought then—as I do now—that if we are to have a world in which women work beside men, a world in which both men and women can contribute their best, women must learn to give up pandering to male sensitivities. . . . Because of their age-long training in human relations—for that is what feminine intuition really is—women have a special contribution to make . . . and I feel it is up to them to contribute the kinds of awareness that few men . . . have incorporated through their educations. And so, when Reo thought or spoke or wrote well, I was perhaps his most appreciative audience, but I did not applaud where I felt applause was not due; I criticized in situations in which I thought improvement was possible, and I was silent when I believed nothing could be done.

In 1936, Mead married another anthropologist, Gregory Bateson, and the couple collaborated on a study of the Balinese people. Mead and Bateson refuted the myth that the Balinese were a happy, complacent people whose highly developed arts were an expession of inner tranquility. On the contrary, they observed, artistic expression was an outlet for anger and anxiety among the Balinese. In Bali, Mead and Bateson developed new techniques of note-taking and of photographing their data, which made field work easier for later anthropologists. Their book, *Balinese Character*, is profusely illustrated with the photographs they took.

In December 1939, Margaret Mead gave birth to a daughter, Mary Catherine Bateson. She was one of the first women to use natural childbirth techniques and to insist on having her baby with her in the hospital room as much as possible.

Eventually, after 15 years of marriage, Margaret Mead and Gregory Bateson split up and Margaret went to live with another woman anthropologist. Mead established herself as an observer of the American scene with *And Keep Your Powder Dry.* Throughout the fifties and sixties, Margaret Mead lectured, wrote, taught anthropology at American universities, and worked at the Museum of Natural History, establishing a Hall of Peoples of the Pacific. She made several trips to New Guinea and to Bali for further research.

An unusually spry septuagenarian, Margaret Mead gave as many as 110 lectures in a 12-month period. Her subjects covered a wide range of vital issues, including education and culture, personality and culture, cultural aspects of problems of nutrition, mental health, family life, ecology, cultural change. Besides to her anthropological studies, Margaret Mead wrote a biography of her friend Ruth Benedict, and a moving memoir of her own life, *Blackberry Winter.*

As a writer, Mead was noted for her lucid, literate style. Once, when asked why *Growing Up in Samoa* reached a mass audience while the works of other social scientists rarely penetrate beyond the groves of academe, Mead replied, "Because I wrote it in English." Her humor and sagacity were undiminished when she died, on November 15, 1978, after a year-long fight against cancer.

Hannah Arendt (1906-1975)
POLITICAL SCIENTIST

As an intellectual and moral force, Hannah Arendt has left her impact on all thoughtful men and women. But, as one of the first female editors-in-chief in the book publishing industry (at Schocken Books), and as the first woman professor at Princeton University, her life and work are especially significant for women. An allegedly electrifying teacher, Dr. Arendt was, in the classroom, in her writings, and in her personal impact on artists, intellectuals, and political thinkers, one of the most influential figures in post-World War II America.

Although the phrase "the banality of evil," which Hannah Arendt coined with reference to the trial of Adolph Eichmann in Jerusalem, is widely used, her name is not as widely known as are the names of other contemporary philosophers such as Simone Weil, Simone de Beauvoir and Herbert Marcuse. Yet, Hannah Arendt was one of the primordial thinkers and great political philosophers of our time. Her books, which include *The Origins of Totalitarianism* (1951); *Men in Dark Times* (1955); *The Human Condition* (1958); *Between Past and Future* (1961); *Eichmann in Jerusalem* (1963); and *The Life of the Mind* (1978), are distinctive for their trenchant analysis of the modern world, stamped with corrosive irony, and coruscating wit. Hannah Arendt's essays on the Vietnam War, race relations, civil disobedience, and other stark issues, mark her as one of the most insightful commentators on the American scene. Her field of knowledge was immense. She has written with equal cogency on the French and the American Revolutions, on existential philosophy, and on modern German literature. A true citizen of the world, Hannah Arendt's prose style is notable for an apposite use of quotations and phrases drawn from many cultural traditions and languages. She is that rare writer whose voice is intensely personal, yet carries an authority untainted by subjectivity.

Hannah Arendt was born in Hanover, Germany on October 14, 1906, the only child of Jewish parents. As a child, Hannah heard discussions about the anarchist Rosa Luxembourg, whom she later wrote about in *Men in Dark Times.* The Rosa of Hannah's childhood memories was not "Red Rosa," the brilliant Communist desperado of political tradition, but a gentle, saintly woman, whose jailors bid her goodbye with tears in their eyes when she left prison.

Hannah attended the local public schools and the Gymnasium, or high school. She matriculated at the University of Koenigsberg, where her fields of concentration were classics, philosophy, and theology. After obtaining a bachelor's degree in 1924, Hannah studied philosophy at the University of Marburg, under the existentialist Martin Heidegger, and at the University of Freiburg, under the phenomenologist Edmund Husserl. Hannah also studied theology and Greek, and at the age of 22, obtained her doctoral degree from the University of Heidelberg, where her philosophical mentor had been the psychological existentialist Karl Jaspers. Her doctoral thesis, on Saint Augustine's concept of love, published as a book in 1930, was widely reviewed and signalled German intellectuals that an important new intelligence was among them.

In Hannah Arendt's subsequent writings, she adhered to the Augustinian concept that love of one's neighbor as a manifestation of God is paramount over lesser forms of love. Although never a practitioner of any particular religion, Hannah Arendt was deeply spiritual. She states, for example, in *Men in Dark Times,* that atheists were "fools who pretended to know what no man can know," and maintained a sardonic stance toward "those who find religious and theological questions 'interesting'". Her essay on Pope John XXIII indicated Dr. Arendt's dedication to Christian values.

Hannah Arendt was taciturn on the subject of her first marriage to a German writer, Guenther Stein, with whom she coauthored an article on the German poet Rilke. Her second husband was Heinrich Bluecher, a philosophy professor and writer.

In the early 1930s, Hannah Arendt published articles in German magazines on the sociology of knowledge, on Kierkegaard, 19th- century Jewry, and other subjects. Because she was inconspicuous politically, and neither a Zionist nor a practicing Jew, Hannah Arendt was asked by German Zionists to collect data about Nazi anti-Semitism. While copying anti-Semitic statements from German periodicals in a Berlin library, Hannah Arendt was arrested by the Gestapo and imprisoned. Fortunately, the commissar of the prison took a liking to Hannah Arendt, and obtained her release.

In 1934, Dr. Arendt fled to Paris, where she became an administrator for the Youth Aliyah, founded by Henrietta Szold to help Jewish youth in German-occupied countries resettle in Palestine. After working for the Aliyah for six years, Hannah Arendt was arrested by the Vichy government and interned at a prison camp for aliens at Gurs. She escaped from the internment camp, and through friends was able to obtain an American visa. In 1941, Hannah Arendt and her husband, Heinrich Bluecher, arrived in the United States as political refugees.

Although still not a member of any synagogue, Hannah Arendt by now felt her Judaism as a political identity—her only identity. She began to write a column for the German refugee magazine *Aufbau*, urging the formation of a Jewish army for self-defense. From 1944 to 1946, Dr. Arendt was research director of the Conference on Jewish Relations. She also published a number of articles in Jewish magazines on racism, totalitarianism, and imperialism.

From 1946 to 1948, Hannah Arendt worked as chief editor at Schocken Books, a small but prestigious trade publishing company in New York City. Dr. Arendt edited two volumes of Karl Jaspers' book *The Great Philosophers*, and was responsible for the publication of several other important volumes, including the Max Brod edition of Franz Kafka's diaries, which she helped to translate. In 1947, a collection of six of her own essays, which included an article on Kafka, was published in Heidelberg, under the title *Sechs Essays.*

As executive secretary of the Jewish Cultural Reconstruction from 1949 to 1952, Hannah Arendt was responsible for the recapture and reallocation of cultural property purloined from European Jews by the Nazis. During this period, Dr. Arendt wrote *The Origins of Totalitarianism,* published in 1951. In this seminal discussion, Dr. Arendt traces the origins of Nazism and Stalinism to 19th-century imperialism and anti-Semitism. This controversial thesis established Hannah Arendt as an important political scientist.

Acclaim of her formidable intellectual talents came in various forms. In 1952, Hannah Arendt was awarded a Guggenheim fellowship, and two years later she received a grant of $1,000 from the National Institute of Arts and Letters. In 1953, Dr. Arendt was invited to come to Princeton University as an outside lecturer— Princeton was not yet prepared to hire women as members of its tenured faculty. During the fifties, Dr. Arendt also taught at other universities, including Berkeley, the University of Chicago, Brooklyn College, and Columbia University.

Finally, in 1959, Dr. Arendt was offered and accepted the position of Visiting Professor of Politics at Princeton. At Princeton, Hannah Arendt earned the respect and affection of students and colleagues. The poet Randall Jarrell was a frequent visitor to the Arendt-Bluecher home. Dr. Bluecher was at this time a professor of philosophy at Bard College in New York. Hannah Arendt credits Jarrell with introducing her to the giants of English and American literature.

The invitation to join the Princeton faculty was perhaps inspired by the warm critical reception of Dr. Arendt's second major book, *The Human Condition,* published in 1958. In this work, based on a series of lectures that she gave at the University of Chicago in 1956, Dr. Arendt propounds the thesis that there are three types of human activity— labor, work, and action. In ancient times, Arendt maintains, the emphasis was on action, comprising man's social role. It later shifted to work, the production of durable objects, and is now tilting heavily toward labor, the energy expended on acts of mere physical survival. *The Human Condition* is a deeply pessimistic work, deploring the decline of the Greek concept of friendship and the Christian concept of the primacy of the soul.

Hannah Arendt's best-known work is the highly controversial *Eichmann in Jerusalem: A Report on the Banality of Evil*, published in 1963. Covering the trial by the Israeli courts of former Nazi henchman Adolph Eichmann, Dr. Arendt portrays this executioner of untold thousands of Jews as a nondescript petty bureaucrat, who was "only following orders" issued by his superiors. She reiterates the Augustinian doctrine that evil is not an active force in itself, but merely the absence of good. Dr. Arendt proclaims the collective guilt of all who passively acquiesced in the Nazi reign of terror.

She later drew parallels between Nazi Germany and the United States of the Vietnam War era, and advocated engagement in anti-war activities by concerned Americans. Her articles on American politics were published in the *New York Review of Books*, to which Dr. Arendt was for many years an active contributor. The Watergate scandal was regarded by Dr. Arendt as further evidence of the ascendancy of the bureaucrat in the modern age.

In her latter years, Hannah Arendt was University Professor of Political Philosophy at the New School for Social Research in New York City. Every Thursday afternoon, at her apartment on Riverside Drive, she held colloquies with her friends, reading and discussing Plato and other classical writers.

Modest as Dr. Arendt was, her estimable contributions to moral intellectualism did not go unnoticed. She was the recipient of a number of honors in her lifetime, including the Lessing Prize given by the city of Hamburg, Germany in 1959, and the German Academy's Sigmund Freud Prize for scholarly prose in 1967.

In *Men in Dark Times*, Hannah Arendt wrote:

Even in the darkest of times we have the right to expect some illumination, and that such illumination may come less from theories and concepts than from the uncertain, flickering, and often weak light that some men and women, in their lives and work, will kindle under almost all circumstances and shed over the time-span that was given them on earth.

There is nothing weak about the light shed by the work of Hannah Arendt.

Rachel Carson (1907-1964)

ECOLOGIST

Rachel Carson did not coin the word *ecology*, but it was she who made it a household word. A marine biologist and science writer, Carson detonated an "environmental revolution" with her book *Silent Spring*, a well-documented polemic against the indiscriminate use of pesticides. Her books, *Edge of the Sea, Under the Sea Wind*, and *The Sea Around Us*, are among the most beautifully written works of natural history ever published. Carson was the most influential conservationist of the 20th century. The *New York Times* has called her "one of the most influential women of her time."

The author of *Silent Spring* was born on May 27, 1907 in Springdale, Pennsylvania, and passed her childhood there and in neighboring Parnassus. Her mother, a former schoolteacher, was 36 years old at Rachel's birth, and Rachel's brother and sister were so much older than she that she had the sense of being an only child.

Mrs. Carson transmitted to her daughter her own love of literature and music, and "Schweitzerian feeling for all life." One of Rachel's earliest memories was of sitting in a highchair on the porch, listening to the song of the meadowlarks. Mother and daughter took many long walks together in the woods near their farm. Together, they observed plant and pond life, and became amateur bird watchers. All her life, Rachel retained a love of birds, becoming a director of the Washington, D.C. chapter of the Audubon Society.

Rachel Carson won her first writing award at the age of 10,   She was a studious, introverted child, who received more attention from her teachers than from her classmates. She spent much of her youth wandering alone in the Allegheny Valley.

Rachel won a scholarship to the Pennsylvania College for Women at Pittsburgh in 1924. She took a biology course in her sophomore year and became so fascinated by the study of natural life that she decided to major in zoology. After graduating *magna cum laude*, she spent the summer at the Marine Biological Laboratory at Woods Hole, Massachusetts. Here, for the first time, Rachel Carson saw the ocean, the subject of her most lyrical prose.

In 1931, Carson joined the zoology faculty of the University of Maryland. She earned a Master of Arts degree at Johns Hopkins University in 1932.

Rachel's father died in 1935, and on her shoulders fell the financial responsibility for her mother and two nieces. Rachel's salary was insufficient to support this extended family, so she decided to get a government job. The only woman to take the Civil Service examination in 1935, she achieved the highest score of all the candidates. In 1936, Carson joined the Department of the Interior, as an aquatic biologist with the Bureau of Fisheries.

Rachel spent her leisure hours writing newspaper features on nature. In 1937, her article called "Undersea" was published in the *Atlantic Monthly*. This essay was to serve as the basis for Carson's first book, *Under the Sea Wind*, which appeared in 1941. Subtitled "a naturalist's picture of ocean life," and widely praised by the critics for its informative content and pellucid style, the book sold only a few thousand copies.

In 1940, the Bureau of the Fisheries merged with the Bureau of Biological Survey to form the United States Fish and Wildlife Service. The stated purpose of the new department was "to insure the conservation of the nation's wild birds, mammals, fishes and other forms of wildlife . . . with a view to preventing the destruction or depletion of these natural resources, and to promote the maximum present use and enjoyment of the wildlife resources." After the departmental reorganization, Rachel Carson was promoted, and in 1947 she became editor-in-chief of the bureau's publications.

During the war years, Rachel Carson supplemented her modest government salary by writing articles for magazines. Although by nature timorous and retiring, she occasionally attended parties given by her Washington colleagues, and went on bird-watching expeditions with friends. An habitual bedtime reader, she was particularly fond of Herman Melville's South Sea adventure tales, and Henry David Thoreau's naturalist writings.

Fascinated by the life of the ocean, Rachel Carson immersed herself in research and writing. She researched her subject meticulously and wrote slowly, making frequent revisions. In 1950, Carson published a selection from the manuscript she was working on in the *Yale Review*. The essay, entitled "Birth of an Island," won a $1,000 award from the George Westinghouse Foundation.

While she was spending all her free time in intensive work on her manuscript, Carson produced 12 government pamphlets on *Conservation in Action.* In these booklets, Carson decried the unnecessary waste of natural resources in the United States, and called for a responsible nationwide policy of conservation to prevent a permanent depletion or extinction of wildlife.

After years of work, Carson completed her manuscript, and in 1952 *The Sea Around Us* was published. A comprehensive treatment of the biological, chemical, geographical, and historical aspects of the sea, its islands, and its inhabitants, the book was an instant bestseller. Acclaimed by the critics as "a beautiful book" and "a joy to read," *The Sea Around Us* won a National Book Award, and remained on the best seller-list for 86 weeks. It was also made into an Academy Award winning documentary.

The Sea Around Us earned its author numerous fellowships and speaking engagements, and enough royalties to enable her to resign her government post and become a full-time writer. Rachel bought a coastal retreat in Maine where she lived with her niece and her niece's son, Roger. Here she could study nature and write about it. In 1955, Carson published *The Edge of the Sea*, a popular guide to seashore life.

One day, in 1957, Rachel Carson received a letter from some

friends in Massachusetts complaining that some anti-mosquito pesticide sprayed on their two-acre nature sanctuary had decimated the birds as well as the mosquitoes. This letter was the impetus for *Silent Spring.*

For the next four-and-a-half years, Rachel Carson stockpiled evidence showing how modern technology and agri-business were destroying the natural world. She consulted authorities from all parts of the world, as well as drawing on her own experience in the Department of the Interior. She attended hearings on gypsy-moth spraying in Long Island and on the 1959 cranberry scare in Washington. These hearings resulted in a ban on the sale of cranberries sprayed with aminotriazol.

In 1960, Rachel Carson learned that she had cancer and would have to undergo massive radiation treatments. Realizing the cancer was irreversible, and although suffering from a number of other ailments, including partial blindness, did not deter her from her work on *Silent Spring.* When the book appeared, in 1962, it caused an overnight sensation.

Claiming that chemicals "are the sinister and little-recognized partners of radiation in changing the very nature of the world—the very nature of life," Rachel Carson warned that if industrial spraying continued to be uncontrolled, a silent spring would dawn, unrelieved by the song of birds or the leaping of fish in streams. Carson documented her assertions with examples of chemically induced damage in animals, plants, helpful insects, and even human beings. She did not oppose limited use of pesticides and herbicides to curb the insect population, but firmly denounced the excessive use of DDT and other poisonous substances, warning that human food supplies were in serious danger of being contaminated. She also suggested that pesticides might be a cause of cancer. *Silent Spring* charged that the testing of poisonous chemicals was insufficient and enumerated the various dangerous substances for sale on supermarket shelves.

Silent Spring was the catalyst for what is now called the "ecological revolution." More than 300,000 copies of the book were sold within the first three months of publication. Carson was inundated with mail; some letters were laudatory, some vituperative.

Many politicians took up the conservationist cause, using statements from Rachel Carson in their campaigns. Carson also acquired congressional enemies; one, for example, who derided her concern about chemically induced genetic damage as inappropriate for a spinster. Big Business denigrated the book as "baloney," and alleged that the soft-spoken naturalist was a Communist tool.

Rachel Carson found herself at the forefront of an environmental crusade. In spite of deteriorating health, she picked up the gauntlet, and carried the fight into the state legislatures. By the end of 1962, over 42 bills had been introduced into state legislatures to curtail the use of insecticides. The Department of Agriculture called for the registration and labeling of all pesticides under its supervision, and refused to allow products suspected of causing harm to be released until proved safe. In 1963, when President Kennedy ordered his Science Advisory Committee to investigate claims of rampant and irresponsible use of insecticides, Rachel Carson's crusade was vindicated. The committee decreed that the indiscriminate deployment of poisonous chemicals was "potentially a much greater hazard than radioactive fallout." A subcommittee on environmental hazards was convened, to establish a provident policy of conservation.

Shortly before her death, Rachel Carson was named Conservationist of the Year. She died on April 14, 1964, but the ecological movement that she spawned lives on, steadily growing in size and influence. A Rachel Carson Seacoast Fund and a Rachel Carson Fund for the Living Environment have carried on Carson's fight to preserve our natural resources and wildlife. Carson's Maine laboratory was purchased by the Department of the Interior and transformed into a 4,000-acre Rachel Carson National Refuge.

When she appeared before the Congress of the United States in 1963, Rachel Carson had declared, "I deeply believe that we in this generation must come to terms with Nature." Through her writings, Carson was the prime mover in forcing man to come to terms with Nature, and with our reckless disruption of natural processes. Singlehandedly, Rachel Carson raised the national consciousness, making us aware of the interrelation of all living things.

Bette Davis (1908-   )
MOTION-PICTURE ACTRESS

In 1930, the term "Hollywood actress" was practically a contradiction, defining a location more than a profession, involving histrionics rather than acting. If you were an actress you wouldn't be in Hollywood; and if you were in Hollywood, you couldn't act. A woman who achieved stardom in a screen role was forever after typecast in that role. The only choice available to a movie actress was between the glamor role of the sex siren and the walk-on role of the eccentric. Then came Bette Davis.

By winning a hard-fought battle to secure challenging, diversified roles and quality scripts, Davis succeeded in upgrading American films. Adding new dimensions to the image of Woman on the Hollywood screen, she blazed the trail that Joanne Woodward, Jane Fonda, and Diane Keaton are still widening today.

Named after her mother, Ruth Elizabeth Davis was called Bette, after the heroine of Balzac's *Cousin Bette*. Born in Lowell, Massachusetts on April 5, 1908, Bette was the elder of two daughters of patrician parents. Her father, a graduate of Harvard law school and a patent attorney, left his wife when Bette was seven. After that, Bette and her sister, Barbara, accompanied their mother on her hegira across New England and New York in search of governessing positions. The Davis sisters attended a girls' boarding school in the Berkshires, then moved to New York City when their mother enrolled in photography school there. Bette became a Girl Scout leader. She completed her formal education at Cushing Academy, where she waited on tables to help pay her tuition. Here she also developed a crush on fellow student, Harmon Nelson, who was later to be the first of Bette's four husbands.

Although she had only twice been to the theater, Bette determined on a career as an actress.

Mrs. Davis wrote to actress Eva LeGallienne, who ran the only inexpensive but good drama school in New York, and obtained an interview for Bette. The formidable LeGallienne had the neophyte actress read in the role of a 65-year-old Dutchwoman, and then dismissed her as "frivolous little girl." Bette Davis was crushed. "If ever I could have become a mental case it was at that time," she later admitted.

Undaunted, Mrs. Davis next went to the manager of the John Murray Anderson School of the Theater and announced: "My daughter Bette wants to be an actress. I haven't the money to pay her tuition, but will assure you that you will eventually have it." Miraculously, Bette was accepted at the school, and eventually obtained a scholarship there. In addition to acting, she studied dance with Martha Graham.

Bette Davis's first professional acting experience was with the George Cukor winter stock company in Rochester, New York, in 1928. She was assigned a one-line part, and at her mother's urging, also understudied a meatier part. It was a lucky gambit, for the actress sprained her ankle and Bette Davis stepped in to replace her. Indeed, Bette Davis seemed destined to acquire most of her best film roles as an 11th-hour stand-in for indisposed actresses.

Bette Davis made her New York debut as a farmer's daughter in the two-act drama *The Earth Between*, in 1929. Brooks Atkinson of the *New York Times* pronounced her "an entrancing creature." That autumn, Bette played on Broadway in *Broken Dishes*, and earned plaudits from the critics and a contract from Universal Studios.

When Bette Davis saw her first screen test, she "ran from the projection room screaming." Henceforth she insisted on applying her own makeup, and used paint so sparingly, that when she arrived on the West Coast, the Universal publicist who was sent to meet her at the station saw no one who looked even "faintly like an actress," and returned to the studio alone. Bette straggled in later with her mother, her constant companion in her early years in Hollywood.

"What happened to the car you were sending to meet my train?" Bette asked the Universal personnel. The publicist's remark was repeated to her, and Davis retorted, "I had a dog with me—you should have known I was an actress." This crack was the first of the mordant ripostes that were to become Bette Davis's trademark.

When the 22-year-old Davis was introduced to Universal panjandrum Carl Laemmle, Jr., he stared at the innocuous wisp of a girl in disbelief, and muttered, "What audience would ever believe that the hero would want to get *her* at the fade-out?" Another gander at the future star of *Jezebel* failed to show him her potential; Laemmle added, "I can't imagine any guy giving her a tumble." When the gamy girl asked what sex appeal had to do with acting, she was told, "You don't know Hollywood, sister."

In the next few weeks, Bette Davis got to know Hollywood well enough to wonder what she was doing there. Dubbed "the little brown wren," Davis was subjected to myriad minor indignities in the effort to metamorphose her into a peacock. Her legs were subjected to minute scrutiny and pronounced barely acceptable. She was used as a guinea pig to screen-test 15 male actors, who had to prove their mettle in the pretended seduction. Later, Bette compared the experience to being "a mattress in a bawdy house." Next, she was given a bathing suit and ordered to pose for cheesecake photographs for the fan magazines. Even her name was found unsuitable. "A great name for a secretary," said the Universal publicity department. But Bette Davis would not be rechristened Bettina Dawes: "I refuse to go through life as 'between the drawers.'"

Bette Davis's early career in films was inauspicious, to say the least. She made her movie debut in 1931, as the unmemorable "good sister" in *Bad Sister*. Her male co-star was another tyro— Humphrey

Bogart. Davis's next films, *Seed* and *Waterloo Bridge* offered no greater opportunity or challenge, and then Universal loaned her out to other companies, for three more bombs.

In 1932, Universal declined to renew Bette Davis's contract. Broke, bitter, and befuddled, the obscure young actress prepared to return to New York. Enter the discerning George Arliss, the grand old man of stage and screen, and apparently the only individual in Hollywood who could view the starlet reputed to "have as much sex appeal as Slim Somerville" without laughing. As a prestigious Warner Brothers star, Arliss was allowed to designate his own leading ladies, and chose as the heroine of *The Man Who Played God* Bette Davis. The studio brass instantly squawked. "I don't care what she looks like," snapped Arliss, "this girl has the makings of a great actress." Grudgingly, Warner Brothers offered Bette Davis a contract. It was the beginning of a tumultuous 18- year association.

Davis's performances in *The Man Who Played God* and subsequent Warner films were well received by the critics, but it was not until *Of Human Bondage*, in 1934, that she drew her first rave notices. As the sullen, slatternly waitress, Mildred Rogers, in the film version of the Maugham classic, Davis sent thrills of horror up the spines of the spectators. "I despise you," she jeered at protagonist Leslie Howard. "Do you know what you are? A cripple! A cripple!" *Life* magazine proclaimed Davis's delineation of the Cockney slut as "the best performance ever recorded on the screen by a U.S. actress."

Bette Davis had had to make her own break to do *Of Human Bondage*. Brought up on the prose of Emerson and Thoreau, Bette Davis relished *Of Human Bondage* as the first literate script she had encountered since coming to Hollywood. She pestered Jack Warner relentlessly, every day for six months, until he consented to release her to RKO. The rival studio was most keen to get Bette for the role of Mildred because none of their established actresses would touch the part, fearing that the public would identify them with the thoroughly despicable character forever after. Indeed, it was fear of this fate that made Warner Brothers reluctant to free Bette for the role. Of course, it was exactly in this role that Davis established herself as the most promising actress in Filmdom.

On her return from RKO, she begged Warner Brothers for comparable roles instead of the inane ingenues and vacuous vamps that were her usual fare. But to little avail; the best of a bad lot was playing opposite hero Franchot Tone in *Dangerous,* as the besotted Joyce Heath, a quondam actress on her way to Skid Row. Davis considered the heroine of *Dangerous* "mawkish and maudlin," and "worked like ten men" to give the character credibility. She succeeded: in 1935, *Dangerous* won her the Oscar she ought to have been awarded for *Of Human Bondage.*

Davis got her first decent role from Warner Brothers in 1936, as Gaby Maple, the city-struck heroine of *The Petrified Forest* in the film version of the Sherwood Anderson drama. However, even after this memorable movie Warner Brothers continued to offer the now-popular star nothing but mediocrities. Claiming it was a question of self-respect, the spunky actress went on strike. The studio retaliated by suspending Davis for three months; then added insult to injury by offering her more rubbishy scripts, which the intransigent star refused.

In 1936, Davis defied Warner Brothers and signed up with a British film company. Her American bosses brought suit and won; Bette Davis lost $60,000 in salary: 45,600 sterling in damages; and 25 pounds of flesh during the ordeal of the trial. Returning to Beverly Hills, the defeated renegade was welcomed home by Warner Brothers. Though she had lost the battle, Bette Davis had won the war: from then on, Hollywood took her seriously, and Warner Brothers offered her more worthwhile roles. In 1936, Davis starred with Bogart in *Marked Woman;* in 1937, she was a boxer's moll in *Kid Galahad;* in the same year, she competed with her friend Olivia de Havilland for the affections of Leslie Howard in *It's Love I'm After.* The scripts were hardly literary masterpieces, but at least they were no longer unmitigated garbage.

Finally, in 1938, came *Jezebel,* the watershed of Bette Davis's career. Davis's performance as the brash Southern belle was a *tour de force,* and won her a second Oscar. The following year, she triumphed again, first in *Juarez* and then in *Dark Victory.* She successfully opposed the director, who wanted her to play the demented heroine in *Dark Victory* in a histrionic manner by displaying her frenzy through exaggerated gesticulations of the hands. Davis demurred, choosing to show her emotions with her eyes alone. Her exophthalmic orbs had initially been regarded as a liability in Hollywood, but she had shown that she could use them to advantage, hypnotizing audiences into swallowing drivel by the sheer intensity of her gaze. Playing the part her own way, Davis created in *Dark Victory* what she called "my favorite and the public's favorite role."

In the forties, Bette Davis produced a panoply of memorable performances in films like *Now, Voyager, Deception,* and *A Stolen Life,* which she also co-produced. As the faded beauty in *Mr. Skeffington,* she drew tears from the audience with the acknowledgment at the closing that "A woman is beautiful only when she is loved." As the imperious Regina in Lillian Hellman's *The Little Foxes,* Davis electrified audiences and reviewers alike.

In 1941, Bette Davis became the first woman to be elected president of the Academy of Motion Picture Arts and Sciences. When she was forced to resign the post for trying to institute reforms, Davis turned her energies to founding the Hollywood Canteen, where entertainers waited on and performed for American GIs during World War II.

In the fifties, Bette Davis continued to demonstrate her versatility and consummate artistry not only on the screen, but on Broadway and television as well. Her best roles, however, were still in the movies, where they ranged from Queen Elizabeth in *The Virgin Queen* to a frumpy Bronx housewife in *The Catered Affair.* In the sixties, after suffering a paucity of good roles, Davis made a stunning comeback in the ghoulish film *Whatever Happened to Baby Jane?*

The seventies mark Bette Davis's fifth decade of stardom. While steadfastly pursuing her career, she has throughout her life sustained a number of personal tragedies. During her first marriage, she reluctantly underwent an abortion because her husband could not pay her maternity expenses and was too proud to let her pay. Her second husband died prematurely, and her other marriages dissolved in bitterness because the role of "Mr. Davis" was unendurable to her spouses. Davis also had to undergo painful jaw surgery that interrupted and almost ended her career when it was rumored that she had cancer of the jaw. However, she prevailed and continued to act, and raised three children, two of them adopted, as well as caring for her sister Barbara's children during Barbara's several nervous breakdowns.

Bette Davis is perhaps most identified with the role of Margo Channing, the acerbic bitch-goddess in *All About Eve*, but the actress probably best reveals her talent in her least flamboyant roles. No one can top the psychological depth in her subtle portrait of the spinster aunt who cannot betray her identity to her illegitimate daughter in *The Old Maid*. "I tried to open the hearts of the women I played." Tried, and succeeded. In *Watch on the Rhine*, Davis demonstrated her capacity for restraint; and in *The Man Who Came to Dinner*, she showed a gift for low-key humor in sharp contrast to the hyperbolic high drama that is considered vintage Davis.

Bette Davis well deserves the title First Lady of the Screen. Given a vehicle worthy of her abilities (and more often than not she had to fight for such parts), Davis was superb. When foisted into one of Hollywood's bromidic excuses for human drama, she somehow managed to make her role plausible. The lines she has immortalized in her long career are legion: as, for example, "Ah'd love to kiss you but ah jes washed mah hayah" (*Cabin in the Cotton*), or "What-ta-dump" (*Beyond the Forest*), or "Fasten your seatbelts—it's going to be a bumpy evening" (*All About Eve*).

Davis has used her extraordinarily mobile face to enhance her characterizations—a flash of the eyes defined the spirited heroine of *Jezebel*; a tuck of the mouth captured the prim Charlotte Vale of *Now, Voyager*. She has shunned a glossy patina and has striven for authenticity. In *Watch on the Rhine*, she matched wills with the director, insisting that she be allowed to wear cotton stockings rather than silk; in *Bordertown*, she realistically smeared her face with cold cream upon rising from bed in the morning—scandalizing the rest of the cast. For her Elizabethan costumes in *The Virgin Queen*, Davis studied Holbein's famous portrait of the British monarch, and, suppressing personal vanity, had her head shaved to accommodate Elizabeth's elaborate orange wig.

A quintessential actress, Davis's salient virtues are taste, intelligence, and style, and she has displayed them in an incredible assortment of roles. Heroine or harridan, loyal or lethal, pathetic or pernicious, Bette Davis has played them all—and played them compellingly.

Among her colleagues, she is as noted for her fairness and generosity as for her talent. Davis insisted on enhancing Mary Astor's part in *The Great Lie* at the expense of her own role in the interest of adding plausibility to the script. In her prime, Davis went out of her way to show consideration for elderly actresses who had been reduced to bit roles, even to those who had snubbed her when she was a struggling starlet.

Every screen actor is indebted to Bette Davis for the stature and dignity that she added to the profession. Every filmgoer is indebted to her for improving the quality of American movies. Even today, with the American cinema in the throes of a new renaissance, there are few actresses to equal Bette Davis—and none who surpass her.

Simone Weil (1909-1943)
PHILOSOPHER AND HUMANITARIAN

STRANGE SUICIDE. REFUSED TO EAT ran the headline in the *Kentish Express.* Thus was the death of Simone A. Weil, French teacher, philosopher, and writer reported. She died at age 34 at the Grosvenor Sanatorium, near Ashford, England. The senior medical officer testified that:

She tried to persuade Professor Weil to take some food and she said she would try. She did not eat, however, and gave as a reason the thought of her people in France starving. She died on August 24 and death was due to cardiac failure due to degeneration through starvation.

The coroner's verdict was suicide by starvation. But in a deeper sense, Simone Weil died of love, love for her beleaguered compatriots in Vichy, France, whose rationed allotment of food she was unwilling to exceed, though ill with tuberculosis and worn down by mental stress. Born into the *haute bourgeoisie,* Simone Weil took it upon herself to suffer with those that she saw suffer—with workers in the factories and vineyards of France, with soldiers and nurses on the battlefield in Spain, with American blacks in Harlem, and finally, vicariously, with her people in German-occupied France. Simone Weil distilled the wisdom of her own suffering into some of the most original philosophical writings of our time. Her notebooks have been compared to Pascal's *Pensées;* her essays and books led André Gide to characterize her as "the most truly spiritual writer of this century." T.S. Eliot and Leslie Fiedler have likened Simone Weil to a saint. But perhaps the most apt definition of Simone Weil's genius came from her students at the French girls' high school where she taught. They called her Mother Weil, in French *Mère Weil,* pronounced *merveil,* which translates as *marvel.*

Simone Weil was born in Paris on February 3, 1903. Her father was a well-to-do Paris physician. The Weils were nominally Jewish, but they raised Simone and her older brother, Andre, as intellectual agnostics.

Even as a small child, Simone was unusually idealistic. She was five years old at the outbreak of World War I, and voluntarily gave up her sugar ration for the soldiers fighting at the front.

Throughout adolescence, Simone was given to fierce cogitations on the meaning of existence. Simone wrote to her close friend, Father J.-M. Perrin:

At the age of fourteen I fell into one of those fits of bottomless despair which come with adolescence; and I seriously thought of dying because of the mediocrity of my natural faculties. The extraordinary gifts of my brother, who had a childhood and youth comparable to those of Pascal, made me forcibly aware of this. What I minded was not the lack of external successes, but the having no hope of access to that transcendent realm where only the truly great can enter, and where truth dwells. I felt it better to die than to live without truth.

She wrote in her diary that at the center of the human heart was a longing for truth, or absolute good, which "is always there and is never appeased by any object in this world." This idea was to be the cornerstone of Weil's later philosophic works.

A brilliant student, Simone Weil attended the best Parisian high school, the Lycée Henri IV, and was one of the elite of French students accepted at the École Normale Supérieure, the most prestigious and most selective institution of higher learning in France. The only other woman in Simone's class at the École Normale Supérieure was also named Simone—Simone de Beauvoir, who later became a celebrated French feminist writer. A militant leftist, Simone Weil was widely known at the university as "the red virgin." In 1931, Simone Weil earned her doctorate and was sent by the French ministry of education to teach at a lycée for girls at Le Puy, and later to another lycée, at Roanne. As a professor of philosophy, Simone imparted to her students her socialist idealism, and also taught them higher mathematics and science. Outside of school, she participated in a workers' study circle at St. Étienne, where she came to know the leading trade unionists of the province. During a miner's strike, Simone Weil kept only that portion of her teacher's salary equivalent to the miners' unemployment compensation, donating the rest to a fund for the strikers and their families. She also ran a soup kitchen for workers in her home.

Simone Weil began to contribute essays to magazines, criticizing the dehumanization and exploitation that characterized modern society. She deplored the brutalization imposed by compartmentalization of labor, not only on manual workers, but also on scientists and intellectuals:

One could count one one's fingers the number of scientists in the entire world who have a general idea of the history and development of their own particular science. There is not one who is really competent as regards sciences other than his own . . . there are no longer, strictly speaking, any scientists, but only drudges doing scientific work, cogs in a mechanism which their minds cannot embrace as a whole. . . .

Simone Weil disapproved of her fellow left-wing intellectuals because of their detachment from the working classes. She herself sought direct experience with the problems of the average worker, and as a high school teacher, had worked after class in the potato fields. In 1934, she took a leave of absence from teaching and worked as an unskilled worker on the assembly line where her job was to raise and lower a shutter. The physical misery of the job was intensified by the migraine headaches with which she was plagued.

The special misery of women workers was to preoccupy her at

her next two jobs, at the Forges de Basse-Indre and the Renault factory. Male workers, she wrote, at least had the hope of promotion into more challenging jobs, but "women are stuck with completely mechanical tasks that demand only quickness."

In 1936, civil war erupted in Spain, and Simone Weil went to Barcelona as a Loyalist sympathizer. When she returned to France, she resumed teaching until the recurrence of intense migraine headaches caused her to resign. But she continued to lecture to workers and to write, producing political tracts, as well as a study of the *Iliad*. Simone Weil's writings on the human quest for beauty, and our futile attempt to possess beauty by possessing the objects in which it resides, are among the most haunting and lyrical of philosophical writings.

During Easter Week 1938, Weil went with her mother to Solesmes to hear the Gregorian chants. She found that the music miraculously abstracted her from the pain of her headaches, and for the first time experienced what she later termed "the divine love." At Solesmes, Simone met an Oxford undergraduate who introduced her to 17th-century English metaphysical poetry. While reciting George Herbert's allegorical poem "Love," Simone Weil had a mystical experience. "Christ himself came down and took possession of me," she said. Although she never formally converted to Christianity, she became a practicing Roman Catholic.

With the collapse of France in June 1940, Simone tried to get to England to join the Free French propaganda effort, but failed. Instead, she went to Marseilles, where she became friendly with Father J.-M. Perrin, a Dominican priest. In Marseilles, Simone became an agricultural worker in a vineyard. She found solace from the arduous work in prayer.

As a Jew, Simone Weil was denied a teaching post in Vichy, France, and her father was barred from practicing medicine. The family emigrated to New York in May, 1942. But Simone still hoped to join the Free French in England. After spending several months in Harlem, praying with blacks at a Baptist church and recording observations in her notebooks, Simone obtained passage to Liverpool on November 10, 1942. From there she went to live in London, where she wrote her most important book, *The Need for Roots.* But Simone was neglecting her health, starving herself in an act of solidarity with her countrymen in occupied France. In April 1943, Simone was admitted to Middlesex Hospital as a tuberculosis patient. From there, she was transferred to the sanatorium at Ashford, where she died of self-imposed starvation on August 24.

The physical and spiritual ills of modern society weighed heavily on this frail idealist and mystic. Simone Weil's philosophical writings are illuminated with her spiritualism. In her book *The Need for Roots*, Weil laments the lack in modern industrial society of a sense of belonging to a collectivity. Our one major obligation toward our fellow human beings, Weil stresses, is to feed the hungry, which also includes responding to the spiritual hunger that plagues modern man.

The absence of roots accounts for the spiritual void which we all inhabit. Weil advocates a rerooting through a belief in an impersonal God, through non-chauvinistic ties at the local and national levels, and through a commitment to true justice, such as was exhibited by the Catholics of Béziers, who died rather than turn the Albigensian heretics over to the Inquisition, or by Homer, who refused to take sides with the Greeks against the Trojans in the *Iliad.*

Weil brilliantly pinpointed the shallowness of contemporary values—our spurious pursuit of success, our degraded sense of justice, which favors the strong over the weak, our worship of money and money-makers, our loss of religious inspiration, and our submission to blind, mechanistic forces, which allows us to absolve ourselves from responsibility for each other. She calls for a renaissance of faith and a rededication to common spiritual and cultural values.

Today, ironically, with the posthumous publication of her notebooks and religious essays, Simone Weil, who so abhorred the cult of personality, is herself becoming a cult among American intellectuals. Leslie Fiedler calls Weil "the saint, the mystic, and the witness of God, of the un-churched, the agnostic, and the intellectual." Weil is also the mouthpiece of truth, which as Blake observed "can never be told so as to be understood and not be believed"—if only we would listen.

Mildred "Babe" Didrikson Zaharias (1913-1956)

ATHLETE

Her nickname was Babe; it should have been Champ. For Babe Didrikson Zaharias was one of the most spectacular all-around athletes in sports history, and the best woman golfer in America. She won awards in basketball; broke records in field and track events; earned gold medals in lifesaving and in figure skating; made astounding throws in baseball and phenomenal punts and passes in football; won prizes in tennis, diving, and bowling.

But Babe Didrikson Zaharias is most often remembered for her golfing feats. She won a total of 82 professional and amateur golf tournaments; established a record 17-game winning streak; was the first American to win the British Ladies' Amateur Championship; and, barely four months after undergoing major surgery, captured the trophy in the U.S. Women's Open by a record-shattering 12 strokes. No wonder the sports press called her "Whatta-gal." Six times—in 1932, 1945, 1946, 1947, 1950, and 1954—Babe Didrikson Zaharias was voted Woman Athlete of the Year by the Associated Press sportswriters; and in 1950, she was designated Woman Athlete of the half-century. When the Athletes of the Century are chosen in the year 2000, it seems likely that the honors will go to two out-standing Babes—Babe Ruth and Babe Didrikson Zaharias.

The woman who was termed by sports columnist Grantland Rice "the athletic phenomenon of all time, man or woman" was born in Port Arthur, Texas, on June 26, 1912.* She was named Mildred Ella, but as the youngest of six children, she was called Baby—until her prowess on the sandlot changed her nickname to Babe.

As a child growing up in Beaumont, Texas, where the Didriksons moved when she was three, Babe was encouraged to develop her athletic talents. Her father, a Norwegian-born carpenter, constructed a gymnasium in the back yard, with bars, weights, and trapezes. Her mother who had been a champion ice skater in her native Oslo, had Babe tie scrubbing brushes to her shoes and scud over the linoleum on sudsy water, thus teaching the girl to skate and getting the floors cleaned at the same time. On Saturdays, Babe was a regular at the local vacant lot, where an informal Little League played baseball. Later, Babe was to describe the difference between all-girl and coed athletics thus:

Girls are nice to each other. Boys are rough with each other, and rougher with girls who crash into their game.

I have been asked if I could give advice to girls on how to be better athletes . . . the only . . . advice I can give is to get toughened up playing but DON'T GET TOUGH. There's a lot of difference there.

At Beaumont High School Babe became the top scorer of the basketball team, the Miss Purple Royals. The team never lost a game with Babe as their shooting forward. In 1930, Babe Didrikson was discovered by a visiting scout, the coach of athletic teams for an insurance company in Dallas, Texas.

Babe Didrikson arrived in Dallas on February 17, 1930, and played her first game with the Golden Cyclones the following day. Within three weeks, she was known as the hottest forward on the women's basketball circuit, and corporate recruiters were vying with one another to lure her away. In her first season, she scored 210 points in five games, and was designated All-American forward.

*Different sources report the year of her birth variously as 1911, 1912, 1913, 1914.

In 1930, Babe also made her debut as a track and field star. She set national records in javelin- and baseball-throwing. In 1932, Babe Didrikson singlehandedly won five field and track events at the Evanston tournament, and placed in two others— racking up 30 points as a one-woman track team for the Employers' Casualty Company. Her opponents were track teams consisting of 12 and more members. Babe catapulted Employers' Casualty to the Amateur Athletic Union National Championship; she also qualified herself for the 1932 Olympics.

Ever since she had watched the 1928 Olympic Games on television, Babe Didrikson had yearned to compete in this international decathlon. In July 1932, she was on the train to Los Angeles, where the Olympics were to be held.

She was the sensation of the 1932 Olympiad, shattering four world records in women's sports. She threw the javelin 143 feet four inches, breaking the previous record by nearly a foot; and in the 80-meter hurdle beat the previous top time of 12.2 seconds with her 11.7 seconds. She took second place in the high jump.

The star of the Olympics was met at the Dallas airport by a citizens' delegation led by the mayor, and escorted through downtown Dallas in a tickertape parade. Some of the male sportscasters, who had been uniformly hostile to the short-haired woman who disdained "brassieres, girdles, and all that junk," now changed their tune. They dubbed her The Texas Tornado, and gave her glowing full-page spreads. Sportswriters Paul Gallico, Damon Runyon, and Grantland Rice became her chief fans.

It was "Granny" Rice, who had coined the famous "not that you won or lost, but how you played the game," that started Babe Didrikson on her golf career in the summer of 1932. Chatting with Westbrook Pegler in the Olympics pressbox, Rice bet that Babe could master any sport she tried. Pegler was skeptical. "What about golf?" he asked. "Sure, why not golf?" Rice retorted. The next morning, he arranged for Babe to play at the Brentwood Country Club. She took to the links the way mustard takes to a hot dog, slamming the ball 250 yards off the tee on several drives. The following day "Granny's" column celebrated Babe's finesse on the fairway: "She is the longest hitter women's golf has ever seen," he proclaimed, "for she has a free, lashing style backed up with championship form and terrific power in strong hands, strong wrists, forearms of steel. . . ."

What had begun as a sportswriters' gag became the turning point of Babe Didrikson's career. Babe Didrikson was one of the few golf champions who had not trained rigorously from childhood. To earn enough money to finance her new and expensive career, Babe went on the RKO vaudeville circuit, shot putting, performing acrobatic stunts, and playing the harmonica with panache. She also pitched baseball exhibition games. She earned enough money to tide her over the next three years, as well as to support her parents and to pay for a college education for her many nieces and nephews.

In November, 1934, after taking golf lessons from professional Tommy Armour, Babe Didrikson entered her first amateur golf tournament, the Fort Worth Women's Invitational. WONDER GIRL DEBUTS IN TOURNAMENT GOLF: TURNS IN 77 SCORE was the local newspaper's report.

The Texas Women's Golf Association was by no means pleased when Babe Didrikson sent in her application for the 1935 state amateur championship tournament. The association was composed of moneyed aristocrats from the local country clubs, and the South Beaumont wonder girl was viewed as an uncouth upstart. "We really don't need any truck drivers' daughters in this tournament," drawled qualifying-medalist Peggy Chandler. Chandler got her come-uppance on the golf course, losing the tournament two-up in the final round to Babe Didrikson. But the Texas bluebloods had their revenge; they caused Babe Didrikson to lose her amateur standing because of her stint in professional vaudeville.

Babe was determined to get back her amateur standing, but she would have to renounce professional golf for three years. First, she must accumulate some financial resources. In 1936, she teamed up with pro Gene Sarazen, and went on a golfing tour of the United States and Australia. Babe quickly established a rapport with the spectators at these exhibitions, bantering good-humoredly with her fans, and tossing off dramatic descriptions of her golfing strategy.

At the Los Angeles Open Tournament in 1936, Babe was paired with burly George Zaharias, a professional wrestler and successful businessman, who was an expert golfer as well. Soon the couple were sharing an apartment in St. Louis. Finally, Zaharias protested,

"Babe, you're too famous for *living together*." They were married on December 23, 1938.

Marriage to the wealthy Zaharias enabled Babe Didrikson to retire from professional golf. While waiting for reinstatement as an amateur, Babe opened a sports-clothing store in Beverly Hills. Babe had won awards for designing women's sports outfits, and throughout her career she designed all her own golfing costumes.

In January 1944, Babe Zaharias regained her amateur golfing status. Her husband renounced his own career to become the Babe's manager, cheering her to victory after victory in all her ensuing tournaments. In 1945, Babe Didrikson won the Western Open, the Texas Open, and the Broadmoor Invitational; in 1946 and 1947, she went on to win every major amateur golf championship. In her qualifying round for the Doherty Cup, Babe Zaharias set a new record with a score of 64—four under men's par and eight under women's par. Her fans roared with glee as Babe whacked the ball 285 yards from tee to green. She could out-drive all other women professionals, and most men professionals. Babe repeatedly out-drove baseball player Ted Williamson in their exhibition matches.

By October 1947 Babe Zaharias had garnered all the women's amateur golf titles. Then, once again, Babe Zaharias turned professional. She also wrote a book, *Championship Golf*, and with her husband, founded the Ladies Professional Golf Association, and was elected president.

By now, Babe Zaharias was a national heroine, who dropped in at the White House and asked President Eisenhower how his wife's golf game was progressing. But Babe Didrikson Zaharias's successes were marred by personal tragedies—her mother's sudden death, her miscarriage, frequent estrangements from her husband, and hostility from the press. The disparaging "Muscle Moll," first hurled at Babe by the sports columnists, was taken up by some Texans. One sportswriter insisted ". . . in athletics women didn't belong, and it would be much better if [Babe] and her ilk stayed at home, got themselves prettied up, and waited for the phone to ring."

In 1950, Babe discovered that she had cancer. Refusing to be defeated by illness, she won two major tournaments within months after her first operation. She also became an active member of the

Cancer Crusade, establishing a Babe Didrikson Zaharias Fund to support cancer research and treatment.

Babe went through hospitalizations and operations with indomitable courage. She continued to win tournaments until her physical deterioration became severe. On October 26, 1955, she played her last round of golf. Retiring to her house in Tampa, Florida, Babe dictated her autobiography, and established an annual Babe Didrikson Zaharias Award for the woman who did the most for amateur sports in America. Then, on the morning of September 27, 1956, her husband at her side and her golf clubs in the corner of her hospital room, Babe Didrikson Zaharias went to present her final score card to the Great Scorer in the Sky.

When Babe's death was made public, eulogies filled the sports columns of every newspaper in the nation. Perhaps the most moving summary of Babe's achievements was delivered by her friend and fellow golfer, Patty Berg:

Babe changed the game of golf for women—not only by bringing along the L.P.G.A. [Ladies Professional Golf Association], but by her kind of golf. She came along with that great power game, and it led to lower scores and more excitement. She even changed the swing. . . . And she brought all that humor and showmanship to the game. She humanized it. . . . Our sport grew because of Babe, because she had so much flair and color. . . . Her tremendous enthusiasm for golf and life was contagious—even the galleries felt good when Babe was around.

Diane Nemerov Arbus
(1923-1971)

PORTRAIT PHOTOGRAPHER

In November, 1972, all previous attendance records at the Museum of Modern Art in New York City were broken, as 3,000 visitors a day jammed the museum to view a posthumous retrospective of Diane Arbus's photographs. A few months earlier, Arbus had set another precedent as the first photographer ever to be represented at the Venice Biennale art exhibition, where her ten colossal black-and-white portraits were the *piece de resistance* of the American Pavilion.

A fashion photographer for the major part of her professional life, Diane Arbus's reputation rests on the non-commercial photographs she took during the last decade of her life. She forged a style which syncretized the best features of documentary photography with the symbolism of Albert Stieglitz, and has been the major influence of the 1970s on photographers in the United States and western Europe. Singlehandedly, Arbus changed the emphasis in photojournalism from politics to psychology, from places and circumstances to people.

As a portraitist, Diane Arbus ranks with Titian, Rembrandt, and Rouault. As *Time* magazine's Robert Hughes remarked, ". . . Arbus did what hardly seemed possible for a still photographer. She altered our experience of the face." In recognition of Arbus's artistry, *Artforum* magazine used her *Portrait of a Pro-War Parader* on its cover—the first time a photograph graced the cover of an art magazine. Diane Arbus's powerful presentations of ordinary people whom she termed "the quiet minorities" are unique. Arbus confronts us with "the thing itself; unaccommodated man," defying us to pluck out the heart of another's mystery, while forcing us to know ourselves.

The photographer who chose as her subject the common man belonged to an uncommon family. Diane Nemerov was the daughter of David Nemerov and Gertrude Russek Nemerov, proprietors of a fashionable clothing emporium on Fifth Avenue in New York City. Diane's brother, Howard Nemerov, became a noted 20th-century poet. Diane, the second of three children, was born on March 14, 1923, and grew up in one of New York's most elegant neighborhoods, Central Park West. She attended the Fieldston and Ethical Culture schools, where her teachers encouraged her to become a painter. But Diane felt her paintings were facile and self-indulgent, and hated hearing her canvases praised: "I didn't want to hear I was terrific. I had the sense if I was so terrific at it, it wasn't worth doing." As a photographer, Diane was to embrace the credo "a man's reach must exceed his grasp." "The thing that's important to know," she wrote, "is that you never know. You're always sort of feeling your way." Diane's definition of a photograph was "a secret about a secret. The more it tells you, the less you know."

But Diane's artistic ambitions were kept in abeyance for many years. At the age of 14, Diane fell in love with struggling photographer Allen Arbus. The Nemerovs felt that their daughter was too young to become romantically entangled, but Diane and Allen saw each other secretly for four years, and on April 10, 1941, they eloped. Her parents, accepting the marriage as a *fait accompli*, hired the couple to design advertisements for their store. Diane would come up with ideas for pictures, and her husband would take the photographs. Thus began a highly successful collaboration in fashion photography, which endured for nearly 20 years. During this period, Diane gave birth to two daughters, Doon and Amy.

In 1959, Diane Arbus left her husband, and installed herself and the two children in an apartment in Greenwich Village. She had become disaffected with the specious glamor of the fashion world, and decided to study serious photography with Lisette Model, known for the "human concern" of her photographs.

During the early sixties, Arbus began to take on photography assignments for the media. Her photographs illustrated articles in magazines, and other national publications. But Arbus felt that photojournalism was not her forte. A gregarious individual, Diane sensed that she had something new to say about people, and about the human condition. She wanted to make the kind of statement with her camera that her favorite writers, Kafka, Rilke, and Borges, had done with their pens.

"We've all got an identity. You can't avoid it," Diane wrote in her notebook in the mid-sixties. She had begun the notebook in 1959 and it soon became a compendium of stories of the romances, tragedies, and deaths of the people she encountered on her photographic safaris. Diane always tried to gain the confidence of the people she asked to pose for her photographs by exchanging confidences with them. She never tried to capture her subjects unawares; rather, she allowed them to pose, encouraging them to relax, be themselves, and permit her to capture their identities on film. This approach marked a radical break with the dominant Cartier-Bresson school of photography, whose idea was to "catch" and "frame" the subject at a hypothetical "decisive moment." Unlike most photojournalists, Arbus was not trying to portray a slice of life, but an eternal psychological truth.

A typical entry in Arbus's diaries lists the subjects that she planned to photograph: *diaper derby, lady wrestling, Timothy Leary's wedding, waiting room, tattoo parlor, Gloria Vanderbilt's baby, masquerade ball, hermit, convention, roller derby, sleepless people.* Soon, however, Arbus felt an increasing need to narrow the range of her subjects to represent "some generalized human being, so everyone will recognize it." She chose her archetypal figures from a segment of humanity that had not been widely photographed before; the celebrity and the man in the street were already clichés.

Daringly, Diane Arbus chose to make human oddities her special domain. There were the congenital oddities: twins, triplets, midgets, giants, physically and mentally damaged people. There were the sexual oddities: homosexuals, lesbians, transvestites. And there were the social oddities: nudists, hustlers, sports pros, and burlesque queens. Though she also photographed suburbanites, babies, and children, Diane Arbus gained recognition largely as the photographer of human aberrants. However, there is nothing voyeuristic, lurid, or sordid about Arbus's photographs. She did not take pictures of child molesters, murderers, rapists, or other hard core criminals. Nor did she portray her burlesque queens on exhibition before leering audiences, or her transvestites cruising Ninth Avenue for pick-ups. Rather, she showed these people in ordinary situations—the strip-teasers at their dressing tables putting on make-up, the drag queens in repose taking off their stockings. She photographed deviants, not devils, and her purpose was not to outrage, but "to see life steadily and see it whole."

As Arbus explained, "There is a quality of legend about freaks. Most people go through life dreading they'll have a traumatic experience. Freaks were born with their trauma. They've already passed their test in life. . . ." Arbus's "freak," like Coleridge's Ancient Mariner, was "a person in a fairy tale who stops you and demands that you answer a riddle." The riddles were the mystery of human diversity; the human need to assume masks, both literal and figurative; the perplexity of what is done to us and what we do to ourselves.

Touched by the frenzy with which strangers sought to make human contact, Arbus haunted dance-halls and photographed their habitués, steeped in meretricious splendor. She was also fascinated by the compulsion of one sex to adopt the appurtenances of the other— women smoking cigars, men donning female apparel, "like anyone would try on what the other person had that he didn't have. It was heartbreaking." By confronting the viewer with the stranger specimens of humanity, Arbus conveyed the idea that we are all fundamentally strange to one another: "It is impossible to get out of your skin and into somebody else's," she said. And yet, our mutual alienation breeds a sympathy that binds us together.

To supplement her income as a free-lance photographer and writer, Diane taught photography at the Parsons School of Design and at Cooper Union. Diane Arbus had submitted a portfolio of her work to the Department of Photography at the Museum of Modern

Art in New York City. In 1967, John Szarkowski, the director of photography at the Museum of Modern Art, made Diane Arbus the central figure in an exhibition of three young photographers entitled "New Documents." The critics who covered the show acclaimed the purity, candor, originality, and integrity of Arbus's work. The impact on other young photographers was immense, but Arbus was repelled when they produced travesties of her work. Arbus had no interest in the bizarre for its own sake, as many of her sensationalist imitators did. Her special interest was "a sort of contemporary anthropology;" Arbus used misfits and nonconformists as the anthropologist uses primitive people, to distinguish between man's inherent characteristics and the cultural norms he establishes.

"My favorite thing is to go where I have never been," Diane Arbus was fond of saying. "For me there's something about just going into somebody else's home." On July 26, 1971, Diane Arbus went to "the undiscovered country from whose bourn no traveler returns." When her body was discovered, wrists slashed, in her apartment in the Greenwich Village artists' community of Westbeth, Diane's friends were shocked. "Gentle" was the word they most often used to characterize Diane. Why had she chosen to execute such violence against herself? Artistic disappointment? Personal bereavement? Arbus's suicide remains incomprehensible. As she herself said, "Somebody else's tragedy is not the same as your own."

During her lifetime, Diane Arbus was a controversial artist. When *Contemporary Art* ran a series of her photographs, the magazine was besieged with angry letters and subscription cancellations. But after her death, Diane Arbus became a cult figure, especially for women in their twenties and thirties who canonized Arbus along with Sylvia Plath, Anne Sexton, and other women artists who died by their own hand. The Arbus showing at the Venice Biennale created a world-wide demand for expositions of her work. The 1972 Museum of Modern Art retrospective traveled throughout the United States and Canada for three years. And the Arbus legend continues to grow.

"Make people think they're thinking and they'll love you. Make them really think and they'll hate you," critic Logan Pearsall Smith once remarked. What is disquieting and discomfiting about Diane Arbus's photographs is that they really make us think, and about subjects that we would prefer to evade. By refusing either to romanticize or satirize her subjects, or to render any moral, political, or value judgments whatsoever, Arbus throws the burden of what to make of them on the viewer. Like Flaubert's perfect artist, she is present everywhere and visible nowhere in her photographs. What we perceive often tells us more about ourselves than about either Arbus or her "freaks."

Why did Arbus so often choose anomalous men and women as her prototypes of humanity? Why did Yeats speak through Crazy Jane, or Rouault through circus clowns? Why do behavioral scientists study man through experiments with chimpanzees and ants? The exaggerated role-playing of Arbus's "freaks" makes us conscious of our own more subtle role-playing. Arbus shows us the relation of normalcy to abnormalcy.

Diane Arbus said that "freaks" filled her with "a mixture of shame and awe." Her photographs inspire the same sentiments in most observers. Yet the "freaks" have accepted their difference, while we inexplicably wince at the sight of three Russian Dwarfs enjoying a *gemütlich* evening in their living room, or stare transfixed at a picture of two nudists sprawled out on chairs, their faces as familiar as the faces we see in the supermarket.

Arbus often used "freaks" to highlight the gap between illusion and reality, but she also captured phantasmagoric beauty. There is the photograph of a little flower girl who has strayed from a wedding party and stands against a misty backdrop, like some fey creature. A nocturnal view of a castle at Disneyland is eclipsed by shadow, and we almost believe ourselves before some Bavarian castle in the Middle Ages.

Arbus had to develop new techniques to portray her truths. She posed her figures frontally before the camera so that their faces, especially the eyes, seem paramount. There is a minimum of ambiance and artifacts—nothing to distract us from the human figures, who are blown up to epic proportions. Their hugeness hypnotizes us; we are implicated in their condition though not of it. No photographs have ever been as rich in psychological and metaphysical implications as Arbus's portraits.

Helen Frankenthaler
(1928-   )
PAINTER

Helen Frankenthaler is living proof of John Stuart Mill's hypothesis that, given the same opportunities as male artists, great women artists will emerge. Helen has been lucky enough to enjoy the rare confluence of natural endowment and favorable circumstance. The daughter of wealthy, cultured parents, Helen was made to feel "special" from the day she was born. She was educated at some of the best American private schools, where gifted teachers recognized and encouraged her genius. The result: today, Helen Frankenthaler is one of America's most celebrated contemporary painters, with works in the permanent collections of every major art museum in the United States and in many European galleries. She is recognized as a major influence on her contemporaries and on younger artists. As the originator of "stain painting" and Lyrical Abstractionism, Frankenthaler belies the old myth that women artists are derivative rather than original.

Helen was born on December 12, 1928. She was the third and youngest daughter of New York State Supreme Court Justice Alfred

Frankenthaler and German-born Martha Lowenstein Frankenthaler.

From childhood, Helen showed a propensity for the visual arts. She remembers filling the sink with water and making "wonderful designs" in it with her mother's nail polish.

Helen attended New York City's most prestigious private schools. At Dalton High School, she studied painting with the noted Mexican painter Rufino Tamayo. Helen became Tamayo's favorite pupil, primarily, she later maintained, because she painted "such good Tamayos."

Her older sister introduced Helen to Dali's *Persistence of Memory*, and to her first artistic epiphany. As she gazed at the surrealist painting, Helen was struck by the power of the human imagination to transmute a real image into something wondrous and transcendent. Later, Frankenthaler's own paintings would be lauded for their magical aura.

Helen's father died in 1940, and to the adolescent girl the world seemed to come crashing down. But when she entered Bennington College after graduating from Dalton, Helen felt herself reborn. At Bennington, Helen studied painting with Cubist oriented painter Paul Feely. She soon found herself discarding the bold Mexican colors and themes she had adopted from Tamayo in favor of the analytic cubism of Braque and Picasso.

The Bennington faculty included psychologist Erich Fromm and critic Kenneth Burke. Poet W.H. Auden and novelist Ralph Ellison were also at the Bennington campus. Helen became intrigued by the mythic aspects of literature, and enjoyed drawing parallels between literature and art. Her paintings are often invested with a literary quality, and she has been characterized as a "poet's painter."

During the Bennington work programs, Helen studied in New York City with painter Wallace Harrison, and at the Art Students' League under the tutelage of Vaclav Vyactil. She spent a brief period at Columbia University Graduate School studying art history, and enjoyed a course given by Meyer Schapiro, the doyen of New York art historians.

Helen Frankenthaler was initiated into the New York art world by critic Clement Greenberg, whom she met when she was asked to arrange a benefit exhibition for Bennington College. Greenberg did not like Frankenthaler's contribution to the show, the Picasso- influenced *Woman on a Horse,* but he recognized her talent. Through Greenberg, Frankenthaler met avant-garde artists Willem and Elaine de Kooning, David Smith and Franz Kline, among others. Greenberg also escorted Frankenthaler to the popularartists' hang-outs, the Cedar Tavern and the Artist's Club, where she became friendly with abstract expressionist painters Grace Hartigan, Larry Rivers, Joan Mitchell, Alfred Leslie, and with poets Kenneth Koch, Frank O'Hara, and John Ashbery. At Greenberg's recommendation, Frankenthaler studied for three weeks with Hans Hoffmann, the guru of the New York School of painters, in Provincetown.

The year 1951 contained some highlights. Frankenthaler was the youngest artist included in the "Ninth Street Show." She was exhibited in "New Generation," a group show at the Tibor de Nagy Gallery, and later had her first solo showing, also at the de Nagy Gallery. But perhaps the most significant occurrence of the year was Frankenthaler's first exposure to Jackson Pollock at an exhibition at the Betty Parsons Gallery, an experience she compared to finding herself in the center ring of Madison Square Garden. Bowled over by the physical impact of Pollock's action-painting, *Number One,* and magnetized by the intimacy of *Autumn Rhythm,* Frankenthaler felt that Pollock had opened up a whole new terrain in painting. One of the first to appreciate Pollock's significance, she began to visit the artist and his wife, Lee Krasner, at their studio in Springs, Long Island. In her own art, Frankenthaler began to focus on creating "explosive landscapes," adapting many of Pollock's and Krasner's techniques to her own ends. Like Pollock, Frankenthaler abandoned easel and brush and laid the canvas on the floor, where she could work on it from all sides, spilling the paint directly onto unsized, unprimed canvas.

But Frankenthaler was no mere imitator. After assimilating influences from old masters, as well as from contemporaries such as Pollock and Arshile Gorky, in 1952 Frankenthaler made her own revolutionary contribution to painting technique—stain painting. Diluting her paints so thin that the color soaked right into the canvas, Frankenthaler achieved a unity between image and medium; her forms appeared to be painted not merely *on* the canvas, but *in* it.

Frankenthaler put together the unique palette that was to launch a revival of color in American painting, which had been dominated by black and white, and neutral tones. Doing water colors on a trip to Nova Scotia, she figured out a way to capture the luminous, transparent effect of the aquarelle in the delicate corals, pearly blues, and pale mauves and greens of her oil paintings. The Frankenthaler painting that announced to the art world that an important and daring artist was in its midst was *Mountains and Sea*. An abstract work, *Mountains and Sea* nevertheless suggests the Nova Scotia landscape. The muted, diaphanous gray-greens, warm pinks and faded blues of the painting, the revolutionary use of blank canvas to create the illusion of light and openness, the original spontaneous forms created from "bleeding" outlines rather than from circumscribed drawn lines, all announced *Mountains and Sea* as a radical departure in modern art.

Soon the New York critics were commenting on Frankenthaler's unique and bizarre palette, novel juxtapositions of colors in defiance of the impressionists and fauves. Not all the reviews were complimentary. Some critics dismissed Frankenthaler's approach to form—her choosing to work from images created by the paint stains, rather than using paint to fill in preconceived outlines—as "flimsy" and "unserious."

In 1959, Frankenthaler was vindicated when her painting *Jacob's Ladder* took first prize at the Paris Biennalle. By the end of the next decade her work hung in every New York museum, as well as in art museums in other American cities and in the capitals of Europe.

In 1958, Frankenthaler married another major New York painter, Robert Motherwell. Frankenthaler and Motherwell were looked on as the "royal couple" of modern art. But in 1971, they were divorced.

Frankenthaler continued to experiment with new ideas and techniques. She switched from oil paints to acrylics, and began to paint more controlled forms, with increasingly opaque colors. Her palette still reflected a broad spectrum of hues, however, and she became a more uninhibited colorist, though never for mere color's sake.

A dynamic artist, enjoying new challenges, Frankenthaler has achieved renown as a sculptor as well as a painter, and has designed bookcovers and tapestries and painted tile mosaics. Her paintings are remarkable for their versatility. Her pictures capture a diversity of moods, from the dreamy to the kinetic, and exploit a variety of techniques. Critics have praised her for never repeating herself; she makes each painting a new adventure.

Helen Frankenthaler has had an enormous influence on other painters. Her experiments with staining and with exposing raw canvas were widely copied and adapted. Frankenthaler challenged the traditional view of composition, which located the interest of the painting at the center. She would often leave huge blanks in the middle of her pictures and concentrate on the previously neglected corners of the canvas. Her impromptu juxtapositions of symmetrical and asymmetrical forms and her fresh use of color offer refreshing relief from academic and commercial trends in modern art.

Like all great art, Frankenthaler's work appeals on two levels, the intellectual and the emotional. An art historian, standing before a Frankenthaler canvas, can trace elements from great painters from the past, and enjoy the way Frankenthaler can carry on a dialogue with her predecessors while making her own unique contribution to artistic tradition. But any museum visitor, even a child, who has never seen a Rubens or Matisse or Pollock, can stand before *Blue Territory* or *Eden* or *Mother Goose Melody* and feel the sheer visceral delight that imaginative use of color and form evoke. Frankenthaler's abstract landscapes offer the viewer an immediate and multisensual appeal. Her colors sing; her forms are tangible; her lines and shapes zig and zag across the canvas with perceptible motion; her bleeding swatches of color explode on the eye with the same gush of sweetness that a ripe mango yields to the tongue and palate. Added to this direct sensuous appeal, Frankenthaler's paintings are intellectually stimulating as studies in spatial dynamics, color production and arrangement, and textural tension.

Frankenthaler's paintings have been described as *lyrical, pristine, dramatic, hedonistic, exuberant, lucid, intelligent,* and *disciplined.* Their ability to transmit a mirthful and yet somehow melancholy quality reminds us of the melodies of Mozart, and their limpid grace, of the poems of Shelley and Sidney. Her landscapes seem to revel in form as Renoir's nudes revel in flesh. In every picture, color and form undergo what Shakespeare would describe as "sea change . . . into something rich and strange."

Index

Acknowledgments

The author wishes to express appreciation to:

High Fidelity magazine, for permission to quote from "Rosa Ponselle Reminisces," interviewed by J.A. Drake, April 1977, pp. 75-78. All rights reserved.

The Macmillan Company, for permission to quote from *Twenty Years at Hull House* by Jane Addams, copyright 1910, renewed 1938 by James W. Lynn.

Harper and Row Publishers, Inc., for permission to quote from *The Long Loneliness* by Dorothy Day, copyright 1952.

William Morrow and Company, Inc., for permission to quote from *Blackberry Winter* by Margaret Mead, copyright 1972.

I would also like to take this opportunity to give special thanks to Beatrice Hart and Donna Kelsh for their editorial assistance, and to Helen Frankenthaler and Margaret Levine, of the American Foundation of the Blind, who read and corrected the chapters on Helen Frankenthaler and Helen Keller, respectively.

Picture Credits